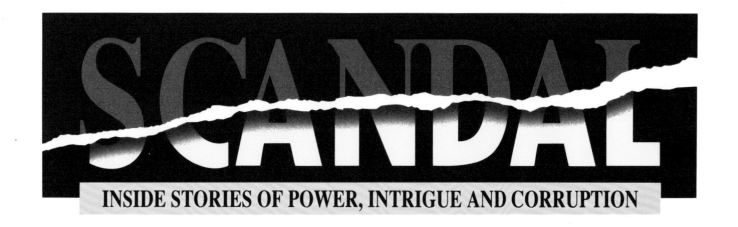

SCANDAL

INSIDE STORIES OF POWER, INTRIGUE AND CORRUPTION

BLITZ EDITIONS

This material appeared originally in
weekly partworks entitled Scandal.

Published by Blitz Editions
an imprint of
Bookmart Limited
Registered Number 2372865
Trading as Bookmart Limited
Desford Road
Enderby
Leicester
LE9 5AD

ISBN 1 85605 028 9

CONTENTS

INTRODUCTION

From time to time, somewhere in the world, a case erupts into the public consciousness. Usually, it involves the famous, the powerful, the rich. Out of a web of gossip, sexual indiscretion or political intrigue, a human story emerges. Perhaps someone dies; perhaps there is a cover-up. Certainly there is a scandal.

A blaze of publicity follows. Press and television commentators have their day. Often there is a court case. And then, before the full ramifications of the story are known, the controversy disappears.

Time passes and the public is left with a jigsaw of a story with significant pieces missing. We can never be sure whether we have been presented with a convenient but incomplete version of events. Questions are left unanswered. Why did those involved do what they did? What effect on history did their actions have? Why do people in positions of power risk everything for a fleeting sensation? What happens when the Establishment is determined to blur the facts? Were the right people brought to justice?

Scandal travels down the corridors of power and explores the alleyways of human frailty. What happened to the people whose vulnerability, greed or lust spun them down from the height of power to the depths of disgrace? Where are the lesser figures who seemed so critical to the case at the time? Who really suffered? Did the media present a balanced picture of the case?

Now, Scandal re-examines a whole series of critical cases, many of which have changed the fabric of modern society. Through the perspective of time, Scandal presents the inside story of what really happened so you, the reader, can form your own judgement.

THE PROFUMO AFFAIR

Two worlds collided in the summer of 1961, when a British Cabinet minister and a young nightclub showgirl met by chance on an aristocrat's Buckinghamshire estate. Others present that fateful weekend included a Russian diplomat, known to be a spy, and a successful osteopath and artist, whose easy charm had secured him a place in London's high – and low – life. As they all enjoyed a hot Sunday around the estate swimming pool, no one could have known that this pleasant social interlude was sowing the seeds of a national sex-and-security drama – and personal disaster

John Dennis Profumo, *Minister for War in the Conservative Government; an aristocratic 'golden boy' tipped for even higher ministerial office.*

Christine Keeler, *a 19-year-old Murray's Club showgirl who came to London and exchanged an unhappy past for excitement and adventure.*

Eugene Ivanov, *the assistant Naval Attaché at the USSR embassy. A cultured Russian who enjoyed the high life, he was watched as a spy by MI5.*

Dr Stephen Ward, *the society osteopath who mixed in influential circles and who was known for introducing pretty young girls to the aristocratic set.*

Mandy Rice-Davies, *a teenage model from Birmingham and a dancer at Murray's. She shared Christine Keeler's ability to attract rich, older men.*

ONE

INDISCRETION

A HOT JULY NIGHT IN 1961, A YOUNG SHOWGIRL CAVORTING NAKED AROUND A SWIMMING POOL, AND A CABINET MINISTER. THIS POTENT COMBINATION WAS THE START OF A CASUAL FLING THAT THREATENED TO ENDANGER NATIONAL SECURITY

A rare weekend away from affairs of state found 'Jack' (John) Profumo – War Minister in a Conservative government that had held power for 10 years – and his actress wife, Valerie Hobson, at Cliveden House, Buckinghamshire. Just one hour's drive from London, Cliveden was the grand family seat of the Astors, one of Britain's richest non-royal dynasties. Profumo's close friend, Lord (Bill) Astor, often held extravagant parties there, attended by rich and influential members of government and high society. On this particular July night, around 30 distinguished guests had gathered for dinner.

Nineteen-year-old showgirl and model, Christine Keeler, was one of the guests that weekend at a smaller, less formal, party on the Cliveden estate. It was held at a Tyrolean-style riverside cottage which Lord Astor rented to his osteopath, Stephen Ward, for a pepper-corn rent of £1.00 per annum. The 47-year-old Ward and Keeler lived together in London, as flatmates rather than lovers, and she was a regular weekend visitor to his Cliveden retreat.

That Saturday evening – 8 July 1961 – was uncomfortably hot. Ward had a standing invitation from Lord Astor to use the Cliveden swimming pool, and his party was glad of the opportunity to cool down there.

Keeler chose an ill-fitting swim-suit from several provided by Lord Astor for his guests, and Ward laughingly suggested that she take it off. Moments later, she was naked and diving into the pool, much to the delight of Ward's other guests.

It was getting very late when a group of Astor's guests, catching the sounds of splashing and laughter drifting up from the pool, decided to wander down and take a look. The host and Profumo walked ahead of the others.

They were confronted by a naked, dripping and highly embarrassed Keeler, vainly grabbing a towel to cover herself. Ward, ever the practical joker, had flung her swimming costume into nearby bushes. It was a bizarre scene. Lord Astor made the introductions, Mrs Profumo, ironically, offered Keeler a swim-suit, and Ward and his companions were invited up to the house.

PARTY GAMES

Once at the house, Profumo took Keeler on a guided tour. He was, Keeler recalled, 'a type I find it hard to say no to; I didn't terribly mind being alone with him. There were some suits of armour in one room, and, on a dare, I let my companion dress me up in one. He paraded me in front of the others. Everybody laughed like hell. I am quite certain that the guests forgot their problems for a few hours that evening. Lord Astor invited us to return the next day for an afternoon swim.'

Sunday dawned even hotter than the previous day. Keeler, who had returned to London

DATEFILE

JUNE 8 1961
MI5 visit society osteopath Stephen Ward about his association with Russian attaché Ivanov

JULY 8 1961
Christine Keeler meets John Profumo for the first time

JULY 12 1961
Ward mentions Profumo link to MI5

JUNE–JULY '61

Above: The impressive main house on Bill Astor's Cliveden estate. Parties held there were lavish, harking back to pre-war aristocratic opulence.
Right: The estate swimming pool, to which Stephen Ward's set had free access, and which was the setting for Christine Keeler's fateful meeting with War Minister, John Profumo.

Far left: The classic shot of showgirl and model Christine Keeler, which once hung in London's National Portrait Gallery. Left: The Minister for War, John Profumo, viewed by some as a future Prime Minister, dancing with his wife, Valerie Hobson. Lord Astor had introduced Profumo to Keeler's 'flatmate', the osteopath Stephen Ward, in 1956, when he took him round to Ward's Devonshire Street consulting rooms.

THE IVANOV CONNECTION

CLOSE-UP

overnight, made the journey back to Cliveden. She was accompanied by two girlfriends and Ward's friend Ivanov – Assistant Naval Attaché at the Russian Embassy. They made directly for the pool.

COMPETING FOR KEELER

Profumo and Ivanov vied for Keeler's attention during boisterous water games. Keeler says, 'I liked Ivanov. He was a *man*. He was rugged, strong and agile. But somehow, when we decided to have a water piggy-back fight, it was Jack Profumo's shoulders I climbed on.'

Ward's recollections were to prove uncannily prophetic: 'Ivanov and JP had a race down the pool, supposedly without using their legs. Profumo shot ahead – using his legs.' Profumo then joked, 'That'll teach you to trust a minister of the Crown!'

What the Soviet diplomat made of all this, Ward could only speculate. 'There it all was,' he wrote, 'his dreams come true. There was the Minister, the President of Pakistan, duchesses, peers and officials of oil companies. Well, it was difficult to explain that this was not the hatching of any dreadful plot concerning oil, the Far East and all points west. I could see the sort of report that was going back to the embassy.'

By the end of the weekend, Profumo had managed to get Keeler's telephone number from Ward

– but it was with the Russian that she drove home that night.

Keeler's account of what happened next, back in the living room of Ward's flat, may be the fantasy of a young girl flattered by a powerful man's attention: 'Suddenly he was kissing me...I was as surprised as I was pleased. I'd always wanted him...We crashed across the room...he was just kissing me with all the power of a man in a frenzy of passion, and we half fell into my bedroom...I threw caution to the winds. We had been together.'

Ivanov, talking in 1990 from retirement at his home in Gorky, finally reveals that he did actually sleep with Keeler, although his account is more one of a routine execution of KGB orders. Ward heard Keeler's account the following morning, on the Monday after the Cliveden weekend, but later wrote in his memoirs, 'She said she would like to have had intercourse with him. I have always believed myself that she never did.' However, at the time, Ward's response to Keeler's revelation was: 'My goodness! What with Eugene on one hand and your new friend [Profumo] on the other, we could start a war!' This particular joke was to backfire tragically on Stephen Ward over the following two years.

POLITICAL DYNAMITE

Jokes aside, Ward shrewdly realised that knowledge of a Profumo-Keeler-Ivanov triangle could be lethal in the hands of the wrong people. On the

In March 1960, Captain Eugene Ivanov (shown above with an American Naval Attaché's wife) was posted to London's Soviet Embassy as Assistant Naval Attaché. This dark, tall 37-year-old was more sophisticated than most Russian diplomats in those days. The British security service, MI5, quickly identified him as a Soviet intelligence officer using diplomatic cover.

Ivanov drank a good deal and, though married, was 'something of a ladies' man.' MI5 thought him vulnerable to being 'turned' and determined on a plan of entrapment through sexual compromise. An introduction to Ward was the perfect start. Through Ward, probably an unwitting lure, Ivanov would meet desirable women. Ward was also open-minded on the USSR and Communism, often talking of dialogue between nations.

MI5 were very active during the early 1960s – the height of the 'Cold War' between East and West. The superpowers were at loggerheads over control of Berlin, and Britain and the USA were concerned about the Soviet build-up of nuclear arms. In this climate, all Soviet embassy appointments were automatically viewed with suspicion.

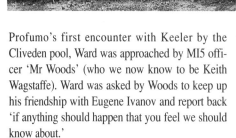

same Monday that Keeler told him about her night with Ivanov, Ward arranged a Wednesday meeting with Keith Wagstaffe, an MI5 contact who had been monitoring Ward's friendship with the Russian as a matter of course.

Ward had been introduced to Ivanov, over lunch at the Garrick club, by the Managing Editor of *The Daily Telegraph*, Colin Coote. Coote had long-standing connections with MI5. Ivanov spent the months after this lunch meeting sampling the delights of Ward's decadent London, visiting his Wimpole Mews flat, and meeting his many girls, including Keeler. Ward's close friendship with

Profumo's first encounter with Keeler by the Cliveden pool, Ward was approached by MI5 officer 'Mr Woods' (who we now know to be Keith Wagstaffe). Ward was asked by Woods to keep up his friendship with Eugene Ivanov and report back 'if anything should happen that you feel we should know about.'

When Ward met Wagstaffe on the Wednesday after that Cliveden weekend, he told the MI5 officer that the War Minister, Keeler and the Russian attaché had been present at the Sunday swimming party. Such a meeting was noteworthy enough, but, at one of his meetings with Keeler at Ward's flat, Ivanov had expressed an interest in a vital security issue – when the Americans were going to arm West Germany with atomic weapons. Keeler claims that Ward said to her, 'Why don't you ask Jack?' They all laughed at such a preposterous idea.

Meanwhile, Profumo wasted no time in pursuing Keeler. Their first 'date' was a drive around London in the ministerial limousine. Although the young woman did not find John Profumo handsome, his aura of power both impressed Keeler and appealed to her.

Profumo began to visit Keeler at Ward's Wimpole Mews flat. He would usually take her for a drive until the coast was clear. She recalls, 'Jack and I became lovers the third time he came around...We started laughing and talking as usual, then there was one of those electric potent silences...without a word we were embracing and he was kissing me.'

Despite possible worry about his wife,

Above left: Christine Keeler has revealed that this snap of her at the Cliveden pool was taken by John Profumo. Just a few weeks later he would send her a 'farewell' letter (above right), which read:
'Darling, In great haste and because I can get no reply from your phone – Alas something's blown up tomorrow night and I can't therefore make it. I'm terribly sorry especially as I leave the next day for various trips and then a holiday so won't be able to see you again until some time in September. Blast it. Please take great care of yourself and don't run away.
Love J'

Ivanov seemed to be based on a shared love of bridge and high living, and, being a social gadfly, he delighted in roaming through London with a real live Russian in tow.

On 8 June 1961, exactly one month before

Profumo once took Keeler home, a grand Nash house in Regents Park. 'It was late,' said Keeler. 'The butler and the rest of the staff were in bed...We crept round the lovely rooms. And then we got into their bedroom...' The couple had sex, said Keeler, on the Profumos' bed. The Minister exuded power. Sleeping with Profumo was, she reflected later, the way other people might feel about making love to a

> *Our meetings were very discreet...We never once dined out, or had a drink in a pub, or went anywhere...He was worried about the press finding out about us. And, above all, he was worried about Valerie.*
> Christine Keeler on Profumo

INSIDE VIEW

WARD'S CLIVEDEN SET

Right: Stephen Ward, the host of weekend parties at the cottage that were rumoured to involve sexual 'high jinks', had become a close friend of Bill Astor. Astor's third wife Bronwen, his wife at the time of the poolside episode, strongly disapproved of Ward's influence on her husband.

The main picture shows the exterior of Ward's cottage. The interior (below) had no 'mod-cons' – heating was supplied by oil fires run off bottled gas and an outside spring served as the refrigerator. Top left: This informal summertime gathering of 'Ward's Set' included Keeler (to left of table) and Ivanov (standing).

During the 1950s, Ward had been a frequent visitor to the privileged world of Bill Astor's Cliveden home. It was July 1956 when Ward, cruising down the river in the Cliveden motor launch with Astor's second wife, Philippa, spotted a dilapidated cottage in the grounds. Ward instantly fell in love with it. In return for a token rent of £1.00 per annum, Ward was to be on hand, when-ever required, to offer Bill Astor osteopathic services.

For Ward, the cottage came to represent 'a haven from the turmoil of London.' He set about tackling the wilderness of a garden and decorating the run-down and damp interior with his girlfriend of the time, model Maggie Brown. Friends dropping in were expected to 'muck in', eating make-shift meals and contributing lively conversation.

film-star such as Marlon Brando.

The couple also made love in his car, and, once, in Regents Park. His presents to her included a Flaminaire cigarette lighter and £20 'for her mother' – a polite way of paying for her services. Keeler later summed up the liaison as 'a very well-mannered screw of convenience; only in other people's minds, much later, was it "An Affair".'

WARNING SIGNS

However, on 9 August, when the 'affair' was barely a month old, Profumo was warned about his liaison by the government's Cabinet Secretary, Sir Norman Brook. On the advice of Sir Roger Hollis, head of MI5, who had heard of the Profumo-Keeler-Ivanov triangle from Keith Wagstaffe, he wanted to warn Profumo to be careful what he said when he met Ward. The osteopath was a sometimes indiscreet chatterbox, and might pass on snippets of information, dropped during casual conversation, to Ivanov.

MI5's greater purpose, however, was that Profumo might be a 'lead-in' to Ivanov, as part of a 'honeytrap' operation to compromise the Russian sexually, and thus encourage him to pass secrets or defect. Profumo turned down MI5's request. Caught out in sexual folly, Profumo must have known that his glittering career and marriage were at risk – helping the MI5 scheme was just another unnecessary complication.

Within hours of seeing Brook, Profumo sat down to write what was to be his 'goodbye' letter to Keeler (see opposite page). Profumo spent the summer recess with his family. As far as he was concerned, the matter was resolved.

Mandy Rice-Davies, Keeler's close friend at the time and also a showgirl at Murray's club, said that she was totally unaware of any Keeler-Ivanov affair.

GOOD-TIME GIRLS

FOR CHRISTINE KEELER AND MANDY RICE-DAVIES, LONDON OFFERED AN ESCAPE FROM THEIR SMALL-TOWN PASTS AND ENTRY INTO A HEADY WORLD OF CLUBS, SEX AND GLAMOUR

Much of Christine Keeler's childhood was spent with her mother and stepfather in two converted railway carriages in the Berkshire village of Wraysbury. Life in the caravan allowed little privacy; although she was close to her mother, she felt threatened by her stepfather's attentions – she even kept a knife under her pillow, in case he forced himself upon her.

TASTING INDEPENDENCE

In 1957, at the age of 15, Keeler took a job as a model at a dress shop in London's Soho quarter. She commuted there daily from Wraysbury. One day, the shop's sweeper, a Ghanaian student, invited her to his flat, where she lost her virginity to him. Says Keeler: 'I can't say I was stimulated by the experience.'

At 16, Keeler was dating American GIs from military bases in the Wraysbury area. One of the men was Jim, a black sergeant from Laleham Air Force base. Months after he had left for the States, Keeler discovered she was pregnant.

She tried to abort the baby herself with a knitting needle. It was a bloody and bungled affair, and the child was born prematurely on 17 April 1959. It survived just six days. That summer Keeler left Wraysbury, staying briefly in Slough with a friend before heading for London.

SHOPGIRL TO SHOWGIRL

While waitressing at a restaurant in Baker Street, Keeler met Maureen O'Connor, a girl who worked at Murray's Cabaret Club in Soho. She introduced Keeler to the owner, Percy Murray, who hired her almost immediately as a topless showgirl. As expected of showgirls, Keeler was soon sitting with the customers between acts, encouraging them to buy more drinks.

One night, a rich Arab customer came to Murray's. He was accompanied by a starlet and a second man – Stephen Ward. Leaning over to Keeler, Ward said, with great charm, 'You were wonderful in the show.' He asked what she was doing later. Keeler tried to avoid giving him her 'phone number, but Ward was insistent and managed to get hold of it before leaving the club that night.

Mandy Rice-Davies pursued a modelling career when she came down to London. This flimsy negligee (right) is a far cry from the matronly outfit (inset) she wore for her first modelling picture, taken in Birmingham when she was 15 years old.

The next day, Ward called Keeler three times. She fobbed him off, but he turned up at Wraysbury to charm her mother. On their second date, Ward asked Keeler to move into his flat in Bayswater.

Ward had much to offer Keeler. She was an attractive woman alone in a big city and he could give her security and an unde-

A DYNAMIC DOUBLE-ACT

Christine Keeler met Mandy Rice-Davies at Murray's Cabaret Club in London. 'It was dislike at first sight,' Rice-Davies recalls, and Keeler felt the same. Nevertheless, they both found themselves at the same parties and the two became companions. Their first photo together (left) was taken in a booth at Heathrow Airport when Rice-Davies had dark hair. They functioned well together in company and seemed to complement each other – Rice-Davies was shrewd and had a head for money, Keeler did not and was generally disorganised.

They also worked well in the bedroom, taking part in threesome sex scenes with men. Keeler says this became a speciality. She says neither were a bit bothered by group sex – it amused them and brought in money for clothes and entertainment.

SHARING RACHMAN'S FAVOURS

Peter Rachman was a ruthless property dealer who had affairs with Keeler and Rice-Davies. He met Keeler first, in 1959, when Ward brought her round to his flat in Bryanston Mews, Paddington, hoping for Rachman's help with flat-hunting.

Within days, Keeler had left Ward and moved into Rachman's flat, where he visited her daily for sex. Rachman was clinical in his lovemaking, making no pretence at passion. Keeler gave up her Murray's job, relying on Rachman for money and expensive presents that

included a sports car. She liked Rachman's lavish lifestyle, but not his jealousy. After six months, she broke with him and returned to Ward.

Rachman met Rice-Davies at the end of 1959, shortly before she and Keeler moved to a flat at Comeragh Road, Barons Court. At their flat-warming party, he left with Rice-Davies's telephone number and called a couple of days later. For 18 months he was her lover, keeping her supplied with all the luxuries and money that the girl from Solihull could desire.

Peter Rachman (inset) was 41 when he met Rice-Davies. Here, the two of them celebrate the 1961 opening of his 'La Discothèque' club. The toilet seats echoed the sleazy atmosphere.

manding friendship. Unlike most other men, Ward did not pester Keeler for sex. She recalled that they were soon living like 'brother and sister'.

Some time after meeting Keeler, Ward decided that he wanted to move to a larger flat. The one person that he knew could help was Peter Rachman

– later to be exposed as London's most unscrupulous property racketeer.

MANDY RICE-DAVIES

In 1960, Mandy (born 'Marilyn') Rice-Davies was 16 years old. Though she grew up in Solihull near Birmingham, her parents were Welsh – her mother, a miner's daughter, her father, an ex-policeman working for the tyre company, Dunlop. At 15, but looking older, she began to model clothes at Marshall & Snelgrove, a Birmingham department store.

Before she turned 16, Rice-Davies lost her virginity to a graduate of Trinity College, Dublin. He was helping his parents run their shop in the sum-

mer holiday, and the event, she remembers, took place 'in the room above the sweet shop next to the Odeon cinema.'

Some months later, Rice-Davies was in London, posing as a model at the Earl's Court launch of a new car called the Mini. The pay for the week was £80; that, plus receptions and glamorous launch parties, gave her a taste of the high life. rice-Davies packed her bags and headed south.

A HOST OF ADMIRERS

On her first day in London, Rice-Davies was hired as a dancer at Murray's Cabaret Club. Here, the 16-year-old Rice-Davies found many wealthy, often middle-aged, admirers. They included Walter Flack, millionaire partner of the property magnate, Charles Clore (who was to have sex with Keeler for money), and Eric, Earl of Dudley. The Earl showered Rice-Davies with flowers, sent her a case of pink champagne and took her for drives in his Jaguar.

Another admirer was New York millionaire Robert Sherwood. He advised Rice-Davies to go back to Solihull. Rice-Davies, caught up in London's exitement and glamour, chose to ignore him.

A teenage Christine Keeler poses for the camera while on holiday abroad (inset). A few years later she posed again (main picture), but this time as a topless showgirl at Murray's Cabaret Club in London. Part of her costume consisted of fake birds – here coyly used to cover her partial nudity. It was at Murray's that she met Stephen Ward and Mandy Rice-Davies.

WEST END

A BURST OF GUNFIRE IN A LONDON BACKSTREET MARKED THE BEGINNING OF THE END FOR WARD AND PROFUMO. JUST WHEN THE EVENTS OF 1961 SEEMED TO BE FADING, CHRISTINE KEELER'S LOVE-LIFE YET AGAIN SPELLED DISASTER

By the summer of 1962, the Profumo-Keeler-Ivanov story was beginning to seep out into society circles. July's issue of *Queen* magazine made a vague reference to the rumours in a gossip column snippet – 'called in MI5 because every time the chauffeur driven ZIS drew up at her *front* door, out of the *back* door into a chauffeur driven Humber slipped...'

AN ANONYMOUS INFORMER

In early November, an anonymous caller told George Wigg, a Labour MP who was known to dislike Profumo, to 'forget the Vassall case [the Admiralty Spy]. You want to look at Profumo.' Wigg took note. It was mid-December, though, by the time Profumo's secret life began to come out into the open.

Among Christine Keeler's lovers were two West Indian rivals for her attention, Aloysius 'Lucky' Gordon and Johnny Edgecombe. Gordon

GIRLS IN SHOTS DRAM

By MIRROR REPORTER

THE two girls pictured above—Christine Keeler, 20 (left), and Marilyn Davies, 18—leaned out of e window of a mews luxury flat yesterday

into the lock of the door leading to the flat.
Two more shots were heard as Christine and Marilyn looked out of the window.

phoned Dr. Ste the owner of the has his surgery Devonshire-street.
Dr. Ward said

Davies found themselves the centre of a shooting incident at Ward's Wimpole Mews flat (right). Edgecombe, Gordon's successor as Keeler's lover blasted the door of the house with a revolver that previously belonged to Keeler.

No one could have known that a jealous lover would be the trigger to a major national scandal. In December 1962 Keeler and Rice-

was jealously infatuated with Keeler. He had assaulted her in the street and had also, Keeler alleges, held her hostage for two days with an axe. Keeler dropped charges she had brought for the latter incident in response to appeals from Gordon's brother – he feared that Gordon would get a long sentence because of his criminal record for violence.

When Keeler at last rejected Gordon, she

bought a revolver to protect herself from him. John Edgecombe was also enlisted by Keeler to act as her minder. On 27 October 1962, Edgecombe and Gordon met in a face-to-face confrontation at a Soho club. Edgecombe slit Gordon's face with a knife, inflicting a wound needing 17 stitches.

For the next few weeks Edgecombe went into hiding from the police, while Keeler, in fear for her life, changed address to avoid Gordon.

DATEFILE

DECEMBER 14 1962
Johnny Edgecombe fires revolver shots outside Ward's flat

JANUARY 29 1963
Captain Eugene Ivanov leaves London posting to return to Moscow

MARCH 15 1963
Daily Express front page puts Profumo rumours next to Keeler disappearance story

DEC '62-MARCH '63

SHOOT-OUT

JOHNNY'S TALE

Profumo's affair with Keeler is believed to have ended with the Minister's final letter to Keeler in late 1961. But, according to Johnny Edgecombe (right), the West Indian musician who became Keeler's lover and minder, it was still going on well into the summer of 1962.

'This chick looked as if she had some class,' recalled Edgecombe on his first meeting with Keeler in the summer of 1962, 'and I asked her what she was doing running around with a cat like Gordon...To turn it around she told me about Profumo.'

'If she needed some bread,' Edgecombe continued, 'she could always ring up and arrange to see Jack. She would go off and see him, and he'd give her some money. I don't think it was a lot, fifteen or twenty pounds maybe. Yes, she was sleeping with him – she wouldn't see the guy for anything else. I don't know how many times she rung him...'

'Jazz singer' Lucky Gordon held Keeler in a grip of terror, watching her night and day. Keeler met Gordon at the El Rio café, when she bought marijuana from him. She claims that Ward encouraged her to make the approach.

raised the alarm, and Wimpole Mews was quickly swarming with police and journalists. Edgecombe, who managed to make off in a taxi, was later arrested at his Brentford flat. The press, excited by the action, had no idea of the story that was about to be unleashed.

The episode proved a catalyst. Keeler's story of sexual and political intrigue poured forth to interested parties. Michael Eddowes, a solicitor friend of Ward, who later played a prominent part in its exposure and was responsible for alerting the Americans to security aspects of the affair, was one such person. Keeler also informed the former Labour MP, John Lewis, who, unknown to her, was an avowed enemy of Stephen Ward.

After hearing Keeler's amazing testimony, Lewis believed that he was finally in a position to ruin Ward. It so happened that he was also a horse racing acquaintance of Profumo's critic, Labour MP George Wigg.

In early January 1963, Lewis told Wigg the details of Keeler's story – including Ward's

Edgecombe realised that he could not remain in hiding indefinitely and asked Keeler to help him find a solicitor before surrendering himself to the police. But Keeler, jealous of the fact that Edgecombe had taken another lover, made a decision that was to precipitate the exposure of the whole Profumo story. She told Edgecombe that she would not help him and that she planned to

testify against him in court.

In the early afternoon of 14 December 1962, Edgecombe, wild with rage, showed up outside Ward's Wimpole Mews flat. Keeler, there visiting Mandy Rice-Davies, refused to let him in. Incensed, Edgecombe blasted the door with the revolver that had once belonged to Keeler. Neighbours, hearing the startling commotion, alleged request that she should try to obtain information from Profumo regarding the possible delivery date of nuclear warheads to West Germany. In Wigg's opinion this represented a clear-cut security risk and he began to build up a dossier on Ivanov. Meanwhile, Lewis continued to feed the police with accusations that Ward was running a call-girl service. Once again, his allegations were entirely bogus, but this time they would be taken seriously.

Events now began to gather pace. The sixteenth of January 1963 was the date set for the Edgecombe committal hearing. Two days later Ward saw his friend Ivanov for what was to be the last time. On 22 January, Keeler told her story to the *Sunday Pictorial*. It included all the intimate details of the affair and the allegation that Profumo had left himself open to 'the worst type of blackmail – the blackmail of a spy'. Eugene Ivanov left the UK one week later, a departure 'much regretted' by his friends and undertaken with 'the connivance of MI5'.

The ever-increasing pressure on Ward and Keeler began to affect their relationship. On 26 January, they had a row which was to have bitter consequences, particularly for the osteopath. By coincidence, a Detective Sergeant Burrows had called to take Keeler's statement with regard to the Edgecombe hearing. Still angry, she blurted out her tale to the bemused policeman. Besides giving out details of her relationship with Profumo and Ivanov, she also claimed that Ward was a 'procurer for gentlemen in high places', as well as being 'sexually perverted'.

When rumours of a forthcoming story in the *Sunday Pictorial* reached Ward, his first thought

The background picture shows Christine Keeler in happier times, before events got out of control. Right: Chief Inspector Samuel Herbert (left) and Detective Sergeant John Burrows, soon to be assigned to a Ward investigation. Keeler had lifted the lid on Ward's lifestyle by chattering on distractedly to Burrows when he made a routine call at her flat to ask her to be a witness at Edgecombe's trial.

INSIDE VIEW
BEARING A GRUDGE

John Lewis (far left) and George Wigg (left) were men with revenge in mind. Both were eager to expose the Profumo scandal – one for personal reasons, the other political.

John Lewis was described as a 'nasty piece of work', 'evil and unscrupulous' and 'corrupt'. He had been trying to ruin Ward since the 1950s, when Lewis' wife, an ex-model, had come to Ward for advice over the disintegration of her marriage. Nothing improper occurred then, but when Ward later introduced a female business associate of Lewis to a was to warn his friends Lord Astor and Jack Profumo. Over the next few days, strenuous efforts were made to try and keep Keeler's revelations out of the papers. First, Profumo asked Sir Roger Hollis, the head of MI5, to issue a 'D-Notice' to stop publication, presumably on the grounds that publication of the story would have represented a threat to national security. Hollis, reportedly, had no desire to see his department tainted by a public scandal and decided to stay out of it.

JOSTLING FOR POSITION

There followed a series of complex negotiations between Keeler and the legal representatives of Ward and Profumo. What actually happened remains obscure, but in essence, it was proposed that she drop her story and leave the country in return for a compensatory payment of £5000. The alternative explanation is that she was being lured into a trap, whereby she would have left herself open to a charge of extortion. Either way, the deal fizzled out.

As news of these happenings reached the Government, Profumo was seen by the Prime Minister's Principal Private Secretary, Timothy Bligh, and Chief Whip, Martin Redmayne. Profumo lied that the affair had been no more than 'a giggle in the evening', and that sexual intercourse had not taken place. 'I am a man of the world,' said Redmayne, 'and I know if you hear a lot of rumours that somebody is sleeping with a girl, there is generally something in it.' However incredible Bligh and Redmayne must have found Profumo's assertion, their sense of public school honour meant that they had no option but to take his word for it – as a trusted colleague and fellow gentleman.

Bligh also arranged a meeting with MI5 to ask why the Government had not been informed earlier. He was given the brush-off. MI5 claimed they had no idea that Profumo had been sleeping with Keeler. In fact, Stephen Ward, ever anxious to do the right thing for Britain, had kept them closely informed on this matter right from the outset. He even managed to persuade an assistant editor of the *Sunday Pictorial* that Christine Keeler's story contained material inaccuracies, and that its publication would be bound to attract a major libel suit.

But the rumours were spreading fast. An obscure newsletter, *Westminster Confidential*, printed a thinly veiled reference to the scandal in its March edition. The readership was composed mainly of MPs, so the affair soon became common knowledge on the backbenches. Interestingly, the information had been supplied by the right wing Tory MP, Henry Kerby, an ex-MI6 officer who was now used by MI5 as an informant in Parliament.

When, on 14 March, Johnny Edgecombe finally appeared in court, Christine Keeler was nowhere to be seen. A week earlier she had travelled to Spain with a

lesbian Swedish beauty queen and the two had an affair, Lewis vowed to destroy him.

George Wigg, ex-soldier and Labour MP, had been betrayed by Profumo in the House of Commons. The two opponents had agreed to cooperate on an issue that was important enough to be kept above the squabbles of party politics. But when it came to the debate in July 1962, Profumo went back on his word and publicly belittled Wigg. He left behind an extremely bitter and dangerously angry man.

BACKDROP

LONDON NIGHTLIFE

The fateful appearance of Gordon and Edgecombe in Keeler's life revealed another side to the energetic nightlife both she and Ward led. While rubbing shoulders with millionaires and sugar daddies at Mayfair's glitzy watering holes, they were also among the first whites to venture into the emerging West Indian nightspots of Notting Hill.

Left: Keeler at a London night spot with, left to right, friends Paula Hamilton-Marshall, Bruce Brace and Paul Mann, with whom she escaped to Spain. Above: Out clubbing with gangland boss Ronnie Kray (to the left of Christine).

The El Rio café in Notting Hill was where Keeler had her first meeting with Gordon. It was a raffish hang-out for the young West Indians of the immigrant wave, thick with the smell of marijuana and a place where drugs could be bought easily. Then there was the All-nighters club in Soho, the haunt of American GIs, where the music was ahead of its time – a mix of American soul and Jamaican Ska.

At the other end of the scale were the clubs where money mattered, places such as the Black Sheep and the Kray twins' Esmeralda's Barn, dotted around the square mile of London's Mayfair. The regulars consisted of aristocrats, MPs filling in time during all-night sittings, actors winding down after the last curtain and assorted characters with money to burn. Murray's Club, where Keeler had worked as a showgirl and where the performers danced topless, was at the top of the list. Visitors had included Winston Churchill, Princess Margaret – and Minister of War, John Profumo.

The story was not accurate. Profumo had discussed resignation weeks earlier – with the Chief Whip, not the Prime Minister – and had decided against it. Profumo was able to tell reporters now gathered outside his home, 'There is no truth in this story at all – I have not seen the Prime Minister. I have been working on the Army estimates.' It did not matter that the story was garbled. The story remained front-page news from this moment on. It was fuelled by some curious burglaries.

MYSTERY BREAK-INS

The break-ins had started in early February, during Profumo's efforts to suppress the truth. Two photographs, both taken at the Cliveden swimming pool, vanished from Ward's London flat. One picture, showing Ward with three girls, had been snapped by Profumo. He had later added a caption 'The New Cliveden Set. "J".' The second photograph showed Profumo with two girls, one of them Keeler.

Trevor Kempson, then a 21-year-old freelance journalist, now admits that he was the culprit in the burglary at Ward's country retreat. He broke in, turned the place upside down and finally found pictures of Ward and Keeler inside a jar of coffee. He tried to sell the photographs to the *Daily Mirror*.

OVER THE EDGE

By now, few in the world of politics believed the dam could hold. It was about now that Conservative MP William Shepherd wrote to the Prime Minister, demanding action on the 'immorality in the government'. Macmillan asked him to give his information to the Chief Whip, Martin Redmayne, and he did. Shepherd remembers the conversation. 'As I was about to leave I said, "What are you going to do about Jack?" And he says, "If anyone says a word about Jack in public, we will sue for damages..."'

What the mandarins of the Conservative Party wanted would soon be academic. Labour MP George Wigg had shown his bulging dossier to his political boss, the future Prime Minister Harold Wilson, and Wilson cleared him to bring the matter into the open. Wigg now looked for a way to raise the Profumo case under protection of parliamentary privilege, and fate offered an ideal opportunity.

> *If you hear a lot of rumours that somebody is sleeping with a girl, there is generally something in it.*
>
> Michael Redmayne to John Profumo

couple of friends, Paul Mann and Kim Proctor. In 1989, it was alleged that Mann had been paid £3000 by anonymous officials to 'spirit Christine Keeler out of the country'. On his return, he was taken to Whitehall and advised to 'forget the whole incident'. The main effect of Keeler's absence was to re-awaken press interest in her original allegations.

As for Edgecombe, he was found not guilty of the assault on 'Lucky' Gordon but received a seven-year prison term on the lesser charge of possession of a firearm. He has always maintained that the conviction was racially motivated and served over five years of his sentence before being released. 'The British people wouldn't wear a situation,' Edgecombe believes, 'where a government minister was sleeping with the same chick as a black guy.'

For John Profumo, who must have long wished the earth would open and swallow up Christine Keeler, her disappearance now spelt disaster. It provided a way, at last, for the press to link the Keeler-Edgecombe case with the name of John Profumo. The *Daily Express* did it on 15 March 1963, by means of a clever trick on the newspaper's front page. One column away from a picture of Keeler, captioned 'Vanished', the newspaper ran a picture of Profumo next to the headline 'WAR MINISTER SHOCK – Profumo offers his resignation for personal reasons and Premier asks him to stay on.'

BACKDROP WARD AND KEELER'S LONDON

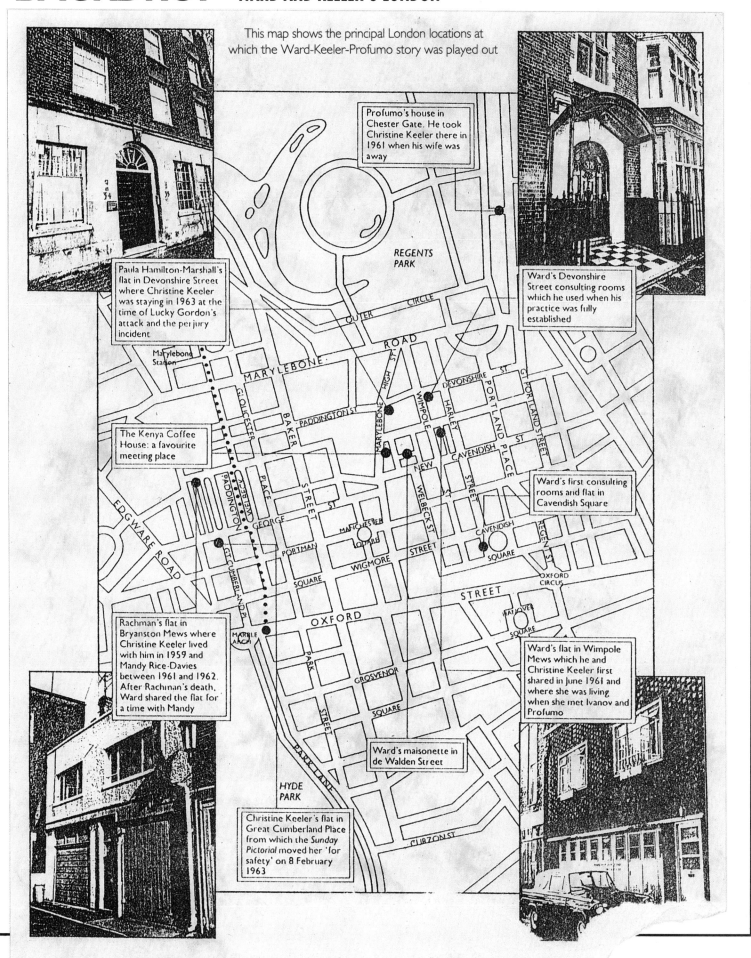

This map shows the principal London locations at which the Ward-Keeler-Profumo story was played out

Profumo's house in Chester Gate. He took Christine Keeler there in 1961 when his wife was away

Ward's Devonshire Street consulting rooms which he used when his practice was fully established

Paula Hamilton-Marshall's flat in Devonshire Street where Christine Keeler was staying in 1963 at the time of Lucky Gordon's attack and the perjury incident

REGENTS PARK

The Kenya Coffee House: a favourite meeting place

Ward's first consulting rooms and flat in Cavendish Square

Rachman's flat in Bryanston Mews where Christine Keeler lived with him in 1959 and Mandy Rice-Davies between 1961 and 1962. After Rachman's death, Ward shared the flat for a time with Mandy

Ward's flat in Wimpole Mews which he and Christine Keeler first shared in June 1961 and where she was living when she met Ivanov and Profumo

Ward's maisonette in de Walden Street

HYDE PARK

Christine Keeler's flat in Great Cumberland Place from which the Sunday Pictorial moved her 'for safety' on 8 February 1963

SUMMER OF '63

AS BRITAIN SWELTERED THROUGH THE LONG HOT SUMMER OF THE PROFUMO REVELATIONS, THE COUNTRY STOOD AT THE CROSSROADS BETWEEN OLD IDEALS AND NEW TRENDS. LIFE WOULD NEVER BE QUITE THE SAME AGAIN

The dramatic Profumo story coincided with a period of major transition between the old world and the new. Public fascination was not simply a matter of titillation over the sex, spies and politics that the scandal offered. It also provided a focus for growing resentment against the old order and offered an opportunity to expose the Establishment's hypocrisy.

DYING VALUES

There was a growing sense that the old guard was on its way out and that a new generation

The 'twist' was the dance to be doing throughout Britain's burgeoning club scene (above), while modesty continued to be observed up and down the country's packed beaches (main picture).

would solve the world's problems. In May, Sir Winston Churchill announced his retirement from the House of Commons at the next election,

Left: Kennedy states: 'Ich bin ein Berliner' ('I am a Berliner') in his summer speech to the West Germans, while Martin Luther King champions black rights (below).

while MP Anthony Wedgwood Benn renounced his viscountcy, later becoming plain Tony Benn.

The Conservative Government was reeling from a succession of dramatic spy cases that had rocked confidence in the nation's security service. Admiralty clerk, William Vassall, was found to have given secrets

to the USSR and former diplomat Kim Philby defected to Moscow. Two years before, George Blake had been sentenced to 26 years for spying. It seemed that the Profumo revelations provided the icing on the cake.

'Youth' was becoming the universal symbol for an awaken-

DECLINING STANDARDS

At the time of the Profumo scandal, various public figures were called upon to comment on Britain's changing morality:

It is the duty of public people...to set a good example and give a lead in life. When they don't it is deplorable and they no longer deserve to rule.

Lady Longford, Historian

The moral fibre which made Britain great is disappearing. The trouble is a total lack of discipline.

Sir Vivien Fuchs, Explorer

Left: Dusty Springfield in 1963. Having tasted great success as part of The Springfields trio, she went on to pursue a solo career when the group split up in 1963. Her classic hit of the year was 'I Only Want To Be With You'.

Right: Sean Connery as agent 007 in the huge May 1963 box office hit From Russia With Love. The first Bond film, Dr No, had been slow to find large audiences when it first came out in 1962.

ing that had started to touch every part of society since the beginning of the decade. In the wake of violent civil rights riots across the USA, Reverend Martin Luther King made his historic 'I have a dream' speech in August 1963. In Berlin, the American President John F Kennedy declared solidarity with the people of West Germany against the threat from the Communist bloc.

In Britain, Prime Minister Harold Macmillan and his Cabinet, including John Profumo, typified the traditional 'Establishment'. Harold Wilson, the Huddersfield-born Opposition leader, was more effectively catching Britain's new mood. He tried to model himself on the dynamic and youthful American President, and called for a revolution in science and technology – the areas where Britain was falling most visibly behind the rest of Europe.

A NEW BRITAIN ?

Post-war values, which had remained virtually intact during the 1950s, were being chal-

lenged at every level. A new and sharper satire, showing little respect for society's leaders and elder statesmen, was beginning to flourish. The magazine *Private Eye* was launched, and 'That Was The Week That Was' had appeared on BBC television in late 1962. Irreverence was the order of the day.

Sex was coming out of the closet. Matters which had been judged indecent before were now openly debated, while the indiscretions of public figures were fast becoming the preoccupation of the press. This new openness had begun in 1960, when the authorities had unsuccessfully tried to ban sections of

D H Lawrence's 'pornographic' novel *Lady Chatterley's Lover*. On 19 June 1963, the sexual revolution took another major step – the first British-made oral contraceptives became available on prescription.

INTO VOGUE

A series of innovations in fashion, design, music and dance were also underway. During the early 1960s, Mary Quant and John Stephen opened their boutiques along Chelsea's King's Road – which was now turning into the new fashion centre. Much to the disapproval of the other Sunday newspapers, the *Sunday Times*

had issued its first colour supplement in 1962, featuring the work of photographer David Bailey and a new model, Jean Shrimpton.

Following their first number one hit 'Love Me Do' in 1962, 1963 turned into the year of *The Beatles* – two huge number one hits dominated the summer charts. Radical innovation and change was coming from below at an unprecedented pace.

Below: A flavour of older values shows in this 1963 women's magazine advertisement. Meanwhile, fashions were changing from tailored dresses into trends that formed the vanguard of the 'swinging sixties' (insets).

DECEPTION

JOHN PROFUMO WAS TRYING TO LIE HIS WAY OUT OF TROUBLE, BUT THE NET WAS CLOSING AROUND HIM TOO FAST. ON 22 MARCH 1963, IN FRONT OF A PACKED HOUSE OF COMMONS, HE STEPPED BEYOND ANY HOPE OF REDEMPTION

A debate took place in the House of Commons on the evening of 21 March 1963, concerning two reporters who had gone to prison for refusing to reveal their sources during the enquiry into William Vassall. Vassall was the homosexual Admiralty clerk who had been jailed for 18 years for spying for the Soviet Union. This lucky combination of issues – national security and press reporting – gave George Wigg the opportunity to speak on a related, but entirely different, matter.

FORCING THE ISSUE

Just before midnight, Wigg addressed the Commons: 'There is not an honourable member in the House, nor a journalist in the Press gallery,' he said, 'who, in the past few days, has not heard rumour upon rumour involving a member of the Government Front Bench. The press has got as near as it could – it has shown itself willing to wound, but afraid to strike...That being the case, I rightly use the privilege of the House of Commons

– that is what it is given me for – to ask the Home Secretary...to go to the dispatch box – he knows that the rumour to which I refer related to a Miss Christine Keeler, and Miss Davies, and a shooting by a West Indian – and, on behalf of the Government, categorically deny the truth of these rumours...'

Pandemonium broke out behind the scenes. Chief Whip, Martin Redmayne, woke the Prime Minister up after 1 am to tell him that it was vital for Profumo to give a personal statement to the House before the newspapers ran Wigg's speech all over their front pages. Profumo's 'phone was off the hook, so an official car had to be sent to collect him. The Minister for War had taken a sleeping tablet, and was still in a stupor as the car sped back through the night to Westminster.

CRISIS MEETING

Profumo found himself before five men who formed the backbone of the British Establishment. There were Sir John Hobson, the Attorney-General, and William Deedes, Minister without Portfolio. Both were old Harrovians, like Profumo. There too were Chief Whip Redmayne; Solicitor-General Sir Peter Rawlinson; and Leader of the House Iain Macleod. The Home Secretary, the man responsible for police and security matters, was conspicuous by his absence.

Profumo reasserted his innocence. But there were those in the room that evening who thought it likely that he was lying. As a fellow Conservative was to say, Profumo 'was not a man ever likely to tell the absolute truth in a tight corner.' However, by 4.30 am, a statement had been concocted. Profumo went home, to a house still besieged by reporters.

Shortly after 11.00 am, flanked by Harold Macmillan, Profumo rose to tell the historic lie that would not be forgiven:

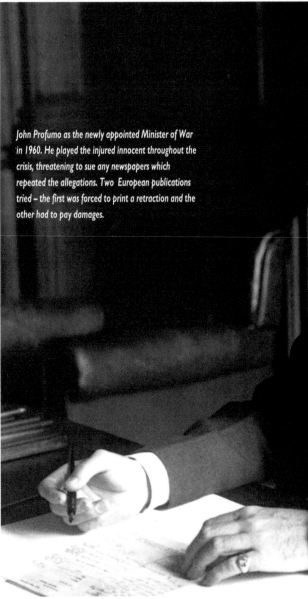

John Profumo as the newly appointed Minister of War in 1960. He played the injured innocent throughout the crisis, threatening to sue any newspapers which repeated the allegations. Two European publications tried – the first was forced to print a retraction and the other had to pay damages.

'My wife and I first met Miss Keeler at a house party in July 1961, at Cliveden. Among a number of people there was Dr Stephen Ward, whom we already knew slightly, and a Mr Ivanov, who was an Attaché at the Russian Embassy. Between July and December 1961 I met Miss Keeler on about half a dozen occasions at Dr Ward's flat when I called to see him and his friends. Miss Keeler and I were on friendly terms. There was no impropriety

AND DISGRACE

CLOSE-UP

THE PRIME MINISTER WHO NEVER WAS?

himself to be photographed with her. That night he went to a dance at Quaglino's with his wife.

George Wigg left the Commons 'with black rage in my heart because I knew what the facts were.' He would not rest until he had forced the Government to face the truth. In the background were other men, all dedicated to the exposure of Profumo, or Ward, or both. There was Ward's deadly foe, John Lewis, solicitor Michael Eddowes, and the chiefs of MI5, scheming to mask their own involvement.

Wigg then appeared on BBC television and spoke of a continuing security issue. One of the viewers was Stephen Ward. Stung by the implication that he had endangered national security, Ward saw Wigg the next day. He provided a briefing that Wigg recorded on paper. It was, Harold Wilson was to say later, 'a nauseating

whatsoever in my acquaintance with Miss Keeler...I shall not hesitate to issue writs for libel and slander if scandalous allegations are made or repeated outside the House.'

Profumo left to the cheers of the Conservative faithful and the Prime Minister walked with him, his hand on the younger man's shoulder. The same afternoon, Profumo found time to go to the races, at Sandown Park, with the Queen Mother. He allowed

document, taking the lid off a corner of the London underworld of vice...blackmail and counter-blackmail...together with references to Mr Profumo and the Soviet Attaché...'

On 29 March, Michael Eddowes called Scotland Yard to say he had important information. He gave a special Branch officer an aide-memoire, based on the information Keeler had given him after the Edgecombe shooting, alleging that it was Ivanov – not Ward as all other accounts have it – who had asked Keeler to pump Profumo for information about the delivery of nuclear warheads to Germany. The Special Branch man, according to Eddowes, said that the information would be put in front of the Prime Minister.

MI5 COVER-UP

On the same day, the head of MI5, Roger Hollis, was called in by Home Secretary Henry Brooke. Although MI5 already knew about the Keeler affair and that Profumo had lied to the House of Commons, Hollis did not share his knowledge with the Home Secretary. To do so would have revealed MI5's use of Ward in their scheme to entrap

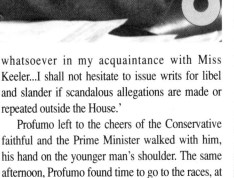

The grandson of an Italian baron, John Profumo was born to Conservatism. He believed he belonged to a natural ruling class and led a social life taken up with polo, horse shows, house parties and fêtes.

His family had settled in England at the turn of the century and styled themselves as English country squires, with a country seat near Stratford-upon-Avon, where Profumo was MP (right) from 1950 until his resignation. Profumo went to Harrow and Brasenose College, Oxford and was elected as a Member of Parliament at the precociously early age of 25.

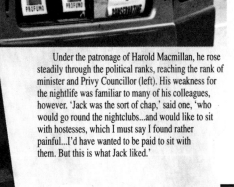

Under the patronage of Harold Macmillan, he rose steadily through the political ranks, reaching the rank of minister and Privy Councillor (left). His weakness for the nightlife was familiar to many of his colleagues, however. 'Jack was the sort of chap,' said one, 'who would go round the nightclubs...and would like to sit with hostesses, which I must say I found rather painful...I'd have wanted to be paid to sit with them. But this is what Jack liked.'

DAILY EXPRESS

PROFUMO
QUITS: I LIED

He gives up War Minister's job
and seat in House of Commons

His denial of impropriety with
Christine Keeler was untrue...
'I misled you,' he tells Premier

*Who's going to believe the word
of this whore against the
word of a man who has been
in government for ten years?*

John Profumo to journalist Chapman Pincher

Profumo had tried and
failed to ride the storm and now had to face the
jeers of the public (right). His resignation (above) was immediately
accepted by Prime Minister Macmillan.

Eugene Ivanov.

Instead, the head of MI5 threw Ward to the wolves. He told Brooke that Ward had asked Keeler to get information from Profumo on nuclear warheads. The Home Secretary wanted to know if there was a case for prosecuting Ward under the Official Secrets Act. Hollis evasively replied that the evidence was shaky. But he had planted the idea that the buck should be passed, not to the Minister of War, but to the 'provider of popsies', Stephen Ward.

Brooke now turned the guns of the Establishment on Ward. Was there, he asked the

Sir Roger Hollis (left), the
head of MI5 who knew about
Profumo but did not tell the
Government.

Police Commissioner, Sir Joseph Simpson, a police interest in Ward? Simpson said there might be some basis for prosecuting him in connection with his girls, but the evidence would be hard to get. There now began a vice investigation out of all proportion to Ward's alleged offences.

Two days before the Brooke meeting, the Criminal Investigation Department began receiving anonymous mail. It alleged that 'Ward was living off immoral earnings of girls'. Significantly, the public was never allowed to see the letters. There is only one serious candidate for the poison-pen writer – John Lewis.

The first statements taken in the police investigation of Ward came from Christine Keeler.

They contained details of her relationship with Profumo which – as Lord Denning later admitted in his laborious prose – 'one would think...not likely to have been invented.' The police now knew, if they had not known already, that Profumo had lied in Parliament – but that was not the issue Their job was to get Ward.

'I became aware that the police had started asking questions,' Ward wrote. 'It only came home to me most gradually that these questions were directed against me...now the full horror of the situation came home to me, and I started to feel hunted.' Ward flailed around for help. On 7 May, he met the Prime Minister's secretary, Timothy Bligh, with an MI5 man sitting in.

For Lucky Gordon, Christine Keeler was still a dangerous obsession. In April 1963, he had to be restrained by the police (left) when he tried to confront her after her appearance in court for failing to attend the Edgecombe trial. Two months later he was to appear in court himself, charged with assaulting Keeler at her friend Paula Hamilton-Marshall's flat in London.

'You see,' said Ward hopefully, 'the facts as presented in Parliament were not strictly speaking just like that...I made a considerable sacrifice for Mr Profumo...I feel I should tell you the truth of what really happened. I know myself here that there is a great deal of potentially extremely explosive material in what I've told you.'

WARD'S DESPERATION

Ward was becoming increasingly desperate about the scale of the investigation. 'The Marylebone police are questioning my patients and friends in a line which is extremely damaging to me both professionally and socially...Over the past weeks I have done what I could to shield Mr Profumo from his indiscretion about which I complained to the Security Services at the time.'

His assertion that he had told MI5 about Profumo's affair with Keeler while it was still going on was simply denied. 'There is no truth,' MI5's

Director General Hollis had long since reported to the Prime Minister's office, 'in the story that the Security service was informed of Mr Profumo's alleged visits to Ward or to Miss Keeler.' It was a lie, of course, as several former MI5 officers would shame-facedly confirm nearly two decades later.

In the meantime, *The People* newspaper was preparing to step into the gap left by the *Sunday Pictorial's* decision to drop the Profumo story. Editor Sam Campbell intended to expose Profumo as a liar. He told the Police Commissioner, and the Commissioner warned the Government.

On Friday, 31 May, the Lord Chancellor, Lord Dilhorne, told Profumo he would interview him in a week's time. The minister responded by going to Venice with his wife – on holiday. Before the weekend was over, a telegram from Dilhorne destroyed any illusion that his lie would hold up: would he please return to London? Profumo talked through the night with his wife, then decided to go home and tell the truth.

TIME FOR THE TRUTH

Profumo told Timothy Bligh that he had indeed slept with Keeler. His resignation letter, written at once, read, in part:

'Dear Prime Minister

I said that there had been no impropriety in this association. To my very deep regret I have to admit that this was not true...I have come to realise that,

by this deception, I have been guilty of a grave misdemeanour...I cannot remain a member of your administration, nor of the House of Commons...I cannot tell you of my deep remorse...'

Harold Macmillan wrote back:

'This is a great tragedy for you, your family and your friends. Nevertheless, I have no alternative but to advise the Queen to accept your resignation.'

John and Valerie Profumo successfully went into hiding for several days. Astonishingly quickly, as one observer noted, 'Profumo was far from the stage, heading back fast towards obscurity.' Ward

Prime Minister Harold Macmillan (right) admitted after his retirement that he suspected that Profumo had been lying to him about his relationship with Keeler. But he felt that – as a colleague and a fellow gentleman – he had to accept the Minister of War's word.

was at Bryanston Mews when the resignation news came through, with the press at his door. He was now at his wits' end, harried by reporters and abandoned by his rich friends. When a former patient offered Ward sanctuary at his home in Watford, Ward gratefully accepted.

He emerged blinking into the light and squeezed into his Jaguar, only to find the street blocked by press cars. Frantic, Ward drove straight into one of the vehicles, bulldozing himself an escape route. The man with the unflappable charm was finally snapping.

On 8 June, Ward was arrested at Watford by two policemen. He was taken to Marylebone Police Station and charged: 'That he, being a man, did on divers dates between January 1961 and 8 June 1963, knowingly live wholly or in part on the earnings of prostitution at 17 Wimpole Mews, contrary to section 30 of the Sexual Offences Act 1956.' Other charges were to follow.

Profumo had lost his career, but much worse was to befall Stephen Ward. He had become the scapegoat for the Government's embarrassment and of a security service ruthlessly determined to cover its tracks. While Profumo had been allowed to disappear from circulation, Ward was forced to remain in the full glare of publicity, hounded by the press, exposed to the moral disapproval of the public and deserted by the people he thought were his friends.

CLOSE-UP THE MINISTER'S WIFE

Valerie Hobson married John Profumo in December 1954 at a quiet but fashionable wedding service in Knightsbridge, London (left). He was then 39 years old and she was 37. She came from a conservative and Protestant background in Country Antrim, Northern Ireland, where her father was a Naval Commander.

She had been divorced for two years before marrying Profumo, having been previously married to a film producer, Anthony Havelock-Allen. She was herself a well-known actress and had starred in a string of films including *Kind Hearts and Coronets*, *The Spy in Black* and *Great Expectations* (left, inset with John Mills). Her marriage and subsequent retirement from acting was seen as a considerable sacrifice, since she had just landed the lead role in the West End stage version of *The King And I* and her career was reviving after a prolonged low patch.

Christine Keeler

CHRISTINE KEELER'S LIFE HAS BEEN LIVED AWAY FROM THE SPOTLIGHT EVER SINCE THE PROFUMO CRISIS. IN JUNE 1990, IN AN EXCLUSIVE INTERVIEW GIVEN AT THE BASIL STREET HOTEL IN KNIGHTSBRIDGE, LONDON, SHE TOOK THE OPPORTUNITY TO TELL HER OWN STORY

The early childhood of Christine Keeler, she recalls, living in a caravan in Wraysbury, was largely uneventful and ordinary. But this innocence was shattered, she maintains, by a period of sexual overtures from her stepfather that was eventually to force her to leave home: 'He had a big crush on me from about the age of 12 till I was 15. I used to go to sleep at night and be scared that he'd come and grab hold of me. I felt that he was madly in love with me. On one occasion, when my mother went into hospital, he tried to kiss me and rubbed my chest with 'Vick' saying it was because I had a cold...I didn't want to leave my home, but I had to.'

ON WARD

After a brief stay in Slough, she moved to London, where she eventually began working at Murray's Cabaret Club in the West End. It was here that she met Stephen Ward: 'I was what you call a showgirl...I didn't have any clothes on, but I didn't take them off in public. Stephen was charming, terribly well-spoken. He had a command of the English language and was very persuasive. He had

❝ Never once has there been a thrill about being Christine Keeler. ❞

that gift of getting people to do what he wanted – just his voice would make you go stupid.' Christine found him 'not handsome but pleasant looking. He was far too old for me, but he had a very good physique.'

Once she moved in with him, her account of their day-to-day life together is very different from the common impression of endless wild parties. 'He needed me for company and to wait on him, make his coffee, get something to eat...I was like the au pair, although he didn't pay me. I used to keep the place clean and, if anyone came round, I'd be quiet while they talked. In the evenings I used to go out [to Murray's] and he used to wait for me to come back.' She believes he discouraged her from making a career in modelling – 'He'd say "stay in bed; we'll go for lunch." He used to hold me back – he wanted me to be with him.'

She says that in her relationship with Ward there was '...absolutely no sex whatsoever. He wasn't a very sexual man at all – he had a few girlfriends here and there. He took me to a sex party once – I didn't enjoy it and even then I didn't have anything to do with him.'

While her initial admiration for Ward was total, the idea that he was her 'Pygmalion' figure, grooming her for great things, has been exaggerated. 'I worshipped him, he was like my father. Whatever Stephen said, I did. I thought he had my best interests at heart...I suppose he did make me speak a little better. Obviously there was a bit of grooming living with somebody like that, but then my stepfather brought me up to speak properly and be well-mannered.'

ON ESPIONAGE

With hindsight, Keeler is convinced that if she was being groomed for anything, it was for a far more sinister role. Contrary to what many commentators on the Profumo case think, she is sure that Stephen Ward was acting as a paid agent for Soviet Intelligence. She even suspects that he was the Fifth Man, the undiscovered last link in a chain of British double agents working for the Soviets. 'Stephen was definitely spying,' she says, 'and the embarrassing thing

was that no one was aware of it...he was getting money from the Russians. I knew that he was doing it, but it didn't seem that serious. He was setting me up because he wanted me to find information. He left it...so that if ever I said anything, he could say, "it's not me, it's her." I was used. I was an innocent.'

ON IVANOV

Her involvement with Ivanov was nothing more than a one-night stand, an act of impulse on her part which was not encouraged by Ward. She says that she slept with Ivanov because she felt jilted by another man: 'I was upset, because I was actually going out with a chap called Noel Howard-Jones...Stephen didn't know this and he would have been most jealous. Along came Noel with this young beautiful girl [to Cliveden]. I was absolutely choked. I came back to London with Eugene and that's why I jumped into bed with him. There wasn't really any sort of relationship. He was quite a good-looking chap compared to most of Stephen's friends...but he was still too old for me. After the incident he didn't come round for a while and when I did see him, we didn't look into each other's eyes.'

ON PROFUMO

Keeler's version of the Profumo liaison – 'he was a flirty sort of chap...very intelligent...a very nice man,' – is matter-of-fact: 'I knew it wasn't going to last, I didn't want to be serious with him. Jack [Profumo] wanted me to move out of Stephen's place and I thought, "Oh God, no way; I'll probably land up as some MP's whore..." and I didn't want to do that.'

'Stephen was horrible to me really because he was setting me up. Ivanov had asked Stephen to find out when the Germans were going to get the bomb and he wanted me to find out information [from Profumo]. He was setting me up to blame me if it came out about him asking me to get information about Jack [Profumo]. I was being pushed by Stephen into something I didn't want to do.'

ON DENNING

She believes that the report by Lord Denning on the Profumo case was a cover-up which played up the sex angle in order to hide the truth about the risk to national security: 'Lord Denning left all of these things

❝ Stephen was definitely spying... and the embarrassing thing was that no one was aware of it. ❞

out. He dragged in an incident [the Man in the Mask party] which had nothing to do with the Profumo affair whatsoever'. The report was 'just a set-up to make it into a sex case...I was the scapegoat.'

Keeler has mixed feelings about her friendship with Mandy Rice-Davies. 'We were absolute dynamite together. What she wouldn't do I would and what I wouldn't do she would. We were just young, just like anybody really.' But 'Stephen didn't like Mandy, he thought she was mercenary. The only thing Mandy was interested in was Mandy.' The friendship became less intense once Mandy began living with Peter Rachman:

'Stephen didn't like Mandy and Peter didn't like Stephen. They weren't part of us, they were different types of people. They were going to night clubs and gambling – they were low people...seedy.'

ON KEELER

The whole episode with Lucky Gordon, leading to her prison sentence for perjury, leaves nothing but bad memories for Keeler. 'Gordon was just obsessed with me although I didn't want to know him. He was never my boyfriend...he was very lucky that he came across me when I didn't have my gun, otherwise I would have shot him. By the time I got out of prison, I was mentally very wounded. I got all the blame, filth and dirt. I felt dirty and ashamed – for nothing.'

Looking back over her life, Keeler says, 'I think Stephen was about the only person that I've ever lost who has been really close to me. I have not been very good at relationships; I don't have them any more.' When she reflects on the 'celebrity' status she has achieved in the wake of the scandal, Keeler's summing up is stark but realistic; 'Never once has there been a thrill about being Christine Keeler.'

Christine Keeler (right) believes she has emerged 'pretty level-headed' from a life that has see-sawed between high society and bankruptcy.

THE TRIAL OF

ON 22 JULY 1963, STEPHEN WARD FACED HIS ACCUSERS AT COURT NUMBER 1, THE OLD BAILEY, CHARGED WITH LIVING OFF IMMORAL EARNINGS. TO MANY, IT SEEMED AS IF THE ESTABLISHMENT WAS OUT TO GET HIM BY ANY MEANS

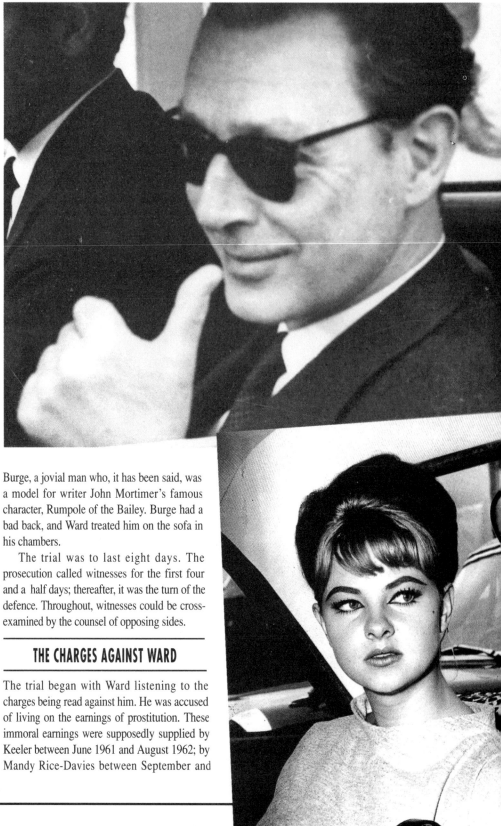

For the crowds, ten deep, that gathered outside the Old Bailey – London's Central Criminal Court – Stephen Ward's trial looked like being the 'trial of the century' or at least a national entertainment. People had even queued overnight for a seat in the court's small public gallery.

Inside, the ritual began with the arrival in court of the sheriff and alderman, and the judge, Sir Archibald Marshall. Nicknamed 'the Hen', Marshall held stern, old-fashioned values. He 'could hardly be expected to make allowances for the renegade son of a canon,' wrote a chronicler of the Old Bailey. 'His demeanour and the very inflection of his voice implied moral disapproval...'

The prosecuting barrister was Mervyn Griffith-Jones, a man capable of moral outrage at the slightest failing. He was so out of touch with the modern world that at the 1960 *Lady Chatterley's Lover* obscenity trial, he had solemnly asked the jury whether it was 'a book you'd want your wife and servants to read.'

Stephen Ward's defence counsel was James

Burge, a jovial man who, it has been said, was a model for writer John Mortimer's famous character, Rumpole of the Bailey. Burge had a bad back, and Ward treated him on the sofa in his chambers.

The trial was to last eight days. The prosecution called witnesses for the first four and a half days; thereafter, it was the turn of the defence. Throughout, witnesses could be cross-examined by the counsel of opposing sides.

THE CHARGES AGAINST WARD

The trial began with Ward listening to the charges being read against him. He was accused of living on the earnings of prostitution. These immoral earnings were supposedly supplied by Keeler between June 1961 and August 1962; by Mandy Rice-Davies between September and

off

DATEFILE

JULY 22 1963
Beginning of Stephen Ward's trial at the Old Bailey. Christine Keeler is the first witness for the prosecution

JULY 23 1963
Mandy Rice-Davies testifies against Ward

JULY 25 1963
Stephen Ward gives evidence

JULY 30 1963
Justice Marshall's summing up

JULY '63

STEPHEN WARD

December 1962; and by two others, Ronna Ricardo and Vickie Barrett, between January and June 1963. There were two other charges: of procuring a girl under 21 to have intercourse; and attempting to procure a girl under 21 to have sex with a third person.

To convict Ward, the prosecution had to do three things: prove that Ward was providing Keeler and Rice-Davies with 'goods and services' for carrying out the trade of prostitution; prove that the two girls were prostitutes; and have Keeler's and Rice-Davies' evidence corroborated by independent witnesses.

The prosecution began with Griffith-Jones' opening speech, which portrayed Ward as a monster of depravity. This lasted one and a half hours.

The best evidence mustered against Ward came

While Ward managed to look a model of composure as he set off for the first day of the trial (left), Rice-Davies and Keeler (below) arrived with the prospect of giving prosecution evidence against their former friend and 'father-figure'.

from the prosecution's two most important witnesses – Christine Keeler and Mandy Rice-Davies. They had been under great pressure from the police. Keeler had been endlessly interrogated and to prevent Rice-Davies making trips abroad, the police had twice arrested her at Heathrow Airport on trivial or false charges.

STAR WITNESSES

Keeler was the first witness to appear. She wore a mustard-coloured outfit, and her long, copper hair hung down to her shoulders. Said Ludovic Kennedy in his 1964 book *The Trial of Stephen Ward* 'despite the tarty high-heeled shoes, she was tiny, a real little doll of a girl...one could see at once her appeal to the animal instincts of men.'

Griffith-Jones attempted to establish that Keeler was a prostitute in league with Ward. He prised out of her the fact that she had had sex about six times, at Ward's Wimpole Mews flat (the scene of the first two charges), with a Major James Eylan. He had paid her about £15 on each occasion. Ward knew nothing of the payments. She had sex with John Profumo several times. 'On one occasion,' said Keeler, 'he gave me money to give to my mother.'

Keeler had also had sex – for £50 – with a man referred to in court only as 'Charles'. She has since confirmed that this was Charles Clore, the millionaire financier. Some of this money she gave to Ward, 'to pay my debts,' she said.

Mandy Rice-Davies, testifying on day two, said she had sex 'about five times' with a man referred to throughout the trial as 'the Indian doctor'. This was Emil Savundra, the crooked, Ceylonese-born head of Fire, Auto and Marine Insurance. Savundra, Rice-

Defence counsel, James Burge (above) was witty and genuinely likeable, but he proved no match for prosecution counsel, Mervyn Griffith-Jones (left). A product of Eton and the Brigade of Guards, he heaped disapproval on Ward – Griffith-Jones could have made 'a honeymoon sound obscene', said Burge.

Davies said, gave her money after sex – between £15 and £25 a time. Rice-Davies also spoke of the one occasion on which she had slept with Lord Astor.

Like Keeler, Rice-Davies admitted having given Ward money occasionally – 'just a couple of pounds, or something like that, but it was not in return for him introducing me to men. You have to pay where you live.' Again, Rice-Davies, like Keeler, had contributed to the general day-to-day expenses at the Wimpole Mews flat, including the food bills – 'in all about £25.'

MEETING THEIR MEN

The prosecution made a big issue out of how the girls met their men, in order to establish whether Ward was introducing girls to men expressly for sexual services. John Profumo and Lord Astor had come on the scene as a result of Ward's socialising. Keeler said she met James Eylan by herself, though Ward, she said, did actually introduce her to Charles Clore. He also allegedly

A LOVER OF DECADENCE

During the trial, the Crown prosecutor described Ward as 'thoroughly immoral'. It is true that Ward was no angel. Many of the parties he attended, for example, rapidly turned into sex games, but this had nothing to do with the charges that had been brought against him. 'These parties,' Ward said, 'nearly always started in the same way – a few drinks, and one or other of the girls would start the ball rolling – usually one would offer to do a striptease. That was enough.'

The parties could last for days, kept going with the aid of pills, such as Benzedrine or Methedrine, ground up and added to guest's drinks. The people who attended them were often rich and famous; they included Tory MPs, a member of the Royal family and, on one occasion, American singer Bing Crosby.

Some of the gatherings were devoted to masochism and sadism. Ward was a frequent guest at the parties of Mariella Novotny. One of the most famous, held in 1961, was the 'Man in the Mask' party. Mandy Rice-Davies recalls: 'Mariella was there wearing a kind of corset, and carrying a whip. Naked people were everywhere...' There was also a man in a rubber mask, who, writes Novotny, 'was strapped between wooden pillars. A whip was placed in front of his naked figure. As each guest arrived they gave him one stroke...' Later, he served them all dinner. The man has never been positively identified.

BACKDROP

suggested that an encounter with Clore would not go unrewarded.

In the witness box, Rice-Davies spoke about her relationship with the Indian doctor, Savundra. According to her, she met Savundra with Ward at a Marylebone coffee bar. Ward, she said, had already rented out her room to the doctor for £25 so that he could use it for a daytime assignation with his girlfriend. It was the following day that Emil Savundra turned up at the flat and the two of them – Rice-Davies and the doctor – had sex.

Keeler had her own highly damaging testimony about Savundra. According to her, Ward had made the suggestion that she should 'entertain' him once a week – in return for money. The plan never came off, however.

The true facts might have come out had the men themselves been called as witnesses, yet John

Profumo and Lord Astor, spoken of almost reverentially in court, were never called. Nor was Emil Savundra. Charles Clore's surname was never revealed. Only Major James Eylan had the courage to appear. His 10-minute appearance in the witness-box established one thing for beyond any doubt. In her relations with him, Christine Keeler had indeed prostituted herself. However, it was also clear from Eylan's evidence that Stephen Ward was in no way involved.

POLICE PRESSURE

Ronna Ricardo, produced by the prosecution on the third day of the trial, appeared with her hair dyed red and wearing a pink sweater. She readily admitted she was a prostitute. She was known as 'Ronna the lash', and specialised in flagellation. Earlier, in a statement to the police and at the Ward committal proceedings, she had implicated the osteopath in a series of sex episodes that had involved money.

Two days before the trial, however, Ricardo retracted her first statements. 'At no time,' she said, 'have I received any money on Stephen Ward's premises, or given money to him.' She lied because she had been led to believe that the police might take her baby daughter and younger sister out of her care.

'Are you suggesting,' asked Judge Marshall at the Old Bailey, 'that the police had just put words into your mouth?'

'Yes,' Ronna Ricardo replied.

EVIDENCE

The court also heard the testimony of a prostitute called Vickie Barrett, said to have visited Ward's flat over a period of many weeks, and to have provided sex for money for several men. Perhaps purely by coincidence, Barrett had been arrested for soliciting on 3 July, the same day that Ward was committed for trial. In her diary, allegedly, were the names of Stephen Ward and five others. Thus the police had made their connection.

Vickie Barrett told the court that she had met other middle-aged men at the flat, that she had

All I have left between me and destruction is a handful of friends, my legal advisers, the integrity of a judge, and twelve men on a jury.

Ward before the trial

A ZEALOUS PURSUIT

Once the Metropolitan Police had been told to find evidence against Ward, they pursued him with a zeal for which there is no parallel – except, perhaps, the murder of a fellow policeman. Inspector Herbert revealed the fantastic industry that had gone into his prosecution.

'The policeman in charge,' says playwright Michael Pertwee, a friend of Ward's, 'had spent most of his recent past operating in Soho against pimps and blackmailers, and his methods were pretty dubious.'

Ronna Ricardo (right), a witness for the prosecution, confirms this. 'The police knew I hung around with Stephen,' she says. 'They said they would do me on immoral earnings...I couldn't take this pressure from the coppers.'

The police pursuit was out of all proportion. The 1956 Wolfenden Report shows how such cases were normally treated. Of 131 people found guilty of living on immoral earnings in one year, 117 were dealt with by magistrates and 13 were conditionally discharged, fined or put on probation.

beaten several of them with a horsewhip – at a rate of £1 a stroke – and that Ward had kept the money they paid. One of these men, Barrett alleged, was Ward's artist friend, Vasco Lazzolo – a successful society portait painter with a taste for young women and prostitutes. (Lazzolo later admitted that he had in fact met Vickie Barrett, but never at Stephen Ward's flat.)

THE ACCUSED SPEAKS

On the afternoon of the fourth day, after Burge's opening speech, Ward took the stand as the first witness for the defence. He took the oath firmly in his rich, resonant voice. One of the major issues he dealt with

was the financial arrangement between him and the girls. What money had they allegedly given him? This was at the heart of the charges – that Ward lived off immoral earnings.

The only payments, he said, in answer to Burge's questioning, had been occasional contributions to the rent, the telephone, and the electricity bill. Keeler had been living rent-free at Wimpole Mews and he had, in fact, given Keeler £70-£80 as a loan.

Rice-Davies paid £6 a week rent for her room, but had only given Ward enough for the first month in advance. After that she paid nothing. For the two months that she stayed

Crowds gathered daily outside the Old Bailey to catch a glimpse of Ward (far left), the 'wicked, wicked creature' on trial. At the same time, Mandy Rice-Davies (left) seemed to be making the most of playing up to the press. When told that Lord Astor had denied her claim that they had slept together, she replied to the laughter of the court, 'Well, he would, wouldn't he?'

Prostitute Vickie Barrett (right) claimed that Ward had set her up with men at his flat. Ward admitted he had slept with her himself, but that the rest was 'a tissue of lies from start to finish.'

Sunday Mirror

PEOPLE IN THE CASE—SKETCHED BY STEPHEN WARD

THESE are among the pictures which have been drawing the curious to the Museum-street galleries in London's Holborn. These are the famous—and notorious—faces named during the week in the Old Bailey trial of osteopath-artist Stephen Ward. Ward sketched them all—although Mandy Rice-Davies added some individual touches to hers. Missing from the gallery: Christine Keeler. Her Ward sketch is in the hands of her mother.

MANDY RICE-DAVIES

IVANOV THE RUSSIAN

SYLVIA PARKER

DOUGLAS FAIRBANKS

SALLY NORIE

LORD ASTOR

Justice Sir Archibald Marshall (left) had previously been a criminal lawyer in the Midlands. He now found himself dealing with a gallery of exotic personalities (above) involved in the Ward accusations.

> '*It was by any standards a feeble case. It consisted mainly of uncorroborated statements by proven liars: it was a hotch-potch of innuendoes and smears covered by a thin pastry of substance.*'
>
> Ludovic Kennedy, writer and political commentator

at Wimpole Mews with her parents, recovering from a suicide attempt (following Peter Rachman's fatal heart attack in November 1962), her total contributions had been a mere £24. Plus about £5 or £6 for the telephone.

The prosecution did not challenge this evidence. To one observer, the writer Ludovic Kennedy, the whole charge seemed ludicrous. He wondered how they could continue asserting that Ward was living on Rice-Davies' earnings. Not least when Keeler had said on the first day of the

trial, 'I usually owed him more than I ever made.' The show, however, went on.

On the fifth day, it was the prosecution's turn to cross-examine Ward. Griffith-Jones repeatedly dwelt on Ward's promiscuity. 'So we start this story, do we,' he said, 'with a man of 48 or 49 chasing two girls of 16?' Although this attack on Ward's morals strongly influenced the jury, it was not what Ward was actually on trial for.

When asked about Barrett's evidence, Ward said it was 'a tissue of lies from beginning to end.' He vehemently denied her claim that she had gone with men at his flat for money, and that he had kept the cash. He admitted knowing Barrett, and Ronna Riccardo, and having sex with them. That was all; he had merely been their client.

One of the last witnesses was Frances Brown. Under Griffith-Jones' cross-questioning she admitted visiting both Lazzolo and Ward at their respective homes, along with Barrett. Barrett had had sex with both men, during which she (Brown) had either 'helped' or 'looked on', but she knew nothing of Ward taking money.

Judge Marshall's summing up for the jury took up most of Tuesday afternoon, 30 July. The printed version of the summing-up seems clear and balanced. This is not how it came across in court. Those who were there remembered how Marshall's tone of voice and emphasis belied what he said. A French reporter, for *France-Soir*, put his finger on it: 'Monsieur Marshall,' he said, 'is a puritan, and Ward, the roué, the libertine, the cynic, appalled him...every time M. Justice Marshall explained to the jury the questions they would have to answer, his voice gave it away: M. Marshall did not like Ward, for he had brought a scandal upon England.'

THE LAST WORD

For the first two charges (living off immoral earnings), Justice Marshall told the jury they must decide three questions: Were Keeler and Rice-Davies prostitutes? Did Ward know they were? Did he knowingly receive from them or others money for 'the introduction and facilities for sexual intercourse which he provided?'

Lord and Lady Astor flank the famous classical guitarist Segovia and his wife at a concert party on the eve of the Ward trial. Astor was fast distancing himself from Ward and – though he had given him £5000 to cover his defence costs – had asked him to move out of his cottage at Cliveden.

THE LUCKY GORDON LINK

CLOSE-UP

On the morning of 30 July, as Ward's trial was ending at the Old Bailey, word came through that 'Lucky' Gordon had just been freed at the Court of Criminal Appeal, nearby in the Strand. The previous month he had been found guilty of assaulting Keeler (at the flat of her friend, Paula Hamilton-Marshall).

After Gordon's trial, at which Keeler testified, it was discovered she had given perjured evidence. In a tape-recording made with her business manager, Robin Drury, she reportedly

Marshall told the jury that, to decide a man was guilty of living off a prostitute, it must be shown that he knowingly assisted her, and received money for it. Then the judge pointed out that Ward had been abandoned by his friends. 'There may be many reasons,' he said, 'why Ward has been abandoned in his extremity. You must not guess at them, but this is clear: if Ward was telling the truth in the witness-box, there are in this city many witnesses of high estate and low who could have come and testified support of his evidence.'

told a story different to the one she told at Gordon's trial –one she repeated at Ward's. Keeler had denied that anyone else was present at the assault. On the recording, she apparently admitted that two other men had been there, and that another man caused her main injuries.

The jury at Ward's trial may never have brought in the verdict they did had they known of Keeler's lies. But the prosecuting counsel, Griffith-Jones, did not make the facts plain. He suggested she could have told the truth – but that Gordon had been released simply because of new evidence from the two key witnesses.

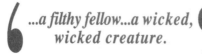

Although Ward had been warned to expect nothing from the Establishment, he had hoped from the start that Lord Astor would come to his aid, to restore his 'good name'. Astor, however, stayed silent, not only on the advice of a solicitor friend, but – now that he had become a 'fervent Christian' – on the 'spiritual direction' of a bishop. Now that most of his friends had deserted him, Ward belatedly realised their true calibre.

FADING HOPES

In a cruel way, the judge managed to turn against Ward the fact that none of his high-society friends had the courage to come and speak up on his behalf. It was a broadside that had a great effect on the jury.

The summing up was unfinished when the court rose, as usual, at half-past four in the afternoon. Ward was shattered by the judge's attitude. He asked his solicitor, Jack Wheatley, for a considered opinion of his chances. 'Guilty – and a two-year sentence,' Wheatley replied.

> **...*a filthy fellow...a wicked, wicked creature.***
>
> Mervyn Griffith-Jones, Crown prosecutor, describing Ward to the jury

THE MAN WHO LOVED WOMEN

Wine-glass in hand, an urbane and casually dressed Stephen Ward attends an exhibition of his sketches. Apart from being a skilled osteopath, Ward was an accomplished portrait artist. His sitters included members of the British royal family and well-known politicians.

Born in 1912, Ward was the son of a Hertfordshire vicar and an Irish mother whose family were landed gentry. From his father, he inherited a strong belief in social equality; from his mother, social aspirations. As she told a close friend: 'One day my boy will be famous.' She could not know the irony of her remark.

EDUCATED FOR SECRECY

Ward was sent to Canford, a lesser public school in Dorset, and its code of behaviour left a profound mark. Forty years later, Ward recalled a dormitory incident in which a boy's skull was fractured. Ward refused to divulge the culprit, taking the blame himself and receiving a beating in front of the whole school. During the Profumo affair, this was still a bitter memory. 'They expect me to go along with this stupid public school convention that good chaps don't tell. Well, I didn't tell once, but not this time...'

After Canford and short-lived jobs in London, Germany and France, a family friend encouraged Ward to study osteopathy in the USA. The warmth and hospitality of the American people made a deep impression, allowing him to shed his British inhibition. His eventful travels there were almost beatnik-like, reflecting a bohemian streak.

LOVE BY PROXY

In Chicago, Ward explored the brothel district. This fascination with the seamy side of sex had emerged earlier in the red light areas of Hamburg and Paris.

Ward's interest in women was mostly voyeuristic. At sex parties he watched rather than participated; with his women he enjoyed discussing their sexual exploits rather than having intercourse with them himself.

A MARRIAGE OF INCONVENIENCE

In July 1949, Ward married 21-year-old model Patricia Baines at Marylebone Registry Office. They were photographed outside afterwards (left). Hardly knowing Ward, she only discovered on their Paris honeymoon how they differed. He believed in open marriage and was neither the financial nor social catch she thought he was. Both parties were uncomfortably mismatched – the marriage lasted just six weeks.

HIGH-SOCIETY HEALER

During the Profumo affair, the newspapers suggested that Ward was a quack doctor. This was quite untrue. In fact, Ward was a highly qualified osteopath who had studied at Kirksville College in Missouri, USA, passing his examinations with credits. To do so, he had to study all branches of conventional medicine, including surgery and gynaecology. These skills gave him entry into high society and his clients soon included European royalty, maharajahs and famous figures such as Winston Churchill and Elizabeth Taylor (insets), Frank Sinatra and millionaire Paul Getty. Says one friend, Ward 'wanted to

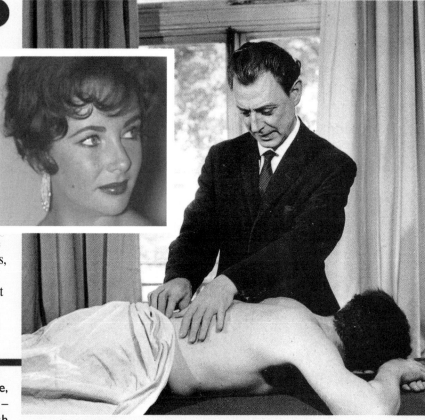

impress his acquaintances and be accepted in society.' Nevertheless, Ward found real pleasure in alleviating pain and it is clear that his patients found him a sympathetic person who took his work seriously (right).

Emotionally, Ward was keenly affected by rejection. Unable to stop the marriage of an early sweetheart on his return from the USA in the late 1930s, he said: 'This was my first brush with pain...I decided that I would never again become so seriously involved with anyone.' After his second great love, Eunice

Bailey, married someone else, Ward tried to commit suicide – perhaps his second such attempt (the first may have occurred in the army in 1945).

From the late 1940s onwards, Ward's various flats became magnets for young women looking for a place to stay. The atmosphere was relaxed and parties there were attended by people as

The first of Ward's protégées was Vicki Martin (left). Known as the 'Golden Girl' of society circles, she died in a car crash in 1956. Another protégée was Pat Marlowe (below), model, actress and jet-setting businesswoman. She committed suicide in 1962. One of his great loves was Margaret Brown, pictured here with Ward at his Cliveden cottage (far left). Under his wing she became a top international model.

varied as typists, prostitutes and even royalty.

The girls themselves, says writer Frederic Mullally, loved Ward 'as a girl might love an elder brother or a father. Stephen used girls [to gain entry to society parties], but he never abused them...he flourished in the sensual hothouse of a home forever strewn with discarded nylons, lip-printed tissues, cosmetic debris.'

Ward's friend, Ellis Stungo, adds: 'He never lived off the girls or ran a call-girl service...he was so generous and wanted to help people.'

LATTER-DAY PYGMALION

During the Profumo affair, when the stage-show *My Fair Lady* was playing, Ward was dubbed a Pygmalion, a modern Professor Higgins who created his ideal woman. This referred to the years when Ward seemed to groom a succession of young women for social success. Ward rarely fell in love with his cre-

ations, but he genuinely liked women as people and had platonic friendships with many. The most famous of these was Christine Keeler, whom he met at Murray's Club in 1959.

INSIDE KNOWLEDGE

Ward had another side. His attendance at high-society parties that involved group sex and sado-masochism gave him inside secrets. Says journalist Warwick Charlton: 'Many highly placed men shared his sexual liking...he gained confidences from his patients in his consulting room...if a few patients had their sexual needs attended to at the same time by the way of a few little parties and introductions, well, that was life wasn't it?'

As the scandal evolved during late 1963, Ward continued to shield his friends from exposure. Even in court, he minimised damaging testimony. He always thought they would come to his aid. They never did.

REPERCUSSIONS

ALL THROUGH THE TRIAL, WARD WAS VILIFIED BY THE PROSECUTION. THE JUDGE'S SUMMING-UP WAS THE FINAL BLOW. WARD NOW KNEW THERE WAS NO HOPE LEFT. IT WAS TIME TO TAKE MATTERS INTO HIS OWN HANDS

The jury's decision (above) came while Ward was lying in a coma in hospital – it was a verdict which carried a possible maximum sentence of seven years.

DATEFILE

JULY 30 1963

Stephen Ward takes overdose

JULY 31 1963

Jury pass guilty verdict on Ward

AUGUST 3 1963

Ward dies at St Stephen's Hospital

DEC 6 1963

Christine Keeler jailed for nine months for perjury

JULY– DEC '63

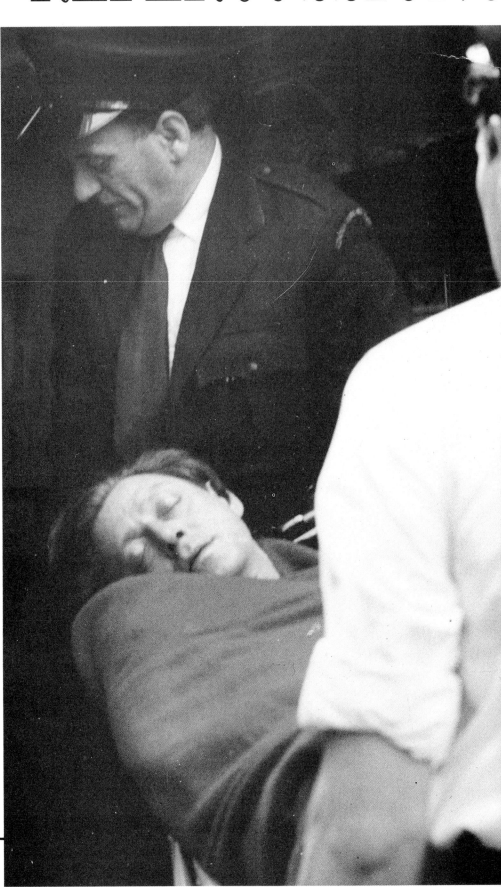

It was the evening of 30 July 1963, the second to last day of the trial. The judge was only half-way through his summing-up. Stephen Ward went to a coffee bar with his current girlfriend, a young singer, Julie Gulliver. They then went back to the Chelsea flat of the man giving Ward shelter during the trial, advertising executive Noel Howard-Jones. There, in Mallord Street, Ward began writing letters to be delivered 'only if I am convicted and sent to prison.' He handed 12 of them over to Howard-Jones. Gulliver thought Ward looked 'noticeably upset' and uncharacteristically restless.

> *I tried to do my stuff, but after Marshall's summing-up I've given up all hope... I'm sorry to disappoint the vultures.*
>
> Stephen Ward's last letter to Noel Howard-Jones

Ward saw Tom Mangold, one of the few journalists he still trusted. Mangold drove to Mallord Street, where he found Ward at the end of his tether. 'He felt absolutely betrayed.' He asked Mangold to post the letters he had written. The journalist knew they were suicide notes and refused to post them; one was addressed to Mangold himself. 'Well,' Ward told him, 'take your letter, but don't open it till I'm dead.'

Julie Gulliver stayed with Ward until about ll.30 pm, when he drove her back home, hugged her and said a final 'goodbye'.

At 8.30 the next morning, the telephone woke Howard-Jones. He knew the 'phone was next to his guest, Ward, who was sleeping in the lounge. Yet the 'phone kept ringing. He stumbled out to take the call. After he hung up, he told the inquest, 'I turned around and saw him. I thought he was dead. His face was a purple colour. His mouth was open...I slapped his face, and he breathed just once. I tried an amateur type of respiration.' As soon as Ward began breathing, Howard-Jones hurriedly telephoned for an ambulance.

Twenty minutes later, Ward was admitted to St Stephen's Hospital, a few streets away on Fulham Road. He was unconscious and did not respond to stimuli. After an hour, his condition was 'good enough for him to be transferred to a ward'. The doctors thought that he might pull through.

THE TRIAL GOES ON

At the Old Bailey, the court reconvened. Judge Marshall said: 'I want it to be understood that Ward shall be immediately put under surveillance. Bail is withdrawn from now, and the normal steps shall be taken to secure greater security.' Like most of his statements at the trial, the judge's words seemed unreal. He continued his summing up as if nothing had happened.

The jury deliberated all afternoon. Shortly after 7 pm, they came back with a decision. They declared Ward guilty on the first two counts of living on the immoral earnings of Keeler and Rice-Davies. Many thought this was an amazing verdict. It may have been possible to argue Ward's guilt

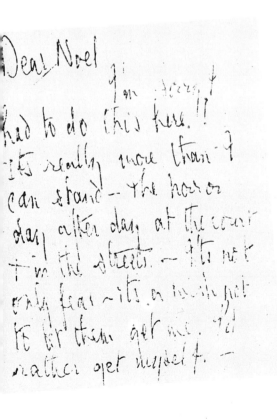

Noel Howard-Jones (above) whose house Ward was staying at during the trial, was the first to discover him after his overdose. Lying beside Ward was a note (left): 'Dear Noel,' it read, 'I'm sorry I had to do this here! It's really more than I can stand – the horror day after day at the court and in the streets – it's not only fear, it's a wish not to let them get me. I'd rather get myself.' It went on to say, 'Incidentally, it was surprisingly easy and required no guts. I'm sorry to disappoint the vultures.' Ward was rushed unconscious from the house (left) to nearby St Stephen's Hospital.

THE DENNING REPORT

On 21 June 1963, almost three weeks before Ward came to trial, the Prime Minister, Harold Macmillan, set up a judicial inquiry into the security aspects of the Profumo Affair. It was headed by Master of the Rolls, Lord Denning, who Macmillan hoped would be able to check 'the flood of accusations and rumour.'

Denning later wrote: 'I saw Ministers of the Crown, the Security Service, rumour-mongers and prostitutes. Some of the evidence I heard was so disgusting... that I sent the lady shorthand writers out, and no note was taken.'

The report came at the end of 1963. But if the public were looking for a juicy read, they were to be disappointed. The inquiry was at best a damage limitation exercise and at worst, a whitewash. Profumo, the Government and British Intelligence were let off lightly. Ludicrously, Denning was to damn Ward as 'the most evil man I have ever met.'

according to legal technicalities, but few believed he was a pimp. To them, the outcome seemed a travesty of natural justice.

One juror later said of their deliberations: 'Most of us had already made up our minds when we heard about all the perversions and sex. You've got to remember that we weren't as liberal-minded as we are today. It was very disgusting to us. What swayed us was the prosecution lawyer, Griffith-Jones. He had such an air of utter supremacy that when...[Ward] went into the dock he was already done for before he opened his mouth...We were told that Ward was guilty...and the judge guided us towards the fact that he was indeed guilty.'

The judge postponed sentence until Ward could appear. But Ward had taken a dangerous overdose of barbiturates and did not look likely to survive. A pill bottle had been found at his side. The autopsy later indicated that Ward had taken the equivalent of 14 to 20 1.5 grain sleeping tablets.

At St Stephen's Hospital, Ward clung to life. A prison officer sat nearby to see he did not escape –

a totally unlikely event. Then his condition began to deteriorate. A tracheotomy was performed, and later he was given a heart massage. At 3.45 on the afternoon of 3 August, after 79 hours in a coma, Ward died.

The funeral took place a week later at Mortlake Crematorium. Only his brother Raymond, his sister Patricia, two cousins, his solicitor and Julie Gulliver were present. A large wreath of white roses, dedicated to 'Stephen Ward, a victim of British hypocrisy', was sent by 21 British writers and artists, including playwright John Osborne and critic Kenneth Tynan.

THE REACTIONS

Another wreath was laid on Cheltenham War Memorial. A note upon it read: 'We three girls of Cheltenham Ladies' College have laid this wreath as tribute to dear Dr Stephen Ward, who dared to live...as a human being and not just as a dummy. An outraged society revenged itself upon him.'

Mervyn Griffith-Jones, the prosecuting counsel, is said to have wept when told of Ward's death; as did Ward's defence counsel, James Burge. 'He was very affected,' says a former colleague. 'He never seemed to be the same man again...' Burge later said: 'Ward's case was rigged...Judge Marshall murdered Stephen Ward. It's as simple as that.'

One of Ward's suicide notes was sent to Marshall. On receiving it, the judge paled, repeating, 'But he was guilty, you know, he was guilty.' Another note went to Vickie Barrett. 'I don't know what it was or who it was that made you do what you did,' he wrote. 'But if you have any decency left, you should tell the truth...' A reporter, Barry O'Brien, called on Barrett immediately after Ward's death. 'It was all lies,' she said of her sworn testimony. 'But I never thought he would die.' Barrett later retracted her retraction.

One man who seemed indifferent to the trial was Lord Astor. At the height of the scandal, he showed up at Ascot looking – as a gossip columnist in The *Daily Express* reported – 'urbane and relaxed'. His Lordship toasted the winning jockey in champagne, then drove to Cliveden for a party.

Rice-Davies took Ward's death badly. 'I was stricken with anger and remorse and sorrow.' Keeler was hysterical with grief. Ward had been her closest friend, and she had never experienced death before. Keeler was later to spend six months of a nine month sentence in Holloway prison for the perjury offence arising out of Lucky Gordon's

trial and conviction. She welcomed it, saying it was 'a bit of peace. I was psychologically exhausted...'

How Profumo, the man at the centre of the scandal, reacted to Ward's death is not known. He slipped quietly into affluent obscurity .

Prime Minister Macmillan admitted that the scandal had 'inflicted a deep, bitter and lasting wound'. Four months after Profumo's resignation, Macmillan, too ill to carry on, handed the premiership over to Lord Home. Exactly one year later, in October 1964, 13 years of Conservative rule came to an end when Harold Wilson narrowly won the General Election.

Profumo believed he could get away with it because he did not think anyone would dare to publish the truth. No one, he believed, would challenge the ruling class to which he belonged. Only a few, however, have raised their heads above the parapet and printed the truth.

SUICIDE OR MURDER ?

There was also the question as to whether Ward's death was, in fact, suicide. A former MI6 operative, who knew Ward, firmly believes that he was murdered, perhaps to prevent him revealing the sordid activities of the British Establishment. He says: 'The establishment's view has always been to take a tough line against such people – squash them!' In this way the Establishment protects its own and someone had to pay. That someone was Stephen Ward.

The Profumo scandal took place at a significant moment in history, when Britain was discarding old values and plunging into massive social change. Certainly from then onwards, the social and personal life of any politician was likely to attract media attention. This was an attractive proposition for the tabloids, eager to expose sexual revelations even when there was no security angle.

INSIDE VIEW

GOVERNMENT IN CRISIS

Satirical magazine Private Eye had a field day with the Government sex scandals. The infamous Keeler chair picture was transformed – as was Harold Macmillan – by cartoonist Scarfe (left).

By the summer of 1963, the Macmillan government was tottering. It had been badly damaged by a series of scandals, including the Profumo Affair. Another crisis that threatened its stability in 1963 centred on a photograph produced at the Duchess of Argyll's sensational divorce hearings.

The picture showed the Duchess performing fellatio with an unknown man at her London home. The top of the photo had been cut off, so that the man's head was missing. German newspapers claimed he was a Conservative minister, Duncan Sandys.

In June 1963, Sandys admitted to Macmillan that though 'he was not the headless man...he had been involved with the lady...' Sandys offered to resign but was stopped at the last moment. An inquiry into the 'headless man' rumours by Lord Denning cleared Sandys, but it was a close call. Had the incident been made public, it would probably have proved the last straw for a government that was to fall one year later.

THE DEATH OF MARILYN MONROE

As early risers switched on their radios on Sunday 5 August 1962, they were greeted by shocking news – Hollywood's greatest 'goddess' was dead. To news editors worldwide, rushing to get the story of a film legend's apparent sleeping pill overdose into print, it was possibly just another headlining story. To others, it may have been the tragic final chapter of a more sinister book. Were there those that had good reason to keep this book firmly closed? What role did the two men at the highest level of the United States Government play in the final, complex years of Marilyn Monroe's life?

Marilyn Monroe, 1926–1962, the quintessential Hollywood star. Torn by deep-seated emotional problems, she was closer than her public guessed to the machinery of American power politics.

ONE

THE MISFIT

BY 1960 MARILYN MONROE HAD BECOME AN ICON FOR MILLIONS OF CINEMA–GOERS. BEHIND THE SCREEN IMAGE, HOWEVER, HER PRIVATE LIFE WAS A WORSENING TANGLE OF DEPRESSION, PILLS, AND ILL HEALTH

It was late in July 1960. The heat in the desert near Reno, Nevada, was edging over 100 degrees when Marilyn Monroe began making what was to be her last completed film. About a group of cowboys who earn their living by rounding up wild mustangs, it focuses on a lonely, troubled woman who comes to Reno seeking a divorce and falls in with the men. The film was, appropriately enough, to be called *The Misfits*. Planned as a celebration of great talent, the film included such stars as Eli Wallach and Montgomery Clift. The male lead was played by Clark Gable, now ageing, but still the heart-throb of a generation of women.

Marilyn was its centrepiece. Her screen persona was unique – a combination of knowing sexuality, innocence and vulnerability. These characteristics, together with intelligence and sincerity, also drew people to her in real life. But Marilyn had complex emotional problems. As these intensified while filming *The Misfits*, so she entered the darkest period, the last two years, of her life.

When work on the film began, the 34-year-old actress was visibly run-down. She had left New York to fly west to Nevada, but her clothes were dishevelled and stained and she had bags under her

The Misfits was Marilyn's last film. The script had been written especially for her by her husband Arthur Miller, who based it on a short story of his that had been published in Esquire magazine. It offered a thrilled Marilyn the chance to play alongside her girlhood idol, Clark Gable (left, with Marilyn on the set) who, she had always believed, resembled her father. Although the filming was punctuated by many difficulties – heightened by the break-up of the Monroe-Miller marriage – there were moments of relaxation when Marilyn's radiance shone through (right).

eyes. She had been drinking too much and 'popping' pills – mostly sedatives prescribed by a variety of doctors. She suffered bouts of intense depression and destructive rages. 'She'll be in an institution in two or three years, or dead,' John Huston, director of *The Misfits*, told Marilyn's third husband, Arthur Miller.

But Miller, the author and screen-writer of the film, was helpless. Their marriage, once tender, was collapsing. Soon her drugged stupors were a regular sight. Marilyn had for several years been notorious for lateness, tantrums and forgetting her lines. Her films ran over-budget, but made fortunes. Now, growing ever more dependent on sleeping pills downed with vodka and champagne, she left film crew and co-stars to wonder daily whether she would turn up for work at all.

Earlier in 1960, Marilyn had had an affair with the French actor Yves Montand during the making of the comedy, *Let's Make Love*. Marilyn had been publicly shamed by the dignity shown by Montand's wife, Simone Signoret, herself a distinguished actress. 'If Marilyn is in love with

my husband, it proves she has good taste. For I am in love with him too,' Miss Signoret had said. Montand returned to his wife. Rejected by Montand and outclassed by his wife, the episode had been a crushing blow to Marilyn's self-esteem. She had committed herself to a highly publicised infidelity – and lost.

RIFTS WITH MILLER

On the set of *The Misfits*, Marilyn's conflict with her husband became open warfare. On director John Huston's birthday, they had a violent row in front of the entire company. Marilyn also spread a false rumour that her husband was having an affair with Huston's script assistant, Angela Allen. Allen believed this enabled Marilyn to 'work out her own guilt over Montand.'

Once during filming, Marilyn left Miller stranded in the desert without any means of getting back to his hotel. 'It was sheer malice, vindictiveness,' John Huston said. 'It was shameful.'

'Doesn't he look marvellous?' Marilyn enthused about Gable to one interviewer. 'We were rehearsing a very long scene, and he started to

DATEFILE

JULY – OCT 1960
Shooting of Marilyn's last film, *The Misfits*

JANUARY 20 1961
Marilyn divorces her third husband Arthur Miller

JANUARY 1962
Marilyn buys her first home – a bungalow in Brentwood, a suburb of Los Angeles

JULY '60 – JAN '62

tremble, just the slightest bit. I can't tell you how endearing that was to me. To find somebody – my idol – to be, well, *human*.'

Gable was more than an idol to Marilyn. Although she had never had a real father, her mother had always kept a photograph of the man she claimed

> ' *What the hell is that girl's problem? Goddam it, I like her, but she's so damn unprofessional.* '
>
> Clark Gable on Marilyn while filming *The Misfits*

was Marilyn's father. He bore a resemblance to Gable and sometimes, in company, Marilyn began repeating a childhood fantasy – that she was none other than the daughter of the great film actor.

ILLNESS AND DISRUPTION

On 26 August, Gable played a scene in which, as the cowboy Gay Langland, he tells Marilyn, playing the divorcee Roslyn: 'Honey, we all got to go sometime, reason or no reason. Dyin's as natural as livin'; man who's afraid to die is too afraid to live...'
To an already vulnerable Marilyn, this speech may have had a depressing effect. On the following day, she was found almost unconscious after another heavy cocktail of alcohol and drugs. Her stomach was pumped and she was carried to an aircraft wrapped in a wet sheet to protect her from the baking heat.

After being flown to Los Angeles, she spent 10 days in Westside Hospital, tended by psychiatrist Dr Ralph Greenson. Yves Montand was briefly in California during this period, and Marilyn made constant efforts to reach him by telephone. He would not accept her calls. 'I think she is an enchanting child...' he told Hollywood columnist Hedda Hopper. But, he continued, '...nothing will break up my marriage.'

When, in November 1960, the shooting of *The Misfits* was over, Marilyn and Miller flew back to New York on separate flights. On 11 November, in an exclusive interview with show business columnist Earl Wilson, Marilyn revealed that her marriage was over and a divorce would follow.

A few days later, Clark Gable died of a heart attack. He had long suffered from a weak heart, but his pregnant widow, Kay, felt that the strain of working with Marilyn had contributed to the attack.

Meanwhile, Marilyn was still clinging blindly to the hope of a reunion with Montand. He was known to have had a trip to New York scheduled for late in December 1960. Marilyn assumed they would meet.

Shortly before Christmas, Marilyn received a telephone call from France. It was Simone

CLOSE-UP

THE SICILIAN

Joe DiMaggio, Marilyn Monroe's second husband, was an authentic American hero, the greatest baseball player of his own or any other age. The son of poor Sicilian immigrants who settled in San Francisco, DiMaggio had retired from sport a wealthy man when he and Marilyn met in the spring of 1952. Suave, confident and, at 37, 12 years older than Marilyn, DiMaggio brought the promise of steadfast, protective love into her life. But the price was a possessive jealousy and disapproval of her public exhibitionism.

They were married on 14 January 1954 in San Francisco and divorced on 27 October in the same year (above, a highly distraught Marilyn stands with attorney Gerry Giesler at the announcement of the break-up). But the bond between them was never broken. The tormented DiMaggio never ceased trying to bring about a reconciliation between them, though his ruthless methods – such as hiring private detectives to follow Marilyn and her friends – chilled many who knew him.

DiMaggio, who loathed the public intrusion into the brief marriage, has never broken his silence about Marilyn. 'Guys have the right to go to the end in privacy,' he has said.

Marilyn's second to last film was Let's Make Love, a musical that received poor critical reviews. The only memorable aspects of the film were Marilyn's song-and-dance routines, which included a sensational rendering of Cole Porter's song 'My Heart Belongs to Daddy'. (The picture here shows Marilyn on the set.) It was during filming that she started an affair with its co-star, Yves Montand (left, with Marilyn). He was married to actress Simone Signoret and he quickly returned to her when the affair became public knowledge.

PERSPECTIVE

RUNNING WILD

The peak of Marilyn Monroe's film career had been the comedy *Some Like It Hot*, directed in 1958 by Billy Wilder. Marilyn played a naive singer (above) and ukelele player in a female band which hires two male musicians, disguised as women in order to escape gangsters in Chicago. Marilyn drove her co-stars, Tony Curtis and Jack Lemmon, to fury with her lack of professionalism and delays. One scene, involving a line of three words – which Marilyn could never seem to remember – had to be shot 65 times. Curtis, the son of a Jewish tailor, was to say that kissing Marilyn on set had been 'like kissing Hitler.'

But the final result won accolades and profits for all concerned. Marilyn's song, *Running Wild*, performed in the film on a train journey from Chicago to Florida (top left), showed the brilliance of her timing, and flair for projecting innocence and worldly humour at the same time. It also made the most of her inimitable voice.

Signoret, pleading with Marilyn to leave her husband alone. However, Montand did not get to New York. He cancelled the trip at the last minute. Marilyn was devastated.

Soon afterwards, her maid, Lena Pepitone, said she found Marilyn by a window ledge in the bedroom, holding the outside moulding. The maid quickly gripped her by the waist. 'Lena, no. Let me die. I want to die. I deserve to die,' Marilyn had cried. 'What have I done with my life? Who do I have? It's Christmas.'

A DOUBLE WATERSHED

The twentieth of January 1961 saw two important events in Marilyn's life – one personal, one national. Her divorce to Arthur Miller was finalised, and a dashing Democratic Senator from Massachusetts, John F Kennedy, was inaugurated as President of the United States.

Marilyn herself had occasionally taken up political causes. She was a sponsor of SANE, the National Committee for a Sane Nuclear Policy, and she was a registered member of the Democratic Party. In addition, Marilyn's long relationship with Arthur Miller had brought her into contact with his free-thinking political and social ideals.

Much more significantly, she knew the President personally. A few weeks before Kennedy's inauguration, she told a confidant that she had recently had 'a date with the next President of the United States.' The way she talked about it left him in no doubt that Marilyn meant she had had sex with John F Kennedy.

In February 1961, *The Misfits* opened to poor reviews and the next day, still unable to cope with setbacks, Marilyn entered the Payne Whitney Psychiatric Clinic in New York.

Arriving in a thick fur coat, she was placed in a section for 'moderately disturbed' patients. But the door was locked from the outside and Marilyn was allowed only limited use of the telephone in her suite. 'Open that door!' she screamed. 'I won't make any trouble, just let me out! Please! Open the door!' When her appeals were rejected, Marilyn stripped off all of her clothes and stood,

THE WRITER

The Last Scenes In A Hollywood Love Story

MARILYN'S MARRIAGE BREAKS UP

From JOHN GOLD

NEW YORK, Friday.

THE marriage of Marilyn Monroe and Arthur Miller, her tall, pipe-smoking, playwright husband, is over. The couple are to get a friendly divorce soon.

'It's all over. There's no possibility of reconciliation. There will be an announcement soon,' Miller told professional associates a few hours ago.

Reporting this in the New York Post today, Earl Wilson, a leading American columnist, said the glamorous star had separated from Miller nine months ago.

They had met several times since then in the actress's apartment in New York, the last coming last week and their marriage, which took place in June, 1956.

Wilson said no third person was involved in the marriage break-up and neither Miller nor the 35-year-old actress have planned to marry anyone else.

Friends of the star who described her as devastated by the collapse of her third marriage said reports of her interest in Yves Montand her French matinee idol, were ridiculous.

THEIR FILM 'The Misfits'

Montand, who starred with Marilyn in 'Let's Make Love,' was reported to have returned to France saying 'she has a schoolgirl crush on me.'

Ironically, the marriage between the deeply ambitious, socially conscious Miller and the beautiful star blew up as filming came to an end on 'The Misfits,' a film specially written for Marilyn by Miller.

Friends believed that one of the main causes of the shattered romance was the inability of either the star or her shy, introspective husband to have any privacy.

Miller hinted at the problem when he arrived in England shortly after the

Arthur Miller, Marilyn's third husband, was already the most distinguished playwright in America when they met in Hollywood in 1950. His play *Death of a Salesman*, written in 1948, remains a moving portrayal of a man destroyed by the pressures of commercialism. Jewish, and from New York City, Miller offered Marilyn a warm, forgiving love, and a settled home life.

They were married on 29 June 1956 after Miller, at 41, had divorced his first wife. Marilyn, then 30 years old, was to experience several settled years with Miller, but her instability gradually wore him down and his creative skills grew stagnant. He struggled to find a way to love her, without being consumed by her neuroses. Sensing this, she tested him more and more severely until Miller was too exhausted to keep her away from drugs, or to help her through depressions.

On the set of *The Misfits*, Miller met the photographer Inge Morath, who would eventually become his third wife. In his 1987 autobiography

Timebends, he spoke in detail about the difficulties and joys of life with Marilyn, and their attempt to reconcile the two 'disjointed' worlds in which they tried to live, balancing world-wide fame with domestic privacy.

---

fully naked, by the window.

The hospital staff then took her to a more secure ward. Marilyn later claimed that undressing was a stunt to win her freedom. The staff saw it as a symptom. 'She made us all feel like we wanted to hold her in our laps,' one nurse said.

During the rest of 1961, Marilyn suffered several physical ailments. In May, she underwent gynaecological surgery in Los Angeles, during which it was discovered that her Fallopian tubes were blocked. In June, she

After The Misfits opened in February 1961, Marilyn went into the Payne Whitney Psychiatric Clinic in New York. From there she wrote a desperate, almost incoherent, two-page letter to her drama coach Lee Strasberg and his wife, Paula, pleading for help. The first page (above) refers to her 'two idiot doctors' and claims that she is 'locked up with all these poor nutty people – I'm sure to end up a nut if I stay in this nightmare...' Right: Marilyn leaves hospital after a gall-bladder operation later in the year.

was treated in New York for an inflamed gall-bladder. She also had an ulcerated colon.

She did no film work at all during 1961. Her New York apartment became squalid. There were dog stains on the carpet, and the place was littered with half-empty pill bottles. Marilyn, increasingly foul-mouthed, saw no friends and did not go out.

In July 1961, Marilyn was back in Los Angeles, staying at her apartment on Doheny, a few blocks south of Sunset Strip, where she had lived in the early 1950s. Now she began seeing her psychiatrist Dr Greenson constantly. Earlier, in May, after her Payne Whitney experience, Greenson had opened his Santa Monica home to her, contrary to the strict traditions of orthodox psychiatry. He felt he needed to offer the 35-year-old Marilyn a sense of family and security.

From about September, Marilyn's life seemed to lose direction, with random promiscuity and heavy pill-taking. Her address book, covering late 1961, contained

the names of 36 doctors, all separate sources of drugs. Dr Ralph Greenson had nurses stay in her apartment day and night to control her medication, since he believed she was suicidal.

NEW HOME, SAME LONELINESS

At Christmas, 1961, DiMaggio came to stay with Marilyn. They were happy enough for a few days, but he did not stay. After the holidays were over, he flew back to New York.

At the end of January 1962, Marilyn bought a Mexican-style, single-story bungalow in Brentwood, a Los Angeles suburb. By the standards of other Hollywood film stars, it was modest and inexpensive, but Marilyn had made no films for the past year and her percentage of profits from past films had yet to come in. Indeed, when she bought

> *...her performance as a dramatic actress was extraordinary, but I'm not sure all that torture was worth the result, all that agony. It's not worth anything.*
>
> Arthur Miller, Marilyn's husband and writer of *The Misfits*

the house, she had little ready money. On signing the papers, she wept at having to buy it alone.

The buying of her first home coincided with a new phase in Marilyn's life. As the spring of 1962 wore on, she dialled a Washington number with increasing regularity. It was the work number of the President's brother, the Attorney-General, Robert Kennedy.

NORMA JEANE – THE GIRL WHO BECAME MARILYN MONROE – WAS RAISED IN A BLEAK WORLD OF FOSTER HOMES. HER QUEST FOR LOVE AND STARDOM TOOK HER FROM MODELLING TO BIT-PARTS AS A HOLLYWOOD STARLET

A CHILD OF MOVIELAND

Norma Jeane was born in Los Angeles on 1 June 1926, at the city's General Hospital. The child was baptised with the surname Mortensen. Her mother, Gladys, appears on Marilyn's birth certificate as Gladys Monroe – her maiden name. Gladys had, in fact, been married twice by the time Norma Jeane was born. Her first husband, Jack Baker, left her in 1923. She then married a Martin Edward Mortensen, whose name appears on Marilyn's birth certificate as her father. But he and Gladys had parted by the time of Marilyn's birth, and Gladys was living alone.

There has been much controversy surrounding the real identity of Marilyn's father, but the true facts emerged only a few years ago ('A Father Revealed' see p41). According to one interview with Marilyn, her real father 'walked out and left her [Gladys] while I was getting born.' Norma Jeane had no experience of stable family life. Gladys, unable to cope with motherhood, returned to her job as a film cutter, and the child was brought up mainly by foster parents.

Though absent, Gladys provided for Norma Jeane financially and, when they met, spoke forcefully to her daughter of her religious beliefs. Gladys adhered to the doctrines of Christian Science with its emphasis on redemption from sin, patience and humility. Although Marilyn stayed a partial adherent of Christian Science into young adulthood, it was no fixation. She later converted to Judaism to marry the playwright, Arthur Miller.

MENTAL TROUBLES

When Norma Jeane was about seven, she lived with her mother for several months. But Gladys soon suffered a deep depression, followed by a violent outburst, and she was immediately committed to an asylum.

Mental instability ran in Gladys' family. Her maternal great-grandfather had hanged himself when aged 82, and her maternal grandfather suffered a form of insanity associated with syphilis. Gladys' mother had died in an asylum and 'manic-depressive psychosis' was named as a contributory factor.

A ROOTLESS EXISTENCE

Gladys' friend Grace McKee became Norma Jeane's legal guardian, but the little girl was still farmed out to various foster parents. All in all, Norma Jeane's childhood was a saga of dislocation, in which she passed through at least 10 foster homes, and a two-year spell in the Los Angeles Orphans' Home.

When Norma Jeane was about 11, she went to live with Grace McKee, by now married

Norma Jeane (above, centre foreground) sits cross-legged on the floor with a group of other Twentieth Century-Fox starlets in 1946. The distinguished Life photographer Philippe Halsman, who took the picture, said: 'I remember that one of the girls was an artificial blonde by the name of Marilyn Monroe, and that she was not one of the girls who impressed me the most.' She had just adopted her new screen name and signed a six-month contract with the company.

to a man named Doc Goddard. She was enrolled at Emerson Junior High School and, four years later, went to Van Nuys High School. It was at this last school – according to Marilyn – that she first slept with a boy. Her awareness of sex, however, dated from much earlier. Marilyn alleged that at the age of eight she had been assaulted by a man who boarded at one

Norma Jeane (above right, aged about 18 months) spent most of her infancy and childhood in a succession of foster homes. In 1933, she finally went to live with her mother, Gladys (above, with Norma Jeane).

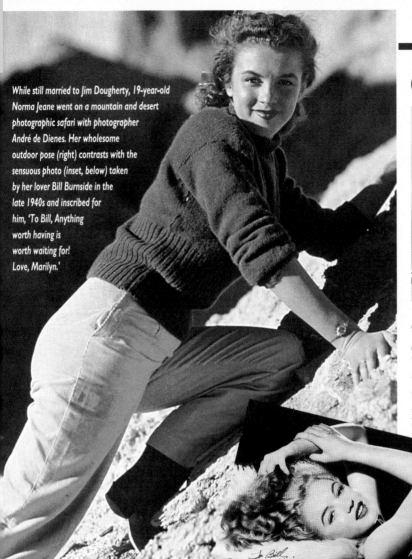

While still married to Jim Dougherty, 19-year-old Norma Jeane went on a mountain and desert photographic safari with photographer André de Dienes. Her wholesome outdoor pose (right) contrasts with the sensuous photo (inset, below) taken by her lover Bill Burnside in the late 1940s and inscribed for him, 'To Bill, Anything worth having is worth waiting for! Love, Marilyn.'

OPENING SHOTS

The camera and Norma Jeane discovered each other during World War II. In 1944, she was working at Radio Plane, a factory that built aircraft for target practice. One day, an army film unit sent a photographer, Private David Conover, to the plant 'to take morale-boosting shots of pretty-girls' for *Yank* magazine.

Conover singled out Norma Jeane from the other women at the factory. 'Her eyes,' Conover recalled, 'held something that touched and intrigued me.' He first photographed her on the assembly line. Then, during the lunchbreak, he persuaded her to change into a tight red sweater, and offered her $5 an hour as a freelance model. At the factory, Norma Jeane earned $20 for a whole week's work. While keeping her job, she joined Conover for several photo sessions (for example, above left) that launched her as a cover girl.

PROMISE OF STARDOM

The first review of Marilyn's film acting by an authoritative journal appeared in the *Motion Picture Herald* after the release of her third film, *Ladies of the Chorus* (above), on 22 October 1948. 'One of the brightest spots is Miss Monroe's singing,' wrote the *Herald*'s critic Tibor Krekes. 'She is pretty, and with her pleasing voice and style, shows promise.'

of her foster homes. Shortly before her death in 1962, she was still repeating this story.

In 1942, Grace and Doc Goddard decided to move East, but without 15-year-old Norma Jeane. The solution was to find her a husband. Grace liked the look of Jim Dougherty, her neighbour's 21-year-old son, then a night-shift fitter at Lockheed Aviation. He and Norma Jeane had dated a couple of times.

WIFE AND PIN-UP

Dougherty's mother suggested the marriage idea. When she explained that the alternative was to send Norma Jeane back to the Los Angeles orphanage, he agreed.

Following a short courtship, the wedding was held on 19 June 1942, less than three weeks after Norma Jeane's 16th birthday made it legal for them to marry. Just over a year later, Dougherty joined the Merchant Marine. Norma Jeane also helped the war effort. In 1944 she took a job at a plant producing miniature target planes, where she inspected parachutes and sprayed fuselages.

By early 1946, the marriage was over; while Dougherty was at sea, Norma Jeane had been unfaithful to him. She had also decided to become a movie actress.

During the war, Norma Jeane posed for magazine photographers looking for pretty-girl pictures to cheer the troops in Europe and Asia. She was a successful pin-up girl, appearing on the covers of such 'girlie' magazines as *Swank*, *Sir* and *Peek*.

By the time Norma Jeane's divorce from Dougherty went through, in August, 1946, she had won the promise of a contract as a stock player at Twentieth Century-Fox — thanks to the enthusiasm of the company's casting director Ben Lyon and its chief of production Darryl Zanuck.

TINSELTOWN HOPES

Los Angeles was a city of dreams. It was there, while Norma Jeane was growing up in the 1930s, that the Hollywood film industry entered its heyday, promising dazzling wealth and stardom.

In the 1950s she remembered how, as an aspiring actress, she watched the cars roll down Sunset Boulevard. 'I used to think,' she said, ' that there must be thousands of girls sitting alone like me, dreaming of becoming a movie star. But I'm not going to worry about them. I'm dreaming the hardest.'

A sex symbol in public, Marilyn pursued her love of literature in private. Here (above) she tackles a modern masterpiece, James Joyce's Ulysses.

Lyon, said she should have a new name. He suggested Marilyn, after the actress Marilyn Miller, and Norma Jeane decided to keep her grand-mother's surname, Monroe.

STEPS TO STARDOM

Twentieth Century-Fox sent Marilyn to the Actors' Lab, near Hollywood's celebrated Sunset Boulevard. She found favour with the tutors, Morris Carnovsky and his wife, for being punctual and conscientious, but gave no hint of her future success.

Early in 1947, Marilyn Monroe made her film debut, playing an extra in the lightweight comedy, *Scudda Hoo! Scudda Hay!* A scene in which she paddled a canoe survived the cutting-room floor, but most of her dialogue did not. In the finished version, she was heard to say just one word: 'Hello.' This debut was followed by the role of Eve, a waitress, in her first released film, *Dangerous Years* (1947), in which Marilyn had three whole lines.

In August 1947, Twentieth Century-Fox ended her contract. This may have been because she was dallying with another contract player, Tommy Zahn, whom Zanuck was grooming to marry his own daughter.

In 1946, at her first screen test, wearing a sequined gown and high heels, Norma Jeane was instructed to walk across the set, sit down, light a cigarette, put it out, go upstage, look out of a window, come downstage and exit.

'This girl,' the cameraman Leon Shamroy was to say, 'had something I hadn't seen since silent pictures. She had a kind of fantastic beauty like Gloria Swanson...she got sex on a piece of film like Jean Harlow...she was showing us she could sell emotions in pictures.'

Within a week, Norma Jeane Dougherty was signed on with Fox as a contract player. The casting director at Fox, Ben

Marilyn clutches the Henrietta Award for the Best Young Box Office Personality of 1951 (right). In the following year it was revealed that Marilyn had posed for a series of nude calendar shots in 1949. The affair embarrassed her employers, Twentieth Century-Fox, though the publicity harmed neither Marilyn nor the company. In a version of one of the calendar pictures (below), her nudity has been obscured by strategically placed pieces of lace, painted onto the photograph.

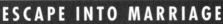

ESCAPE INTO MARRIAGE

Norma Jeane and Jim Dougherty were wed in 1942 (left). The reception was held at an Italian restaurant in Hollywood. There was no honeymoon.

The newly-weds knew almost nothing about each other. Dougherty, the less complicated of the two, patiently overlooked early culinary disasters, such as raw fish and a spoonful of salt in the coffee.

Their conflicting accounts of the marriage may be due to the different ages at which they spoke about them. In her early days of success, Marilyn Monroe was to say: 'I was a peculiar wife. I disliked grown-ups...I liked boys and girls younger than me. I played games with them until my husband came out and started calling me to bed.' There is a hint

of selectivity in such memories. The new movie star may have needed to forget any simple, homespun happiness of the kind which, 20 years later, Dougherty recalled. He also insisted that Norma Jeane had ardently wanted a baby. She herself had claimed the opposite, saying she had feared the child would end up in an orphanage.

In 1952, Marilyn posed for this seductive photograph (below) when Twentieth Century-Fox loaned her to RKO studios to make Clash by Night, *a sophisticated melodrama. In a review of the film, Marilyn was described as 'the new blonde bombshell of Hollywood'.*

The mystery surrounding the identity of Marilyn's missing father was finally solved in 1987 by Anthony Summers, author of the acclaimed Marilyn biography, *Goddess*. Summers first interviewed a Presbyterian minister, Dr Donald Liden, who said that the man in question – a southern California dairy farmer called Gifford – had told him in a sick-bed confession that he was Marilyn Monroe's father. Further details emerged in a series of interviews with Gifford's surviving relatives.

Charles Stanley Gifford, the son of an affluent ship-building family, was born in Newport, Rhode Island, in 1897. While working for a Hollywood film laboratory as a sales supervisor, he met Marilyn's mother, Gladys, who was working there as a film cutter. She soon fell for the 27-year-old, Clark Gable look-alike (right) – and bore him a daughter, Marilyn.

By then, however, Gladys and Gifford had parted. Gifford dropped out of view, eventually setting up a dairy near the small farming town of Hemet, south-east of Los Angeles. Reluctant to hurt his third wife, Mary, by acknowledging he had had a child out of wedlock, he kept Marilyn's existence a secret.

When Marilyn tracked Gifford down to his farm in 1950, he refused to see her – a decision that left Marilyn embittered. Gifford died in 1965 and the story of Marilyn's paternity stayed hidden for a further 22 years.

After half a year, Marilyn's admiring, 70-year-old boss at Twentieth Century-Fox, Joseph Schenck, helped her get a six-month contract at Columbia Pictures, at the rate of $75 a week. There, Marilyn was trained by Natasha Lytess, the head drama coach who became closely attached to her student. She was quick to see that, alongside Marilyn's helpless child persona, there existed a shrewd businesswoman.

A BLOSSOMING CAREER

At Columbia, Marilyn also met 32-year-old Fred Karger, the director of music, who not only was her musical coach, but came to be the most important love in her life. They became lovers, but he would not marry her. 'When he said, "I love you" to me, it was better than a thousand critics calling me a great star,' Marilyn said later.

In *Ladies of the Chorus* (1948), Marilyn was given a chance to talk, sing and dance. One of her songs was 'Every Baby Needs a Da Da Daddy.' By the age of 23, according to Jimmy Starr, then a writer for the *Los Angeles Herald-Express*, Marilyn had 'learned a trick of cutting a quarter of an inch off one heel.' The result was the celebrated Monroe wiggle.

Early in 1949, Groucho Marx, of the Marx Brothers comedy team, needed a 'sexy girl' for a walk-on part in the film *Love Happy*. She had to 'cause smoke to issue from my ears.' Marilyn got the part.

Meanwhile, Marilyn pursued involvement with other older men. These included Henry Rosenfeld, a wealthy dress manufacturer, who became a comforting friend in later years, and Johnny Hyde, the powerful Hollywood agent who used his connections to launch Marilyn's film career. Hyde fell deeply in love with Marilyn, and wanted to marry her, but Marilyn would not. She loved him dearly, but was not in love with him.

With Hyde's help, Marilyn was soon back at Twentieth Century-Fox to play a gangster's mistress in her first important film, John Huston's *The Asphalt Jungle*. Her next notable role was as an aspiring starlet in *All About Eve* (1950).

CALENDAR NUDE

Marilyn was still obliged to make lightweight films, and her career was threatened in the early 1950s by the discovery that she had posed nude for a photographer (Tom Kelley) in 1949. Executives at Twentieth Century-Fox were alarmed at the potential damage to their starlet's image. Posing naked was not the way nice girls behaved. The nude pictures appeared in the first-ever edition of *Playboy* in 1953.

In spite of the calendar affair, Twentieth Century-Fox now realised they had a star on their hands. After making the 1952 film *Monkey Business* with Cary Grant, Marilyn was soon able to afford a $750-a-month suite at Los Angeles' Bel-Air Hotel.

On her 26th birthday on 1 June that year, Marilyn received piles of congratulatory telegrams and gifts from the some of the mightiest names in Hollywood. Norma Jeane had made it.

US troops in Germany voted Marilyn 'Miss Cheesecake of 1951', in honour of their number one pin-up. She celebrated by offering a piece of real cheesecake to actor Edward G Robinson (above).

THE PRESIDENTIA

MARILYN'S RISE TO FAME AS A HOLLYWOOD SEX SYMBOL WAS PARALLELED BY THE RISE TO SUPREME POLITICAL POWER OF THE KENNEDY BROTHERS, JOHN AND ROBERT. BOTH MEN WERE TO FALL UNDER MARILYN'S UNIQUE SPELL

I
n the summer that Marilyn Monroe made *The Misfits*, Senator John ('Jack') Kennedy was close to becoming the youngest man, and the first Roman Catholic, ever to be elected President of the United States.

On 13 July 1960, Kennedy was nominated as the Democratic Party's candidate for the presidential elections in November. His rise heralded a new era in American public life, which had grown stagnant during the 1950s.

John Kennedy came from a family of vast wealth and power, and this seemed to prepare him for the mantle of the highest office in the land. He was charming and energetic, and appealed to many young Americans.

Kennedy, however, lived on the edge of scandal. He was a compulsive womaniser. If a majority of Americans had known how he flouted the ethics of both family life and his religion, Kennedy's presidential campaign would have been wrecked. Because of this, his trysts with Marilyn Monroe in the summer and autumn of 1960 were carefully concealed from public view.

With his youthful good-looks and dynamic charisma, President John Fitzgerald Kennedy – here (right) seated at his desk at the White House – represented a break with the dowdier image of the previous Eisenhower administration. At 43, Kennedy was the youngest elected chief executive in American history. Above right: In May 1960, while still the Senator from Massachusetts, John ('Jack') Kennedy was photographed reading a newspaper account of his West Virginia election victory on the 'Glory Road' to the White House. He had just defeated Senator Hubert Humphrey from Minnesota.

DATEFILE

JULY 13 1960
John F Kennedy nominated as Democratic Party's candidate for US presidency

JANUARY 20 1960
John Kennedy inaugurated as 35th president of USA

FEBRUARY 1 1962
Marilyn attends a dinner party for Robert Kennedy at the Lawfords' house

JULY '60 APRIL '61

Two days after Kennedy's nomination, the Hollywood film star Peter Lawford threw a party to celebrate his candidacy. Marilyn arrived with the actor Sammy Davis Jr.

Both Lawford and Davis belonged to Hollywood's so-called 'Rat Pack', a circle of performers led by the singer and actor Frank Sinatra, who

Robert Kennedy (right) stands with his brother-in-law Peter Lawford (centre) and Frank Sinatra at a Los Angeles airport in 1961.

TOUCH

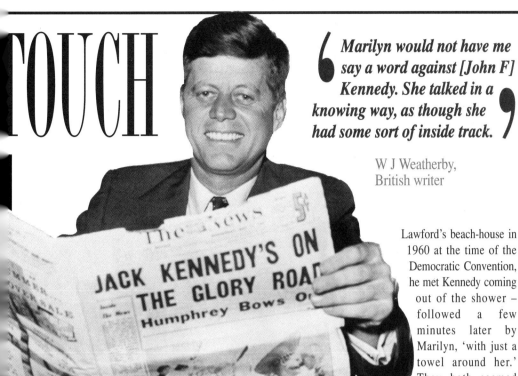

> **'Marilyn would not have me say a word against [John F] Kennedy. She talked in a knowing way, as though she had some sort of inside track. '**

W J Weatherby,
British writer

Robert Kennedy, the US Attorney-General. Rumours of an affair with Marilyn Monroe in 1962 threatened to open him up to blackmail and exposure by organised crime.

Lawford's beach-house in 1960 at the time of the Democratic Convention, he met Kennedy coming out of the shower – followed a few minutes later by Marilyn, 'with just a towel around her.' They both seemed unconcerned about it, but Kennedy's relationship with Marilyn threatened to unleash a campaign crisis.

Through her marriage to Arthur Miller, Marilyn was used to meeting politically-minded people. But she came to hold Kennedy in awe because he was brilliant, articulate and close to holding extraordinary power.

When the writer, W J Weatherby, quietly suggested that even Kennedy could not speak and act wisely all the time, she replied, 'Oh, he does.'

AN UNDERWORLD LINK

In August, 1960, Sinatra invited the cast of *The Misfits* to hear him sing at the Cal-Neva Lodge overlooking Lake Tahoe. This casino and resort complex, which Sinatra was in the process of buying, was to bring into question his reported association with one of the most powerful underworld figures in America, Sam Giancana, head of the Chicago Mafia.

Giancana owned a part of the Cal-Neva. He was also well-disposed towards John Kennedy's candidacy. On Election Day, 5 November, he used his influence to help Kennedy win Chicago and, with it, the state of Illinois. With these votes, Kennedy won election to the White House by a narrow margin over his Republican rival, Richard Nixon.

Marilyn and the President continued to see each other before and after his inauguration in

By the time Marilyn had begun her screen career, the Mafia and other criminal groups had gained widespread influence in Hollywood. They had moved in on the industry before World War II because it brought in enormous profits.

In Marilyn's time, a man called Johnny Roselli was the 'representative' who guarded the Mafia's interests in Hollywood. In the 1950s, Marilyn Monroe and a number of other actresses were the victims of an old-fashioned extortion racket run by a gangster from Los Angeles named Mickey Cohen. The women would be seduced while a recording was made. Copies of the tape would then be sold at high prices unless the victim paid to keep matters quiet.

In 1959, while the Los Angeles District Attorney kept Cohen under surveillance, his agents saw Marilyn several times in the company of Cohen's henchmen. One of those agents, Gary Wean, has said he listened to one such tape of Marilyn, and that the purpose must have been extortion.

January 1961. She was often seen entering the Carlyle Hotel in New York, where Kennedy stayed, by Jane Shalam, a member of a well-connected New York family whose apartment overlooked the hotel. 'When she took her makeup off, and had her hair back, you wouldn't know it was her,' Jane Shalam has said. On other occasions, Marilyn would travel alone wearing a wig and dark glasses, or be accompanied by an escort, to meet Kennedy at parties.

But since late 1960, with her marriage to Miller ending, she had also been having an affair with Frank Sinatra. For much of 1961, she was to be directly linked both to the country's head of state and, through Sinatra, to one of its most ruthless mobsters, Sam Giancana. As for having knowledge of presidential matters, she did give the impression to a number of friends that she had inside information of Kennedy's plans.

The attitude of John Kennedy towards sex is now well established. He once confided: 'Dad told

was a friend of John Kennedy. Lawford was also the husband of Kennedy's sister Patricia.

At the party, according to the seasoned Hollywood bartender, Ross Acuna, 'Monroe and the Kennedy boy were pretty close together.' One of Kennedy's senior campaign advisers, Pete Summers, remembered seeing them earlier in a more compromising state. When visiting

Marilyn Monroe made several visits to the Cal-Neva Lodge, a gambling and resort complex straddling the California-Nevada border (hence its name) beside Lake Tahoe. In this picture, Marilyn enjoys a conversation with Frank Sinatra (right) at the Cal-Neva, where he sometimes performed. With the breakup of Marilyn's marriage to Arthur Miller at the end of 1960, Sinatra embarked on an affair with Marilyn.

> *He...clipped two gorgeous emerald earrings on Marilyn's ears. They kissed so passionately that I was embarrassed to be standing by.*

Lena Pepitone, Marilyn's New York cook, on watching Frank Sinatra and Marilyn meet for a date, 1961

all the boys to get laid as often as possible.' In this, he took his father's advice whenever he could. Marilyn was just one of many Hollywood actresses with whom he had affairs; he inherited his fascination with the film world from his father, Joe, who had had a much publicised affair with the famous Hollywood actress, Gloria Swanson.

John Kennedy's attitude differed in degree from that of his brother Robert ('Bobby') Kennedy. In 1960, the 35-year-old Attorney-General had been married for 10 years and had seven children. He had also been named 'Father of the Year.' Robert was not quite so spotless – he had extramarital affairs with at least four women. Nevertheless, with Marilyn, Robert's commitment may have been greater than a simple 'fling'.

ROBERT AND MARILYN

Sources disagree as to exactly when Robert Kennedy and Marilyn first met. Some believe it was in February 1962. On the first of that month, Marilyn attended a dinner party at Peter Lawford's home given in honour of Robert Kennedy, who was about to begin a world tour, accompanied by his wife, Ethel. Danny Greenson, the son of Marilyn's psychiatrist, Dr Ralph Greenson,

John Kennedy poses with his wife Jacqueline (seated, right) and his parents, Joseph and Rose, in November 1960, on the day after his election to the presidency.

CUBA - THE MAFIA CONNECTION

President Kennedy had made enemies in both the CIA and the Mafia through the failure in 1961 of an invasion of Cuba that was financed and directed by the US government. Since 1959, Cuba – a Caribbean island only 217 kilometres south of Florida, USA – had been governed by the Communist revolutionary, Dr Fidel Castro. His close ties with the Soviet Union alarmed many Americans.

On 17 April 1961, Kennedy gave the go-ahead to a force of some 1500 anti-Castro Cuban exiles, trained by the CIA, to invade Cuba at the Bay of Pigs, on the island's southwest coast. The men were transported in American merchant vessels escorted by US destroyers. However, air cover by US planes was forbidden by President Kennedy at the last minute.

On landing, the invaders were routed by Cuban troops and more than a thousand men were captured and held hostage. The Mafia were particularly angered by the failure of the invasion, since Castro had shut down their lucrative Havana casinos and drug trafficking. Some criticised Kennedy for not giving his fullest support to the invasion.

During 1961 and 1962, the Chicago mobsters Sam Giancana and Johnny Roselli and other members of the Mafia plotted with the CIA to assassinate Castro, in defiance of the President's orders. Giancana was the man who owned part of the Cal-Neva Lodge, where Marilyn Monroe was a regular guest. (He is seen, left, handcuffed to a chair after his arrest in 1957 in connection with the murder of a banker.)

ACKDROP

recalled that Marilyn had prepared a list of political issues to discuss at dinner.

'They were left-of-center criticisms...' Danny Greenson said. 'She wanted to impress him [Robert]...' A few weeks later, during her trip to Mexico, Marilyn told an expatriate friend in Mexico City, Fred Vanderbilt Field, that she and Robert had had 'a very political talk' alone after dinner. She said they had discussed whether the Kennedys could fire J Edgar Hoover as head of the FBI (Federal Bureau of Investigation), which dealt with US internal security. Her Mexican lover, José Bolaños, says Marilyn mentioned that she and Robert had talked about Castro's Cuba.

Other sources believe that Marilyn and Robert Kennedy met earlier, in 1961. Deborah Gould, Peter Lawford's third wife, believes that the affair began when Robert was sent as his brother's 'messenger boy' to tell her the affair with the President was over. 'Marilyn took it quite bad,' Gould says, 'and Bobby went away with a feeling of wanting to get to know her better...it led into an affair between Marilyn and Bobby...he fell head over heels.'

From spring 1962, Marilyn began making numerous calls to Robert Kennedy's office at the Justice Department in Washington. Kennedy's personal secretary, Angie Novello, says her boss always took Marilyn's calls or returned them soon afterwards. 'He was such a sympathetic kind of

'They were dancing very closely, with their bodies very close together, and it looked rather romantic.'

Stanley Tretick, photographer for *Look* magazine, on Marilyn Monroe and Robert Kennedy

person...he was well aware of her problems.' Novella adds, 'He was a good listener and that, I think, is what she needed more than anything.'

DANGEROUS AFFAIRS

Marilyn's secret involvement with both John and Robert Kennedy, which probably overlapped at certain stages, was known or guessed at by many friends and associates. One of those she talked to about her relationship with Robert Kennedy was Anne Karger, mother of Fred, Marilyn's great love of years before. Her New York friend, Henry Rosenfeld, and her masseur, Ralph Roberts, also knew about the Kennedys. She was also often seen in Robert Kennedy's company at the Lawfords' home in Santa Monica.

Neither the President nor the Attorney-General, however, seemed to care, behaving as though nobody could touch them. Yet there were forces, such as organised crime, that were looking for ways to discredit the administration. And Marilyn's relationship with the Kennedys offered an opportunity for damaging revelations.

INSIDE

VIEW

BOBBY AND THE MOB

Marilyn Monroe's friendships with figures linked to the underworld was of direct concern to the Kennedy brothers. In the late 1950s, Robert Kennedy had acted as chief counsel to a senate committee investigating organised crime. As Attorney-General, he launched a crackdown against the Mafia, subjecting many of its leaders to harrassment and prosecution.

Many leading underworld figures had supported John Kennedy's campaign for the presidency because of their acquaintance with his father, Joseph P Kennedy, who had made a fortune through illicit sales of whisky during the Prohibition era of the 1920s. The underworld did not realise that Robert (left) would be appointed Attorney-General.

The Kennedys' involvement with Marilyn Monroe exposed both brothers to the danger of blackmail by certain mobsters, inside and outside Hollywood, who were seeking to gain a hold over the two most important men in the land – the President and his brother, the Attorney-General.

A SOCIETY ON

A GROWING URGE FOR SOCIAL CHANGE MARKED THE MOOD OF AMERICA IN THE EARLY 1960S. AS PROTESTS FOR CIVIL RIGHTS FLARED THROUGHOUT THE USA, YOUNG PEOPLE ACROSS THE CONTINENT BEGAN TO BUILD THEIR OWN VERSION OF THE AMERICAN DREAM

The United States of the early 1960s was a land suffering racial injustice, the fear of nuclear war and a complacency born of immense material wealth. While many young, white Americans found an outlet for their energy in fast cars, rock 'n' roll and a new dance craze, the twist, the country's black population was stepping up its non-violent protests against decades of discrimination.

The black rights leader, Dr Martin Luther King Jr, challenged the segregationist laws of the Deep South, which even prevented blacks from eating in the same restaurants as whites. He also attacked the power of mobsters who kept the black ghettoes supplied with heroin.

Educated white liberals, too, were inspired by Dr King. Thousands of them joined blacks on their civil rights marches through the South, and many were beaten senseless by racist mobs or corrupt, small-town police officers.

A CULTURAL CAMELOT

The inauguration of John F Kennedy as America's new president in 1961 launched a brief era when, for the first time in US politics, wealth, style and radical ideas merged. At the centre of the political estab-

Above: A woman pickets the White House in 1962. Main picture: A vast, multi-racial crowd gathers before the Lincoln Memorial, Washington DC, in August 1963. The rally was intended to speed the passage of civil rights legislation through the United States Congress.

lishment, the Kennedys created a legend – half fact, half myth – of a new Camelot, a reference to the legendary place where King Arthur held court with his Knights of the Round Table.

The Kennedy White House held evenings of poetry and folk music, elegant fashion shows and raucous midnight bathing. Much of the best in this renaissance was the work of the First Lady, Jacqueline Kennedy, who

The early 1960s saw American women beginning to challenge their stereotyped roles and express themselves more freely. However, the ideal of the fulfilled suburban housewife (right) and the wholesome 'Miss Teenage American' (far right) lingered on as reminders of the 1950s view of American womanhood.

wore evening clothes designed by top couturiers in Paris, and brought to American public life a sense of dignity and an ideal of modern beauty.

The shift in social attitudes was reflected by the entertainment world. Folk singers, such as Bob Dylan, Joan Baez, Pete

THE MARCH

Two irreverent entertainers of 1960s America were Mort Sahl and Lenny Bruce. The Montreal-born Sahl, seen here (right) in a comic routine dressed as 19th-century strongman 'The Mighty Sandow', specialised in social and political satire. Avant-garde comedian Lenny Bruce (below) often fell foul of the law for obscenity in his comedy acts.

was ending. Women's sexual liberation entered a new phase with the introduction in 1961 of the birth control pill. Americans were becoming more promiscuous, and more self-analytical, as they entered the age of 'personal relationships'. Nevertheless, the overall mood of the nation was positive, reflecting a belief that with will and energy the social problems of society could be overcome.

In 1963, the 22-year-old folk singer Bob Dylan (below) stirred a new generation of Americans with his powerful songs of conscience.

ture who baked apple pies, doted on her parents-in-law and planned family holidays beside the perfectly blue seas off California.

Young American girls were abandoning the 'cute' pin-up looks of the late 1950s – all bright red lipstick, shining white teeth and flowery swimsuits. They replaced this image with a more natural look that suited them in their quest for their own identity. This search for a truer self started to lead some people into religious sects, or to Indian systems of meditation, whose teachers had already begun to settle in California.

The age of 'dating'

Seeger and Peter, Paul and Mary sang protest songs with acoustic guitars, while stand-up satirists, like Lenny Bruce and

Mort Sahl, drew packed nightclub audiences to hear them ridicule racial and religious prejudice. This style of comedy often made audiences uneasy, since its barbs spared no one. Still, America was laughing, even though a lot of it was at sterile, formula television comedies.

It was a time when millions of women began to reject the myth of the American housewife – a contented, smiling crea-

THREE

SOMETHING

MARILYN'S RELATIONSHIP WITH THE KENNEDYS WAS NOW THREATENING TO PROVIDE THE MAFIA WITH MATERIAL FOR BLACKMAIL. HER CAREER WAS ALSO FALTERING. IN 1962, SHE EMBARKED ON A FILM THAT WAS TO PROVIDE A FITTING EPITAPH TO HER DECLINE

Marilyn Monroe's connection with both the Kennedy brothers and Frank Sinatra's circle of acquaintances was drawing her into a web of intrigue which threatened to affect the presidency of the United States. Sam Giancana, the mobster boss who knew Sinatra, was being investigated by Attorney-General Robert Kennedy's own Justice Department. And Marilyn herself had been present at Peter Lawford's house, along with Frank Sinatra and others, when Robert Kennedy had explained why the President could no longer be seen with the singer.

CARELESS TALK

Marilyn did not seem to grasp the significance of her position in these events. She failed to see that she posed perhaps the biggest risk of all. She still made mischievous comments about her affair with the President to a number of friends. To her masseur and friend, Ralph Roberts, she gossiped on the telephone, 'I think I made his back better.'

Touches of Marilyn's former screen magic were few and far between during the filming of Something's Got to Give. *Her contract with Twentieth Century-Fox was already seven years old and the sum she grudgingly had to accept for her appearance in the film – $100,000 – was well below what she could have expected by 1962.*

DATEFILE

APRIL 1962
Marilyn begins filming *Something's Got to Give*

MAY 19 1962
Marilyn sings at President Kennedy's Madison Square birthday party

JUNE 8 1962
Marilyn fired from cast of *Something's Got to Give*

JUNE 26 1962
Robert Kennedy visits Marilyn – for the last time?

APRIL–JUNE '62

HAD TO GIVE

> *'She was the light and the goddess and the moon... But everything else all together too, including Hollywood and the girl next door that every guy wants to marry.'*
>
> Bert Stern, photographer, on Marilyn

Unknown to Marilyn, plans were underway to install bugging equipment in her new house in California. A friend of hers named Arthur James was approached: 'The request was that I should get Marilyn away from the house for a while, perhaps for a weekend at my place in Laguna Beach,' he says. 'I told them I wouldn't do it.' James, however, did not warn Marilyn. 'I figured she worried about things enough anyway, and if they wanted to bug the house, they would find a way.'

The approach had been made, through a go-between, by a man named Carmine DeSapio, a corrupt New York city politician with links to the Mafia. DeSapio was also known to have connections with Jimmy Hoffa, the head of America's largest labour union, the Teamsters' Union. Hoffa was an avowed enemy of Attorney-General Kennedy, who was trying to prosecute Hoffa on corruption and extortion charges.

UNDER SURVEILLANCE

Confirmation that Marilyn's house was actually bugged in the early summer of 1962 has come from several people who were close to the operation. Jimmy Hoffa had regularly employed an expert in electronic eavesdropping named Bernard Spindel, whose assistant, Earl Jaycox, says that in 1962 Spindel had told him of the existence of two reels of tape which together could hold 12 hours of recordings. Jaycox says he was told the tapes contained private conversations between Marilyn and both John and Robert Kennedy.

Whether or not Marilyn was aware of this surveillance is not known, but she was certainly becoming acutely conscious of her privacy. She had started making any important 'phone calls from public telephone booths instead of her home and carrying a heavy purse of coins around with her for that purpose. She also claimed to a friend that she had had her neighbours 'checked out'.

Emotionally she was becoming increasingly unpredictable, regularly seeing her psychiatrist Ralph Greenson, and displaying to her friends an anxiety about everyone and everything that

THE 'WRONG DOOR RAID'

Rumours that Joe DiMaggio was bugging Marilyn's house in 1961 may not be as ridiculous as they seem. The possessive attention that he showed towards his ex-wife (seen with her, above, in April 1961) had started only a matter of days after their marriage ended when, on 5 November 1954, he was allegedly involved in an assault which became known as the 'Wrong Door Raid'.

Marilyn was with her new lover Hal Schaefer at the apartment of her friend, Sheila Stewart, when a private detective who was hired by DiMaggio to keep her under surveillance spotted her car and contacted DiMaggio. DiMaggio was with Frank Sinatra at the time and within minutes the two of them had arrived outside the apartment. But it was the occupant of the ground floor apartment, Mrs Florence Kotz, who suffered. Her front door was broken down and men rushed in to take photographs. Realising their mistake, Sinatra and DiMaggio fled, while Marilyn and the others sat upstairs. Kotz later sued Sinatra, DiMaggio and a number of private detectives and accepted a settlement of $7500.

INSIDE VIEW
JIMMY HOFFA

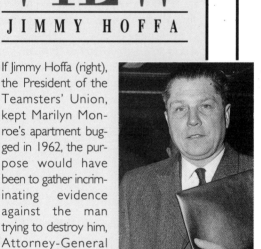

If Jimmy Hoffa (right), the President of the Teamsters' Union, kept Marilyn Monroe's apartment bugged in 1962, the purpose would have been to gather incriminating evidence against the man trying to destroy him, Attorney-General Robert Kennedy. Hoffa had enlisted the support of the Mafia in gaining control of the union and turning its pension fund into a cash-source for organised crime. Kennedy had been pursuing Hoffa long before he began his drive against organised crime in 1961.

In May 1962, Hoffa was indicted for extortion. Later that summer, his henchman, Edward Partin, became a government informant when he heard Hoffa discuss a plan to have Robert Kennedy murdered. This was in July or August 1962, the period when the Attorney-General saw Marilyn for the last time. Hoffa eventually served five years in jail. In 1975, he disappeared and is presumed to have been murdered.

Dr Timothy Leary (above), the psychologist who was asked by Marilyn to introduce her to the new drug, LSD.

seemed to verge on paranoia. To one friend, poet Norman Rosten, her manner was one of 'controlled desperation'. Talking to him about Frank Sinatra she asked, ' He's nice isn't he?' Rosten later reflected that 'the tone in her voice was not eagerness, but panic.'

Marilyn's ex-husband, Joe DiMaggio, continued to take a close interest in Marilyn's life. 'DiMaggio keeps an eye on me, sort of,' she told Norman Rosten. 'If I have any trouble, I just call on Joe.' But his interest in her went further than that, and often verged on the obsessive. There is evidence that, in 1961, he too had installed eavesdropping equipment in her house.

> ' *Marilyn... was convinced that this* [Something's Got to Give] *was the one that would bring her back.* '
>
> Nunnally Johnson, Scriptwriter

In May 1962, approaching her 36th birthday and depressed by her decline as a movie star, Marilyn began making the comedy *Something's Got to Give* with Dean Martin, another member of Hollywood's 'Rat Pack'. Her approach to the film was ambiguous. She had little faith in the film itself but was convinced that it was her opportunity for a revival on the big screen. In view of her state of mind at the time, there was little ground for optimism. But her contract with Twentieth Century-Fox made it impossible for her to refuse the work.

Marilyn's vague sense of dread was evident from the outset of filming. She was sent the script with a request that she put 'XX' by any line to which she strongly objected. Marilyn for some reason interpreted this as a sign that she was soon to be double-crossed. The film's producer, Henry

Weinstein, later described her as 'one very ill, very paranoid lady.' She harboured suspicions that her co-stars were trying to upstage her and became convinced that her fellow actress in the film, Cyd Charisse, was trying to copy her by having the same colour hair as her. Even the 50-year-old actress playing the part of the housekeeper had to have her hair darkened to avoid trouble with Marilyn.

'Remember, you've got Marilyn Monroe,' she told the scriptwriter, Walter Bernstein. 'You've got to use her.' Bernstein tried to placate her by including a scene in which Marilyn wore a bikini, and by removing any lines which implied that her screen husband, Dean Martin, could look twice at any other woman. But during a total of 35 days' filming, Marilyn only turned up to the studios for 12 of them. More than once she was seen retching near the studio entrance, which producer Henry Weinstein generously interpreted as an extreme fear of going before the cameras: 'We all experience anxiety, unhappiness, heartbreaks,' he said. 'But this was sheer, primal terror.'

LSD EXPERIMENT

Weinstein, like most Hollywood people, would have been aware of Marilyn's personal problems. But it is unlikely that he knew that she had taken the hallucinogenic drug lysergic acid (LSD). In the summer of 1962, one of President Kennedy's mistresses, Mary Meyer, went to see a Harvard University psychologist called Dr Timothy Leary. Though later to become a figurehead of the 1960s mind expansion culture, Leary was then quietly engaged in academic research into drugs. Miss Meyer told Leary that she was keen to find out about LSD.

HOLLYWOOD VISIT

In May 1962, Meyer persuaded Dr Leary to come to Hollywood to discuss LSD with various doctors and celebrities. After a party there, Leary had gone to sleep in a bedroom, only to be woken up by Marilyn Monroe. 'She wanted me to introduce her to LSD,' he said. He warned her about the drug's power, but the following night she persuaded him to give her a very small amount. She and Leary

In New York, Marilyn sang 'Happy Birthday' at President Kennedy's 45th birthday party. Introduced by Peter Lawford (inset), Marilyn was wearing a $5000 sparkling rhinestone dress, with nothing on underneath.

Dean Martin and Marilyn (left) on the set of Something's Got to Give. Obsessed with her health, Marilyn walked out of the studio once on hearing that Martin had a cold.

arrival on stage but, at his first introduction, she failed to appear. Lawford's second attempt was followed by a drum roll, but she still did not come out on stage. Finally, Lawford announced 'Mr President, the late Marilyn Monroe.' This time, virtually propelled on stage by Lawford's agent, she appeared. For 30 unnerving seconds, however, she was silent before at last singing her lines faultlessly.

RENEWED DESPERATION

Back in Hollywood on 1 June 1962, Marilyn celebrated her own birthday, her 36th, with the film crew of *Something's Got to Give*. But within two days, desperation had overtaken her again. She rang Dr Greenson's son and daughter, sounding heavily drugged, and they came straight over to her house. Marilyn was extremely depressed and spoke to the Greensons about being ugly, having no one who loved her and being used by people. According to Danny Greenson, 'she said it wasn't worth living any more.' She was inconsolable and the Greensons could do nothing more than call in a psychiatrist colleague of Dr Greenson's to see her.

MOVIE DISASTER

For the producers of Twentieth Century-Fox, who were looking at the first rushes from *Something's Got to Give*, the truth was beginning to dawn on them that they had a financial disaster on their hands. The director, George Cukor, was dismayed by what he saw and on 8 June the executives took the decision

to fire Marilyn. Almost immediately afterwards the movie was cancelled. Marilyn was sued for half a million dollars by the studio and, when Dean Martin announced that he would not work with any other actress, he too was sued.

Marilyn's response was outwardly unperturbed. She sent off a succession of telegrams, including a strange and slightly wistful message to Robert Kennedy and his wife, turning down an invitation to visit them: 'I would have been delighted to have accepted your invitation honoring Pat and Peter Lawford. Unfortunately I am involved in a freedom ride protesting the loss of the minority rights belonging to the few remaining earthbound stars. After all, all we demanded was our right to twinkle.'

On 26 June, Robert Kennedy, wearing slacks and an open shirt, visited Marilyn alone in Brentwood for about an hour. She 'did not seem bubbly or excited by his visit,' her housekeeper, Eunice Murray, said. It was the last time, prior to the day of her death, that anyone claimed to have seen Marilyn and Robert Kennedy together. By early July 1962, Marilyn would wake in the night, and sit with tears streaming down her face.

walked along Venice beach in a frame of mind that Leary described as 'joyous'. But for someone in Marilyn's fragile mental state, the exposure to such a powerful drug was potentially disastrous.

In the meantime, her behaviour on the film set became even more wayward. The producers, to their anger, could not prevent her leaving to go to President Kennedy's birthday party at Madison Square Garden in New York on 19 May. Marilyn had been asked to sing 'Happy Birthday Mr President,' but, faced with the prospect of appearing before 15,000 people, Marilyn's nerve nearly gave way. Dr Greenson's daughter, Joan, gave her a copy of the children's story *The Little Engine that Could* to reassure her when her confidence wavered.

> *Marilyn...thought her phone lines might be tapped... she seemed very paranoid.*
>
> Robert Slatzer, ex-lover of Marilyn's

On the night of the performance, Marilyn became increasingly drunk to steady her nerves. With the auditorium packed, John Kennedy sat smoking a cigar in the Presidential box, his feet up on the rail. The First Lady, Jaqueline, was not with him.

Peter Lawford was there to announce Marilyn's

PERSPECTIVE

SELLING THE BODY BEAUTIFUL

Although *Something's Got To Give* was never completed, one scene from the film achieved its own immortality, and proved that Marilyn never lost her instinct for getting the maximum publicity out of her sexuality.

During the filming of a swimming pool scene (right) in which Marilyn was supposed to be naked, the cameraman complained that the flesh-coloured bikini she was wearing was too obvious. Marilyn's answer was to dispose of it altogether, providing photographers with the first nude shots of Marilyn for a dozen years. Within a month, *Life* magazine had published a suitably discreet selection, but before more revealing shots could be shown, Marilyn herself had to be

consulted. Her approach was simple. As long as the pictures reached a wide enough audience, she was unconcerned and only deleted a few of them. Hugh Hefner of *Playboy* magazine paid $25,000 and the eventual worldwide sales reached $150,000.

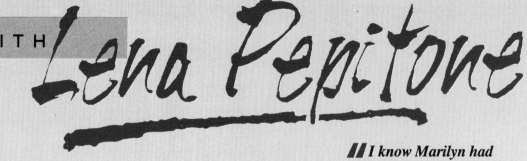

LENA PEPITONE WAS MARILYN'S NEW YORK COOK DURING THE LAST TURBULENT FIVE YEARS OF THE STAR'S LIFE. HERE, LENA TELLS *SCANDAL* HOW THE TWO WOMEN'S SPECIAL RELATIONSHIP GAVE HER AN INSIGHT INTO MARILYN'S MUCH-PUBLICISED PERSONALITY

Lena Pepitone came to America from Italy, settled in New York City with her husband, Joey, and gave birth to two sons. When she decided that she wanted to get a job, she found herself turning up for an extraordinary appointment:

'A local employment agency sent me on an interview to Park Avenue. I remember being overwhelmed by the tall buildings and glamorous surroundings. Arriving at my appointment, I waited for the mistress of this magnificent apartment to greet me. To my shock and surprise it was Marilyn Monroe – and she was completely naked. She said to me, "Sit down, we're both women, it doesn't matter." We talked for five minutes, then, to my astonishment, she told me to begin work immediately.'

Having started to work for Marilyn in October 1957, Lena quickly realised that her film star employer was both a complicated

> **▌▌** Marilyn was always in a state of conflict with herself...and, more than anything, she wanted a child. **▌▌**

and an extremely lonely woman:

'She needed to talk over her opinions on just about anything...I soon discovered that Marilyn was always in a state of conflict with herself: she was a sex symbol, but couldn't handle the men in her life; she loved being in the public eye, but treasured her privacy; and, more than anything, she wanted a child.'

ON MARILYN AND CHILDREN
There have been many conflicting stories about whether or not Marilyn had any abortions, or indeed if she had any children. In one story that Marilyn told Lena, the film star claimed that:

'She tried to escape her unhappy childhood by getting a housekeeping job at the age of 13. The man of the house violently raped her and, although people claimed she had an abortion, I know Marilyn had the child because every month I sent a cheque to a special orphanage under orders of strict secrecy.'

Marilyn's longing to bring up a child of her own showed in her affection for Lena's sons:

'Myself, my husband Joey and our sons became a family for Marilyn. She adored my boys and let them romp around the house as if it was their private playground. I remember Arthur Miller getting very angry at Marilyn for allowing the boys to pound the keys of their Steinway grand piano as if it were a special toy.

'Marilyn would send her limousine to collect the boys – on their arrival, stacks of new toys would be waiting for them and the refrigerator would be filled with treats. The boys would always show Marilyn their report cards, and she would reward them with gifts if they had got high grades.

'Many arguments would break out between Marilyn and Arthur Miller over my children. He found them a nuisance, while she would defend them as if they were her own.'

ON MISCARRIAGES AND DEPRESSION
Lena dates Marilyn's downward slide into despair from her second miscarriage with Arthur Miller, at the end of 1958. She remembers that a symptom of Marilyn's post-miscarriage depression was rapid weight fluctuation. This meant that Lena, an accomplished seamstress who made many of Marilyn's

clothes, was constantly altering her employer's clothes – or making new ones. Lena recalls one bitter episode:

'Marilyn lost her temper.because she could not get into a blouse that I had just finished making. She ripped the blouse off and threw it on the floor. We had a furious argument. It was around this time I threatened to leave – Marilyn burst into tears, apologised and begged me to stay on.'

ON SAVING MARILYN'S LIFE
By December 1960, with her marriage to Miller over, Marilyn's depression was reaching dangerous proportions. Lena remembers going round to Marilyn's apartment on Christmas Eve 1960. She was taking gifts from her husband Joey and her children, and planned to ask Marilyn to spend Christmas with her:

'When I entered Marilyn's room, I saw an empty bed and Marilyn had one foot on the window ledge. I pulled her down and we fell onto the bed, both of us crying hysterically. This time, Marilyn put her depression down to the death of Clark Gable [her co-star in The Misfits had died the previous month] – which she blamed herself for.'

ON THE PRESIDENT'S BIRTHDAY PARTY
On one particular occasion (19 May 1962), Lena was on hand for an unusual dressmaking task – when Marilyn was asked to sing 'Happy Birthday' at the President's grand birthday celebrations at Madison Square Garden:

'She selected a gown that was two sizes too small and insisted on wearing it no matter what I said about it. It was my job to see that it fitted her properly, which was impossible, and we argued about its suitability for the occasion. When we arrived at the Garden, the dress split at the seams. I had to sew it again and again.

'Finally, long after her scheduled time of appearance, she sauntered on stage. I remember the two of us cursing at each other in Italian, and me sticking her in the rump with a pin as she walked out on to the stage. We later laughed at her grimaces in photographs of the occasion.'

> **▌▌** I know Marilyn had the child because every month I sent a cheque to a special orphanage under orders of strict secrecy. **▌▌**

ON MARILYN, MEN AND DIMAGGIO
Lena soon developed a sixth sense about the onset of Marilyn's depressions:

'She was usually depressed by getting her hopes up for love affairs which never blossomed. She desperately wanted to share her life with a man, but she was always treated like an object.

'Marilyn and DiMaggio remained friends for a long time [after their divorce in October 1954]. He would come over for dinner and console her as a good friend. Joe was a real friend and a great gentleman. He told me, in Italian, how much he still loved Marilyn.'

ON THE FINAL MONTHS
During the growing desperation of her last months, Marilyn became prone to dramatic mood swings. Lena recalls one sudden upturn in Marilyn's mood:

'She was fired from the film [Something's Got to Give, in June 1962] because of her erratic moods, and for not showing up at work, or being ill. I would get her to talk constantly at that time, trying to help her through. It seemed that she went from bad to worse, until, one day, she called me and said, "Lena, we're going to celebrate. I just personally re-negotiated my contract with the studio, and this film is going to be great." She went on to explain that she was now totally in control of her life and wanted to throw a huge party for her friends.

'I began the preparations for the party, relieved at last that she seemed to be better, when, one morning in early August 1962, I was called by the Los Angeles Police Department to be told of Marilyn's death. A part of me has never quite recovered. When I went to Marilyn's New York apartment to collect my personal possessions, the police wouldn't let me in. To this day, they have not been returned.'

Lena Pepitone (right), whose husband and sons provided Marilyn with a surrogate family.

FAREWELL

THE LAST WEEKS OF MARILYN'S LIFE WERE MARKED BY WILD MOOD SWINGS. ABANDONED BY THE KENNEDYS, SHE RENEWED CONTACTS WITH OLD FRIENDS AND LOVERS, BUT MARILYN'S BELIEF IN HERSELF AND HER SENSE OF HER OWN WORTH WAS EXHAUSTED

Towards the end of June 1962, Marilyn took part in photographic sessions for several major magazines, sometimes working through the night. In one of the sessions, for *Vogue* magazine, she wore furs, posed nude behind a see-through scarf, and finally dropped the scarf entirely.

She also made a series of taped interviews at her home with a reporter for *Life* magazine, Richard Meryman. He noticed how 'pasty and lifeless-looking' her face was. Marilyn spoke as though her peak as a famous beauty had passed. 'Fame will go by,' she told him, 'and, so long, I've had you, Fame.' Her life, she added, was in her work and 'in a few relationships with the few people I can really count on.'

Meryman felt the despair when he entered Marilyn's house. 'There was something creepy, something sick about it,' he says. Marilyn was clinging to her privacy and, in so doing, created 'a fortress feeling...of being embattled.' The actress refused to allow her home to be photographed.

DATEFILE

JUNE 1962
Marilyn holds photo and interview sessions with *Life*, *Vogue* and *Cosmopolitan* magazines

MID-JULY 1962
Lawfords take Marilyn to Cal-Neva Lodge for a weekend break. She has a near-collapse from drink and pills overdose

JULY 30 1962
Marilyn makes an eight-minute call to the Justice Department

AUGUST 5 1962
At 3.30 am Marilyn's housekeeper notices her light is still on and alerts Dr Greenson

JUNE–AUGUST '62

In the months before her death, Marilyn became less in control of herself than ever before. However, she was still greatly adored by her fans. Here (above), at the annual dinner of the Hollywood Foreign Press Association on 5 March 1962, she was presented with the Golden Globe Award for being the world's favourite actress.

In early July, Marilyn fell into a depression deeper than any she had suffered before. She visited psychiatrist Dr Ralph Greenson almost every day, and saw her general physician, Dr Hyman Engelberg, at least twice a week.

At this time, July, there was no word from the Kennedy brothers. Marilyn's efforts to telephone them ended in failure. The impact on Marilyn was deeply wounding. In spite of their past relationship with her, the Kennedys were treating her as though she had never existed.

Marilyn hinted strongly to friends that she had recently become pregnant by one of the Kennedys, but had miscarried after a few weeks. To her friend, Arthur James, she suggested that Robert

had been the father. To others, Marilyn coyly refused to say which brother was responsible.

In late June, Marilyn had offered a clue to her close friend, the photo-journalist George Barris. She told him: '...when a man leaves a woman when she tells him she's going to have his baby, when he doesn't marry her, that must hurt a woman very much, deep down inside.'

Whether genuinely pregnant or not, Marilyn

TO FAME

At the end of June 1962, Marilyn did a series of photo sessions with Vogue photographer Bert Stern. Ensconced at the Bel-Air Hotel in Los Angeles with only Stern and bottles of champagne, she posed nude behind a diaphanous scarf (left), and lay seductively on a rumpled bed (above right).

PERSPECTIVE

YET ANOTHER MARRIAGE ?

Some of the more disputed claims about Marilyn Monroe's life have been made by a man who knew her for much of her Hollywood life. Robert Slatzer, a young writer from Ohio, met her in 1946 when she was still calling herself Norma Jeane Mortensen.

Slatzer and Marilyn were occasional lovers and intermittent friends for many years (he is seen below right with a photo of himself and Marilyn taken in 1952). Slatzer introduced Marilyn to *The Rubyáiát of Omar Khayyam* and the works of Edgar Allan Poe. She gave him Kahlil Gibran's *The Prophet*. Slatzer was close to Marilyn during her involvement with Joe DiMaggio. The two men even turned up for a date with Marilyn on the same night – a small fiasco caused by Marilyn getting 'her schedules mixed up.'

Slatzer has claimed that he and Marilyn married in the Mexican border town of Tijuana on 4 October 1952. He says the marriage took place on impulse, while DiMaggio was away in the east. They drove down to Mexico in his 1948 Packard convertible and found 'a lawyer behind a storefront right on the main street' to conduct the brief civil ceremony.

When Marilyn changed her mind, they bribed the Mexican lawyer in Tijuana to destroy the marriage certificate.

The story is corroborated by actor Kid Chissell who said he was roped in as a witness at the ceremony, and the actress Terry Moore, who said Marilyn had told her about the marriage soon after it occurred.

was suffering deep shock at being cold-shouldered by the Kennedys and the realisation that her attractions could not compete with the demands of raw political realities.

During July, Marilyn had meetings with her former lover, Robert Slatzer. He warned her flatly that Robert would never marry her. But Marilyn was angry and bewildered that the Attorney-General would not accept her calls. She showed

> **'** *Do you know who I've always depended on? Not strangers, not friends. The telephone! That's my best friend.* **'**
>
> Marilyn Monroe to reporter
> W J Weatherby

Slatzer Robert Kennedy's letters to her, written on Justice Department notepaper, and a small red book, parts of which he read with growing alarm.

The 'diary', as Marilyn called it, described her political conversations with Robert Kennedy. Marilyn had written down his comments to her on subjects as sensitive as the failed invasion of Cuba and his efforts to prosecute and imprison Jimmy Hoffa, the Teamsters' union leader.

It was clear to Slatzer that Marilyn had no idea of what the Kennedys' many enemies would do to get hold of her little red book. 'Bobby liked to talk about political things,' she told Slatzer. 'He got mad at me one day because he said I didn't remember anything he told me.'

A creature of the telephone, quick to communicate, Marilyn found it hard to accept that anyone should refuse to accept her calls. Her friend and neighbour Jeanne Carmen once saw Robert looking concerned as Marilyn wrote down

A frequent companion of Marilyn's during the summer of 1962 was her 26-year-old lover, the Mexican scriptwriter, José Bolaños. The couple had met during Marilyn's trip to Mexico in February 1962 (they are shown, left, dancing at a Mexico City nightclub) and he followed her to Los Angeles.

one of his jokes in some private notebook. Robert told her, 'Ah, get rid of that.'

With the diary and the letters keeping alive her memories of Robert, and her importance to him, Marilyn ignored Slatzer's advice to forget the Kennedys. But the pain of rejection took its toll.

Around the middle of July 1962, Peter Lawford and his wife, Pat, took Marilyn for a weekend at the Cal-Neva Lodge, where Sinatra was performing. Marilyn cut a forlorn figure. 'She wasn't well,' says Mae Shoopman, who worked at the reception desk. 'She kept herself disguised pretty much, kept herself covered with a black scarf, and stayed in her room a good deal of the time.'

Afraid of lonely nights in her Cal-Neva cabin, Marilyn slept holding a telephone receiver that was linked to the main switchboard. Late at night, an operator suddenly heard her rasping breath coming through on the line. Marilyn was near-collapse after another dose of champagne, vodka and sleeping pills.

Sinatra and the Lawfords quickly arranged for her to return home for treatment. Time was running out for Marilyn. Unable to sleep, she would call on Ralph Roberts in the middle of the night for a massage, or telephone Dr Engelberg. She also argued with friends who had given generously to her, such as housekeeper Eunice Murray and her acting coach Paula Strasberg.

By the last week of July, Marilyn seemed to be losing her grip. She visited the Cal-Neva Lodge once more, looking more miserable than ever. Frank Sinatra reportedly took photographs of her that weekend, which he later burned. The photographs, according to a witness, showed Marilyn in utter disarray.

Marilyn's pride added to her injuries. She had infuriated Robert Kennedy by phoning his home in Virginia. On Monday, 30 July, she rang the Justice Department for the last time and, on this occcasion, may have spoken to Robert Kennedy. The call lasted eight minutes. On Wednesday, 1 August, Marilyn's former husband, Joe DiMaggio, outraged by reports of sex parties and drug-taking at the Cal-Neva Lodge, quit his job and flew west. He still had hopes of a future with Marilyn.

DINE OUT OR TAKE AWAY ?

Robert was due in California that first weekend in August. Marilyn rang Peter Lawford, who gave her the telephone number of his wife, Pat, the Kennedys' sister. She was visiting the Kennedy clan in Massachusetts, and Lawford thought Marilyn could find out from her how to contact Robert when he came west.

The Attorney-General flew to California with his wife, Ethel, and four of their children, on the Friday afternoon. He was due to make a speech to the American Bar Association on the Monday. Although the Association provided a suite at San Francisco's St Francis Hotel, the Kennedys stayed 60 miles south of the city at a ranch owned by attorney John Bates.

That same Friday, Marilyn saw both Dr Greenson and Dr Engelberg, and spent at least part of the evening with her press secretary, Pat Newcomb. The atmosphere was tense. Pat was to say that they dined at a restaurant in Santa Monica. But, in events that have never been fully explained, Marilyn also ordered during the day

> *I don't mind being burdened with being glamorous and sexual. We are all born sexual creatures...it's a pity so many people despise and crush this natural gift. Art, real art, comes from it...*
>
> Marilyn Monroe to *Life* reporter Richard Meryman

large quantities of expensive food from a delicatessen, and that night had food brought in from the exclusive La Scala restaurant.

The proprietor of La Scala, Jean Leon, who had worked at the Villa Capri restaurant frequented by Sinatra and DiMaggio, accompanied the delivery that Friday evening. He observed that Marilyn and Newcomb had a guest at the house, but to this day refuses to say who it was.

There is no reliable record of what happened at Marilyn's house in Brentwood between the food delivery from La Scala and dawn on Saturday, 4 August, when she rang her neighbour, Jeanne Carmen, in a state of fear. 'She said some woman had been calling all night, harassing her and calling her names, then hanging up,' Jeanne recalls.

INSIDE VIEW
TELEPHONE LIFELINE

During her last week of life, Marilyn lived by the telephone, ringing people in the fashion and film businesses, discussing new projects and telling Lena Pepitone, her maid in New York, that she was planning a party for September.

Many long-standing friends, such as Marlon Brando, received messages that Marilyn had called. Brando returned the call and they chatted for some time; he managed to make her laugh. (Brando is seen, left, with Marilyn at a film première in 1955.) Marilyn even disturbed a gynaecologist, whom she had not seen for years, at his golf club. Despite her personal crisis, she still remembered to send her neighbour, Jeanne Carmen, a birthday card.

Shrewder friends saw through this cheerfulness. On Friday, 3 August, her friend and writer Norman Rosten, speaking to Marilyn on the 'phone from New York, noticed how she leapt frenetically from one topic to another. Anne Karger, the mother of Marilyn's sometime lover Fred Karger, received a call in which Marilyn announced she was going to marry Robert Kennedy.

THE ENIGMATIC FRIEND

He's been ignoring me. I've been trying to reach him on the telephone, and I just can't get to him.

Marilyn on Robert Kennedy, quoted by Robert Slatzer in his book *The Life and Curious Death of Marilyn Monroe*

Marilyn first met her enigmatic press aide, Pat Newcomb (above, left), during the making of *Bus Stop* in 1956. Newcomb was a 25-year-old from the East Coast with a degree in psychology. She was handling Marilyn's press for a while on behalf of Arthur Jacobs, Marilyn's public relations agent. The women were very alike physically and took to each other at once. But they fell out almost as quickly. Marilyn suspected her of trying to steal a man-friend. As a result, Newcomb had to leave the location. A similar issue was to cloud their relationship again in the last 24 hours of Marilyn's life.

The two women met up again towards the end of 1960, after Marilyn had completed *The Misfits*. Marilyn's press aide and friend, Rupert Allan, had left her employ and she agreed to take Newcomb back. Apart from being efficient as a press aide, Newcomb now became one of Marilyn's closest friends.

When *Life* reporter Richard Meryman interviewed Marilyn in 1962, he remembered the ever-present Newcomb as being 'obsessively loyal, totally devoted.' Marilyn, however, gave him the impression she was only keeping Newcomb on sufferance. To this day, Newcomb refuses to comment when asked about Marilyn, the President and the Attorney-General.

Marilyn told her that the caller had said something like, 'Leave Bobby alone, you tramp. Leave Bobby alone.' At 8 am Eunice Murray arrived for work, to learn that Pat Newcomb had stayed overnight.

An hour later, Marilyn, still wracked by insomnia, was sipping some grapefruit juice. 'She looked sick, desperately sick,' says Norman Jeffries, Mrs Murray's son-in-law, who used to help with heavier household tasks. 'I thought...maybe she was scared out of her mind.' Marilyn retreated to her bedroom and the telephone. As the morning wore on, she rang her masseur, Ralph Roberts, and received a regular weekend call from Sidney Skolsky, the Hollywood writer.

AFTERNOON TORMENT

Skolsky knew something of Marilyn's dramas with the Kennedys and – wanting 'a witness' – asked his daughter Steffi to listen on an extension. Steffi remembers Marilyn saying she expected to see Robert Kennedy at Peter Lawford's house that evening, and also that 'Pat's jealous of me.'

Pat Newcomb, was, reportedly, herself deeply in love with Robert. Throughout the day, Marilyn seemed furious with her. Near noon, Agnes Flanagan, Marilyn's hairdresser, arrived and, soon after, a package was delivered. It contained a toy tiger. Agnes Flanagan watched as Marilyn went to sit by the pool, holding the stuffed tiger. She seemed 'terribly, terribly depressed,' said Flanagan. The significance of the tiger, however, remains a mystery.

Marilyn returned to her bedroom. At 4.30 pm she rang Dr Greenson, who thought she sounded 'depressed and somewhat drugged.' He drove to the house to find Marilyn furious that Pat Newcomb had slept until midday, because she, Marilyn, had had 'such a poor sleep'. Soon, he learnt that her meeting with one of the 'very important people' – her term for the Kennedys – was off. It tormented Marilyn that, although her beauty was renowned across the world, she had no date for a Saturday night.

COUNTDOWN TO DISASTER

After about two and a half hours, Marilyn grew calmer. Pat Newcomb left and Greenson asked Mrs Murray to stay the night. He left at 7.15 pm. Twenty-five minutes later, as the psychiatrist was shaving for a dinner party, Marilyn rang again. Greenson, pleased to hear her sounding more cheerful, told her to sleep well and to call him the next morning.

Sometime after 8 pm, Marilyn's former lover Henry Rosenfeld rang from New York. He thought she sounded 'groggy.' At about 9.30 pm, Marilyn rang her friend, hairdresser Sidney Guilaroff. She told him she was 'very depressed' and rang off without saying good-bye.

Over the next 30 minutes, Marilyn was telephoned by José Bolaños, the Mexican who had been her lover that year. Then she called Jeanne Carmen, begging her to come round. Jeanne did not go. At 3.30 am on Sunday, 5 August, the telephone rang at the Greensons' home, less than two miles away in Santa Monica. Ralph Greenson listened as Eunice Murray told him that, unusually for that hour, Marilyn's bedroom light was still on. Greenson told her to bang on the door. She reported that there was no answer.

When Murray told him she had gone round to the front of the house, and seen Marilyn through the window lying quietly on the bed, Greenson said he would be over immediately. He reached the house in five minutes to find Marilyn's bedroom door locked from the inside.

Marilyn's temper could be ugly. When, in July 1962, Twentieth Century-Fox discussed a possible revival of Something's Got To Give, Marilyn summoned her acting coach, Paula Strasberg, back from Europe to help in negotiations. But Marilyn spurned her and abused her for doing nothing. In this photograph, taken in June 1962, Marilyn and Strasberg talk on the film set.

GODDESS AND

AS A MOVIE GODDESS, MARILYN MONROE WAS FOR MANY THE EMBODIMENT OF GLAMOUR AND SEXUAL ALLURE. YET SHE WAS ALSO A PERSON WITH VERY HUMAN STRENGTHS AND FAILINGS, WHO STRUGGLED AGAINST GREAT ODDS TO FIND FULFILMENT IN HER CAREER AND PRIVATE LIFE

Talking in 1954, when she was already a household name, Marilyn Monroe described how Norma Jeane – the 'sad, bitter child who grew up too fast' – remained within her. 'With success all around me,' Marilyn explained, 'I can still feel her frightened eyes looking out of mine. She keeps saying, "I never lived, I was never loved," and I often get

Marilyn's role in The Misfits (1960) reflected a problem in her own life – how to hold onto faith and confidence in herself and those around her. Here (main picture), during a break in filming, her face captures some of the strain she was experiencing. Inset: At home, Marilyn relied heavily on the telephone to reach out to friends and aquaintances for support and company, regardless of the hour of the day.

confused and think it's I who am saying it.'

Marilyn, who had a lifelong interest in the occult, and often visited astrologers and psychics, would have recognised such duality as typical of a Gemini,

under whose sign she was born – a bright, sparkling exterior hiding a dark, inner despair. This double character could be seen in other ways. To the film-going world, she was a 'screen goddess'; to her close friends,

she radiated a natural warmth, sense of humour and compassion that might have been found in the 'girl-next-door'. Yet Marilyn believed she was more than two people in one. 'I'm so many people...I wish I was just *me!*' she told a reporter close to the end of her life.

EARLY REJECTION

For some understanding of Marilyn's complex nature, one must look to her early, 'Norma Jeane' years – a period she never forgot. Abandoned by her father before she was born, and placed in a string of foster homes by her mother, Gladys, the young Norma Jeane had an emotionally deprived infancy and childhood. Deep feelings of

AN INDEPENDENT SPIRIT

Marilyn Monroe was one of the first Hollywood stars to try to break the monopoly of the big film studios. In January 1955, she announced the formation of Marilyn Monroe Productions. She would hold 51 per cent of the stock, with the rest controlled by her friend, the photographer, Milton Greene. Marilyn said she felt like a 'a new woman' and

would not renew her contract with Twentieth Century-Fox. 'I didn't like a lot of my pictures,' she said. 'I'm tired of sex roles. I'm going to broaden my scope.'

Marilyn had no capital of her own, and Greene and his wife, Amy, financed the deliberately luxurious lifestyle of the new executive. The company never made any films, but it forced

Twentieth Century-Fox to pay more for Marilyn's services. The idea was not entirely a ploy. According to Amy Greene, Marilyn 'was fascinated by women who had made it', especially Joséphine, Napoleon Bonaparte's consort, and Emma, Lady Hamilton, Lord Nelson's mistress who had begun life as a servant girl.

GIRL-NEXT-DOOR

MARILYN'S CHILD – FACT OR FANTASY?

Marilyn Monroe is believed to have died barren, never having given birth to any of the children she craved (the picture below right shows Marilyn and acting coach, Paula Strasberg, admiring a local drugstore owner's baby during filming of *The Misfits*, in 1960). But there lingers a story, told in 1979 by her New York cook, Lena Pepitone, that Marilyn spoke of becoming pregnant in her mid-teens. Marilyn, Pepitone says, hid her pregnancy from her guardian, Grace McKee, for several months. When Marilyn broke the news, McKee arranged for the child to be born in hospital. Pepitone quotes Marilyn as saying, '...I was so scared, but it was wonderful. It was a little boy. I hugged him and kissed him...I couldn't believe this was

my baby...' The child, says Pepitone, was taken away almost immediately.

Marilyn told similar stories to her friends Amy Greene and Jeanne Carmen. According to Carmen, Marilyn worried that she might be punished for giving the child away. Amy Greene has acknowledged that 'Marilyn used to fabricate a great deal...'

rejection and instability left her with a very fragile self-esteem and a difficulty in separating her 'real' self from a fantasy image.

In the opinion of a New York psychiatrist, Dr Valérie Shikhverg, such a background made Marilyn a potential 'borderline' personality – someone who hovers 'on the border

between psychotic and neurotic'. According to Dr Shikhverg, such a person is likely to be emotionally unstable, over-impulsive and dependant on external approval; a 'borderline' also cannot stand being alone, suffers 'depressive, crashlike reactions' to rejection by others, abuses drugs and alcohol, and makes suicide gestures for help. These traits marked Marilyn throughout her life.

As she grew up, Marilyn tried to con-

Marilyn, the starlet, seen here in about 1952, lifts dumb-bells to keep herself in trim for her films. Her jeans and work-outs put her ahead of her time as a woman in early 1950s America.

trol the negative undercurrents in her psyche. Her powerful – almost ruthless – drive for success brought her 'screen goddess' status and a much-desired public recognition. But she also feared being trapped by it. Her love life, in particular, was an area fraught with difficulties.

ESTEEM THROUGH SEX

Marilyn had many brief, almost compulsive, affairs that seemed to contradict her oft-stated yearning for monogamy and motherhood. These may have simply been the result of sudden physical attraction, but there was a strong element of bolstering up her low self-esteem. It seems that Marilyn gained little satisfaction from sex – a view endorsed by her psychiatrist, Dr Greenson.

The men she found attractive were usually older than her. 'Older men are kinder, and they know more,' Marilyn said. In these relationships – and in those with some of the women she befriended – she was drawn by a strong need to be looked after. It is why she found simple enjoyment and security in the family circles of close friends.

THE PULL OF POWER

Marilyn was also attracted to men of power. She was taken up, then rejected, by two of America's most powerful men, the President and Attorney-General. She had assumed that there was a place for her in their lives, but perhaps she proved too much of a liability.

While Marilyn presented to

the world an image of vitality and sensuality and an accomplished sense of comedy, her private life was frequently in despair. The more she sought happiness, the more it eluded her. Her desire to have children was always frustrated. This inability to bear a child may have been due to a womb ailment made worse by early gynaecological damage.

Marilyn's conflicts often overcame her; she had attempted suicide twice by the age of 19 – once by leaving the gas on, once by taking sleeping pills. Was it despair that finally overtook her almost 20 years later?

Marilyn, seen here with her hairdresser in Hollywood, in 1961, was very conscious of looking her best in public. By the last years of her life, her various hairdressers and make-up artists had become some of her closest friends.

DEATH IN

HAVING RUSHED TO MARILYN'S HOUSE IN THE EARLY HOURS OF SUNDAY 5 AUGUST, DR GREENSON PEERED THROUGH A WINDOW TO SEE HER STILL FIGURE LYING ON THE BED. WHAT HAD HAPPENED SINCE THEIR PHONE CONVERSATION A FEW HOURS EARLIER?

M arilyn lay face down on the bed. Her shoulders were bare, and she was gripping the 'phone in her right hand. Dr Greenson realised she was dead as soon as he entered the bedroom after breaking a pane of glass and climbing in the window. 'I could see from many feet away that Marilyn was no longer living,' Greenson said later. 'I suppose she was trying to make a phone call before she was overwhelmed.'

Greenson unlocked the bedroom door from the inside. Mrs Murray was waiting in the corridor. 'We've lost her,' Greenson said. One of Marilyn's physicians, Dr Engelberg, arrived at about 4 am and agreed nothing could be done. He rang the police. Sergeant Jack Clemmons of the West Los Angeles police force took the call at 4.25 am. Incredulous, he went immediately to the house. Mrs Murray showed him into the bedroom, where the two doctors sat waiting. There were various pill bottles on the bedside table, but Greenson showed the officer the one which appeared the most significant. It had contained Nembutal, a

A policeman stands guard outside Marilyn's Brentwood home three days after the discovery of the star's body. Her bedroom lies obscured behind a tree to the left of the photo. Note the stuffed toy animals on the lawn. Is the one farthest from the camera the toy whose delivery seemed to upset Marilyn on the day of her death?

sleeping pill Marilyn had been prescribed, but it was now empty. Greenson thought she had been dead for several hours.

NO SUICIDE NOTE

Nothing had been touched except for the telephone, which had been replaced on its stand, and there was no sign of any suicide note. Mrs Murray had begun cleaning the kitchen and washing some clothes. Sergeant Clemmons had an 'uneasy feeling' about the scene he encountered: 'There was something I didn't understand.'

Soon the house was filled with police officers and staff from the Coroner's office. Outside, in the early light, a small army of reporters has set up camp with cameras, microphones and notebooks. The news of Marilyn's death had flashed around the world at dawn. Everyone in the film business, everyone in a dozen countries who knew Marilyn, or anyone who had met her just once, was asked to comment.

Inside the small house, the Coroner's representative, Guy Hockett, saw that rigor

Star's Life in Photos, Stories

Los Angeles Times MONDAY FINAL

MARILYN MONROE FOUND DEAD

Sleeping Pill Overdose Blamed

Red Super Bomb Kicks Off Series

Nixon Team al Helm of State GOP

Unclad Body of Star Discovered on Bed; Empty Bottle Near

Junta Pledges to Seat Victor in Peru Election

SAD CHILD, UNHAPPY STAR

Help She Needed to Find Self Eluded Marilyn All Her Life

THE NIGHT

As Dr Greenson climbed in through this window, photographed shortly after Marilyn's death, he could see her motionless body lying on the rumpled bed inside.

On the day Marilyn's body was found, a police officer points to an assortment of pill bottles on her bedside table. Could the tall container to the right of the waste bin have contained water with which Marilyn swallowed pills?

mortis, the stiffening of the body after death, had begun some hours before. The body he examined was not that of a beautiful woman but 'a poor little girl that had died, no makeup, fuzzy unmade hair,

a tired body.' The Coroner's team wrapped Marilyn in a blanket, placed her on a stretcher and wheeled her to a waiting station wagon. She was taken to the Westwood Village Mortuary before being moved to the County Morgue in Los Angeles.

THE HUSBANDS' REACTION

On hearing of her death, Marilyn's three ex-husbands kept their feelings to themselves. James Dougherty said quietly, 'I'm sorry,' while Arthur Miller was quoted by a relative as saying, 'it had to happen; it was inevitable.' Joe DiMaggio had known a crisis was looming and had visited Marilyn just a few days earlier. On hearing of her death, he flew to Los Angeles from San Francisco, formally claimed Marilyn's body and began to arrange a quiet funeral. He sat in his hotel room, weeping and raging against Sinatra and his friends, the President and, above all, Robert Kennedy.

CLOSE-UP

MARILYN'S HOUSEKEEPER

Eunice Murray (shown left), Marilyn's housekeeper, said that she saw the light shining under Marilyn's door when she went to bed at midnight, and thought Marilyn may have been making a telephone call. Mrs Murray has since made a number of contradictory statements about how she came to deduce that Marilyn was using the telephone at midnight. On one occasion, she admitted that the pile of the new carpet was too thick to allow the light to shine beneath the door. She has also said that Marilyn seemed 'disturbed' by the call, a statement that conflicts with an earlier account that she had not seen Marilyn since 8 pm. Mrs Murray also made inconsistent statements about whether she first became worried at midnight, or at 3.30 am, when she woke up with a 'sixth sense' that something was wrong.

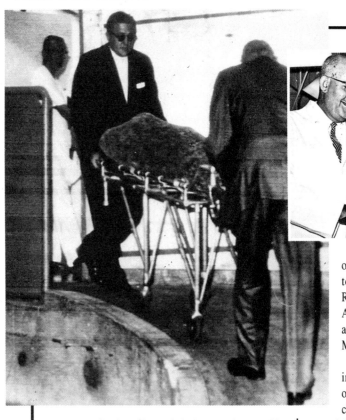

Far left: Marilyn's body is wheeled from the morgue on 6 August 1962 on the way back to the Los Angeles Mortuary. Left: Dr Curphey, Los Angeles Chief Medical Examiner (left), and his deputy, Dr Thomas Noguchi, who conducted the autopsy. Noguchi's report gave mode of death as 'suicide', although he added the word 'probable'.

Marilyn's Hollywood circle seemed stunned by her death. Sinatra said he was 'deeply saddened,' and Peter Lawford, in tears, told a neighbour that he had been the last person to speak to Marilyn.

Not far away, in upstate California, Robert Kennedy and family prepared to leave the ranch and according to their host, rancher-lawyer John Bates, the party would only learn of her death on Sunday evening, after driving into the city. Robert had shown little reaction. 'It was really taken rather lightly.' Bates says. 'It was discussed in sort of an amusing way.'

THE AUTOPSY

At 10.30 am on that Sunday morning, the autopsy on Marilyn Monroe was conducted in the County Morgue by a young Deputy Medical Examiner called Dr Thomas Noguchi. Noguchi sent a number of specimens from Marilyn's internal

Dr Ralph Greenson (third from left), Marilyn's psychiatrist and the man who found her body, at the funeral with, from left, his son Danny, his wife and his daughter, Joan.

organs to the department's specialist in toxicology (the study of poisons), Dr Ralph Abernethy. He also sent Dr Abernethy the empty bottle of Nembutal and seven other pill-containers found in Marilyn's house.

Abernethy found there was no alcohol in Marilyn's blood. This ruled out an overdose of one of her cocktails of champagne, vodka and sleeping pills. But potentially fatal levels of Nembutal and another, less potent, sedative were present in her liver and blood respectively.

THE OFFICIAL VERSION

On 10 August 1962, Noguchi submitted his official report, which stated that the cause of death was 'acute barbiturate poisoning' as a result of an overdose. The official form gave a list for 'Mode of Death'. Noguchi put a circle around 'suicide' but wrote the word 'probable' next to it. On 17 August, the Coroner announced that Marilyn had died of barbiturate poisoning following a self-administered overdose.

Sceptics were quick to identify questions left unanswered by this finding and by the autopsy report. There has been a medical debate over whether traces of barbiturate pills and of their coloured dye should have been found in Marilyn's stomach. Neither were found during the autopsy. Why, it has been asked, is there no police record of a glass of water, often necessary to swallow pills, being found by the bed? One photo of the death scene does show an object that could be a water flask.

Several experts have criticised the conduct of the

autopsy, saying a search for traces of the Nembutal barbiturate should have been extended to the small intestine. Dr Noguchi has since expressed regret that he did not demand such an examination. When he did make such a request, after the case was officially closed, Dr Abernethy told him the relevant samples had been destroyed.

Marilyn had been prescribed 25 Nembutals on Friday, 3 August, the day before she died, by Dr Engelberg. Her neighbour, Jeanne Carmen, recalls that Marilyn had asked her over the telephone at least twice on Saturday 4 August to bring over some sleeping pills. No one knows over what period Marilyn consumed the original 25 prescribed by Dr Engelberg.

It is questionable whether she took them all on the Friday and the early hours of Saturday morning. This was the period covering the delivery of food from La Scala, the visit by the unnamed guest and the calls she claimed she received, warning her to keep away from Robert Kennedy. If she was so disturbed by the calls as to need to take unusual numbers of sleeping pills, why had she not left the receiver off the hook? Her comment to Jeanne Carmen suggested the calls

CLOSE-UP

FINAL RESPECTS

Only 24 people were invited to attend Marilyn's funeral service at Westwood Memorial Park in Los Angeles on 8 August 1962. Her former husband Joe DiMaggio (shown above, grief-stricken, at the funeral, next to his uniformed son, Joe DiMaggio Jnr) who organised the ceremony, had told an official not to let 'those damned Kennedys come to the funeral.' DiMaggio also excluded Frank Sinatra and Peter Lawford, both left fuming at the gates, and many other Hollywood stars. Among those present were the Greenson family, Pat Newcomb and Lee and Paula Strasberg.

The eulogy was read by Marilyn's former acting teacher Lee Strasberg. After the playing of Judy Garland's 'Over the Rainbow', flowers were laid on the coffin, and it was moved to the Mausoleum of Memories and placed in a vault.

After Marilyn's death, a note she had written but not sent to DiMaggio was found in her bedroom. It said: 'your happiness means my happiness.' Throughout the service, DiMaggio wept helplessly, and whispered farewell with the words 'I love you...I love you.'

INSIDE VIEW

THE SLEUTH

A colourful figure who stalked the final years of Marilyn's life was the Hollywood private detective Fred Otash (left). In 1957, he was hired by Frank Sinatra's lawyers to clarify the singer's role in the 'Wrong Door Raid' three years before. Otash was also associated with the bugging of Marilyn's house in 1961, at the behest of parties who wanted confidential information about the Kennedys.

According to Otash, Robert Kennedy rang Marilyn on a bugged telephone after leaving her house on the last afternoon. He invited her to Peter Lawford's home that evening. Otash quoted Marilyn as saying, 'stop bothering me, stay away from me' and rejecting the invitation. Otash has also acknowledged that, in the hours after Marilyn's death, he was hired by Peter Lawford to remove any evidence of Robert Kennedy's links to Marilyn.

---

had continued for a long time. If some of Dr Engelberg's prescription was left over for Saturday, it remains unclear why Marilyn was pressing Jeanne Carmen for more pills.

The deputy District Attorney for Los Angeles, John Miner, attended the autopsy and later had a long professional interview with Dr Greenson. Neither Miner nor Greenson have ever commented publicly on the case but, later in August 1962, Miner wrote a memorandum which he recalls said: 'I believe I can say definitely that it was not suicide.' Miner and Greenson both believed that Marilyn was not in a suicidal frame of mind, despite the shock of her rejection by the Kennedys. Miner's conclusion, if correct, and the unresolved medical questions, leave open two possibilities: accident – or murder.

THE FATAL DOSE

The theory of an accidental overdose assumes that Marilyn mistook her resistance to barbiturates and, after years of abuse, finally took too many. In this case, the fatal dosage would have been swallowed gradually over the course of the day, as the evidence of advanced digestion of the pills appeared to indicate. The evidence in favour of this theory includes the observations of Dr Greenson and another witness at the house on Marilyn's last day, Mrs Murray's son-in-law Norman Jeffries, that Marilyn looked drugged.

Events in Marilyn Monroe's house immediately before and after her death have emerged which were not mentioned during the initial investigation. These events are at such variance with official reports as to

reinforce the suspicions of those who believe that Marilyn was murdered. However, these events only seem to prove that intensive efforts were made to disassociate certain powerful individuals from Marilyn in death, and

> **'** *It was a nasty business, her worst rejection. Power and money. In the end, she was too innocent.* **'**
>
> Film director George Cukor, in 1983

that a cover-up of evidence linking her to these people was ordered.

DESTROYING EVIDENCE

In his 1985 biography of Marilyn, *Goddess* (1985), British author Anthony Summers provides evidence showing that enormous efforts were made to conceal or destroy all traces of the telephone records which could have identified the last person Marilyn spoke to by telephone, and the time of the call. There is evidence to suggest that the records were destroyed by the FBI, at the request of the Attorney-General, Robert Kennedy. Kennedy, according to his host that weekend, John Bates, had seemed quite unaffected when Marilyn's death was discussed on the Sunday evening. But Marilyn's affair with his brother was by this time common knowledge in political, police and press circles. Unless Robert had something to hide in his contact with Marilyn, he could be expected to show keen political interest at least in her death.

A VISIT FROM ROBERT

Anthony Summers' *Goddess* documents a chain of events that supports the widespread belief that

Part of the 'phone records, missing since Marilyn's death and only retrieved in the 1980s, showing calls made in her final days. A detective has written 'Kennedy?' next to calls to Washington RE7-8200, a 1962 number at the Justice Department.

June 20	Brooklyn, N.Y.	875-1367
June 20	Brooklyn, N.Y.	Mrs. Rosten - Collect
June 25	Washington	RE 7-8200
July 2	Washington	RE 7-8200
July 2	Washington	RE 7-8200
July 6	San Diego	OR 6-1890
July 6	San Diego	
July 9	New York City	DiMaggio - Collect
July 9	New York	EL 5-2288
July 16	Washington	MU 3-6522
July 16	New York City	RE 7-8200
July 17	Fullerton	OR 3-7792
July 17		TR 1-3190
July 17	Washington	RE 7-8200
July 17	Washington D.C.	RE 7-8200

LONG DISTANCE
MUNROE PHONE CALLS -
FROM TWO PHONES
4761890 x 472X4830
POB006471
6400 Sunset Hollywood

	7/18	NYC	BR 91195	3
	7/23	WASH (DC)	RE. 78200	1
	7/28	NYC	PL. 92497	10
4830	7/30	NYC	LA. 41000	1
	7/30	WASH. (D.C)	RE. 78200	8
	7/30	BKLN	TR. 51367	13
	7/31	N.Y.C.	TR. 72212	11
	8/3	BKLN	TR. 51367	32
	8/4	ANAHE	GR. 61890	5

Kennedy?

Robert Kennedy slipped away from his family at the ranch on the Saturday afternoon to tell Marilyn in person that their affair was over. Dr Greenson has said in private that he learned Robert Kennedy had been to Marilyn's house before his arrival. This would explain why it took Dr Greenson two hours to soothe Marilyn that afternoon. Marilyn told Greenson virtually every secret she ever had. But the psychiatrist left her house that evening with the firm belief that Marilyn was far from being in a severe, dangerous depression. It is interesting that a number of people, including Arthur Miller and *Life* journalist Richard Meryman, had a sense of doom on Marilyn's behalf while Dr Greenson, a man alert for signs of imminent catastrophe, was close to being astonished by her death.

Anthony Summers, in *Goddess*, records the detailed research by which he discovered that Marilyn almost certainly died well before midnight on the Saturday night of 4 August 1962. He cites evidence that Marilyn made an appearance early that evening at the home of Peter Lawford, and reports on a bewildering variety of conflicting statements made by Lawford. Natalie Jacobs, the wife of Marilyn's public relations agent, Arthur Jacobs, has said that her husband was called out to 'fudge' the presentation of Marilyn's death long before Dr Greenson was roused from bed by a 'phone call from Mrs Murray at 3.30 am.

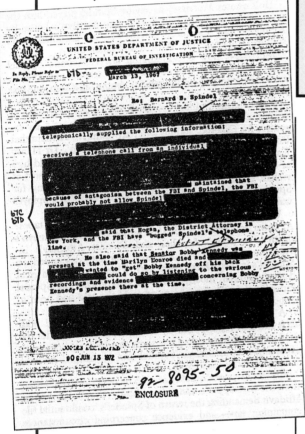

A censored FBI document referring to Bernard Spindel's alleged comment that Robert Kennedy was present at Marilyn's death.

The head of an ambulance company, Walt Schaefer, told Summers that Marilyn actually died at Santa Monica Hospital, having been taken there in a coma by one of his company's ambulances. Years later, Greenson said that she died in a nearby hospital. Was she later brought back to the house, which had perhaps been combed for items damaging to the Kennedys? Deborah Gould, who Peter Lawford married in 1976, has said that he spoke of going to Marilyn's house that night to 'tidy' things up before the police and press arrived.

INSIDE VIEW

THE MISSING TAPES

The final recordings from the bugging of Marilyn's house were stored at the New York home of electronics expert Bernard Spindel (shown on the left of the photograph above). Spindel had arranged for a small microphone to be installed at the Brentwood house on behalf of Teamsters leader Jimmy Hoffa.

In a dawn raid on 15 December 1966, police and New York District Attorney investigators confiscated many of Spindel's tapes. He tried unsuccesfully through the courts to secure the return of the Monroe material, and an attempt by his widow also failed. The tapes' eventual fate is unknown.

A security expert, who asked to remain anonymous for professional reasons, has said recently that Spindel allowed him to listen to one of the tapes before their confiscation. He had heard Robert Kennedy apparently looking for the microphone and angrily insisting it had to be found.

Lawford also mentioned destroying a message he found there that had been scribbled by Marilyn. However, none of these revelations prove murder.

In whatever way Marilyn died, President Kennedy and his brother stood to lose credibility and power if they were publicly linked with her. Robert Kennedy knew of Marilyn's diary entries about his ideas. That indiscretion alone had the potential to damage the Kennedys politically.

WHY MURDER?

If Marilyn Monroe was murdered, it has been suggested that the purpose was to undermine the Kennedys and prevent the President being re-elected in 1964. It has also been suggested that the Mafia and the right wing of the CIA and FBI would have welcomed such a scandal. There has even been a theory that Marilyn was murdered and the stage was clumsily set to make her death look like suicide. When this veneer of suicide began to crack, the theory ran, anyone known to have been near Marilyn's home in the last hours – such as Robert Kennedy – would be implicated.

In the weeks before she died, Marilyn Monroe had achieved a closeness to those in power rivalled by few people. In 1962, millions of people expected nuclear war between the USA and Russia. Robert Kennedy had recently watched the first testing of a hydrogen bomb on American soil, and the Cuban missile crisis, when for a few days the world seemed on the brink of such a conflict, was only a few months away. Cuban

and Soviet intelligence services would have paid enormous sums to hear Robert Kennedy's private thoughts on these issues, and Marilyn almost certainly heard them. It seems that the FBI were fully alert to the security risk posed by Marilyn.

Those who are looking for definitive proof as to how Marilyn Monroe died have yet to find it. Perhaps Marilyn's story teaches us just one thing – that the quest for the truth must continue.

Britain's Daily Mirror *of 8 August 1962 carried what was said to be Marilyn's last picture. It was taken by photo-journalist George Barris, with whom Marilyn was working on her autobiography in the final weeks of her life.*

THE ABDICATION CRISIS

In 1936, King Edward VIII made known his intention to marry Wallis Simpson. The bride who would be Queen was an American, twice-divorced, with her first two husbands still living. She was unacceptable to the British people and government. But the issue went deeper than just Wallis' suitability. The King was prepared to forego his duty for his personal happiness; and during the dark days of World War II and after, tales surfaced of the ex-King's flirtation with Nazism and other disturbing aspects of his life in exile. The question has to be asked: did Wallis and the Abdication Crisis release the British monarchy from an incumbent whose sense of judgement was as lacking as his sense of duty?

King Edward VIII.
He accepted the hand that fate dealt him – to inherit the British throne – until he met the woman against whom even this awesome destiny could not compete.

Wallis Warfield Simpson. *An American 'Southern Belle' who rose higher in society than she ever expected.*

ONE

THE FIRST

WHEN WALLIS SIMPSON EXCHANGED HER FIRST WORDS WITH THE PRINCE OF WALES, THEY WERE BOTH SET IN THEIR WAYS. SHE WAS AMERICAN, TWICE MARRIED AND A WOMAN OF THE WORLD. HE HAD BEEN HEIR TO THE BRITISH THRONE FOR 21 YEARS, AND HAD DEDICATED HIS LIFE TO THE PURSUIT OF PLEASURE.

On 7 April 1920, a ball was held at the Hotel del Coronado in San Diego, California. The guest of honour was the Prince of Wales, the young heir to the throne of Britain whose delicate good looks and charm had made him an international 'superstar'. It was going to be a big night for Wallis Warfield Spencer, the 24-year-old wife of US naval lieutenant Earl Winfield 'Win' Spencer.

She was far away from her native Baltimore due to her husband's posting. The ball was to be a rare bright occasion in a life that was increasingly grim. She had fallen out of love with her alcoholic husband who mistreated her.

In the event, the ball was an anti-climax too. She was only one of thousands who curtsied to the distant Prince, a slight golden-haired figure in white who left as soon as he could with his glamorous entourage.

This could hardly be called a real meeting between Wallis and the Prince of Wales. But it was a connection, and in the mind of the unhappy Wallis it was important. Now she had caught a glimpse of the kind of life she had always imagined for herself. It existed somewhere – it was a possibility.

Their first real meeting remains a mystery; even the two most directly concerned disagree. What is certain is that it was at least 10 years later, in England, and both Wallis and the Prince were very different people.

TWO DIFFERENT PEOPLE

Wallis had spent two fraught years in China when her husband's naval duties took him there. A hoped-for reconciliation with Win had come to nothing, and she went through a protracted divorce in 1927, after which she mostly lived off the kindness of friends. In 1928, she married kindly, rich Ernest Simpson, also American, whose business interests meant he spent much of his time in London. That same year, they set sail for England, and Wallis was free from the smothered existence of a divorcée that Southern American society imposed on her.

The Prince of Wales was no longer young – 40 was in sight. His popularity in Britain and its then enormous empire was greater than ever, but his role as heir to the throne did not seem to have much purpose. He needed excitement and fun. He had mistresses, he liked parties and amusing company – many of his friends were American – and he was in constant, almost adolescent, rebellion against the stuffy atmosphere of his father's court.

Above: Wallis Warfield in 1919, at the age of 23. She had been married to Win Spencer for three years, but the happiness she had expected eluded her. Spencer drank, was jealous of her compulsive flirting with other men and treated her badly.

By 1930, the Simpsons had been in London for two years and were slowly climbing the social ladder. They had reached the periphery of the royal set, and had some friends within it. Sometime in

DATEFILE

APRIL 7 1920
Wallis' first glimpse of Prince of Wales

WINTER 1931
Wallis and Prince of Wales meet

SUMMER 1934
Wallis acknowledged as Prince of Wales' new mistress

JUNE 1935
Simpson marriage on rocks; public still unaware of affair

APR '20–JUNE '35

MEETING

Left: The Prince of Wales and Lady Thelma Furness at the theatre. Although they were always with a group, it was well-known that she was his mistress. Below: The Prince, centre, with Lord Mountbatten on his left, posing with his first tiger kill. Hunting parties like this were highlights of his visits to India.

either the winter of 1930 or 1931, these friends first introduced the couple to the Prince of Wales who was the axis and leader of British high society.

MISTRESS

The Prince remembered the meeting as being in 1931 at Burrough Court at Melton Mowbray, the country estate of Lord and Lady Furness. The American Thelma Furness, a sultry, half-Latin heiress and twin sister of Gloria Vanderbilt, was his mistress and Wallis was her new best friend.

One afternoon, the Prince found himself next to Wallis. Casting around for a topic of conversation he asked her whether she missed American central heating in the cold English winter. Her response took him aback. 'I am sorry, sir,' she replied, 'but you have disappointed me.'

'In what way?' he asked. Wallis' considered response was, 'Every American woman who comes to your country is always asked that same question. I had hoped for something more original from the Prince of Wales.' In his memoirs, the Prince wrote, 'I moved away to talk to the other guests, but the echoes of the passage lingered'.

CHEEKY INFORMALITY

Wallis always maintained that, in fact, the meeting took place a year earlier and she did not remember the conversation. But it does not matter when it was. What that first meeting achieved was that the Prince's interest was piqued by Wallis, who had treated him with cheeky informality, rather than the respect he was used to from all but his closest friends. He would not forget her.

CLOSE-UP

THE FIRST HUSBAND – WINFIELD SPENCER

Earl Winfield Spencer Jr. was attractive to women and eight years older than the 20-year-old Wallis. 'I have just met the world's most fascinating aviator' she wrote to her mother after their first meeting.

They were married on 8 November 1916. On their honeymoon, Wallis discovered that her husband was an alcoholic and a cruel, sadistic man, subject to jealous rages when he would lock her in the bedroom or the bathroom for hours.

Despite his drinking, Win was successful at work. In World War I, as an air station commander in San Diego, he was responsible for 35,000 flying hours flown by his pilots without a single fatality. In 1924 Wallis joined Win in China for a reunion which did not last. They were divorced in 1927. He died in 1950, aged 63.

It was not until seven months later that they met again. Thelma persuaded the Prince to invite the Simpsons to his country residence, Fort Belvedere, for the weekend of 30 January 1932.

That weekend, a friendship was forged and the Prince decided that Wallis would be an amusing addition to his set. Now the Simpsons were on the regular guest list at York House, the Prince's official London residence. They met him frequently for lunch and dinner – often just the three of them together. The Prince's set began to take notice of the Simpsons. They were invited everywhere. Ernest was disregarded, but society figures found Wallis clever and witty.

Right: Wallis achieved the coveted social distinction of presentation at Court on 10 June, 1931. King George V's high moral standards meant divorcées could be presented only if they were the innocent party. Wallis had to obtain her divorce papers from the US as proof. The Prince recalled Wallis' dignity and grace, but no more.

'LOUD AND BRASH'

She was no beauty, however, with her flat, mannish build and bold, square features. The fastidious sensibilities of society's leading photographer Cecil Beaton were offended by her. 'Her voice had a high nasal twang. She was loud and brash, terribly so – and rowdy and raucous. Her squawks of laughter were like a parrot's,' he criticised.

Nevertheless, the Prince was clearly fascinated by Wallis, although Thelma Furness was still his mistress. The situation changed in early 1934 when Thelma went to the United States. She charged Wallis with the duty of looking after 'the little man' for her. This was her intimate nickname for the Prince which many believed referred to his sexual, rather than physical, stature. Little did she know how seriously Wallis would take this duty.

When Thelma returned, looking 10 years younger after a passionate shipboard romance with Prince Aly Khan, whose bedroom techniques eclipsed those of the ardent but sexually insecure Prince, she was greeted coldly by her royal lover. He interrogated her contemptuously about his rival – how could she betray him with an Indian? Thelma innocently asked Wallis whether she knew why he was so different. Her friend simply said, demurely, 'the little man was lost without you.'

WALLIS TRIUMPHANT

At Belvedere the next weekend, Thelma watched astounded as Wallis slapped the Prince's hand when he picked up some salad in his fingers. Thelma flashed Wallis a warning glance; to be so familiar in public with the Prince was to invite dismissal from the royal circle. 'Wallis looked straight at me,' Thelma said later. 'I knew then that she had looked after him exceedingly well. That one cold, defiant glance had told me the whole story.' Next morning Thelma left. She never saw nor heard from the Prince again.

> ❝ *She was loud and brash ... her squawks of laughter were like a parrot's* ❞
> Cecil Beaton on Wallis Simpson

The path to the Prince's affections was finally cleared for Wallis when he just as abruptly dropped his other mistress and friend of 16 years, Freda Dudley Ward, in the summer of 1934.

Wallis was now acknowledged as the Prince's mistress by English society. The general public would be unaware of any relationship, as the press

Above: The Prince of Wales poses formally with his family; he stands far left with brothers Henry, Albert and George. The two Marys – mother and daughter – flank the King. Inset: He relaxes with Wallis on holiday in Biarritz in 1934 when, according to Wallis, they 'crossed the indefinable boundary between friendship and love.'

usually refrained from publishing stories of this nature, unlike today. It was a good subject for gossip, nothing more. She was yet another married woman in a long line and there were bound to be more before the Prince finally chose a suitable future queen to marry.

SECURING HER POSITION

Chips Channon, an MP and social commentator of the time, summed up the general feeling, 'The romance surpasses all else in interest. He is obviously madly infatuated, and she, a jolly, unprepossessing American, witty and an excellent cook, has completely subjugated him. Never has he been so in love. She is madly anxious to storm society while she is still his favourite, so that when he leaves her (as he leaves everyone in time) she will be secure'.

But time went on and there was no sign of the Prince tiring of Wallis. On the contrary, his love

FORT BELVEDERE

The Prince of Wales first took this grace-and-favour residence in 1929. It was love at first sight for the Prince, as he viewed the strange mock-Gothic miniature castle on the edge of Windsor Great Park. Originally built for George II's son, William Duke of Cumberland, it was a 'castellated conglomeration' complete with 'cannon and cannon balls and little furnishings of war'.

When the Prince took it on, it was an 'unstately ruin', which needed almost complete renovation. He called it his 'get-away-from-people house', though he frequently filled it with houseparties of amusing friends. By the time the Prince had completed the improvements it had been rebuilt and altered and enlarged to 14 rooms. There was a bathroom and shower for each bedroom and central heating throughout. He had a steam bath in his own bedroom. The grounds had been cleared of weeds and replanted. The Prince had turned a lily pond into a swimming pool, which was the scene of many summer parties.

became almost frantic. Wallis changed too. Beaton, who had previously found her coarse, now said she was 'immaculate, as fresh as a young girl. Her skin was as bright and smooth as the inside of a shell, her hair so sleek she might have been Chinese'.

In August 1934 the Prince invited Wallis to holiday with his party in Biarritz; Ernest was not invited. Instead her Aunt Bessie Merryman accompanied her as chaperone. It was a magical holiday when, they agreed, they passed 'the indefinable boundary between friendship and love'.

After this, the Prince wanted her as his escort to official engagements, even though this flouted royal protocol. With Ernest, ever in tow for propriety's sake, Wallis was even invited to the Duke of Kent's wedding, and all the parties surrounding it, in late 1934. One celebration she was not invited to was a ball given at Buckingham Palace by King George and Queen Mary, who wholly disapproved of their son's disregard for the dignity expected of

the heir to the throne. They removed her name from the guest list the Prince had submitted. Nevertheless, a furious Edward took Wallis as his escort and presented her to his parents who greeted Wallis with a glassy stare.

By early 1935, the royal court, high society – and the press – knew about the affair. The great mass of the British people knew nothing. A compliant press decided to remain silent on the topic. Instead, the Prince was portrayed as the charming bachelor – with lady friends, of course, but nothing serious.

At the same time, the Simpson marriage was failing, and existed in name only. Ernest was still invited to glittering official functions which the Prince wished Wallis to attend, often forming a bizarre threesome, with Wallis seated between her lover and her husband.

NAZI SYMPATHIES

Aside from the moral question, the Prince's family were increasingly worried about the way 'David' – the family's name for the Prince – was distancing himself from them, and about his maverick ten-

dencies to do and say exactly what he wished, without thought for political or constitutional consequences. In June 1935, the Prince spoke at a British Legion rally saying that the British should 'stretch forth the hand of friendship to the Germans.' It was a public avowal of his admiration for Hitler. That July, Wallis was invited for dinner at the German embassy.

In the mid-1930s, British policy sought to accommodate both the German and Italian dictators, Hitler and Mussolini, in order to retain a balance of power in Europe. But the Prince's and Wallis' Nazi connections were so close that the British Secret Intelligence Services felt it prudent to take note of the friendships Wallis, especially, made with people of fascist persuasion.

CHILLING PROPHECY

As 1935 drew to its close, it was clear to all that the old King was becoming increasingly ill. The prospect of a new king in the new year was very real. King George himself was desperately worried about his heir, and he spoke seriously to the Archbishop of Canterbury about him. 'After I am gone,' he said, with chilling prescience, 'the boy will ruin himself in 12 months.'

PERSPECTIVE
TRAVELLING THE WORLD

As the Prince of Wales grew to manhood, it was shrewdly perceived by his family and the Government that he had what would now be called star quality. This could be used for the good of the country. Without his own wishes being taken into account, he was pressed into service as a roving ambassador.

After World War I, he was kept constantly on the move, touring the world. He visited nearly every country in the Empire, as well as the United States and Japan. Everywhere he went he was fêted like a superstar – making the headlines and drumming up trade for the depressed industries at home.

Life was a blur of smiling faces and hands to be shaken – here he greets New Zealand Maoris. His every comment was treated as if it was of international consequence. It is not surprising that he developed the belief that who he was and what he wanted were the most important things in the world.

AMBITION AND TRADITION

BORN WITHIN A YEAR OF EACH OTHER ON DIFFERENT SIDES OF THE ATLANTIC, WALLIS AND EDWARD TROD COMPLETELY DIFFERENT PATHS EARLY IN LIFE. THEIR COMMON BONDS WERE THE RESTRICTIONS THEY SUFFERED – SHE FOR HER IGNOBLE BIRTH, HE FOR THE EXACT OPPOSITE

B essie Wallis Warfield was born on 19 June 1895 – in Blue Ridge Summit, Pennsylvania – 17 months before the marriage of her parents, Alice Montague and Teackle Warfield, on 19 November 1896. Alice had been sent away from the family home in Baltimore to avoid scandal.

No birth certificate exists and she was not baptised – her birth out of wedlock was a shame that an old Southern family would go to great pains to hide. At the time of Wallis' birth, the American Civil War had been over barely 30 years. Her grandparents' generation were brought up in the old Southern ways.

However, after the premature death of her consumptive father when Wallis was only two-and-a-half years old, family

Above: Wallis in 1915. Like millions of 18-year-old girls at the time, she had a crush on the British Prince of Wales (right, aged 17). She pinned his picture up in her room and followed his every move from news articles she cut out and kept.

attitudes seemed to soften towards Alice and her baby. They were taken in by the formidable Anne Emory, Wallis' grandmother.

POOR RELATIONS

However, it was always made plain that they were the poor relations and so, when Wallis was five, Alice went to live with her sister, the widowed Bessie Merryman, who would become Wallis' confidante during the Abdication Crisis 36 years on.

Despite this upheaval, Wallis had a happy childhood, excelling at school and always striving to be first, as if making up for her bad start in life.

Nevertheless, Wallis' early life was not that of 'poor kid from the other side of the tracks'. Her Uncle Solomon Warfield owned several railroad companies and was a public dignitary. His money sent Wallis to the best schools in Baltimore, from where she graduated in 1913.

It was expected that Wallis would marry early into one of

Left: The centre of Baltimore, a thriving city at the turn of the century. Above: Wallis holds centre stage in 1913, at Oldfields School, the best school in Baltimore.

THE PEOPLE'S PRINCE

In the 1920s, Edward, Prince of Wales, embarked on his famous 'Empire Tours'. He covered thousands of miles visiting even the remotest parts of the still vast British Empire, shaking thousands of hands and being fêted by heads of state. But he took equal interest in the lives of ordinary people, wanting to see things for himself. It was not uncommon, on a tour to a bleak industrial area of Britain, for him to break ranks and enter a working man's house to find out how he lived.

Above: Edward, far left, with his brothers, sister and tutors at Sandringham. Bertie, later to succeed him as King George VI, is in the centre.

Above: Edward with Queen Victoria, who ruled over a quarter of the world's people, many of whom regarded the British monarch as near-divine.

the 'old' families, but she was popular with all the young men in her social circle and had no intention of being tied down.

All this changed in April 1916 when she met Earl Winfield Spencer, a pioneer aviator in Pensacola, Florida. Determined to have a wedding with guards of honour, Wallis accepted his proposal. They were married in the Christ Episcopal Church, Baltimore – a certificate of baptism having been conveniently produced – on 8 November the same year.

A WORLD APART

The birth of Prince Edward on 23 June 1894 was vastly different. He was the eldest son of the Duke of York – later King George V – himself the eldest surviving son of the then Prince of Wales, the future Edward VII. Queen Victoria was still on the throne.

He spent his childhood at Sandringham in the care of nannies. As Duke of Windsor, Edward recalled in his autobiography *A King's Story* that one of

these used to twist his arm prior to taking him to his parents. His father had the reputation of treating his three sons like unruly midshipmen under his command. Years later, Edward could remember the summonses to the Library where he was invariably admonished for some breach of discipline.

NEARER THE THRONE

Edward's life changed when he was six; Queen Victoria died and his parents moved to London. Nine years later, his grandfather, Edward VII, was dead and his father was king.

He was inaugurated as Prince of Wales in a medieval ceremony at Caernarfon Castle in July 1911. Edward remembered that day as 'the first time I realised that while I was prepared to fulfil a role in all the pomp and ritual, I recoiled from anything requiring homage'. Possibly it was Wallis' refusal to pay him such homage that appealed to those early feelings.

Edward was 20 years old at the outbreak of World War I in August 1914. He did not see active service, but he did witness the awful battlefield scenes, visions that made him sympathetic to the plight of the ordinary man during his reign.

Perhaps it was the long years of adulation and the sheer number of Edward's public engagements which finally took their toll, for by the time he met Wallis, he was wilful, spoilt and increasingly disinclined to put business before pleasure.

Left: Although Edward insisted on being allowed to join the army – holding the rank of Major as a battalion commander in the Grenadier Guards – he was kept out of the battle zone.

KINGSHIP

THE DEATH OF HIS FATHER THRUST UPON THE 41-YEAR-OLD PRINCE OF WALES THE BURDEN OF KINGSHIP. THE PLEASURE-FILLED DAYS OF PRIVILEGE WITHOUT RESPONSIBILITY WERE REPLACED BY AFFAIRS OF STATE AND THE GROWING PROBLEM OF HIS EMOTIONAL DEPENDENCE ON WALLIS.

Above: On 28 January 1937, King George V was buried in St George's Chapel, Windsor. His successor, now King Edward VIII, scattered earth over the coffin from a silver bowl and then emerged into the daylight, his 'grey face sad and frightening'.

> *I think I make a pretty good Prince of Wales. But I don't think I'd make a very good king.*
>
> King Edward's self assessment

DATEFILE

JANUARY 20 1936
King George V dies; Edward VIII becomes king.

MAY 27 1936
Edward introduces Wallis to Prime Minister Stanley Baldwin

JULY 16 1936
Assassination attempt on the King

AUGUST 1936
Nahlin cruise with Wallis

JAN-AUG '36

Just before midnight on 20 January 1936 George V died. In the hours and days that followed it was clear that the new king, Edward VIII, was distraught. Frequently at loggerheads with his father, he now displayed a grief that seemed 'frantic and unreasonable' to Lady Hardinge, the wife of Major Alexander Hardinge who became Edward's private secretary. His suffering 'far exceeded that of his mother and three brothers'.

The day after his father's death, Edward flew from Sandringham to London for the Accession Council at St James' Palace. The councillors noted that he looked pale and unhappy, 'very nervous and ill at ease', as he read his declaration. The sheet of paper trembled so violently in his hands that he had to put it down on the table in front of him to read it.

This inexplicable display of emotion was only truly understandable to those who knew that it was for himself he mourned – for the loss of his previous life and the unbearable rigours of the duties that stretched ahead.

GREAT EXPECTATIONS

Meanwhile, the nation waited to see what sort of reign this new monarch would herald. He was modern, informal and seemingly in touch with his people. It was thought he would transform the

The two faces of Edward VIII. Left, he grimaces at having to receive the 1936 season's debutantes. Above, he shows concern over unemployment in Wales as he tours the derelict Dowlais steelworks.

court and stamp his own personality on it, just as his staid father had done when he succeeded the raffish Edward VII.

But when would he begin? The weeks went by and the King showed no sign of moving into Buckingham Palace, the official residence of the monarch. His excuse was to give his mother time to prepare to leave, but his reasons were more selfish. He liked the informality of his own York House and detested the stiff protocol of the Palace.

That the country expected a king at Buckingham Palace did not appear to be a consideration. It seemed that, even in the earliest

days of his reign, he was meeting his own needs first and foremost. He did not move into Buckingham Palace until October.

NEW BROOM

As soon as was decently possible, the King replaced his father's private secretary, Lord Wigram, with Hardinge. Lord Wigram, in fact, was glad to go as soon as deep mourning was over. He did not like the new King's style: his bad temper; his scant attention to duty; the way he demanded the presence of his staff whenever it suited him.

For a short while, the King seemed to take his duties seriously. He read the State papers that were forwarded to him, signing his initials at the bottom of each page as he read. But before long, he found this boring and arduous. Ministerial departments became increasingly worried as documents sent to him in the official red boxes came back unread – or very late – dog-eared and stained with rings from the bases of dirty cocktail glasses.

Equally worrying was that Wallis' influence seemed to grow rather than diminish after the King's accession. Hardinge was very concerned: 'It was

scarcely realised at this early stage how overwhelming and inexorable was her influence on the King. As time went on it became clearer that every decision, big or small, was subordinated to her will. It was she who filled his thoughts at all times, she alone who mattered; before her the affairs of state sank into insignificance.'

CAFÉ SOCIETY

The guest lists for York House and Fort Belvedere were drawn up under Wallis' supervision. Anyone she disliked was dismissed, including members of the King's Household. Instead, London 'café society' became the new 'king's set'. A chattering group of lively and informal party-goers, they were delighted with the relaxed way in which the King allowed his residences to be run; they loved the modern cocktails and American–style meals and snacks that were served. Wallis had done the unthinkable – she had invaded the kitchen and

Above: As King Edward returned from trooping the colour in Hyde Park, London, a man broke through the crowd and pointed a revolver in his direction. He was disarmed before he could fire.

taught the outraged cook to prepare enormous American club sandwiches instead of more traditional English fare.

OUTSPOKEN VIEWS

But there were other matters even more worrying than the social composition of the fledgling court. The King was on rather close terms with the German ambassador, Leopold von Hoesch, given the political developments in Germany and elsewhere (see Backdrop, p.75). The King spoke freely of his belief that

THE SECOND HUSBAND

Ernest Simpson was the son of an English father and an American mother. After studying at Harvard, he came to England in 1915 to join the Coldstream Guards. He rose to be a full lieutenant before leaving in 1919 after the end of World War I.

Four years later, he had become a successful businessman and married a divorcée, with whom he had a daughter Audrey. By 1926 they had separated.

During this time he met Wallis, who was awaiting her divorce from Win Spencer, and proposed, but she turned him down. By 1928 she had changed her mind. They sailed to England and married on 21 July in the Chelsea registry office.

Ernest retained his dignity throughout Wallis' public relationship with the Prince. After their divorce, he married Wallis' former schoolfriend Mary Raffray in November 1937 with whom he had a son, Henry. Ernest died of throat cancer in 1958, aged 62.

Above: Joachim von Ribbentrop was appointed Ambassador to Great Britain in August 1936. His politics were more aligned with the Nazi Party than those of his predecessor, von Hoesch.

the Foreign Office was 'too one–sided' in its attitudes, and had not a 'complete understanding of Germany's positions and aspirations'. He provoked still further criticism when he sent a telegram to Hitler on his birthday, 20 April 1936, in which he wished the Fuehrer well for his future 'happiness and welfare'.

Wallis' own sympathies towards Nazi Germany and her German contacts were also becoming common knowledge in Government circles. There was sufficient suspicion for the security services to feel it necessary to put her

under surveillance. The security services were also increasingly concerned that the King, bored with paperwork and suffering from eyestrain, left State despatch boxes, meant for the eyes of Privy Councillors and the Monarch only, casually around at Fort Belvedere, while all sorts of people came and went as they pleased.

LEAKING INFORMATION

When certain sensitive information found its way back to Berlin via Ambassador von Ribbentrop, who succeeded von Hoesch and was also a frequent guest at the Fort, it was widely suspected that Wallis was the leak. She was on extremely friendly terms with von Ribbentrop, and state matters that the King may have discussed with her may have been repeated to Ribbentrop during one of his many visits to her home at Bryanston Court.

> ❝ *his friendly attitude towards Germany might in time come to exert an influence on British foreign policy.* ❞
>
> Von Hoesch reporting to Hitler

The combination of his cavalier attitude to the despatch boxes, and both his own and Wallis' political sympathies, caused the Foreign Office to act in a manner that was decidedly unconstitutional. Certain sensitive papers were held back from him, and only those papers that officially required his signature were routinely sent in the despatch boxes. The King never noticed the difference.

MARRIAGE INTENTIONS

Barely a month into his reign, in late February or early March, the King had a curious meeting with Ernest Simpson, who desired to know of Edward's intentions towards his wife. The King made his intentions of marriage very clear indeed, and by April, Wallis and Ernest agreed they should separate in the near future.

By May of 1936, the King felt secure enough as monarch to put in train his most dearly held wish: that Wallis should become his wife. On the 27th, he gave a formal dinner party which included Prime Minister

Stanley Baldwin. 'It's got to be done,' he told Wallis. 'Sooner or later my Prime Minister must meet my future wife'. Wallis has said that this was the first time she knew of his intentions to marry her. The curious circumstance of introducing a married woman as his bride-to-be was rendered even more bizarre by the fact that Ernest Simpson was also one of the invited guests.

By common consent the British Press continued to remain silent about the King's mistress. However, as if daring to see how far he could go, the King insisted on publishing the name of Mrs Simpson in the Court

Right: The Daily Mirror, owned by the King's friend, Esmond Harmsworth, would not dare print this headline in its British edition. There was no such reticence in the New York version.

KI M W 'W WEDDIN

LONDON.—Within a few days M
her divorce decree in England, a
Edward VIII, King of England.

King Edward's most intimate frie
and sincerely enamored of Mrs. Simpse
mediately after the coronation he wil

CLOSE-UP STANLEY BALDWIN

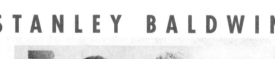

Stanley Baldwin, pictured above with Prince Edward in happier days, was Conservative Prime Minister during Edward VIII's brief reign. He was born in 1867 in Worcestershire and, after managing the family business in heavy industry for a number of years, he entered Parliament in 1908. He was Prime Minister three times, from 1923-1924, again from 1924-1929 and finally from 1932-1937. During the General Strike of 1926, he declared a State of Emergency, organised volunteers to maintain essential services and refused to negotiate until the strike was called off. In 1927, he

secured the passage of the anti-union Trade Disputes Act through Parliament.

His stand against Wallis as King's consort suggests a man who was traditional and, as may be construed by his political stance, unbending. In fact he was known to be kindly and tolerant, and he delayed interfering in the King's private affairs for as long as possible.

Ultimately, Baldwin was motivated by a desire to do what was best for the nation and the Crown. He resigned the premiership in favour of Neville Chamberlain after the Coronation of George VI and retired from politics. He died in 1947.

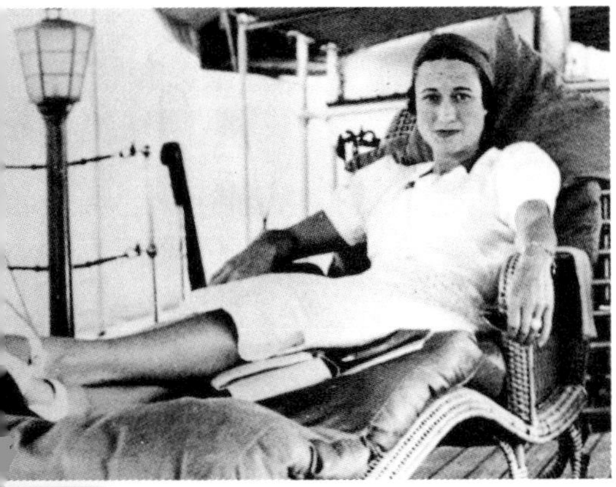

Above and left: The King and Wallis on the *Nahlin*. Droves of the world's – but not the British – press dogged the cruise, reporting his besotted devotion to Wallis. They published pictures of him stripped to the waist – shocking for anyone of consequence and scandalous for the King.

Circulars which announced the guest lists at his dinner parties. The presence of members of his family was requested on many of these occasions, as if he hoped to force their acceptance of Wallis.

Queen Mary was never invited to meet Wallis. His mother bitterly disapproved of the woman whom she termed an 'adventuress' and who, she felt, was not helping her son perform his duties as monarch.

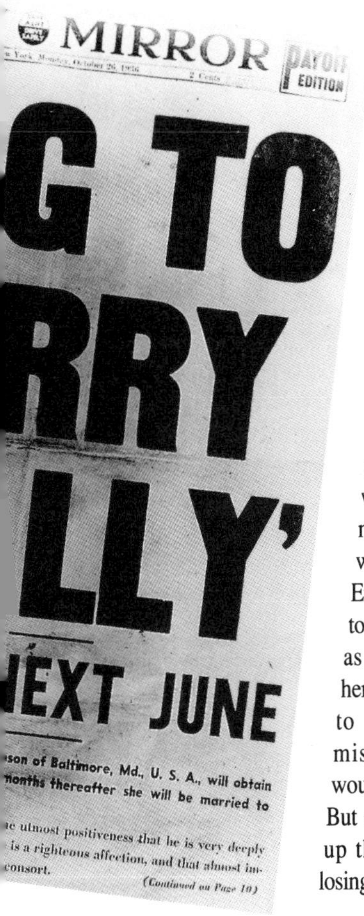

MIRROR
PAYOFF EDITION
2 Cents
G TO
RRY
LLY'
NEXT JUNE
son of Baltimore, Md., U. S. A., will obtain
months thereafter she will be married to
e utmost positiveness that he is very deeply
is a righteous affection, and that almost in-
consort.
(Continued on Page 10)

The real misgivings of the royal family were not without foundation. Earlier in May 1936, Wallis had written to her Aunt Bessie Merryman in Washington, complaining of the stress of her position. Being wife to Ernest and mistress to the King was taking its toll. Ernest did not seem to mind his position as cuckold; she, for her part, was content to be the King's mistress. Marriage would change all that. But she could not give up the King and risk losing all the power and influence she held in society. The letter is a conspicuous admission of Wallis' ambitions.

The official mourning for the old King continued into the summer of 1936, but it was felt the time had come for the new King to show his commitment to his position by publicly assuming the responsibilities of the monarch. He fastidiously attended official ceremonies during June and July, among them the dedication of the Canadian War Memorial at Vimy Ridge in France. He faced personal danger at a military revue on 16 July when a deranged man tried to shoot him.

SUMMER CRUISE

By August, however, he embarked on what seemed a scandalous course at the time. In order to execute a tour of south-east European states, the King chartered a luxury yacht, the *Nahlin*, from an eccentric millionairess, taking a party of friends which openly included Mrs Simpson.

It was an ostentatious display of wealth and frivolity. He had the library on the yacht removed to make space for an extra bedroom, and crates of alcohol. He let it be known that he was taking 3000 new golf balls to practise his swing by driving them off the deck into the sea.

LOOSE CANNON

Foreign Minister Anthony Eden was concerned that political significance could be read into the King's choice of countries to visit, given the recent decision by the British Government to cancel sanctions against Mussolini over Italy's invasion of Abyssinia. The King dismissed this as ridiculous. He was determined to visit Turkey, Greece and Yugoslavia in order to safeguard British interests in the Mediterranean. It was amateurish ventures such as this which created consternation in Government circles. The King was a loose cannon, likely to act unpredictably and not always in accordance with Government policy.

In Great Britain, it was becoming increasingly hard to keep the story out of the papers. Browsers at news-stands were puzzled by the foreign newspapers and magazines which had large chunks cut out of them. Sensational headlines, such as the *Daily Mirror* New York edition's 'KING TO MARRY WALLY', which predicted a wedding a month after the coronation, scheduled for 12 May 1937, were never seen by the majority of ordinary British people.

BACKDROP

FASCIST EUROPE

With hindsight and knowledge of the carnage of World War II, King Edward's fascist sympathies seem outrageous. In 1936, however, with global conflict not even a speck on the horizon, his views were merely ill-advised.

Fascism – extreme nationalism acknowledging the leader principle – and Nazism were ascendant in Europe in the mid-1930s. By far the most high-profile dictator was Adolf Hitler, who had come to power in the German elections of January 1933.

By late 1933 he had eliminated all opposition parties, principally the Socialists and Communists, by force or internment of key figures. 1936 saw a massive rearmament programme and the military repossession of the Rhineland (7 March), in contravention of the Treaty of Versailles which had ended World War I but which Germany regarded as punitive. King Edward urged his government to do nothing.

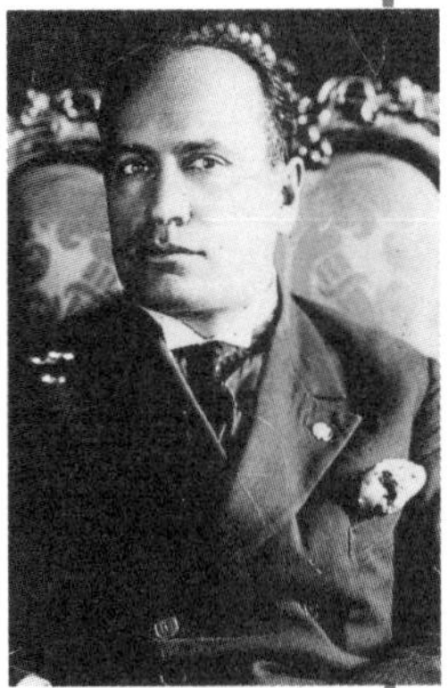

In Italy also, a strong dictator, Benito Mussolini – pictured right as Prime Minister – had arisen (1922). His pretensions to empire-building had resulted in the conquest of Abyssinia (Ethiopia) by 5 May 1936. The British government imposed economic sanctions on Italy as a sign of outrage. These were abolished on 15 June, much to the relief of King Edward, who had always opposed measures against Italy, believing they would drive Mussolini into an alliance with Hitler.

Several, less threatening, dictatorships also abounded in 1930s Europe. King Edward's European cruise on the *Nahlin* – dubbed later by Malcolm Muggeridge as 'the good ship *Swastika*' – took in those countries which were in the Hitler-Mussolini mould, if not in the Hitler-Mussolini camp.

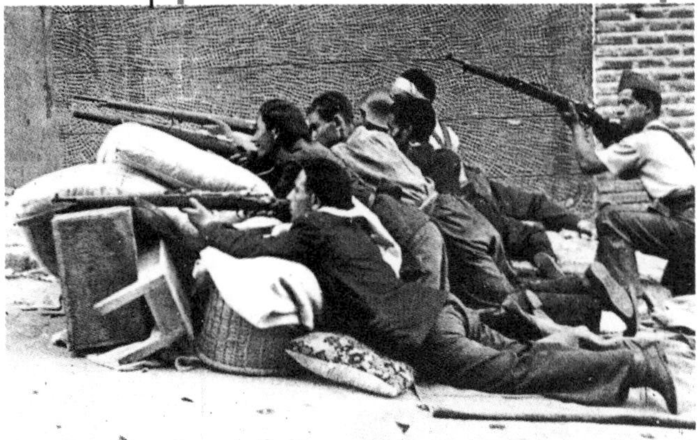

Above: In Spain, the Fascist Party, led by General Franco, caused an uprising against the liberal republican government in July 1936, which precipitated the Spanish Civil War.

His first stop, Yugoslavia, had signed several armaments contracts with Hitler and Mussolini and, at the time of the King's arrival, the Regent, Prince Paul, depended on Germany and Italy for half of his country's imports and exports.

The King went on to meet King George of Greece, whose country had been taken over by the dictator General Metaxas only two weeks before. His tour continued to Turkey, under the dictatorship of Kemal Ataturk; then Bulgaria, where Czar Boris was heavily influenced by both the Italian and German dictators; and finally Austria where, although the Nazi Party was banned, its Chancellor Schuschnigg had entered into an alliance with Hitler guaranteeing mutual political association.

DECADENT

THE WORLD IN WHICH WALLIS SIMPSON ROSE FROM OBSCURE NAVAL WIFE TO SCION OF ENGLISH HIGH SOCIETY COULD NOT HAVE HAD TWO MORE DIFFERENT SIDES. IT WAS THE AGE OF OPULENCE, WHERE STYLE WAS EVERYTHING; IT WAS ALSO THE AGE OF THE DEPRESSION, GRINDING POVERTY, AND THE RISE OF THE DICTATOR.

Above: Josephine Baker's daring style was the rage of 1920s France. Born to poor mulatto parents in the American Deep South, she became a star in Paris wearing little more than strategically placed bananas and feather loin cloths or sometimes nothing at all. Right: Bathing costumes revealing female legs and arms signified a social revolution where women had more freedom.

The 'roaring 20s' were well under way by 1924, a constant party for the well-heeled typified by cocktails and popular jazz. Elsa Maxwell, the society hostess, would travel the world, taking over an entire nightclub or spare palace so her friends, the international smart set, could party along with her. Dances such as the frenzied Charleston and Black Bottom originated in Harlem, and heralded a new era of sexual free-

Left: After the restricting clothes of the Edwardian era, post-Great War fashions were looser in style, and did not accentuate the female form.

dom. Dr Marie Stopes set up the first birth control clinics in London. The 'look' for women was a boyish, flat-chested, snake-hipped figure, topped by a neat head with sleek silky hair. Hemlines crept up higher as the 1920s wore on, and women also raided men's shops for cardigans, ties and cravats. Art Deco was the fashionable art form, and it continued to be popular far into the 1930s.

HUNGER MARCHES

There was a world of difference between the brittle partygoers and the deprived members of the working classes. The rest of British society suffered desperation, dole queues and hunger marches in the 'Land fit for heroes' that was promised after World War I. In Europe, politics were polarised; in 1922, the fascist Mussolini came to power in Italy and in 1924, hard-line

Communist Joseph Stalin took control in the USSR. In 1926, the General Strike crippled Britain when five million workers downed tools.

In the same year, the world's heart throb of the silent screen, Rudolph Valentino, was mourned by millions when he died. Two other international stars, Donald Duck and Mickey Mouse, made Walt Disney's fortune. His *Steamboat Willie*, which was released in 1928, was the first animated 'talkie'.

The new wonder of aviation, recovering from its destructive role in the Great War, caught the public's imagination. In 1927, Charles Lindbergh made his historic non-stop solo flight across the Atlantic, while Amy Johnson made several record-beating

Amy Johnson

flights, from England to Australia in 1930 and to Cape Town and back to England in 1936.

FINANCIAL RUIN

The end of the 1920s was marked by the Wall Street Crash in 1929, which ruined investors overnight and led to a world-wide depression that lasted until 1932. The crash of the money markets ushered in the Depression, which wiped

New Orleans 'black music' – Jazz – stormed from the obscurity of ethnic culture to sweep across America. Partygoers danced to the big-band sounds of Count Basie, right, and Duke Ellington.

AND DESPERATE

attempts made headline news round the world. The world seemed obsessed with speed.

out most of the social gains of the 1920s and brought hardship and unemployment to millions throughout the world – three million in Britain alone.

SHADOW OF HITLER

Poverty brought political upheaval. In January 1929 and again in 1930, hunger marches, such as the Jarrow March by the unemployed in Britain, dwarfed the earlier demonstrations of 1922. Britain's Labour Government had to surrender power to the Conservatives in 1931. In the United States, President Roosevelt was swept into power in 1930 with the 'New Deal'.

In 1930, the National Socialist Party (Nazis) became Germany's second largest

Above and above right: The Wall Street Crash ushered in a period of deprivation that meant different things to different people. A stockbroker sells his car to subsist, while millions of working men queued at soup kitchens for their very survival.

party, promising restoration of national pride to a demoralised people. On 30 January 1933, Adolf Hitler became Chancellor. On 23 March, he took control of the legislation, the budget, the constitution and all foreign policy with a total suspension of democratic liberties.

Political rumblings were not confined to Europe. In 1934, Mao Tse-Tung led 90,000 members of the peasant revolutionary party on an 8000 mile trek to Yenan. 'The Long March' became a central part of China's Communist legend.

Meanwhile the Big Bands played on, the booming jazz sounds tried to lift the spirits throughout the 1930s until their fall from popularity in the 1950s. Count Basie, the US jazz pianist, bandleader and composer, was one of the great stars of the

Above right: Joseph Stalin with Lenin in 1919.
Right: Hitler and Mussolini reviewing German troops in 1937. Bottom: Mao Tse-Tung on the 'Long March' which began his struggle to power.

period. The film world was revolutionised by the advent of sound – or 'talkies' – and colour. 1936 saw the greatest of them all – *Gone With The Wind*.

OBSESSED WITH SPEED

In 1935, Sir Malcolm Campbell beat all his previous land-speed records in his racing car 'Bluebird', averaging 301 miles per hour. He had consistently beaten his own records every time (eight in all) since he set the first one in 1924. His

WAR CLOUDS

As the 1930s wore on, peace became more and more precarious. In 1936, insurgent nationalists started the Spanish Civil War. It lasted until 1939 when General Franco overthrew the Republican Government. 750,000 people died on both sides. The threat of war hung over the whole of Europe. In 1938 Neville Chamberlain, the British Prime Minister, visited Hitler in Munich to express concern over the German invasion of Sudetenland. He returned with the famous 'Peace for our time' paper, signed by Hitler, declaring the 'desire of our two peoples never to go to war with one another again.' On 3 September 1939, Britain declared war on Germany.

THREE

A LOVE GREATER THAN DUTY

ABDICATION

THE SUMMER CRUISE ON THE *NAHLIN* BROUGHT MATTERS TO A HEAD. TALK FROM ABROAD WAS BOUND TO REACH BRITAIN SOONER OR LATER. THE KING WAS DETERMINED TO MARRY WALLIS SIMPSON, DESPITE OPPOSITION FROM THE GOVERNMENT THAT HE COULD NOT DO SO AND REMAIN ON THE THRONE. A DIFFICULT CHOICE LAY AHEAD

The King paid little heed to warnings about the effects of rumours surrounding his friendship with Wallis. His private secretary, Hardinge, finally sought help from the Prime Minister. However, Baldwin made it clear he was reluctant to interfere in the King's private life. He pointed out to Hardinge that no serious constitutional issue was likely to arise while Wallis remained married to Ernest Simpson.

DIVORCE AT IPSWICH

By early autumn, however, the Simpsons' marriage had disintegrated completely. Divorce was pending. Wallis' solicitor advised her to agree to the petition being heard outside London because the backlog of cases could mean a year's delay. He arranged for the hearing to be conducted at Ipswich in October. Hardinge was now able to

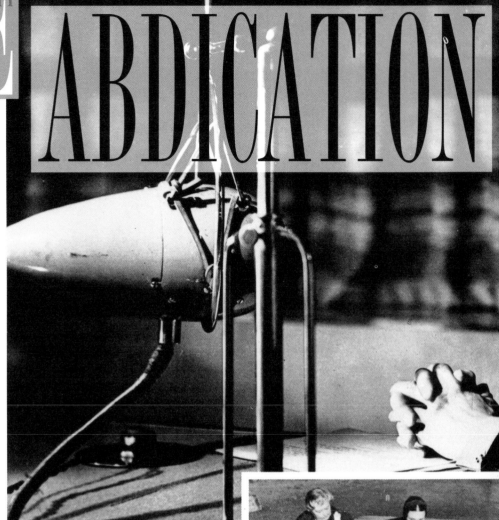

Above: The King prepares to broadcast his farewell speech to the nation from the BBC radio studios. Right: Wallis with her Aunt Bessie Merryman, left of picture, at Fort Belvedere during the crisis.

convince Baldwin to act, at least to ask the King to put a stop to the divorce proceedings. The King professed to be shocked at the idea that he or the Prime Minister could intervene in such a matter. 'I have no right to interfere with the affairs of an individual,' the King maintained. 'It would be wrong were I to attempt to influence Mrs Simpson just because she happens to be a friend of the King.'

The divorce hearing went ahead. The British press were still silent on the matter but foreign reporters swamped the Suffolk town. On 27 October, the Ipswich court heard Wallis' petition for divorce from Ernest on grounds of his adultery. As was common practice then, he had done the gentlemanly thing and provided 'evidence' of an affair. The closed hearing took 19 minutes, at the end of which Wallis had her decree nisi. Before the summer of 1937 she would be free

> *Do you really think I would be crowned without Wallis at my side?*
>
> King Edward to Ernest Simpson

to marry again. The quiet divorce was headlined round the world. 'KING'S MOLL RENO'D IN WOLSEY'S HOME TOWN' was one of the coarser pronouncements, but the message was repeated in various forms and many languages. British newspapers, in deference to a plea from the King, confined themselves to simple statements of fact.

But behind the silence was a restlessness. The editor of the *Morning Post* had warned that he was not prepared to keep quiet much longer. The editor

OCT-DEC '36

of *The Times*, Geoffrey Dawson, went to see Hardinge with a letter he had received from an Englishman living abroad, setting out the damage the stories were doing to the Crown. He also brought a sheaf of articles that had appeared in American newspapers about the certainty of marriage between the King and Mrs Simpson.

On the 16 November Baldwin made his most determined attempt to reason with the King. 'I pointed out to him that the position of the King's wife was different from the position of any other citizen in the country; it was part of the price which the King had to pay...his wife becomes Queen. The Queen becomes the Queen of the country and therefore, in the choice of a Queen, the voice of the people must be heard.'

BOMBSHELL

Then the King dropped his bombshell. 'I intend to marry Mrs Simpson as soon as she is free to marry,' he said. 'If I could marry her as King, well and good...but if the Government opposed the marriage...then I am prepared to go.'

The next day the King related his decision to his mother, Queen Mary. The old lady, still deeply

DIVORCE DECREE FOR MRS. WALLIS SIMPSON

UNDEFENDED SUIT

A decree nisi, with costs, was granted by Mr. Justice Hawke, at Ipswich Assizes yesterday, to Mrs. Wallis Simpson, of the Beach House, Felixstowe, and of Cumberland-terrace, London, N.W., against Mr. Ernest Aldrich Simpson, of Bryanston-court, W. The petition was undefended.

Mrs. Simpson was represented by Mr. Norman Birkett, K.C., and Mr. Walter Frampton.

The marriage took place in July, 1928, at the Chelsea register office and there are no children of the marriage. Mrs. Simpson's case was that the marriage was happy until 1934, when her husband began to stay away at week-ends.

Adultery was alleged between Mr. Simpson and a woman at the Hotel de Paris, Bray, near Maidenhead, on a date in July this year.

Evidence was given by servants at the hotel in support of the petitioner's case.

Above: The 28 October edition of the Daily Telegraph carried this non-committal account of Wallis' divorce hearing in compliance with the King's plea that the case should not be sensationalised.

grieving for her husband, could not believe it. Her life had been devoted to duty and she had always put Crown and country first. Over the next few days, the King informed his three brothers. The Duke of York, who was next in line to the throne, was stricken and remained silent.

Within days the King had changed his mind. Esmond Harmsworth, the proprietor of the *Daily Mirror* and the *Sunday Pictorial*, had broached the subject of a morganatic marriage. The King informed Baldwin of his interest in a marriage contract whereby the king's wife does not become queen nor do their children inherit. His reply left him in no doubt as to the viability of the proposition. 'A morganatic marriage would mean a special Bill being passed in Parliament and Parliament would never pass it.'

GOVERNMENT OPPOSITION

The views of His Majesty's Government were well known on the matter, as were the opinions of senior Civil Servants. The Opposition Labour Party and the Trades Union Congress also pronounced that the people would not tolerate Wallis as Queen. It is worth noting that at this time, Parliament appeared to be speaking for a people whose opinion was not yet known, the British press having kept the story from them.

In contrast, the peoples of the Dominions – Australia and Canada – were well aware of the situation, there being no gentleman's agreement to suppress the story in their newspapers. The Governor General of Canada had told Baldwin that 'the condition of Canadian opinion seems to

PERSPECTIVE

'MRS SIMPSON'S JETTY'

On the accession of a new monarch, it was and is the custom and practice of city councils and local boroughs to name new buildings in his or her honour. In line with other British monarchs, Edward would have allowed his name to adorn buildings, bridges and piers in various parts of the British Isles and the Empire.

However, the brevity of his reign meant that opportunities for such dedications were restricted, and that tiny number would have been reduced after his abdication and the scandal associated with it.

Nevertheless, some monuments to his reign do exist.

One such edifice is the King Edward VIII Pier in Douglas, Isle of Man (below). Extended from the old Red Pier, the enlarged construction was graced with the new name in an opening ceremony on 24 May 1936, just three days before Edward introduced Wallis to Stanley Baldwin as 'my future wife'.

However, the King's controversial liaison was the subject of much local gossip, and the Edward Pier was cynically referred to by some Manx people as 'Mrs Simpson's Jetty'.

In spite of the scandal, the pier is known as the King Edward VIII Pier to the present day.

CLOSE-UP

THE INSTRUMENT OF ABDICATION

This document ended the reign of King Edward VIII. It was witnessed by his three brothers, Albert (soon to be proclaimed King George VI), Henry and George, and read:

'I, Edward the Eighth of Great Britain, Ireland, and the British Dominions beyond the Seas, King, Emperor of India, do hereby declare My irrevocable determination to renounce the Throne for Myself and My descendants, and My desire that effect should be given to this Instrument of Abdication immediately. In token whereof I have hereunto set My hand this tenth day of December, nineteen hundred and thirty six, in the presence of witnesses whose signatures are subscribed.'

me to be most anxious and disquieting' and the Australian High Commissioner had stated categorically that 'if there was any question of marriage with Mrs Simpson, the King would have to go as far as Australia was concerned.'

Constitutionally, only the King, not Parliament, could ask the Dominions for their decision. Thinking the matter too delicate, the King gave Baldwin the authority to do so, to the consternation of his supporters. Max Beaverbrook, proprietor of the *Daily Express*, exclaimed, 'Sir! You have put your head on the execution block. All that Baldwin has to do now is swing the axe.'

'THEY DON'T WANT HER'

On 2 December the Press finally broke their silence. At the Bradford Diocesan Conference – usually an unprovocative body – the day before, the Bishop of Bradford expressed regrets that the

Right: The man who sparked off the storm. It was a speech by the Bishop of Bradford , and this report in a Yorkshire newspaper, that brought into the open the rumours about the King and Wallis.

King had not shown more positive evidence of his awareness for the need of Divine guidance. The bishop was referring to the King's less than regular attendance at church – unacceptable for the titular head of the Church of England – but the implication was that his relationship with Wallis was misguided. It was the excuse the Press had been waiting for.

The headlines were adverse and the editorials damning. With the exception of the very few who championed the King, principally Lord Beaverbrook's *Daily Express*, all the British newspapers ran the story of the King's relationship with Wallis. As the King waded through them he conceded sadly, 'they don't want her!'

For the majority of the population the news was a shock. People picketed Number 10 Downing Street with signs reading 'SAVE OUR EDWARD VIII' and 'OUT WITH THE MATCH BREAKER'. Further pickets outside Wallis' house read 'DOWN WITH THE WHORE', 'WALLY GIVE US BACK OUR KING'. In the City the stock market plummeted.

Now Wallis had to leave the country. Her departure – for France – was almost unbearable for the King. His friend and ally Winston Churchill was seriously worried: 'HM appeared to be under a very great strain and very near breaking point.' Churchill had already stated that 'the King's love for Mrs Simpson is one of the great loves of history – make no mistake, he cannot live without her.'

The King spent hours on the phone talking to Wallis, shouting to make himself heard above the static and interference on the line. Wallis wanted him to make a radio broadcast so that he could put his version of the events to the people, but this was

> *You have laid your head on the execution block. All that Baldwin has to do now is swing the axe.*
>
> Max Beaverbrook to King Edward

vetoed as a divisive measure. Baldwin told him bluntly but gently, 'what I want, Sir, is what you told me you wanted. To go with dignity, not dividing the country, and making things as smooth as possible for your successor. To broadcast would be to go over the heads of your ministers...You will be telling millions throughout the world, among them a vast number of women, that you are determined to marry one who has a husband living.'

Meanwhile, acting on advice, Wallis issued a statement saying she was willing to withdraw from the situation if it would solve the problem. Some newspapers eagerly seized on this, 'MRS SIMPSON RENOUNCES KING! CRISIS ENDED!' blared premature headlines. But Wallis had no intention of giving up the King, and he had no intention of letting her do so.

On 7 December the King told the Duke of York of his decision to abdicate. The next day he gave a dinner party, which included the Duke of York and Baldwin, to make the announcement. It was a grim and gloomy occasion for everyone but the soon-to-be-departing King. He prided himself, as he wrote later, on being 'the life and soul of the party.'

But it was not until the following day that the King told Wallis. Until that moment she had assumed he would fight for the throne. That night they talked for hours on the telephone as she begged him not to go through with it.

The Bishop of Bradford said yesterday that the benefit to be derived by the people from the King's Coronation would depend in the first instance on " the faith, prayer, and self-dedication of the King himself." Referring to the moral and spiritual side of that self-dedication, the Bishop said the King would abundantly need the Divine grace if he were to do his duty faithfully, and he added : " We hope that he is aware of his need. Some of us wish that he gave more positive signs of such awareness."

Dr. Blunt must have had good reason for so pointed a remark. Most people by this time are aware that a great deal of rumour regarding the King has been published of late in the more sensational American newspapers. It is proper to treat with contempt mere gossip such as is frequently associated with the names of European royal persons. The Bishop of Bradford would certainly not have condescended to recognise it....

Left: After the story of the King's involvement with Wallis became known to the British people, many blamed the Government for forcing him to consider abdication. Here, ordinary working men protest outside the Prime Minister's residence, 10 Downing Street.

as to what you are going to be called?' His suggestion was that his brother should now become known as the Duke of Windsor.

It was not until two years later that Queen Mary was able to put her feelings into words. 'You did not seem able to take in any point of view but your own' she wrote to her son. 'I do not think you have ever realised the shock which the attitude you took up caused your family and the whole Nation. It seemed inconceivable to those who had made such sacrifices during the war that you, as their King, refused a lesser sacrifice.'

A DARKER REASON

At the moment of abdication, there were other schools of thought which said that Wallis was the Government's excuse for securing Edward's departure. Von Ribbentrop, the German ambassador to Great Britain, stated it succinctly: 'Edward VIII had to abdicate since it was not certain, because of his views, he would cooperate in anti-German policy.'

Whatever the truth of it, he was gone. Author and diplomat, Harold Nicolson, noted how the tide had turned against the ex-King; there was, he said, 'a deep and enraged fury against the King himself. In eight months he had destroyed the great structure of popularity which he had raised.'

That same day the Duke of York had been to see Queen Mary, devastated by the turn of events. 'When I told her what had happened I broke down and sobbed like a child' he recalled. While he was there, a message from 10 Downing Street was delivered, with instructions that the following morning he would be required, together with his brothers, the Dukes of Gloucester and Kent, to witness the signing of the Instrument of Abdication at Fort Belvedere. On 9 December, all three brothers stood in silence as the King signed his last document as monarch.

NO LONGER KING

The next day the Instrument of Abdication was ratified by Parliament. Now, no longer King, 'His Royal Highness the Prince Edward' broadcast his farewell speech to the people. 'At long last,' he began, 'I am able to say a few words of my own.'

It was a moving speech, which he delivered gravely and well. He had written it himself, but Churchill, the master speechwriter, had tinkered with it too. He spoke of the new King and his excellent qualities, noting that his brother had 'one matchless blessing enjoyed by so many of you and not bestowed on me – a happy home with his wife and children.

'You all know the reasons which have impelled me to renounce the throne' he said. 'But I want you to understand that in making up my mind I did not forget the country or the Empire which as Prince of Wales and lately as King, I have for 25

years tried to serve. But you must believe me when I tell you that I have found it impossible to carry the heavy burden of responsibility, and to discharge my duties as King as I would wish to do, without the help and support of the woman I love.'

Wallis listened to the broadcast at the villa in Cannes. She lay on the sofa, her hand over her eyes, weeping silently.

All that remained was the tidying up of the details. The King's loyal friend, lawyer Walter Monckton, negotiated an allowance for the ex-King, said to be £60,000 a year, and arranged for King George VI to 'buy back' Balmoral and Sandringham for a million pounds. As the two brothers went over the details together, the new King said, 'By the way, have you given any thought

Right: News of the King's abdication was published in headlines which suited their origins. The Sacramento Union's is short and to the point, while the Daily Worker introduces an overt republican dimension into its coverage of the crisis.

What the papers said

EDWARD VIII'S LIAISON WITH A TWICE-DIVORCED AMERICAN WOMAN, AND THE SUBSEQUENT ABDICATION CRISIS, DIVIDED THE LOYALTIES OF THE BRITISH PRESS BARONS. STARVED OF THE FREEDOM TO PRINT THE STORY UNTIL JUST EIGHT DAYS BEFORE THE ABDICATION, THEY UNLEASHED THEIR PENT-UP EMOTIONS WITH FERVENT EDITORIALS AND SENSATIONAL HEADLINES

Most of the popular press clung to the notion that anything was better than losing the glamorous and 'supremely gifted' King Edward. Not so *The Times*, which consistently thundered its support for the Government's uncompromising view of the constitutional position.

❚❚ *Is the British Cabinet sure beyond doubt that the abdication of Edward VIII would not strike a terrible blow at the greatest institution in the world..?* **❚❚**

From commencement of British press coverage on 2 December, until the issue was decided, Lord Rothermere's *Daily Mirror* reflected popular support for Edward. Every day it carried a bold legend above the headline stating:

'GOD SAVE THE KING'

As early as Friday 4 December, the *News Chronicle* – owned by the Cadbury family and a supporter of the Liberal Party – carried the headline: 'Latest View is That Only Miracle Can Prevent Abdication'. The paper's editorial presented the view that the King should marry Wallis in his capacity as Duke of Cornwall and that there should be an 'Act of Exclusion' concerning right of inheritance (a morganatic marriage).

NO HASTY DECISION

The editorial concluded: 'The country would only be the loser by any hasty decision which would result in depriving Britain and the Empire of a King who has won their loyalty and affection and whose disappearance from the throne at this moment would deprive the institution of monarchy of a great personality'.

That very day, the Prime Minister, Stanley Baldwin, announced that a morganatic marriage was unknown to British law, would require an Act of Parliament and was out of the question.

The Times edition of Saturday 5 December was emphatic in its support for the Prime Minister.

Many people throughout the Empire, said *The Times*, would be offended and perplexed by the King's proposed marriage; a view which had been endorsed by all the Dominion governments.

The paper made a veiled reference to 17th-century royal-parliamentary struggles. Members of the House of Commons had shown, said *The Times*, that they deeply resented: 'The suggestion, actually made in certain quarters, that here is a chance to keep a good King and discard a bad Prime Minister'.

The Times' editorial concluded: 'There is a widespread desire, not only that this profoundly disturbing difficulty should be rapidly settled, but once settled, it should neither have repercussions nor resurrection'.

On 6 December, the popular Sunday papers were not inclined to give up the King that easily.

They all reported at length, more or less accurately, the basic details of Wallis Simpson's life.

The News of the World's front page talked of deliberations of the gravest import and 'rumour that would have seemed fantastic only a week ago'.

Lord Rothermere's *Sunday Pictorial* echoed the views of its sister paper, the *Daily Mirror*. The headline screamed 'There Must be No Abdication'.

On its front-page, the *Sunday Pictorial* said: 'The people are thinking of it as a love affair, pure and simple. They feel by the million, that they know King Edward as a personal friend, and are backing him as one'.

WE WANT THE KING

The paper's main editorial ended by saying: 'The King wants to marry Mrs Simpson, and we want the King. Our Government, and the governments of the Dominions, will best serve the whole British family if they approach the problem solely from the point of view of making the best of it'.

There was also a centre-page article by the Earl of Cottenham, headed 'The King Must Not Go', in which the author inveighed against British divorce laws.

The *Sunday Express* reported, in bold capitals, that a change in government was not ruled out.

On Monday 7 December, the *Daily Mirror's* headline was: '45,000,000 demand to know'. The paper reported crowds booing Cabinet Ministers at Westminster, and cheering for the King outside Buckingham Palace.

Four questions, printed on an otherwise empty front page in extra large capitals, concluded by asking: 'Is the British Cabinet sure beyond doubt that the abdication of Edward VIII would not strike a terrible blow at the greatest institution in the world – our monarchy — and thereby cause irreparable harm'?

The following day, there was news of Wallis' offer to give up the King. 'End of the Crisis', said the hopeful *Daily Express* headline.

END IN SIGHT

On Friday 11 December, The *News Chronicle* gave up the ghost: its editorial noted that a semi-mystical consensus of state, church, and people had endorsed the view that the King's proposed marriage was an affront to national life.

The biggest news of all, Edward's abdication statement, was given to the nation instantly via the new medium of radio on the evening of 11 December.

On Saturday 12 December, there was nothing for the papers to do but factually report Edward's departure from the country. The *Daily Mirror*, like all the other papers, had features on the new King, George VI, and his wife and children.

The following day's *Sunday Graphic* featured 'wonderful souvenir pictures' of the new King and Queen; with a centre-page article on 'The Happy Married Life Of Our King and Queen'. Ring in the new!

It was over. Edward VIII was yesterday's news.

SOCIETY HOSTESS WHO WON THE KING'S HEART

Mrs. Simpson's Early Years in Baltimore and Her Two Marriages

PRESENTED AT ENGLISH COURT

("News of the World" Special)

AMID the comings and goings of statesmen, deliberations of the gravest import, and rumour that would have worried York House, the centre of the whole stage...

KING EDWARD VIII.

MRS. ERNEST SIMPSON

HOLIDAY CRUISE

AND MR. SIMPSON VISIT

WHAT THE EMPIRE IS THINKING

Australian Parliament to Meet This Week

THROUGHOUT the Empire—and indeed the whole world—the Constitutional crisis is being followed with the gravest concern.

SATURDAY
Dec. 5, 1936 | ONE PENNY

PRIMATE'S ADVICE TO C

The Archbishop of Canterbury, Dr. Lang, has issued the following statement:—

Daily Pictorial

No. 1,184 | SUNDAY, DECEMBER 6, 1936 | Twopence

MRS. SIMPSON SPEAKS
Page 3

Wireless Programmes on Page 32

THERE MUST BE NO ABDICATION

The Voice of the People

THROUGHOUT the nation yesterday there was only one thought, one thing to talk about—the King. Will all yet be well? Will he abdicate? Or—did the King feel that he is forced to...

AT THE WINDOW OF HIS PALACE

GOD SAVE TH

Daily Mirror

No. 10,302. Mon. Dec. 7, 1936. One Penny

45,000,000 DEM TO KNOW—

fully stated and in detail, is the...

Mirror

GOD SAVE THE KING!

NEWSPAPER WITH THE LARGEST NET SALE

L US THE FACTS, MR. BALDWIN!

Suggestions have appeared that if the King decided to marry, his wife would not be Queen...

THE NATION INSIST KNOWING THE KI

Daily Express

164 PAGES | ONE PENNY

TUESDAY, DECEMBER 8, 1936.

D OF THE CRISIS

Mrs. Simpson Authorises Dramatic Statement From Cannes

Am Willing To Withdraw

**BROWNLOW
DS SIGNED
DOCUMENT**

uation Which Has Become Unhappy And Untenable'

News Chronicle

ONE PENNY

FRIDAY, DECEMBER 4, 1936

No. 28,270

THE KING: PALACE CONFER

Latest View Is Only Miracle Can Prevent

ALL PARTIES STAND BY MR. BALDWIN

His Majesty Visits Queen Mary | Dukes Of York, Kent And Gloucester Meet

RRIED CONSULTATION LATE LAST NIGHT

MRS. SIMPSO
FORT BELV

Daily Mirror

No. 10307 | Registered at the G.P.O. as a newspaper | ONE PENNY

LATE LONDON

EX-KING SAILED THIS MORNING IN YACHT

The Son—and His Mother

I CAN'T GO ON WITHOUT THE WOMAN I LOVE

DISTRESS THAT IS FILLING MY HEART

Escort of Two Destroyers

EX-KING Edward VIII broadcast to the world last night from the Augusta Tower of Windsor Castle. He was announced as his Royal Highness Prince Edward.

One Matchless Blessing

WONDERFUL SOUVENIR PORT

SUNDAY GRAPHIC

and SUNDAY NEWS

No. 1,132 | SUNDAY, DECEMBER 13, 1936. | TWOPENCE

CROWDS ACCLAIM KIN AND PRINCESSES

'With My Wife as Helpmeet I Take Up Heavy Task'

The Duke of Windsor

EXILE AND TH

THE REIGN OF KING EDWARD VIII WAS OVER AFTER ONLY 325 DAYS, THE SECOND SHORTEST REIGN IN HISTORY. SOON AFTER HIS BROADCAST HE LEFT THE COUNTRY, BOUND FOR THE CASTLE OF THE BARON EUGENE DE ROTHSCHILD NEAR VIENNA. HE HAD WANTED TO JOIN WALLIS IN CANNES IMMEDIATELY, BUT SUCH AN ACT IN THOSE DAYS COULD HAVE JEOPARDISED HER DIVORCE

The abdication was the beginning of a period of tortured limbo for the Duke of Windsor. Wallis had never wanted him to give up the throne, and now some of their telephone calls were heated and accusatory. It was small consolation that he was receiving sackfuls of letters of support and sympathy. Wallis, too, was receiving mail, but the majority of the estimated 5000 letters she received over the next few months could only be classified as hate mail.

They spoke on the telephone several times a day. Major Edward 'Fruity' Metcalfe, one friend who offered support, said, 'He's just living through each day till he can be with W'.

The Duke had been known for his generosity when he was Prince and King, but now his income was greatly limited. The final settlement had left him with a capital sum of about two million pounds to support himself and his household; for the rest of his life he worried about money and never picked up a bill if he could avoid it.

In March 1937, Wallis moved to the Château de Candé in Monts near Tours, where they were to be married. This was the home of the naturalised American industrialist Charles Bedaux, a self-confessed 'out-and-out Fascist'. Bedaux was to commit suicide in 1944 rather than face a treason trial in the United States for his wartime actions.

When word arrived at the beginning of May that the divorce had become absolute, the Duke was with Wallis by the next day. He had wanted to marry immediately, but they agreed to wait until 3 June so as not to conflict with the Coronation of George VI on 12 May.

Wallis had none of the Duke's qualms about spending money. She ordered 66 dresses from top designers for her bridal trousseau. Her wedding dress and jacket were made by Mainbocher in 'Wallis' blue.

WEDDING PROBLEMS

Lord Louis Mountbatten offered himself as best man, but the Duke turned him down, saying that he wanted his two younger brothers as 'supporters', the royal version of the best man. But by late May it became clear that no member of the Royal Family would attend the wedding. Neither would many of their friends be present; no invitations were issued as the Duke believed they should show their support by inviting themselves. Many misunderstood this, and even Mountbatten stayed away.

A more pressing problem was that they could find no Church of England clergyman prepared to marry them because Wallis was a divorcée.

Above: The Duke and Wallis on their wedding day, with best man, 'Fruity' Metcalfe. Right: The Reverend R. Anderson Jardine, right of picture. Fiercely criticised in Britain for his role, he left to found the 'Windsor Cathedral of Los Angeles' in the US.

DATEFILE

JUNE 3 1937
Wallis and Edward marry at the Château de Candé in France

OCTOBER 22 1937
The Windsors meet Adolf Hitler

JULY 8 1943
The murder of Harry Oakes

MARCH 15 1945
The Windsors leave the Bahamas

JUN '37 – MAR '45

E WAR YEARS

Finally, a complete unknown, the Reverend Jardine, vicar of St Paul's Church in Darlington, offered his services, despite Church disapproval.

Only hours before the wedding, the Duke and Wallis received a blow. A letter arrived from the Duke's brother, King George VI, stating that although the Duke would enjoy royal status, his wife, and any descendants, would not. Wallis would be a Duchess, but could not be styled 'Her Royal Highness'. The Duke burst into tears. 'But they promised!' he said. The unprecedented – and legally questionable – step of denying royal status to the wife of a Royal Duke (see Perspective, p120) was the source of bitterness and an issue of contention for the rest of their lives.

But the rest of the arrangements went smoothly under Wallis' direction. She flew in her own hairdresser and florist, and society photographer, Cecil Beaton. Fruity Metcalfe was best man, and 16 guests attended the service.

Their honeymoon started in Venice, where the Duke gave the fascist salute to cheering crowds who showered them with flowers. Their destination was Austria, the Castle Wasserleonburg, where they were to stay for three months. During this time, the Duke prepared for the expected diplomatic role to be offered to him. In his farewell radio broadcast, he had mentioned his readiness to serve his country. However, he did not take into account the extraordinary difficulty of arranging a job for an ex-King – a uniquely awkward status.

There was concern within the British Government that his potential popularity was much higher than that of George VI, who had yet to gain the affection of the public. Any high-profile role for the Duke was likely to overshadow the new king. Further problems included the couple's known Nazi connections, which were undesirable as far as the British government was concerned.

EX-KING MEETS THE FUEHRER

The year wore on, and still no post was forthcoming – and then, as if to confirm all the British Government's worst fears, the Duke and Duchess undertook a tour of Germany in October 1937, arranged by the fascist Bedaux. They were fêted and entertained by leaders of the Nazi Party, the visit culminating in an audience with Adolf Hitler (see Inside View, p118).

This highly publicised expedition outraged the public and press in Britain and the United

Right: On 11 October 1937, the Duke and Duchess started their 12-day tour of Germany. It was the Duke's wish to inspect the many new factories and worker's living quarters of the Third Reich. Here they are seen arriving at Berlin's Friedrichstrasse Bahnhof.

States. A subsequent tour of the US, already arranged by Bedaux, was now out of the question.

Although hardly admirable, the Duke's Hitler visit has to be seen in the context of the time. Germany was not at war with Britain in 1937. Indeed, Nazism was seen by many at the time to be one solution to the appalling economic and social problems created by the Depression. Many well-intentioned people in all walks of life, who

Top: At the outbreak of war, the Duchess of Windsor offered her services to the French Red Cross, preparing mess kits and clothing for French troops. Above: November 1939: the Duke salutes French troops in the war zone. Because of his Nazi connections, he was deemed too much of a security risk to be given a post in Britain. He was offered the French position more to get him out of the way than to utilise him for the war effort.

would later rescind their views, would be described today as 'romantic fascists'.

Returning from Germany, the Duke and Duchess continued to linger in France where Monckton had negotiated diplomatic status for the couple. This permitted them to live there tax-free, and they were also offered full security protection.

Despite these concessions, the Duke still felt like the 'King over the water'. He was constantly putting calls through to George VI, involving long conversations in which he would offer advice as if he could rule by proxy. This disturbed and distressed his younger brother, and Walter Monckton had finally to tell the Duke to stop.

'LET ME SERVE!'

For the next two years the Duke and Duchess remained in Paris on hold. Then on 3 September 1939, Britain declared war on Germany. The Duke called Monckton. 'I want to offer my services in any capacity my brother deems appropriate,' he said, 'and I must return to Britain.' He sailed to Britain later that month to await orders.

'Any capacity' he had said, and the post offered him was indeed comparatively humble. He was finally offered a position as a member of the British Military Mission to the French General Headquarters at Vincennes. It was also pointed out to him that he could no longer hold his supreme ranks, such as Admiral of the Fleet. He would have to accept the lower rank of Major-General.

The Duke took up his post willingly enough, and likewise the Duchess, who joined the French Red Cross. But barely had they commenced duties when the war intensified: France fell, and they were told to leave for safety's sake. They headed south through neutral Spain and on to Portugal.

There began a murky period in the Windsors' lives, about which the full truth is still not known. Documents captured after the war showed that Nazi agents were watching the ex-King closely and certain overtures were made to him. The Nazi propaganda office broadcast stories about both the Duke and Duchess of Windsor's sympathies saying that the Duke favoured a negotiated peace between Great Britain and Germany.

I N S I D E
VIEW
THE MEETING WITH HITLER

In October 1937, the Windsors embarked on a 12-day tour of Nazi Germany, the highlight of which was an audience with Fuehrer Adolf Hitler. The stated intention was to inspect the Third Reich's industry and social welfare structure, and to meet leading Nazis.

German ambassador to Britain, von Ribbentrop, gave a dinner party in their honour in Berlin. As they toured the German factories the couple were greeted with 'Heil Windsor' to which they replied 'Heil Hitler'. By contrast, a few weeks earlier, von Ribbentrop had given the Nazi salute during an audience with George VI, who did not acknowledge it.

Hitler had been an admirer of the Duke while he was King. On his abdication, the Fuehrer said, 'I've lost a friend to my cause!' The Windsors met Hitler at his summer retreat on the Obersalzburg, Berchtesgaden, on 22 October 1937 (right). Although a fluent German speaker, the Duke was not allowed to talk to Hitler direct and was irritated by the mis-translations of the official interpreter.

Afterwards Hitler said, 'if it had been possible for me to talk to King Edward VIII for just one hour, the abdication of His Majesty could have been avoided. He had a responsibility not only to Britain but to Europe, of which he did not seem to be aware.'

Apparently, the German plan was that if Britain fell, which seemed likely in the summer of 1940, they would hope to persuade the Duke to return as King.

Whether the Duke knew of the plan, and was willing to collaborate with the Nazis, may never be known. He emphatically denied it. Some say that as he assumed a German invasion of Britain would succeed, he felt he might have a real rôle to play in helping his country come to terms with a Nazi Occupation.

CODE-WORD

Evidence suggests that he had talks with a go-between, and was given a code-word that would tell him that an invasion had succeeded and he would be needed. A document, which a senior German source sent to his superiors in Berlin, reads as follows, 'The confidant has just received a telegram from the Duke, asking him to send a communication as soon as action was advisable. Should any answer be made?'

Meanwhile, the British Government sought a suitable job for the Duke. He was offered the

MURDER AND CORRUPTION – WHO KILLED HARRY OAKES?

On 8 July 1943, during the Duke's Governorship of the Bahamas, a prominent member of the white Bahamian community, the fabulously wealthy Sir Harry Oakes (right), was found battered to death and his body half-burned in the bedroom of his palatial house in Nassau.

Oakes was involved in a deal to smuggle millions of dollars out of the Bahamas into a Mexican bank to join funds being laundered for the Nazis. The Duke of Windsor had been persuaded to invest nearly two million dollars in the operation, though whether he knew what the deal really was remains uncertain. Oakes was also in conflict with fellow magnate, Harold Christie, who had double-crossed him in a land deal involving a consortium rumoured to have Mafia backing.

After being informed of Oakes' death, the Duke waited for four hours before acting. As the island only had a small police force, his decision to seek outside investigative help was perfectly understandable. However, instead of Scotland Yard or the American FBI, he contacted the nearby Miami Police Department, in particular, Captain Edward Melchen, who had been his bodyguard on a number of occasions.

At the very least, this was an error of judgement, since Melchen was suspected by the FBI of having criminal associations.

The Duke took an active interest in the investigation from the start, often calling Melchen several times a day.

Melchen soon decided, on the basis of little evidence, that the murderer was Oakes' son-in-law, the playboy Alfred de Marigny, who once said, 'if the British Government felt that the Duke was someone of importance, he would not have been sent to rot on this miserable reef.' Oakes and he had been enemies since de Marigny eloped with Oakes' daughter, Nancy (far right, on their

wedding day). He was a convenient suspect; although the murder had all the hallmarks of a voodoo killing, the arrest of a black suspect would inflame already dangerously high black feelings.

The Nassau police were told to remove all handprints and fingerprints from Sir Harry's bedroom because, as one constable would testify, such prints 'did not match those of the accused'.

As de Marigny waited in jail, the evidence against him continued to be manipulated. Officials who might have helped were moved away to other posts. The trial seemed to be a foregone conclusion. It was only when Nancy called in New York private detective, Raymond Schindler, that Melchen's evidence was shown to be extremely dubious. The jury acquitted de Marigny without delay.

However, the Duke still had him deported as an undesirable. The fact that the real murderer got away with it is largely attributed to the Duke's decision to bring in the Miami detectives.

Whatever the truth behind the case – the FBI suspected Harold Christie of arranging the murder to clear the path for his business investments in the islands – this sordid affair cast a pall over the Duke's whole term of office.

BACKDROP

Governorship of the Bahamas, starting immediately. Usually the last stop on the way to retirement for the holder, this was one of the most lowly colonial service posts he could have been offered. If he distinguished himself there, he was promised, there would be better things to come.

The Duke's five-year term in the Bahamas – commencing in August 1940 – produced mixed results. Both he and the Duchess hated the sweltering humid climate and took every opportunity to get away. During his term of office, the Duke was to make nine extended visits to the United States, usually against the wishes of the British Government. Nevertheless, despite severe misgivings about his political views in official British and American circles, with his undoubted charm and star-appeal, the Duke generally made a good impression on the American public.

NON-ROYAL DUCHESS

It was assumed that the Royal Family's determination not to give Wallis royal status originated with Queen Mary and the new Queen Elizabeth. (now the Queen Mother) It is true that they led the opposition to Wallis, and it was years before Queen Elizabeth came near to forgiving her. She believed that the stress of acceding to the throne shortened her husband's life.

The decision was probably pragmatic. Once a Royal Highness always a Royal Highness. Wallis did not have a good track record in marriage. What if she divorced the Duke and remarried? What if he remarried and wanted his new wife to have the Royal title? The ramifications were unacceptable.

Without royal status, it was not protocol to curtsey to Wallis, though many did so for the Duke's sake. He insisted their staff accorded her the title of Royal Highness, which he felt was hers by right. Others agreed. Burke's Peerage said it was 'the most flagrant act of discrimination in the whole history of our dynasty'.

> ' *I do not believe that in Nassau he is serving the Empire as importantly as he might* '
>
> The Duchess of Windsor on the Duke

Both he and the Duchess clearly believed that his talents were wasted in the Bahamas. 'How can you expect me to wish him to stay here?' an American publication quoted the Duchess as saying. Used to the most glamorous cities and resorts of Europe and America, the Duke and Duchess could perhaps be excused for disliking the narrow world of the local white settler community who formed their social circle in the Bahamas. These people had the normal prejudices of the day concerning the majority black community, who were not considered fit for senior government posts or participation in white social life. In this respect, with his ancient sense of *noblesse oblige*, the Duke probably had a better understanding of black rights than all but the most liberal members of his white Bahamian flock.

In his own way, the Duke tried to do his duty, as he saw it, as an impartial colonial governor although, some say, his efforts did not seem completely without regard for his own interests.

He attempted to limit the power of the local merchant oligarchy who controlled the island's legislature, and he also put forward sensible schemes for economic reform and development. Eventually, the Duke had some success with local constitutional reforms, despite the opposition of

Left: The Duke of Windsor takes the oath of office before taking up his duties as Governor of the Bahamas. The Duchess can be seen to the right of the Duke trying to ward off the oppressive heat with a hand fan. Above: The Duke and Duchess dance with US naval personnel at a military club in May 1943. This was the third of their nine US tours while the Duke was in office.

Left: Although the Duchess of Windsor was known to dislike the Duke's posting to the Bahamas intensely – she refused to live in the official residence, Government House, until the near-derelict building had been completely refurbished – she offered herself once again to the Red Cross. Apparently, she was a tireless worker and devoted much of her time – when she was not making one of her many visits to the United States – to helping the local black population. Here she is pictured with the Duke inspecting field dressings which the Bahamas Red Cross was sending to England.

wealthy settler interests. During the severe riots of June 1942, in which some blacks were shot dead by the small local garrison, he handled the situation rather well. The Duke managed to calm both racial communities with a broadcast which gave the impression that he recognised the social problems involved, but would nevertheless deal firmly with law-breakers.

LEAVING UNDER A CLOUD

However, the murder of the island's wealthiest resident, Sir Harry Oakes (see Backdrop, p119) together with overtones of local corruption and continuing doubts about the Windsors' political wisdom, sullied the Duke's service. The Duke of Windsor's Bahamas stint ended on 15 March 1945, 10 weeks before his term of office expired. Officially it was a resignation, and there is little doubt that the couple were glad to be on their way.

KING GEORGE MAKES HIS MARK

CLOSE-UP

As the Windsors vanished from public view in Great Britain, so the new King and Queen's star rose. By the end of the war they had exceeded the level of popularity the Duke had enjoyed first as Prince of Wales and later as King. When George VI had ascended the throne he had seemed a poor substitute. Public affection for his daughters, 'the little Princesses' helped, as did the charm and accessibility of his wife, Queen Elizabeth.

The King was shy, stiff, and had a stutter that he never quite conquered, which sometimes made his broadcasts an embarrassment. But the war wrought a change in people's perceptions. The King became a focus for heightened national emotions, and his simple piety, dedication to his country, seriousness and honesty, struck a chord with the people. By the end of the war, they had started loving him for himself.

Those in power, who had initially dismissed him as weak and simple-minded, also changed their minds. Churchill, who had championed the Duke of Windsor and sought to keep him on the throne, Wallis or not, and had never ceased to be his friend, said later, 'Thank God I was wrong. We couldn't possibly have got a better King.'

IT HAS ALWAYS BEEN A MATTER FOR INTENSE SPECULATION: WHAT WAS SO SPECIAL ABOUT WALLIS SIMPSON THAT A MAN WOULD GIVE UP A THRONE AND HIS WHOLE WAY OF LIFE FOR HER? SHE WAS NO BEAUTY AND HER TRACK RECORD WITH MEN DID NOT INSPIRE CONFIDENCE IN HER FIDELITY

HOW DID

For the millions who watched the events of the abdication unfold and the enduring love of the Duke of Windsor for Wallis, her attraction seemed inexplicable. She looked middle-aged, hard and unapproachable. Those who knew her said she was good company, an excellent conversationalist and a talented hostess. But this, surely, was not enough to catch a king and enslave him for the rest of his life?

SEXUAL SECRETS

The answer can only be guessed at and is complex. Many assumed that sex figured strongly. A dossier on Wallis' time in China – ordered by Stanley Baldwin from MI6 for King George V in 1935 when it became critical to prevent Wallis from becoming Queen of England – reveals that she was introduced to 'sing-song' houses there by her first husband Win Spencer.

There, according to the dossier, Wallis was instructed in the arts of *Fang Chung*, which involved relaxation of the male partner through prolonged massage, particularly of the genitals. She would have been taught where the nerve centres of the body were, so that the brushing movement of the fingers would arouse the most sexually inert man.

Whether these techniques were sufficient to overcome Edward's extreme lack of virility is doubtful. Even as the young Prince of Wales, he had the reputation of being a poor lover. Thelma Furness made no secret of his lack of prowess when, in retaliation for his deserting her for Wallis, she broadcast his shortcomings throughout high society.

EROTIC GAMES

Sexual expertise has a limited fascination. It does not account for the decades of adoration.

Right: The Duke and Duchess of Windsor in middle age. With his kingdom went much of what had first attracted Wallis (above) to him. 'Believe me,' she once said, 'I would much rather have been the mistress of the King of England than the wife of the Governor of the Bahamas!'

LADIES WHO 'DANCED WITH THE PRINCE OF WALES'

The Prince was introduced to sex in France during World War I. There followed a succession of brief flings before he embarked on his most lasting affair, with Mrs Winifred May Dudley Ward (left), the wife of a Liberal MP, when he was 24. They saw each other almost every day. The affair lasted 16 years, surviving the Prince's other numerous mistresses. These included black singer Florence Mills and Thelma, Lady Furness, who held such sway over the Prince that she had her own personal bedroom at Fort Belvedere.

'There were other girls,' Freda said. 'But it never made any difference to me. Our friendship remained and I loved him, even though I realised that when it ended, it would be to my disadvantage.'

When the Prince fell in love with Wallis, he dropped his other mistresses instantly. He treated Freda particularly badly. She rang him as usual one day, to tell him of her small son's illness. The telephonist, whom she knew well, said in distress, 'I have orders not to put you through.'

SHE DO IT?

PASSIONATE DAYS IN CHINA

Wallis' first affair, in 1923, was with the Italian ambassador to Washington, Prince Gelasio Caetani. Wallis met him while separated from Win Spencer. The relationship was brief, but long enough for her to develop an intense interest in fascism.

A more torrid liaison evolved with Felipe Espil, an Argentinian diplomat. Their affair shocked Washington society – Wallis openly attended functions as Espil's mistress.

The following year, Wallis joined her husband in China. Among her conquests there that she herself owned up to in her autobiography, *The Heart Has Its*

Reasons, were an Englishman called Robbie; the Italian naval attaché to China, Alberto De Zara; an admiral; and Gerry Greene, First Secretary at the British Legation in Peking who became her devoted slave.

But most dramatic was her liaison with another handsome fascist, Count Galeazzo Ciano (below), later to become Italian Foreign Minister. According to Mrs Milton E Miles, the wife of one of Win Spencer's fellow naval officers, Wallis became pregnant by him in the summer of 1925 and had an abortion. This ended her chances of ever having children and was the cause of severe gynaecological problems which dogged her in later life.

On their wedding day Walter Monckton told Wallis that most people in England disliked her very much because the Duke had given up his throne to marry her. However, if she made him, and kept him, happy all his days, all that would change; but if she failed, he warned, the British people would never forgive her.

SENSE OF DUTY

Indeed some say that Wallis' secret was that she withheld sex. Several of their friends were convinced that throughout the affair they never slept together. One close friend thought that Wallis and Edward indulged in elaborate 'sex games' – nanny and child scenes where she was dominant and he was happily submissive.

What is certainly true is that Wallis filled a vacuum in Edward's life. Undoubtedly his mother, Queen Mary, loved

him but her devotion to duty and to following strict royal protocol prevented her from showing that love in any demonstrable form.

RESPECT FOR HIS STATION

The Edward who travelled the country and the world as the Prince of Wales was loved and fêted by millions, but he had no close relationships. Even his mistresses were distanced by their respect for his station in life.

Wallis cut through this. In some ways she replaced the mother he had never really had. She had also learnt to please a man in the southern American way, by discreet flattery. She knew how to build him up to look more substantial than he was. Wallis understood this. She dedicated her married life to bolstering his importance and making him feel he had a rôle. For this he remained deeply in love with her and she, though less obviously in love with him, managed him with tact and skill.

The final crucial element was that the man who was born to rule had a deep need to serve. Edward feared her as much as he loved her, but he found her hold over him deeply satisfying.

She took him over and ruled him completely. In so doing, she gave him a sense of security greater than anything else he had ever experienced in his life. Her satisfaction, however, never matched his.

But perhaps her sense of duty was greater than his, because she continued to give him whatever it was he needed from her till the day he died.

FIVE

A MONOTONOUS SOCIAL CYCLE

THE WANDERING

AT THE END OF THE WAR, THE DUKE AND DUCHESS OF WINDSOR PICKED UP THE THREADS OF THE LIFE THEY HAD MADE FOR THEMSELVES IN FRANCE WHEN THE DUKE WENT INTO VOLUNTARY EXILE. EUROPE AND THE WORLD HAD CHANGED BUT NOT, IT SEEMED, THE ATTITUDES OF THE BRITISH GOVERNMENT.

When they left the Bahamas in 1945, the Windsors were unaware that they had also left their last official position. The Duke petitioned the new Labour Government under Clement Attlee in 1946 for appointments which he saw as befitting his station – ambassador at large in the United States or Viceroy of India. Instead he was offered the Governor-Generalship of Australia – Britain's second-largest dominion and by no means an obscure posting as the Bahamas had been. Unwisely, he turned it down.

With no official capacity to occupy their time, by the late 1940s the Windsors were adrift in a monotonous social cycle as they moved between the United States and their homes in Paris and the South of France. The Duke could never understand why he was turned down for diplomatic office, but the reasons were always the same.

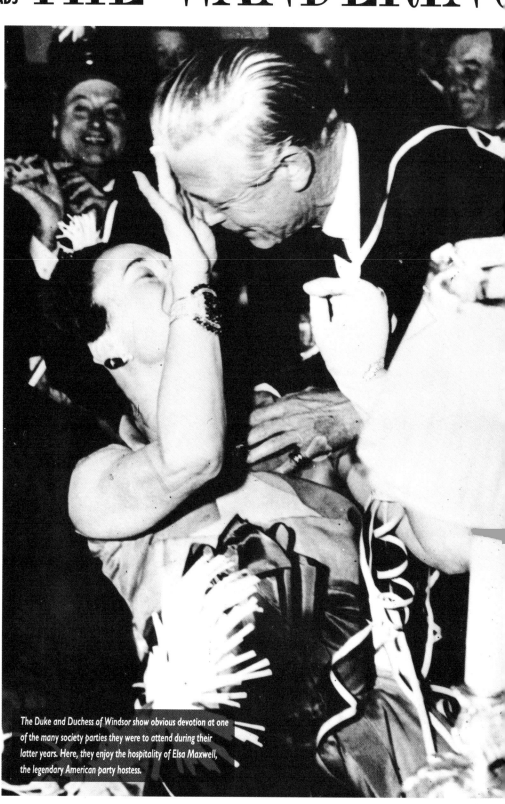

The Duke and Duchess of Windsor show obvious devotion at one of the many society parties they were to attend during their latter years. Here, they enjoy the hospitality of Elsa Maxwell, the legendary American party hostess.

DATEFILE

JANUARY 1946
The Duke petitions the government unsuccessfully for diplomatic office

MARCH 1951
The Duke's autobiography, *A King's Story*, is published

JUNE 3, 1967
The Windsors attend their first official ceremony with the Royal Family

MAY 29, 1972
The Duke of Windsor dies in France

JAN '46-MAY '72

YEARS

SIR OSWALD MOSLEY
*His house—a little gem su...
by allotments.*

The Windsors ar
Mosley's lunch
guests

A CLOSE friendship has developed in the past two years between the Duke of Windsor and Sir Oswald Mosley. The two men have of course known each other since pre-war days, but it is only in recent years especially since they have become near neighbours that they have

A ten-minute drive takes them to their neighbours' house 'Le Temple de la Gloire'

Almost invariably after a quiet period when perhaps attitudes to them were changing, he or the Duchess would do something that would confirm the belief that they were not to be trusted.

PUBLIC GAFFE

One such incident occurred in 1946, when the Windsors were staying in England. A thief got into their suite at Claridge's and stole the bulk of the Duchess's jewellery. Outraged, the Windsors made no secret of their belief that the burglary was some dark plot orchestrated by the royal family to regain Queen Alexandra's jewels. To make matters worse, there were counter-claims that the Duchess had exaggerated what was missing.

The most public gaffe was made by the Duchess. When asked by the Press which pieces she had managed to save because she was wearing them at the time, she said pointedly, 'A fool would know that with tweeds or other daytime clothes one wears gold, and that with evening clothes one wears platinum.' At a time of post-war rationing, these sentiments and the way they were expressed offered no encouragement to the British government to take her seriously as a potential British diplomat's wife, however exalted he may have been.

BAD COMPANY

Perhaps a more disturbing indication of the Windsors' unsuitability for holding high representational office was their choice of company. They seemed to be severely lacking in judgement as to who would be politically and morally acceptable to the British royal family, government and people.

In the early 1950s, when the Windsors had settled permanently in Paris, the Duke renewed his old friendship with Sir Oswald Mosley, the leader of the British Union of Fascists in the 1930s. Scenes of the clashes between his 'Blackshirts' and Jews in the East End of London were forever etched in the minds of the British people. Yet the Windsors chose to enjoy a public friendship with the Englishman most clearly associated with Nazism.

On the moral front, the Windsors' most damaging liaison began in 1947, when they befriended Jimmy Donahue, the fabulously rich and ostentatious homosexual who lived for his sex-life. He spent vast fortunes on male prostitutes and arranging homosexual orgies. During one of these he allegedly castrated a young GI, but the case never came to court because his mother paid the victim a quarter of a million dollars to keep quiet. The Windsors' relationship with Donahue made the headlines in America and the scandal also reached British ears.

FAMOUS FRIENDS

In the latter years of their life together, the Windsors were most famous for the parties they gave and those they attended. They were attracted to people who were rich and successful. Noel Coward, who became their friend in later life, recalled how he had been cut by the Duke in earlier days before he was famous. Multi-millionaires featured on the guest list, people such as the banking heir, George Baker and the railroad tycoon, Robert R Young.

Wallis' dress designers, Coco Chanel and Schiaperelli, became good friends, as did the interior decorator Elsa Mendl. However, all these people were the icing on the cake. Cecil Beaton dismissed most of their friends as 'downright trashy'.

Wallis was an excellent hostess. Herself a talented cook, she knew how to put a dinner party together superbly. Guests were served by footmen dressed in scarlet livery, and each guest had an enamelled box by his or her plate containing cigarettes or a small gift.

The Duke's 70th birthday epitomised the kind of occasions they liked: a dinner dance for about 200 on a *bateau mouche* on the Seine, the climax of the evening being the arrival of a 10-foot-tall birthday cake on a second boat. Most importantly, they did not foot the bill: Nathan Cummings, a self-made millionaire with his company Consolidated Foods, threw the party for them.

Above: Not all the Windsors' companions were 'downright trash'. Here, Wallis is seated next to future president, John F Kennedy.

Above: The Duke working on his autobiography in January 1950. A King's Story was published in 1951 and earned the Duke a much-needed one million dollars.

The three became so inseparable that rumours began to circulate, involving both the Duke and Wallis. She was often seen out with Donahue alone, and some said she was having an affair with him, that he was really bisexual. Others said that the Duke and Jimmy were lovers, and Wallis merely provided the cover for the affair.

It doesn't matter that both of these rumours were probably false, that Jimmy was useful to both of them in their boring exile both as entertainer

> *Donahue destroyed everything he touched..... he destroyed your reputation*
>
> Jerome Zerbe to Wallis

and subsidiser (he paid for everything out of his vast Woolworth fortune). What matters is that their actions gave substance to the rumours. They went everywhere with Donahue and insisted that their friends invited him too. But many people found Donahue's excesses too much to take and dropped their connection with the Windsors. Years later a friend, Jerome Zerbe, said to the Duchess that Donahue 'was a man who destroyed everything he touched. He destroyed your reputation.'

Their *ménage* ended in 1954 when, at a restaurant, Donahue kicked Wallis so hard that he drew blood. The Duke ordered him out of their lives and he, presumably as tired of them as they were becoming of him, made no attempt to apologise.

INSIDE VIEW

THE HOUSE IN THE BOIS DE BOULOGNE

In 1953 the Windsors moved into 4 Route du Champ d'Entrâinement in the Bois de Boulogne. It was a small château, set in two acres of ground surrounded by a high spiked fence and a hedge of rhododendrons. The City of Paris leased it to them at a token rent of about 300 francs (about £10.00 then) per year.

The front door opened on to a gracious marble hall. The high-ceilinged drawing room was decorated in pale blue and silver – including the grand piano. At one end the drawing room gave on to the dining room, with its tiny musicians' gallery, and at the other onto the library, dominated by Gerald Brockhurst's painting of the Duchess.

Their separate suites were on the next floor, the Duchess's in pale tangerine. In its adjoining dressing room hung her exquisitely made clothes – each outfit tagged with the date and occasion when last it was worn – accompanied by around 200 pairs of shoes. The Duke's more spartan quarters were filled with photographs on every surface, 23 of them of the Duchess.

They had a large number of scatter cushions throughout the house,

Main picture: The Windsors' house in the Bois de Boulogne, where they entertained in regal style – even their footmen wore royal livery. Inset: The dining room, whose walls were decorated with Chinese-style paintings.

embroidered with mottoes. Many of these were the work of the Duke, whose hobby was needlepoint, taught to him by his mother, Queen Mary, when he was a boy.

Below: The elegantly furnished drawing room of the Windsors' Bois de Boulogne chateâu. Photographs of the Duke as a young man adorn the antique furniture.

He died in 1966, possibly having committed suicide, with a large quantity of alcohol and barbiturates in his system.

It was during this time that both the Duke and Duchess brought out their autobiographies – unheard of in royal circles. *A King's Story* appeared in 1951 and told of the Duke's early life up until the moment of exile. The Duchess' account of her life, *The Heart Has Its Reasons*, was published in 1956.

In February 1952, George VI died aged only 56, prematurely aged by the stresses of kingship and World War II. His widowed queen, now the Queen Mother, began to refer to Wallis as the woman who 'killed my husband'. Not surprisingly, the Duke alone was invited to the funeral. When his mother, Queen Mary, was dying the next year, he again came alone to be at her side when she died.

ROYAL SNUB

The Duke had hoped that with the passing of his brother and mother there would be a real possibility of him at last finding proper work to do for his country. His niece, Queen Elizabeth II, was young and inexperienced, and he felt that surely now his help would become a necessity. However, the Duke was not invited to her Coronation in June 1953, a snub which signalled that he and Wallis were still not acceptable.

An incident in December the same year would seem to substantiate that view. The Windsors were celebrating New Year's Eve in a New York Club when, at midnight, a tray of paper crowns was circulating. The Duchess snatched two for herself and the Duke. They were photographed wearing them, and as they left the club the Duchess picked them off their heads and said, 'Coronation's over!' With the accession of a monarch who was not

directly involved with the crisis that led to his abdication, the Duke hoped that he might win for Wallis the title of Royal Highness which he so dearly wanted for her and which, he felt, had been unreasonably denied her. To his bitter disappointment, his requests were turned down, and the realisation must finally have come upon him that attitudes were very unlikely to change.

RELAXING OF ATTITUDES

It is understandable that when Queen Elizabeth first came to the throne, she would pay attention to her mother's and her late father's wishes and continue the policy of keeping her uncle, the Duke, at arm's length. But later, she was responsible for much of the relaxing of attitudes towards him. She sent him a telegram on his 70th birthday in 1964, and visited them both when they came to London for the Duke to have an operation on his eye.

She encouraged the younger members of the family, such as the late Prince William of Gloucester, the Duke and Duchess of Kent, and

Above: Wallis and the Duke pose with paper crowns at a New Year's party in New York, December 1953. Left: This is the nearest the Windsors got to the Coronation of Queen Elizabeth II in June 1953. The Duke passes a tray of biscuits at the home of an American heiress, where he and Wallis watched the ceremony on television from the other side of the Atlantic.

Princess Alexandra, to see the Duke and Duchess when they were visiting Paris. Previously, members of the royal family had been discouraged, if not forbidden, to do so.

In 1966, the Queen offered the first official acknowledgement of the Duchess. She invited both of them to the unveiling of a commemorative plaque to Queen Mary. The Duke and Duchess rode in the official procession and were received afterwards by the Queen – and the Queen Mother.

DEATH-BED RECONCILIATION

By spring 1972 it was clear the Duke was very ill. A lifetime of smoking had resulted in cancer of the throat, and he was dying. On 18 May, the Queen called in on her uncle at his house in the Bois de Boulogne during her state visit to France. She was accompanied by Prince Philip and Prince Charles, and they were photographed with the Duchess before going up to the Duke's sickroom. It is said that true to his sense of protocol, he forced himself from his sickbed so he might receive the sovereign with due propriety. Eleven days later he was dead, one month before his 78th birthday.

CLOSE-UP THE FUNERAL OF THE DUKE OF WINDSOR

The military plane carrying the Duke's body was met at RAF Benson, Oxfordshire, by a guard of honour, and was taken to Windsor Castle. Crowds queued for a full day to see the Duke lying in state in St George's Chapel – 2000 people an hour filed past the body to pay their respects.

Wallis had been too ill to accompany the coffin. She flew to Heathrow, where she was met by Lord Mountbatten. He accompanied her to Buckingham Palace where she was to stay as the Queen's personal guest. Wallis did not feel able to attend the Trooping the Colour ceremony, which included a tribute to the Duke, but she watched the Queen ride out at the head of her Household Cavalry from her front window on the Mall. That evening she went with Prince Charles and Mountbatten to see her husband lying in state in the chapel at Windsor.

The funeral was scheduled for 5 June. During the service, the Duchess sat next to the Queen, who helped her find her place in the hymn book when she became confused. The Queen Mother gently took Wallis' arm after the service, as if to show that there was no longer bad feeling between them.

The Duke was buried in the royal burial place at Frogmore, a site he had chosen himself, beneath an old plane tree surrounded by hawthorns, flowering cherries, wild azaleas, and rhododendrons. It was near the garden where he and his brother, Bertie (George VI), used to play as children.

Daily Mail logo

MONDAY, MAY 29, 1972   3p

Duchess of Windsor will fly back with him in RAF plane–and accepts Queen's invitation to stay at Buckingham Palace

THE DUKE COMES HOM[E]

By BRIAN PARK, CHRISTOPHER WHITE and JAMES NICHOLSON

THE DUCHESS OF WINDSOR will fly in the RAF plane bringing the body of the Duke back to England on Wednesday.

Left: Wallis watches the Trooping the Colour from Buckingham Palace, two days before the Duke's funeral. One minute's silence was observed as an 'Act of Remembrance'.

ROCK HUDSON

Rock Hudson was one of the last great romantic screen idols, adored by more than a generation of movie-goers. But in 1985, the carefully cultivated image of a lifetime was shattered by the news that he was a life-long homosexual, dying slowly from AIDS. For many people, it was the first time the disease had taken on a human dimension and it helped to dispel more than five years of public ignorance. Nearly four years after his death, Hudson was at the centre of the AIDS debate again, when an ex-lover took the film star's estate to court on the grounds that Hudson had

THE LAST MONTHS
ONE
SHATTERED

IN 1985, ROCK HUDSON'S FRIENDS AND FANS WERE MYSTIFIED AS THE FILM STAR WENT THROUGH A PERIOD OF DRAMATIC PHYSICAL DETERIORATION. THE EXPLANATION CAME IN JULY, WHEN IT WAS ANNOUNCED THAT HUDSON HAD BECOME THE FIRST CELEBRITY KNOWN TO HAVE AIDS

Paris: Thursday 25 July 1985. Yanou Collart, a French film publicist, walked down the entrance steps of the American Hospital, where a crowd of journalists, photographers and television news crews had been keeping vigil. She read a brief statement: 'Mr. Rock Hudson has Acquired Immune Deficiency Syndrome, which was diagnosed over a year ago in the United States.'

The media horde stood in complete silence during the announcement, then broke up in a noisy dash. Within hours the story was on the evening TV news; the next morning newspaper headlines around the world screamed 'ROCK HAS AIDS'.

> *It's difficult to believe the man is alive. He looks well over a hundred years old.*
> Hudson's nurse at the University of California Medical Center

DATEFILE

JULY 20 1985
Hudson flies to Paris for treatment at the Pasteur Institute

JULY 25 1985
Official announcement given to the press that Hudson has AIDS

JULY 30 1985
Hudson flies back to Los Angeles on a chartered jumbo jet

OCTOBER 2 1985
Hudson dies at home

JULY-OCT '85

MYTH

Rumours about Rock Hudson's obviously poor health had been circulating for months. At the beginning of the year, his appearance on the top-rated TV soap opera 'Dynasty' had shocked fans. The strapping hunk everyone knew was gone; in his place there stood a startlingly thin and inexplicably aged stranger.

Then, in mid-July, Hudson left his Los Angeles home – known to all as The Castle – for Carmel, California, to appear as the first special guest on his favourite leading lady's new TV series, 'Doris Day's Best Friends'. By this time he was desperately ill but still denying it, apparently even to himself.

Everyone present was badly shaken by what they saw; a grey, emaciated, dazed Hudson who was so feeble he could scarcely walk. Rock's normal weight, as a 6ft 5in man, had been around 105 kilos for years; at this time he was down to about 70 kilos. The programme, on which Rock and Doris cheerfully shared reminiscences of their friendship and famous screen partnership, went ahead but was filmed at a slow, subdued pace. Doris said: 'It was devastating. I didn't show what I was feeling, but it broke my heart.'

HOPE OF A CURE

On 20 July, the day after Hudson had returned home exhausted from Carmel, Mark Miller, his personal assistant and friend of more than 35 years, cajoled, urged and half carried him on to a plane for Paris in a last-ditch attempt to seek treatment at the world-renowned Pasteur Institute.

A year earlier, Hudson had seen Dr. Dominique Dormont in Paris and had been treated with the experimental drug HPA-23 for two months. Dr. Dormont had had some encouraging cases of the virus responsible for AIDS being suppressed or slowed in his long-term patients. Hudson was advised by the doctor to continue with the HPA-23 treatment for several more months, but he elected to return to America, where, in October, he had begun filming the television series, 'Dynasty'.

On the last, desperate flight to Paris, Hudson was accompanied by his physical trainer, Ron Channell, who was unaware of the nature of Rock's illness. On 21 July, Hudson collapsed at the Ritz Hotel. Dr. Dormont was away for the weekend and had no idea Hudson was in Paris.

Left: Publicist Yanou Collart reads a statement to the press at the American Hospital of Paris where Rock Hudson was being treated for AIDS. It acknowledged publicly, for the first time, that the star had Acquired Immune Deficiency Syndrome. Above: Earlier, during an episode of the television series 'Dynasty', Rock had to kiss actress Linda Evans, knowing he had AIDS – an act that caused him great anxiety.

LOYAL FRIEND

Hudson first met Tom Clark (above, with Elizabeth Taylor), a publicist for MGM Pictures, in the late 1960s. Eventually he moved into Hudson's home, known as The Castle, where they lived together for 10 years. Clark provided stability and loyalty at a time when Hudson was filled with anxieties about ageing, his fading film career, his switch to television work and his heart trouble.

Clark was his closest confidant. He supervised the household and arranged a pleasant social life with elegant dinner parties and lively special functions.

Then their relationship went a route familiar to many. There were ugly rows, culminating in Clark moving out late in 1983.

In 1985, Hudson took Clark out of his will. Nevertheless, when Hudson's terminal condition was made known, Clark went to the Los Angeles hospital and they made their peace. When Hudson came home, Clark was with him and remained at his side taking care of him and what was left of his life, until the end. It was Clark who finally had to fight off the press hounds from Rock's corpse to guard Hudson's dignity.

CLOSE-UP

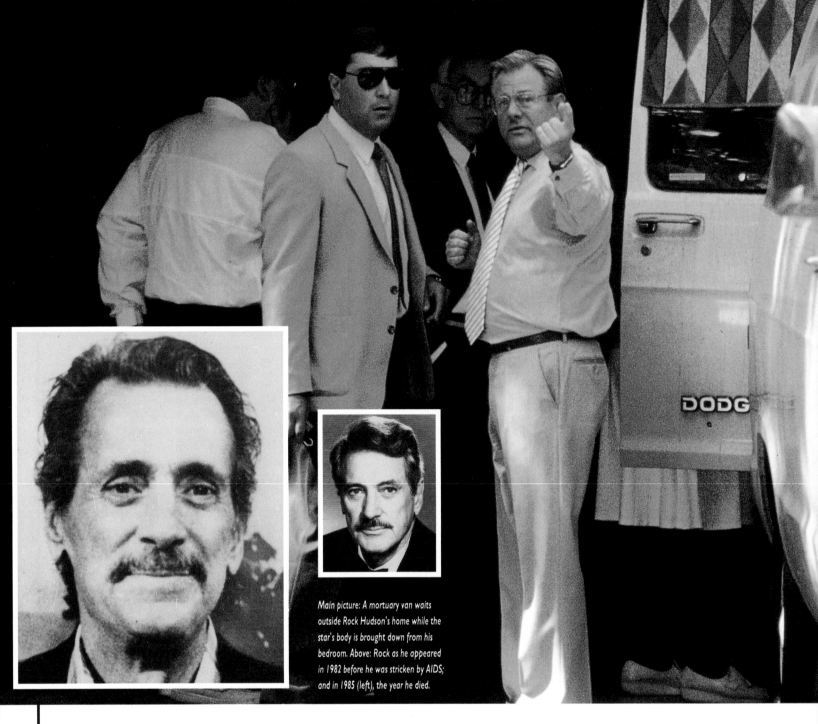

Main picture: A mortuary van waits outside Rock Hudson's home while the star's body is brought down from his bedroom. Above: Rock as he appeared in 1982 before he was stricken by AIDS; and in 1985 (left), the year he died.

Not knowing what to do, Channell rang Miller in Los Angeles, and then had Hudson rushed to the American Hospital. Knowing only that Hudson suffered from a heart condition, and had undergone surgery in 1981, the doctors assumed that the problem had returned. They admitted him to their cardiology unit and began tests.

As Mark Miller raced to Paris, the tests soon revealed the full truth. The hospital administrators were upset. It was not their policy to admit patients suffering from AIDS .

A lengthy conference was held at the hospital between medical staff, Miller, Dr. Dormont, and the publicist Yanou Collart – who had been enlisted from Los Angeles to deal with the growing army of press besieging the hospital.

Hudson's weight was reportedly down to around 57 kilos by now, and he was too weak for the HPA-23 treatment. Eventually it was agreed he would stay in the American Hospital until he was strong enough to be moved, and that a public statement would have to be made.

THE TRUTH REVEALED

The news was taken to Hudson in his private room, where he lay unaware of the growing storm of controversy and too weak to care. Believing that he had but a few days to live, and after 35 years of cherishing his matinée idol image and concealing his homosexuality, he was weary of the effort. Collart read him the simple press statement, and he replied: 'Okay. Go out and give it to the dogs.'

Thus Rock Hudson became the first celebrity publicly acknowledged to have been afflicted with AIDS. Media coverage ranged from 'Star has got the deadly gay plague' and 'Who will it strike next?' reports, to serious political commentaries on the spread of AIDS and the need for governments to address themselves to the problem.

The gay community, whose calls for action and funds to fight AIDS had met with little response for five years, saw in Hudson's case a turning point in public sympathies. And, as the editor of an influential gay newspaper, Brian Jones of San Francisco's *Bay Area Reporter*, poignantly observed: 'Yesterday, most Americans didn't know anyone with AIDS. Today they do.'

In his hospital bed, Hudson apologised to Mark Miller: 'I'm leaving you with a mess. Believe me, it's going to be a real mess. I'm sorry.' They were surprised by what happened in the first days following the public statement. Along with a telephone call from President Reagan, and close

> *I'm leaving you with a mess. Believe me, it's going to be a real mess. I'm sorry.*
>
> Rock Hudson to his friend, Mark Miller

INSIDE VIEW

'ROCKABYE' AND 'BESSIE'

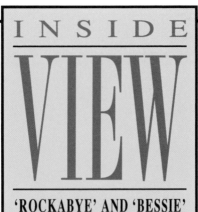

The deep and enduring friendship between Rock Hudson and Elizabeth Taylor began in 1955 when they starred together in the Texan family epic, *Giant*. The two hit it off immediately, and Liz found herself extremely attracted to Rock. She soon realised he was not so inclined, but they were happy working together and passed the tedious off-camera time on location in Marfa, Texas, with such pranks as inventing chocolate martinis and getting so drunk that they had to keep running off the set between scenes to be sick.

Their pleasure in each other's company continued over 30 years. She called him Rockabye and he called her Bessie.

Her devotion to him in his final months was typical of the gutsy Taylor, but she refused to characterise it as anything but his due: 'He was my brother. I loved him.'

friends like Elizabeth Taylor, came telegrams from stars like Frank Sinatra, Marlene Dietrich, even Madonna. The hospital was also deluged with flowers, get-well cards, fan letters and messages of support from more than 30,000 well-wishers.

But the sympathy could not help Hudson. On 30 July, after the doctors concluded there was nothing that could be done for him, he was flown back to Los Angeles on a privately chartered Boeing 747 jumbo jet.

A TIME FOR FRIENDS

At Los Angeles Airport, the wraith-like Hudson was carried by the sombre group to a waiting helicopter and taken to the University of California Medical Center. Hudson stayed at the hospital until 24 August. Mail for him kept flooding in from all over the world; security guards had to be engaged around the clock to keep away journalists and fans. Mark Miller and Elizabeth Taylor put together a visiting roster for the genuine friends who were permitted to see him, although he was unaware of much that was happening. Finally he was discharged to spend his final days at home.

Tom Clark, who had shared Rock's home for 10 years until they parted in 1983, moved back into The Castle to care for him until the end. Elizabeth Taylor came regularly, always cheerful when she was at Hudson's side, but sobbing in distress when she left. Roddy McDowall, Carol Burnett, film producer Ross Hunter and comedienne Martha Raye were among those admitted to sit with him, as was a Catholic priest, Father Tom Sweeney.

Rallying to the crusade against AIDS was suddenly glamorous. Late in September, a glittering crowd of celebrities attended a fund-raising dinner organised by the tireless Elizabeth Taylor and others. Certainly, it was a tribute to Hudson's popularity in Tinsel Town.

On 2 October 1985, just short of his 60th birthday, Rock Hudson died. Almost immediately, his skeletal body – he weighed less than 44 kilos – became the centrepiece of a nightmarish scene that might have come out of a tragi-comedy. Film director Ross Hunter arrived at The Castle gate in tears as attendants struggled to make the body's legs, protruding from the back of the mortuary van, fit inside.

Hunter fainted, and Tom Clark was forced to straddle Hudson's body and hold the back door of the van closed as press photographers leaped on to the roof of the vehicle, pounding on the sides and demanding to photograph Hudson's remains.

FINAL TRIBUTES

Clark stayed with Hudson's body at the Glenview Mortuary, maintaining his vigil until the body was cremated – four hours after Rock's death – and his ashes locked in a vault. There were tributes galore from the film and TV world, including those from Ronald Reagan, Elizabeth Taylor, Doris Day, and Linda Evans.

Two weeks later, the yacht *Tasia II* slipped into the Catalina Channel off the Southern California coast. Tom Clark scattered Rock's ashes over the water. He and the friends who tossed flowers into the waves must have felt this was the end.

But there was far more to come. Within days of Hudson's death, his former lover, Marc Christian, would file a lawsuit against the estate of Rock Hudson, and Mark Miller. The proceedings over the next four years were to expose the intimate details of Rock Hudson's double life, and create drastic new legal implications for AIDS sufferers.

Mark Miller was Rock Hudson's personal assistant and close friend for more than 35 years. Rock said of him: 'He's my man Friday. He makes me laugh. He's my best friend, drunk or sober.'

ROCK HUDSON WAS NOT A BORN ACTOR. IN HIS FIRST FILM, IT TOOK HIM 38 ATTEMPTS TO GET HIS ONE AND ONLY LINE RIGHT. YET WITHIN NINE YEARS HE HAD BECOME THE MOST SOUGHT AFTER STAR IN HOLLYWOOD

THE LAST ROMANTIC

Like many a studio player before him, Rock Hudson was signed for his good looks. Then the handsome young 'he-man' had to learn his profession in public – before the camera. His one-line bit in *Fighter Squadron* (1948) showed little promise of the fabulous career that was to be his. He fluffed his line ('Pretty soon you are going to have to get a bigger blackboard') in 38 takes, and it was another year before he got a second chance. After a passable screen test, Universal Pictures signed him to a five-year contract in 1949, when he was 23 years old.

LEARNING THE TRADE

Universal still practised the old studio method of grooming stars. While giving Rock bit parts in seven routine B pictures in 1950 they kept him busy with lessons in acting, fencing, boxing and singing. Along with the other juveniles and ingenues in the Universal 'school' – Tony Curtis, Jeff Chandler and Piper Laurie among them – he posed endlessly for publicity shots, escorted starlets to premieres and went to all the 'right parties'. He was paid $125 a week.

Way down the cast lists, he began to be noticed with *Winchester '73* in which he played a bare-chested Indian

buck with his hair in plaits. By 1952, in *Bend of the River*, he had worked his way up to fourth in the billing and was at his ease in a string of westerns. He reached top-billing in 1954 in westerns and swashbuckling fare like *The Golden Blade* and *Taza, Son of Cochise.*

Rock had made 25 pictures when he made the leap to major stardom. He achieved recognition as the top romantic idol of his generation in the first of several overwrought melodramas he made with director

In Giant (1956), Rock Hudson (left, with co-star Elizabeth Taylor), played a racist Texas ranch-owner who reforms by the end of the film. During filming, Hudson and Taylor became close friends.

Douglas Sirk. The film was *Magnificent Obsession.* His co-star for his entry to the big-time was Oscar-winner, Jane Wyman, ex-wife of Ronald Reagan. The story was pure soap opera: Hudson played a wealthy playboy inadvertently responsible for the death of Wyman's husband and her subsequent blinding.

Stricken with remorse, the playboy falls in love with her, returns to medical school, becomes a brilliant surgeon devoted to good works and finally performs the operation that saves her life and restores her sight. Audiences adored it.

A GUIDING HAND

Wyman was a real professional and helped carry Rock through the film. He never forgot it. 'Jane Wyman couldn't have been nicer. Jane knew that I was anxious, nervous. And I'd go high on my lines, need 30, 40 takes. Years later I said to her: "You really went out of your way, Jane, to be nice to me when you didn't have to. I want you to know that I do know that, and I appreciate it and I love you for it, and thank you." Then she said something inter-

Left: Rock gets into an amorous clinch with Gina Lollobrigida in Come September (1961). Above: Caught in furs in Lover Come Back (1962).

esting to me. She said: "It was handed to me by somebody. I handed it to you. And now it's your turn to hand it to somebody else".'

Within a year they were teamed again in another tearjerker, *All That Heaven Allows*, for its time a rather daring weepie about a wealthy widow who falls in love with her much younger gardener. It too was a hit, and Hudson was rewarded with a new contract. He was now earning $3,000 a week.

In 1955, the film industry was nevertheless surprised when director George Stevens, casting the sprawling Texan saga of cattlemen and oil barons from Edna Ferber's blockbuster novel, *Giant*, passed over such stars as William Holden and Gregory Peck to borrow Rock from Universal for the role of Bick Benedict. Hudson was thrilled, and rightly so. His performance, which required him to age over 40 years and pitted him against the scene-stealing legend, James Dean, earned

Hudson his only Oscar nomination for Best Actor. It remained his favourite film.

Giant was the biggest box-office hit of 1956, and the four pictures Rock made in quick succession – most notably Douglas Sirk's *Written On The Wind*, which paired him with Lauren Bacall – made him number one at the box-office by the end of 1957. As one of Hudson's co-stars was to observe: 'He became a star; then he learned to act.'

SERIOUS DRAMA

More confident now that he was established, he was keen to tackle more serious drama. The re-make of the Ernest Hemingway classic, *A Farewell To Arms*, was a disappointment to him - a troubled, unhappy production and not a terribly good film, although it did well enough thanks to his popularity.

It was becoming clear, perhaps even to himself, that he did not have the depth to be a great actor. Yet he was by this time a competent one. More importantly, there was something fundamentally likeable about him. He was not equipped to play villains or losers – he simply did

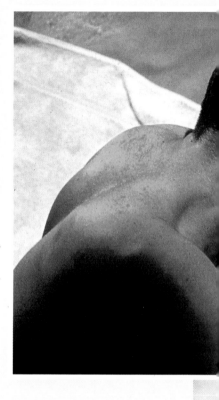

not look like a baddie or Joe Average. Women wanted a man like him, and men wanted to be a man like him.

MOVING INTO COMEDY

At his most popular in weepies, Hudson was reluctant to try comedy. After meeting Doris Day, he agreed to have a go with Universal's low-budget bid to bring back the romantic, battle-of-the-sexes type of comedy that had been big in the 30s and 40s. The result, *Pillow Talk* (1959), became Universal's biggest money-spinner and made Hudson box-office number one again.

After that he was wooed by most of the major studios and offered all types of parts. But he was still happy at Universal. 'It was a wonderful studio,' he would recall. 'The organisation of the studio system was wonderful. You had the publicity department, you had this department, you had that department, at your fingertips.

'They took care of everything – the house you lived in,

Something of Value (1957), directed by Richard Brooks, was filmed in Kenya and was based on the bestselleing novel by Robert Ruark about that country's Mau Mau uprising.

THE MAN WHO DISCOVERED ROCK HUDSON

Henry Willson (right), a theatrical agent, was working as a talent scout for the David O. Selznick studios in 1947. When a gangling Roy Fitzgerald walked through his door, he knew that here was someone he could make a star. 'I was awfully impressed with his size,' Willson recalled. He decided to offer him a contract there and then.

Willson, a plump but dapper man, was a flagrant and aggressive homosexual, greedy for young men and money. He enjoyed plenty of both in the 1950s when his speciality was discovering beefcake actors and

dreaming up nicknames for them. He explained how Rock got his name: 'I thought of the biggest thing around and the Rock of Gibraltar is what came to mind; Hudson came from the river.'

Willson squired him around Hollywood and got him noticed. As Hudson's star rose, Willson clung to him jealously. He made a fortune from Rock, but his complacency in seeking good roles for his client finally drove Hudson away, in 1962, to another agent.

Henry Willson died penniless, in 1978, in a home for show business down-and-outs.

A SPARKLING PARTNERSHIP

The screen partnership of Doris Day and Rock Hudson is one of the most famous in cinema history. Their three romantic comedies - *Pillow Talk*, *Lover Come Back*, and *Send Me No Flowers*, made between 1959 and 1964 - were hugely popular hits and epitomise the early 60s. Light, fluffy concoctions, these sex comedies were not so much sexy as coy and suggestive, but together Day, with her witty comedy talent, and Hudson, with his mischievous air, had an exceptional screen chemistry.

The pair genuinely loved working together. Listing his own favourite films, Hudson invariably named *Giant*, *Seconds*, *Pillow Talk*, and *Lover Come Back*. 'I love the comedies. Doris and I had a ball,' he said.

The feeling was mutual for Doris: 'I adored Rock Hudson. He was one of the most professional actors I ever worked with. He was one of my best friends too. When Rock and I were together, it was just laughter all the way.' They too had pet names for each other. He called her Eunice ('Don't ask me why', she'd laugh), and she called him Ernie; 'because he was certainly no Rock'.

In 1954, Rock played the title role in *Taza, Son of Cochise*, a frontier melodrama set in Arizona and filmed in 3-D and Technicolor.

the shopping, the gardening. If you didn't like the cook that you had, you told the studio; somebody else was hired. It was all done for you; so that the only thing you had to be concerned about was your performance.' Hudson was now earning in excess of $400,000 a picture and slowed down to about two films a year. A few of them were action adventures, but he allowed himself to get stuck in a line of saucy comedies, including two follow-ups with Doris Day and others with Gina Lollobrigida, Claudia Cardinale and Leslie Caron.

CHANGE OF ROLE

His best film of the 60s, arguably of his career, was a radical departure, and the only picture he made away from Universal in 10 years. John Frankenheimer's, *Seconds*, was a chilling suspense drama about a wealthy, elderly man given a new, younger body and identity, only to find himself in a sinister web of deceit and conspiracy.

The film flopped on its release, which was a bitter blow to Hudson. It now stands

Rock Hudson meets an alien in 'The Martian Chronicles', a 1979 television production.

as a cult favourite, and most serious critics regard Hudson's performance as his finest.

From then on it was mostly downhill. Times and tastes had changed. Clint Eastwood, Paul Newman and Steve McQueen, were the Big Three in Hollywood. The studios went into a catastrophic financial decline. Alistair MacLean's cold war thriller, *Ice Station Zebra* (1960), was his last real hit.

Still only in his forties, Hudson was of a type no longer in fashion. He would make less than a dozen films during the rest of his life. But television success, which eluded many other film stars of his generation, was to revive his career.

A GOOD-LOOKING BOY FROM NOWHERE HAD BEEN BUILT UP INTO A STAR AT UNIVERSAL STUDIOS; BUT AS RUMOURS BEGAN TO SURFACE ABOUT HIS QUESTIONABLE SEX LIFE, DRASTIC MEASURES WERE REQUIRED TO PROTECT ROCK HUDSON'S REPUTATION

Rock Hudson was born Roy Harold Scherer Junior on 17 November 1925 in a typical Midwestern American town, Winnetka, Illinois. His father, Roy Senior, who was a garage mechanic with his own small business, was of Swiss-German extraction; his mother Katherine – universally known as Kay – was of Anglo-Irish descent. 'Junior', as he was dubbed, weighed an average five-and-a-half pounds at birth, showing no sign that he would grow into a giant.

Indeed, he appeared to be a thoroughly unremarkable boy. His first few years were uneventful and happy enough, with visits to his grandparents' farm, later a favourite memory for him. When his father's business failed during the Depression, Roy Senior abandoned his wife and their only child to find work in California.

Kay and Junior made the long journey to find him a year later, but he refused to return and requested a divorce. Ironically it was on the bus

Rock Hudson (above) sunning himself at home (1953) and (right) as an 'avid record collector' (1952). Universal Pictures' publicity department kept his face before the public with lots of such photographs of him in standard poses.

DATEFILE

NOVEMBER 17 1925
Rock Hudson, born Roy Harold Scherer in Winnetka, Illinois

MAY 11 1954
Premiere of Magnificent Obsession (the film which made Rock Hudson a star)

NOVEMBER 9 1955
Rock Hudson marries Phyllis Gates

NOV'25-NOV'55

NOWHERE

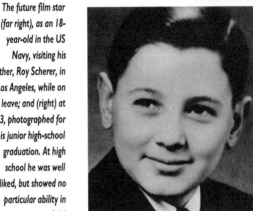

trip back to Illinois that Kay met her next husband, a US marine named Wallace Fitzgerald. He left the service and married Kay when Junior was eight. The boy legally became Roy Fitzgerald – the best thing, from his point of view, to come out of the marriage, since he was able to shed the nickname Junior, which he hated.

Fitzgerald worked at a series of odd jobs and was evidently abusive to both his wife and Roy. Roy found his escape going to the cinema and reading movie magazines; he began to nurture a secret desire to be a child star, and it was a dream he clung to. 'I could never freely say "I'm going to be an actor when I grow up", because that's just cissy stuff', he recalled.

The family was badly off financially. Kay supplemented their income with jobs as a waitress and as a telephone operator. Roy earned his pocket money as a newspaper delivery boy, grocery delivery boy, golf caddy, and chicken plucker.

When Roy was 15, his hated stepfather left for good. So there were no school plays or other activities for the skinny, good looking boy whose smile revealed a crooked tooth. Academically, Roy was average to indifferent.

The future film star (far right), as an 18-year-old in the US Navy, visiting his father, Roy Scherer, in Los Angeles, while on leave; and (right) at 13, photographed for his junior high-school graduation. At high school he was well liked, but showed no particular ability in any field.

He used to work at odd jobs every day after school to help his mother: 'She was mother, father and big sister to me', Rock said, 'and I was son and brother to her.'

NAVY SERVICE

At 18, fresh from school, Roy enlisted in the US Navy. It was early 1944, and after basic training he was sent to the South Pacific for the last year of World War II. He served as an airplane mechanic and saw little action. Discharged in 1946, Roy could not bear being back in Winnetka. Afraid to tell his mother he still dreamed of being a film star, he secretly wrote to his real father, Roy Scherer, asking if he could stay with him in Los Angeles. Scherer agreed, but the two did not get on. Scherer thought the acting bug was a mad fantasy and put Roy to work selling vacuum cleaners. That lasted three weeks, before he was sacked.

He was not accepted at university either – his school grades were too poor. So he took to haunting the film studio entrances, hoping to attract the attention of a producer, and supported himself as a lorry driver. Roy was shy, awkward and lonely, but at the suggestion of an acquaintance he invested in having photographs taken, and delivered them himself to every studio.

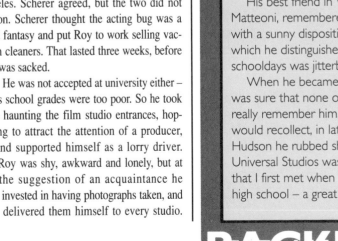

SCHOOLMATES

New Trier High School in Winnetka, Illinois, which Roy Fitzgerald (Rock Hudson) attended, was something of a breeding ground for Hollywood aspirants. Charlton Heston was in the year ahead, while Hugh O'Brian (TV's Wyatt Earp) was actually in the same class. Some years later, the vivacious red-headed actress, Ann-Margret, also attended the school.

His best friend in Winnetka, Jimmy Matteoni, remembered Roy as a prankster with a sunny disposition, but the only thing in which he distinguished himself in his schooldays was jitterbugging.

When he became Rock Hudson, the star was sure that none of his classmates would really remember him. However, O'Brian would recollect, in later years, that the Rock Hudson he rubbed shoulders with at Universal Studios was 'the same kind of guy that I first met when he was a freshman at high school – a great big, likeable warm guy.'

BACKDROP

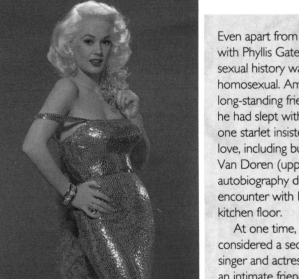

Even apart from his relationship with Phyllis Gates, Rock Hudson's sexual history was not exclusively homosexual. Among his many, long-standing friends were women he had slept with, and more than one starlet insisted they had made love, including busty blonde Mamie Van Doren (upper left) whose autobiography detailed a close encounter with Hudson on the kitchen floor.

At one time, Hudson considered a second marriage, to singer and actress Marilyn Maxwell, an intimate friend for years. They had had a sexual relationship, but he was frank with her about his lifestyle. They agreed that an open marriage – in which he would be free to have male partners as well – wouldn't be happy for either of them.

According to Hollywood legend, a classic but unsuccessful approach was made to Hudson in 1953 by the screen queen, Joan Crawford (lower left). She is supposed to have summoned the young Rock to dinner at her home, and over drinks proposed a moonlight dip. The story goes that, as Rock showered in the poolside cabana, Miss Crawford sprang in on him nude with the novel suggestion: 'Baby, just close your eyes and pretend I'm Clark Gable!'

By chance, an agent called Henry Willson, then a talent scout for David O. Selznick, laid eyes on the boy and liked what he saw. He signed the over-joyed Roy to an exclusive personal contract, got his teeth capped and undertook his Hollywood

Rock Hudson in London (1952) for the Royal Film Première, chatting to glamorous English actress Vivien Leigh (left).

education renaming him Rock Hudson, grooming him, promoting him – and seducing him.

Willson was not Hudson's first homosexual encounter. Many years later, he told friends he had secretly been attracted to men since childhood. When he was no more than nine years old, he said, an adult man had molested him. At the time, however, he told no one. He had frankly enjoyed the experience. In the navy there were more homosexual encounters, naturally furtive.

SIGNED UP BY UNIVERSAL

Soon after his arrival in Los Angeles, Hudson became friendly with a radio producer named Ken Hodge, who introduced him into a circle of homosexual friends who met regularly in comparative seclusion in Long Beach, California, where they partied and, with discretion, hung out at the beach. It was Hodge who encouraged Hudson to send his photograph around town, and surviving members of that Long Beach set believe it was he who dreamed up the name 'Rock Hudson'.

In any case, it was Willson who was Rock's champion in the industry. To celebrate their contract, Willson took Rock to dinner at the swanky Biltmore Hotel in Santa Barbara. Rock was so gauche, he later admitted, that he stacked the dinner dishes on the table when they had finished eating.

While showing off Rock around town, Willson persuaded veteran film director Raoul Walsh to give the boy a screen test. Walsh didn't need much persuading, remarking: 'Even if he can't do anything, he'll make good scenery.' When Walsh gave Hudson a line of dialogue to say in *Fighter Squadron*, Rock was so over-anxious he fluffed it 38 times. Nevertheless Walsh teamed with Willson to make Rock a star. Between them they provided Rock with lessons in acting, speech and movement, and helped him brush up on his social graces. Rock repaid the director by working as a handyman at Walsh's house.

In 1949, their efforts and Hudson's hard work paid off when Universal signed him to a five-year contract. Willson and Walsh recouped their investment in Hudson by selling their contract with him to the studio for $9000. Willson was not about to let him go, however. Remaining Hudson's agent, he made a practice of continually dropping by the studio, ringing him up, and taking Hudson to dinner to keep an eye on him and supervise his progress through the studio system.

WILL TO SUCCEED

At 23, Rock Hudson was very green when it came to acting, but he was determined to be a star and was prepared to work hard to achieve it, taking every opportunity the studio provided to train and improve himself. He did everything he was asked to do, virtually running from one set to another when playing three small-bit parts in different pictures being made simultaneously.

His single-mindedness paid off not only in stardom, but earned him a life-long reputation

throughout the industry for professionalism. He may not have been another Laurence Olivier, but as one actress said in his praise, 'He was one hell of a professional. We loved him; everybody did.' Hudson respected the people he worked with and was invariably, as director Robert Aldrich said of him, 'a pleasure to work with'.

Around the time that he was starting out at Universal, Hudson met the two friends who were to be his closest confidants for the rest of his life – Mark Miller and George Nader, a couple who had met each other in 1947 and remained together from then on. George Nader was a fellow contract actor at Universal, who had a long career as a

George Nader (right), a fellow actor at Universal, was a long-term close platonic friend of Hudson. (Below) Rock Hudson with his manager and mentor Henry Willson , in Italy, on the film set of A Farewell to Arms (1958).

story on the young actor, Rory Calhoun – another client of Willson's – revealing that he was a convicted criminal who had served time in prison for theft. Calhoun's budding career was knocked for six, and he firmly believed Willson 'sold him out' to *Confidential* in a deal to protect Hudson.

The magazine, however, was determined to find out something scandalous about Hudson, and other, more restrained, publications were beginning to publish articles about

Above: Rock Hudson dining out with his wife Phyllis during their brief marriage. Right: Co-starring with the legendary James Dean in a scene from the box-office hit film, Giant (1956).

character actor. Mark Miller, like Rock, was a midwestern boy, a farmer's son who trained to be an opera singer.

Miller and Nader were very much a couple – neither slept with Hudson – but the trio became firm friends. Three men out together was considered a combination safe from suspicion at the time. A trio did not look like a date, whereas two or four men looked 'questionable'.

Hudson's was an essentially boyish nature. In his early studio days his idea of a good time was letting his hair down with Miller and Nader, playing cards and parlour games, water skiing and barbecuing – he was notorious among his friends for burning everything.

As his stock with Universal and filmgoers rose through numerous 'T and S movies' – 'tits and sand', as he called them – he was given more and more coverage in fan magazines such as *Photoplay*, *Modern Screen* and *Movieland*, which were full of tips for female readers on how to nab Hollywood's hunkiest bachelor boy.

PHONEY DATES

Universal and Henry Willson fixed up 'dates' for Hudson that made for good 'fanzine' publicity; he escorted the likes of musical comedy actress Vera Ellen and singer/actress Marilyn Maxwell to premières and banquets. But in 1952, Hudson fell for a big handsome blond Korean War veteran named Jack Navaar, whom he met through Miller and

Nader. In 1953 they began living together. Hudson got Jack to quit his job at an aircraft company, and when he wasn't filming they could often be seen together surfing, eating out or going to films. Word spread around the studio that Navaar was Rock Hudson's 'wife'.

WILLSON INTERVENES

By the middle of 1954, the relationship was shaky. Like Henry Willson, Navaar was in the habit of ringing the studio to check on Hudson. There were stories that when Hudson was away, Navaar was throwing wild parties at their house. While Hudson was in Ireland making *Captain Lightfoot*, Henry Willson got rid of Jack. Willson enlisted his unsuspecting assistant, Phyllis Gates, to accompany Navaar on a trip to the midwest, while Willson told tales to Rock on the telephone.

Soon after, Navaar was approached by a representative from the notorious gossip-mongering magazine, *Confidential*, who offered $10,000 – a vast sum for cheque-book journalism at the time – for 'the goods' on Hudson. Jack Navaar declined. Willson got wind of the proposition, however. Whether it was a coincidence or a scheme of Willson's has never been proven, but the next issue of *Confidential* carried a 'shock horror'

Rock's 'failure to marry'. In the moral atmosphere of 1950s society, this line of speculation made everyone with a financial stake in Hudson's career sick with fear. If Hudson was likely to be labelled a 'fairy', he would just as likely find himself back in Winnetka plucking chickens.

In his search for a suitable wife for a movie star, Willson's gaze rested on his assistant, Phyllis Gates. Phyllis was a pretty, bright Minnesota farm girl who had worked as an air hostess before the lure of California sunshine brought her to Los Angeles at the end of 1959. She had briefly worked for a theatrical agency in New York, which brought her into contact with

Willson. Phyllis was undeniably an asset at his agency, with the poise and charm to help Willson by handling difficult clients and smoothing tense situations. Willson started throwing Phyllis and Rock together at dinners, drives and shopping expeditions.

While their relationship has been characterised as a 'sham', Phyllis and Rock would seem to have been genuinely keen on each other. Mark Miller and George Nader became friendly with Phyllis and witnessed ample demonstrations of puppyish love. Rock and Phyllis were openly physically affectionate and they had a sexual relationship – although, according to her recollections, Rock was, unsurprisingly, scarcely the suave, sophisticated woman-thriller of the silver screen.

NEWLYWEDS

Prompted by Willson, Rock popped the question and Phyllis found herself swept off to be married at the Biltmore in Santa Barbara. Rock's old school chum, Jim Matteoni, was flown in from Illinois to be best man, and Willson cued the newlyweds to ring the gossip columnists with the glad tidings, before letting the couple's mothers in on the news.

Confidential was stymied again. The marriage took place on 9 November 1955. With *Magnificent Obsession* and *Giant* under his belt, Rock was a solid gold star. Willson and the Universal executives could be pleased and relieved by the gushing publicity accorded the wedding. The honeymoon would be brief.

PERSPECTIVE

CONFIDENTIAL MAGAZINE

Sensational gossip-mongering reached previously unprintable depths with *Confidential* magazine, which was launched by publisher Robert Harrison in 1952. Fans with a craving for sleaze were kept agog by the magazine's colourful 'reportage' and outrageous claims. For one cover story, a detective was hired to tail Gary Cooper; the result was photographs of an adulterous tryst with young actress Ursula Andress at a down-market motel. Lana Turner, Frank Sinatra, Marilyn Monroe and Grace Kelly were among the magazine's favourite targets for 'exposés'.

Many of the stories were frankly libellous, but Harrison had a highly paid network of spies and held the upper hand, doing deals to suppress some tales for which he had evidence, and getting away with other dubious allegations.

He met his match in actress Maureen O'Hara, who *Confidential* claimed had been seen making love to a toy boy in the balcony seats at Grauman's Chinese Theatre. In 1957, Miss O'Hara took *Confidential* to court, and was able to produce evidence that she was actually in Europe when the unlikely incident was supposed to have occurred. The jury was divided, but *Confidential* had to pay damages. Liberace, Dorothy Dandridge, and others took actions and won out of court settlements which began to drain Harrison's coffers.

Soon after the 1957 trial, *Confidential* editor Howard Rushmore murdered his wife and committed suicide.

DURING THE EARLY 1980S, AIDS WAS ALLOWED TO SPREAD VIRTUALLY UNCHALLENGED, DUE TO BLINKERED SELF-INTEREST. ONLY A HANDFUL FOUGHT VAINLY TO BEAT AGAINST THE WALLS OF OBSTINACY – BUT THEY REMAINED UNHEARD

POLITICS

In May 1981, the *Morbidity and Mortality Weekly Report* prepared an article entitled '*Pneumocystis carinii* pneumonia in homosexual men'. When it was published, however, it received only a page-two slot, with the phrase 'homosexual men' removed: certain well-intentioned people, it seemed, were anxious neither to offend the gay community nor arouse antagonism towards it. Such an attitude, however, which set the trend for the following years, was dangerous because it obscured the real truth, thereby preventing the necessary actions from being taken.

PROMISCUITY

Without any restraints, promiscuity flourished. A survey taken in July 1982 found that the average infected patient had as many as 1,100 life-time sexual contacts. Some, however, might have as many as 20,000. It was not unusual for such people to experience up to 30 orgasms a night – provided there were plenty of 'poppers' (stimulants) available. Having sex with as many partners as possible meant experiencing life to the full – living 'in the fast lane'. From the bars to the steamy disco floor, ending up at the bathhouses in the early hours, and off to the beaches for the weekend – for most of them, it was simply a question of where

A parody (above) of the famous lines taken from a sonnet by the American poetess, Emma Lazarus: 'Give us your tired, your poor/Your huddled masses yearning to breathe free'. Inscribed on the Statue of Liberty, these lines proclaimed the American ethos – an ideal which fell sadly short when it came to caring for her AIDS casualties (right). The leather boys (below) join a homosexual demonstration.

to get the next sexual 'hit'. And, like drugs, each hit needed to be greater and more meaningful than the last.

Meanwhile, the bathhouse barons grew rich. Bathhouse sex was big business, providing a $100 million industry across the continent. To close down the bathhouses was just not financially viable, argued their owners. Most of them, such as Jack Campbell, who owned a chain of 42 bathhouses, held eminent positions. People were naturally reluctant to offend them.

CESSPOOLS OF DISEASE

When it was pointed out that these bathhouses were potential cesspools of disease, their owners refused even to believe that AIDS was sexually transmissible.

Nor were the bathhouse owners the only ones who failed to act. At an Atlanta convention in January 1983, despite growing evidence to the con-

trary, the blood banks concluded that AIDS posed no threat in blood-transfusions. When finally forced to admit to the possibility of infection through donated blood, they bandied

around a 'one-in-a-million' statistical chance of infection – which few could take seriously. More to the point, perhaps, Dr Aaron Kellner, president of the New York Blood Center,

OF INDIFFERENCE

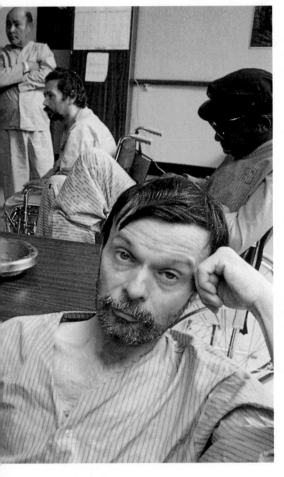

In front of City Hall, New York, gay demonstrators (left) express their amusement at the expense of their mayor, Ed Koch. As Mayor of New York, he alienated the gay community by refusing support to the AIDS campaign when it was most needed. When finally interviewed, in 1983, he merely agreed to help where money was not involved. The tragic results (below) of such indifference from above: a vivid memorial to the AIDS victims, during a 200,000-strong demonstration in Washington, in October 1987.

was the best preventative course. Suddenly, HIM vitamin packs 'maximising the immune system to fight infection', whilst heightening 'sexual potency', flooded the market. With such misleading information, how could the homosexual community be expected to embrace safe sex?

OSTRICHES

Did politicians and officials think that if they buried their heads in the sand, the problem might go away? How many would have to die before they finally took notice? Sadly, it took the death of a celebrity, Rock Hudson, to bring an end to such callous and widespread indifference.

argued that blood screening would cost his center an additional $5 million.

The sad truth was that many stood to lose a great deal, whereas few stood to gain anything at all: perhaps only the victims. It was probably too late for them anyway – the incubation period of a carrier, who might show no visible signs of infection, can last anywhere between a year and ten years. Many homosexuals were themselves reluctant to condone a screening process that would inevitably single them out, making them scapegoats.

Much of the problem had resulted from the insistence throughout that the epidemic

was just a homosexual problem. This was underlined by the original choice of name given to the disease: GRID (Gay-Related Immunity Deficiency). In addition, newspapers and magazines did little to promote awareness of AIDS, believing that homosexual news was unsaleable.

NEW RISK GROUPS

The medical profession soon began to realise that AIDS was not exclusively a homosexual problem: intravenous drug-users, Haitians and prison inmates were amongst the new wave of victims. In New York, AIDS spread outwards into the suburbs, hitting the poor and

undernourished. But indifference reigned supreme.

Significantly, it was only when AIDS began to affect heterosexuals that the media began to show any sustained interest. A similar lack of interest was shown by the Public Health Authorities who, in March 1983, after the epidemic had raged for almost two years, issued their first, meagre warning. Was it sufficient, at this late stage, merely to advise against having multiple partners, and sex with known or suspected AIDS sufferers?

Many homosexuals believed that to stay fit

LIVING A LIE

ROCK HUDSON WAS REACHING THE PEAK OF HIS FILM CAREER BY THE END OF THE 1950S. BUT WITH FAME CAME A GROWING NEED FOR HIM TO DEVELOP AN IMPREGNABLE OUTER SKIN THAT WOULD DISGUISE THE TRUTH ABOUT HIS HOMOSEXUALITY

After a wedding trip to Jamaica, Rock and the new Mrs Hudson returned to his house on Sparrow Lane, and he began filming *Written on the Wind*. Phyllis played the Hollywood wife well, always pretty and beaming on his arm at show business functions, often photographed cooking, capering or canoodling with her husband. Within a few months, however, Hudson and 'Bunting', as he called her, were demonstrably cooler.

Both Phyllis and Hudson were beginning to be wary of Henry Willson. She knew how he operated and could see that he exercised too much control over Hudson, his career, and his money. Apparently, she was still in the dark, however, as to how much influence he had where she was concerned, including her marriage.

By the spring of 1956, there were already moody scenes and signs of male lovers in the background. Phyllis accompanied Rock on location to Africa for *Something of Value*, but he was gradually withdrawing from her.

They officially separated late in 1957, but had seen very little of each other for some time before. Phyllis decided to consult Hollywood's most famous lawyer, Jerry Giesler.

Rock Hudson musing on the set of *A Farewell to Arms* (1957), which was based on Ernest Hemingway's novel. The film was shot in Italy and despite a starry cast was not a critical or commercial successs – many felt Hudson was too weak to be convincing as a soldier-adventurer.

While in Italy (and though still married to Phyllis Gates), Hudson had a romance with a young Italian actor who later followed him back to California. When Gates learnt of the affair she instigated divorce proceedings against her husband.

DATEFILE

AUGUST 13 1958
Rock Hudson and Phyllis Gates divorce

JUNE 13 1972
Rock Hudson appears on stage for first time in San Bernardino in the musical revival *I Do! I Do!*

AUG '58 - JUNE '72

Giesler, according to Phyllis, told her that Hudson and Willson had consulted him just before the marriage. They had come to discuss *Confidential* magazine, and how to suppress a story about an all-male orgy involving Hudson at Willson's house. Giesler had been unable to suppress the story, and advised them that all they could do was sue if it was published. The light finally dawned for Phyllis.

SLANDER CAMPAIGN

Realising that Phyllis might blow the whistle on Hudson's 'other life', Willson attempted to discredit her by initiating a slander campaign against her. Phyllis even claimed to be afraid that Willson might have her physically harmed. Whether from fear or faithfulness, or simply a desire to put it all behind her, she did not expose any of Rock's secrets. She obtained a divorce in 1958 on the suitably subtle grounds of 'mental cruelty'.

She said nothing until publishing a memoir in 1987. In the divorce settlement, which was modest by Hollywood standards, she got the Sparrow Lane house. After the divorce, she never saw Rock Hudson again.

In 1959, Hudson embarked on the first of his smash hit light comedies with Doris Day, *Pillow Talk*. The movie was a new departure for Hudson. With his customary modesty, he was at first reluctant to try a new genre, comedy, and was terrified at the prospect of having to sing. But Doris Day, already an old campaigner in both fields, was the perfect partner.

On the surface, the late 1950s and early 1960s were halcyon days for Hudson. He was a major film star and had houses at Malibu and later, Newport Beach. He bought a sailing boat aboard which, away from the public gaze, he could entertain friends such as the actress Claire Trevor, and film publicists Lynn Bowers and Pat Fitzgerald. His perfect day was to take the boat out to Catalina Island where he would mix lethal martinis and then barbecue steaks.

It was at this period in his life, that Hudson developed an outer skin which enabled him to act not just in front of the cameras, but also during every waking moment. Only with his most intimate

In 1959, Hudson starred in This Earth is Mine, *and celebrated its Los Angeles première at a party at Romanoff's attended by his co-star Jean Simmons (right) and her husband, actor Stewart Granger.*

CLOSE-UP
BOX-OFFICE TRIUMPHS

Rock Hudson's real heyday lasted from 1955 and *Magnificent Obsession* through to 1965 and a string of sex comedies. His track record in the influential, annual Motion Picture Exhibitors of America popularity poll is as follows:

1957 – 1st	1962——
1958 – 5th	1963 – 2nd
1959 – 1st	1964 – 3rd
1960 – 2nd	1965 – 3rd
1961 – 2nd	

No other post-war film star – not even Newman, Redford, Eastwood, Cruise, Schwarzenegger or Ford – has as yet managed to equal Hudson's run.

inner circle could he truly relax. As long ago as 1951, that circle had started with his friendship with Mark Miller, later Hudson's secretary, and George Nader, a successful actor and, eventually, a writer of novels.

WISHING PROBLEMS AWAY

Together with the outer skin came an inner mental toughness. He became expert at willing away a problem. Whether that problem was sex, or money, or a career decision, Hudson could simply make it disappear from his mind. Sadly, as he was to discover in the most tragic way, problems can

not be made to go away. Beneath the surface they fester, waiting for the most inopportune moment to burst into the open – without any warning.

In 1962, Hudson finally purchased the house on Beverly Crest Drive that was to become known as The Castle. To do so he had to sell his boat and beach house. He also had to renew – somewhat reluctantly – his contract with Universal Studios, at a time when he would have preferred to become a free agent. The Castle became Hudson's refuge, the most important feature of his protective skin, and he embarked on a restoration project that was to last him the rest of his life.

The style was Mexican and Spanish, heavy,

A line-up of young women pretend to carry a moustached Rock Hudson on their shoulders for the 1971 movie Pretty Maids All in a Row, an X-rated black comedy directed by Roger Vadim.

dark, massive and masculine. It was once described by a friend as 'early butch.' Hudson loved it, and never tired of buying huge pieces of furniture, pewter candlesticks, or giant statues. It was almost his life's work. 'When the work was done,' said Mark Miller, 'so was the man.'

However, his career nose-dived between 1964 and 1967. The decade had started with the stunning success of *Pillow Talk* and *Lover Come Back*. By 1964, after seven years at No.1 in the Motion Picture Film Buyer's poll, Hudson dropped to No.2. The following year he just made the top ten, and in 1967 failed to make the chart at all. It mattered little that in films such as *Seconds* he was making a new reputation as an actor as opposed to being 'merely a film star'.

There was a new breed of younger film actors, many of them trained by the more intimate medi-

> *There is no Rock Hudson. There are many Rock Hudsons. He projects what will appeal to the person he's with.*
>
> George Nader on Rock Hudson

um of television, who took on the mantle of box office greats. Fashions were changing in favour of 'real actors' who brought a different persona to each role they undertook – actors such as Dustin Hoffman, Al Pacino and Robert de Niro, who were

humorously known as 'the little uglies'.

Of the films Hudson made after 1966, few are remembered today, or even much shown on television. For the most part, the successes – such as they were – depended on the name of the author (Alastair McLean's *Ice Station Zebra*, 1968) or that of Hudson's co-star, for instance, Julie Andrews in *Darling Lili* (1970).

Hudson never ceased striving to extend his career. He stepped on to a theatre stage for the first time in his life, in 1973, in a revival of a the musical *I Do! I Do!*, opposite Carol Burnett and, in London, Juliet Prowse. For this nerve-racking experience he had not only to sing, but to learn to dance. At a time when television was still something that 'real' movie stars did not do, he

INSIDE VIEW

KING OF THE CASTLE

Hudson adored the hideaway home he had created for himself, known to his circle of friends as The Castle. Under Tom Clark's influence, Rock became a generous host and lavish entertainer, and needed a large staff to maintain the house and grounds. Although he paid them little, each of his retainers were part of the family, and they would all eat together in the kitchen, laughing and chatting, with Hudson just another face at the table.

By conventional standards The Castle's 'foot soldiers' were an unorthodox army. Their commander was Mark Miller, now Rock's secretary and confidant, but once an opera singer, dancer and later an estate agent. There was an English butler, James Wright, who, despite having spent most of his working life in America, retained an impeccable and carefully cultivated British accent. Beneath the suave 'Jeeves' exterior, however, lurked a more eccentric character. Not only was his cooking decidedly suspect, but he was rumoured to pick up young men in the street and bring them into the house.

His deputy, John Dobbs, was not only a house servant but also a Shakespearian actor. There was a young part-time gardener named Marty Flaherty who, it was alleged, was 'close' to Mark Miller and had been visiting the house since he was a teenager. The whole bizarre menage was watched over by an elderly Japanese gardener, Clarence Morimito. He would stand impassively in the garden, the typically inscrutable Oriental, observing everything that occurred and saying almost nothing.

Every year, Clarence and Rock would look out for the rare flowering ginger which blossomed in the garden from July to mid-September. In the year Hudson died, it was still in flower in late November, 50 days after his death. 'I think maybe Rock's spirit is in that flower,' said Clarence, breaking his habitual silence.

embarked on a gruelling five year stint (1971-75) in the detective series 'McMillan and Wife', in which he co-starred with the newcomer Susan Saint James, and 'McMillan' (1976-77).

Schedules and budgets were tighter than any Hudson had been accustomed to in his Hollywood prime, but he never complained. The cast and crew still remember his professionalism and spirit of co-operation, and although he had a clause in his contract allowing him not to work late on Fridays, he never alluded to it. At the end of each week's work, he would go drinking with the crew and, as often as not, picked up the bill.

HEART SURGERY

But punishing schedules and the loneliness of hotel rooms were driving Hudson to ever greater quantities of alcohol and nicotine. In 1981, during the making of another TV series, 'The Devlin Connection', about a father and son detective team, Hudson underwent heart surgery. It was a complicated operation, a quintuple heart by-pass, which necessitated major blood transfusions. Surgery took place in the Cedars-Sinai Hospital,

Hudson (right) poses with costumed co-stars Elizabeth Taylor (to his right) and Kim Novak on the set of The Mirror Crack'd (1980). based on Agatha Christie's thriller about murders that occur in an English village during the shooting of an all-star film.

which was located in West Hollywood, where there was a large homosexual population.

Around this time, dark rumours were circulating about a new cancer that was killing homosexuals. No-one then recognised the need to screen blood transfusions – it seemed likely that the 'gay cancer' was sexually transmitted. Exactly when and how Rock Hudson was infected with the HIV virus will never be known, but Mark Miller and many others in Hudson's immediate circle thought it could possibly have been through the blood he received in the Cedars-Sinai Hospital.

Phyllis Gates

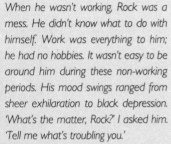

It has always been assumed that Hudson's marriage to Phyllis Gates was a sham, a publicity stunt dreamed up by his ruthless agent Henry Willson to quash rumours about the star's homosexuality, and that Gates's role was that of the innocent dupe. But Hudson, on his deathbed, told a friend that Phyllis was one of the only two people in his life he had ever truly loved.

ON SEX

The first time the love act itself was sublimely passionate, though it ended sooner than I would have liked. Soon he was sleeping like a baby. Rock Hudson naked in my bed. I contemplated that perfect face, that long but ideally proportioned body. How easy it would be to fall in love with him. Or had I already?

My sex life with Rock was far from satisfactory. He knew all the steps to arouse a woman's passion, but he could not contain his own. Like many wives, I tried to be understanding and sympathetic, telling him, 'That's all right, honey.' But I was never very good at acting, and eventually my frustrations came to the surface.

'Can't we try again?' I pleaded after a maddeningly brief encounter.

'One doesn't want hors d'oeuvres after eating dinner,' he replied.

'You're talking about dinner for one!' I exclaimed.

ON MOODS

When he wasn't working, Rock was a mess. He didn't know what to do with himself. Work was everything to him; he had no hobbies. It wasn't easy to be around him during these non-working periods. His mood swings ranged from sheer exhilaration to black depression. 'What's the matter, Rock?' I asked him. 'Tell me what's troubling you.'

'Nothing, nothing,' he said, fading once more into a dark mood.

Those periods of depression alarmed me. I had never known anyone whose very nature could alter so abruptly. There seemed to be two Rock Hudsons: the affable, grinning charmer he portrayed so brilliantly on the screen; and the dour gloomy person he revealed to me. During those low periods, he seemed almost overcome with self-loathing. I couldn't reach him. I could only wait until he climbed out of the pit and returned to his usual self.

ON OTHER ACTORS

Rock didn't care too much for the company of other actors - too much competition perhaps. George Nader was an exception.

George Nader was a founding member of Hudson's inner circle of trusted friends, which for obvious reasons, did not include his wife.

On 30 September 1955 Phyllis moved into Rock's house. It was also the day James Dean died in a car crash. Dean had been working with Rock on the film *Giant*, and it was rumoured that the director was favouring Dean at Hudson's expense.

I was moving my clothes into Rock's house that morning when I heard the telephone ring. Rock answered it. I heard him say a few words and hang up. Then I could hear him sobbing.

Rushing into the living room, I saw his grief stricken-face. I had never seen him so sorrowful before, and it frightened me.

'What's the matter, honey?' I said. 'Is it your mother?'

'No. James Dean.' He started to cry and I put my arms round him. I asked him why the news had shattered him.

'Because I wanted him to die.'

'But why would you want anyone to die?'

'Because I hated him. I was jealous of him because I was afraid he was stealing the picture from me. I've been wishing him dead ever since we were in Texas. And now he's gone.'

Rock couldn't be reached. He was overcome by guilt and shame, almost as though he himself had killed James Dean. I felt lonely, shut out from his innermost feelings. What kind of love did we have anyway, if I was unable to comfort him?

ON MARRIAGE

Rock Hudson tried as hard as he knew how to make the marriage work, in its early days at least. But even on the wedding night there were forebodings.

Midway through dinner, Rock looked at me in a peculiar way. He raised his wineglass and said' 'I toast you, my Bunting. We must always stick together and not let anyone try to pull us apart. You know, Hollywood is full of a lot of vicious people who spread stories and rumours. You must never believe any of them.'

He looked on the brink of tears and I had never been so touched by anything he had said.

'Here's to us,' he continued. 'I love you.'

'I love you, too,' I said, barely able to speak the words because I was so choked up.

Later, Rock was to say, 'I think marriage agrees with me, I feel so good.'

> **There seemed to be two Rock Hudsons: the affable, grinning charmer he portrayed so brilliantly on the screen; and the dour gloomy person he revealed to me.**

ON 'THE OTHER MAN'

Phyllis found out about her husband's homosexuality in the worst possible way, not by outright discovery but through well-meaning gossip.

'Your husband was unfaithful to you in Italy.' [during the filming of A Farewell to Arms].

What? I can't believe it. Who was she?'

'Phyllis, you're so naive. It wasn't a she. It was a he.'

One of my closest friends was telling me this. I had no reason to doubt him. He was not a common gossip or trying to seek favour with me. He knew the distress I was going through and thought he could help. My friend told me that an Italian actor admitted that he and Rock and been lovers during the entire filming of A Farewell to Arms. What hurt me most was to learn that the Italian had been with Rock when Rock telephoned me and professed how much he missed me. Also that the young man had helped Rock select presents for me.

In 1985 Phyllis learned that Rock had AIDS. She was beseiged by reporters, but said nothing. After the hubbub, she reflects:

At last I was alone with my own thoughts, and the impact of the tragedy struck me. I had learned enough about AIDS to realise that he probably wouldn't live much longer. Poor, poor Rock.

Phyllis Gates and Rock Hudson in 1955 (right) – to all appearances the perfect Hollywood couple.

THE WORLD TAKES NOTICE

WHEN ROCK HUDSON WAS TOLD THAT HE HAD AIDS, HE CONFIDED IN ONLY HIS CLOSEST FRIENDS, KEEPING EVERYONE ELSE IN THE DARK. THE MOMENT THE NEWS BROKE, HOWEVER, IT BECAME TRANSFORMED INTO AN ISSUE OF INTERNATIONAL CONTROVERSY

When the story broke, on 29 May 1984, that Rock Hudson had AIDS, the ripples spread far beyond the movie colony. It became a matter of worldwide concern. While Hudson's homosexuality was an open secret in Hollywood, the exposure of his sexuality was a devastating shock to his fans – many of them now middle-aged – who had always regarded him as the epitome of heterosexual masculinity.

PUBLIC AWARENESS

It was not only Hudson himself who was forced 'out of the closet'. His disease was too. Public education on AIDS was in its infancy when Hudson died, but by the end of the 1980s, the risks to the population at large were beginning to be realised. Had Hudson not died in the full glare of publicity, that process of growing awareness would have been very much slower.

However, for one man in particular, the news

On the day before the official announcement that Rock Hudson had AIDS, press attention on both sides of the Atlantic began to gather pace (above), speculating on the exact nature of the film star's illness.

was to have lasting repercussions. In the autumn of 1982, Rock Hudson had met 29-year-old Marc Christian. At the time, Hudson had been living with Tom Clark for nine years, but the relationship had dwindled into one of pleasurable companionship. Hudson, at the age of 57, still enjoyed the thrill of the chase and Christian seemed the perfect prey. Tall, blond, blue-eyed and bisexual, he worked out regularly at the gym to keep his physique in perfect shape. Apparently without a regular job, he had been living with a woman who was even older than Hudson.

DATEFILE

NOVEMBER 5 1983
Marc Christian moves into The Castle

MAY 29 1984
Rock Hudson diagnosed as having AIDS

JUNE 7 1984
Rock Hudson advised by his doctor to 'get his affairs in order'

OCTOBER 28 1984
Rock Hudson starts work on 'Dynasty'

NOV'83-OCT'84

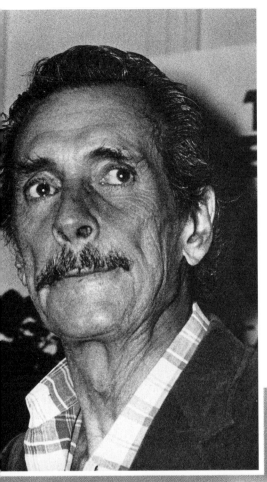

On 27 October, Tom Clark moved out of The Castle. Almost exactly a year later, on 5 November 1983, Marc Christian moved in. At first, everything went smoothly. The staff found him a pleasant change from the more pernickety Tom Clark, and Hudson and Christian were clearly in love.

But the bliss was shortlived. Christian was no empty-headed 'toy boy' but, where once his intelligence had seemed charming to Hudson and his circle, it soon turned into something close to arrogance. He seemed to have some kind of hold over Hudson that had nothing to do with love. It was as though Rock was almost afraid of him. Christian knew too much, and he was too indiscreet. He also began to alienate the staff with his untidiness and irregular hours. He took to staying out all night, once or twice a week, without explanation.

Soon the pair were hardly on speaking terms, and Rock's friends begged him to get rid of the

Left: Rock Hudson returning from his appearance on the 'Doris Day Show'. Below: Hudson's close friend Elizabeth Taylor addressing an AIDS fund raising rally in Los Angeles in September 1985.

one-time lover they were convinced was now simply using him. But Rock, characteristically, blanked out the problem. At the back of his mind he thought that Marc would get the message and leave. He never did.

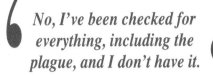

No, I've been checked for everything, including the plague, and I don't have it.

Rock Hudson's alleged response to Marc Christian's question about AIDS.

To complicate matters further, Rock was falling in love with his trainer and masseur Ron Channell. Channell was heterosexual, but the two of them shared the same oddball sense of humour. In between the rigorous exercise sessions Channell mapped out for Rock, The Castle staff would hear the two men roaring with laughter.

In the meantime, Rock had started work on 'Dynasty' in October 1984. The movie star was

formally welcomed on to the set by the stars of the small screen, John Forsyth (Blake Carrington) and Linda Evans, who played Krystle.

FAILING MEMORY

A viewing of Rock Hudson's 'Dynasty' episodes, though, reveals how ill he was. His eyes are staring and deeply sunken in their sockets, his face gaunt, his movements those of a much older man. To his distress, his memory was failing and he often had to rely on cue cards to remember his lines. But with his lifelong capacity to ignore the unpalatable, he would tell friends he thought he looked good in the 'Dynasty' episodes.

The tabloid press were later to accuse Rock of risking Linda Evans' life with their now infamous

A SUMMER IN FRANCE

In August 1984, Hudson planned a visit to France. The trip had a dual purpose. To the world at large, including Marc Christian, the story was that Rock wanted to visit the Deauville Film Festival. He had been approached by a number of film and TV producers in Europe and wanted to discuss possible deals.

To some extent this was true. Aaron Spelling, executive producer of the long-running television series, 'Dynasty', had offered Rock the chance to appear in a short run of episodes. While he was staying at the Ritz Hotel in Paris, 'Dynasty' co-producer Esther Shapiro flew over to persuade him to sign up.

The hidden purpose of the trip to France was to visit Dr Dominique Dormont in his clinic, where he was pioneering a new experimental anti-AIDS drug, HPA-23. After an intensive course of the drug, Dormont told Hudson that the virus had disappeared from his blood. However, Dr Kennamer, Rock's regular doctor, warned him that he should continue the treatment, and that, almost certainly, he was not cured.

When Hudson returned to Los Angeles in September 1984, all the physical evidence suggested that, far from being cured, he was a very sick man. Marc Christian immediately noticed Rock's dramatic weight loss, but, whatever his motives at that time, decided to look on the bright side. 'You're a little thin. You look fine', he said.

screen kiss, despite the widespread belief in the medical profession that the transmission of the HIV virus by kissing is virtually impossible. Rock himself had been horrified when he saw that the script required him to do the kiss, and had literally kept his mouth tight shut to avoid any possibility of transferring saliva. Evans was said to be much distressed by the exaggerated reports of her 'panic'.

By the start of 1985, Rock was giving up on life. His body was covered with sores and rashes and itched continuously. He was losing kilograms in weight almost every week. In July there was the last futile trip to the Paris clinic, and the public announcement that Rock Hudson had AIDS.

DESPERATE LIES

According to Marc Christian, there is no doubt that Hudson lied to him about having the disease. As it took hold, and the symptoms became more apparent, Christian claimed that the lies became progressively more desperate. Less than six months before Hudson died, Christian confronted him directly. 'Do you have AIDS?' The reply had an actor's polish: 'No. I've been checked for everything, including the plague, and I don't have it.' He continued to deny it until July 1985 when the public announcement was made.

Marc Christian contends that he learned that Hudson had AIDS as though he were just a member of the media's worldwide audience. No apology was offered, no explanation given – except from Hudson"s personal assistant Mark Miller, who had continued to play along with the lies. Miller told Christian that he was under orders not to reveal Rock's illness. He added that Hudson had said, 'Look after the kid, I may have killed him.'

AIDS TEST

Christian flew to Paris the morning after the announcement and met Dr. Dormont, a leading authority on AIDS who had treated Hudson. Dormont confirmed that the chances were high that he had contracted the virus, but he would have to wait a week for the results of the test.

Christian tried to see Hudson, but Miller said he was too ill to receive any visitors. Miller dispatched Christian to the South of France to wait for his results.

By the time Christian returned to Dormont's clinic, a week later, Hudson had already been flown back to Los Angeles and was in the UCLA Medical Center. Dormont told Christian: 'All I can say is you are a very lucky man. I found no trace of AIDS in the first test.' Christian then underwent a second set of tests which, in their turn, proved negative.

Strangely enough, as life ebbed away, Hudson became almost a hero. The issue of AIDS, previously tucked away on the medical pages, became front-page news in newspapers around the world. Celebrities who had hesitated to be linked with AIDS charities now flocked to them. Elizabeth Taylor, who had been among the first to put her

Hudson poses (below right) with the stars of 'Dynasty', John Forsythe and Linda Evans. Although still well enough to act, he was already beginning to age noticeably.

BACKDROP

Hudson (above) with his last live-in lover, Marc Christian, who moved into Hudson's house in 1983. Hudson was to lie to Christian about whether or not he had AIDS.

DIAGNOSIS

In January 1984, Hudson noticed a mole on the back of his neck. It seemed unusual to him, and after it persisted he had it removed by surgery. The mole returned, and in May it was again removed by a plastic surgeon. Later that month a biopsy was performed on the tissues, revealing the presence of Kaposi's sarcoma, one of the commonest symptoms of AIDS. Rock Hudson, movie star, was officially informed that he had the disease.

For a week he kept the dreadful secret to himself. Then, on 5 June 1984, he decided that he had to turn to his old friend and confidant (and secretary) Mark Miller. At two o'clock in the afternoon, Rock walked into the lounge at The Castle. He sat down and said: 'I've got AIDS. I've been crying for a week. I don't want anybody to know it.' Miller, devastated, didn't know what to say. 'I'm sorry,' was all he could manage.

Two days later, Miller went with Hudson to an appointment with Dr Michael Gottlieb, a respected immunologist and one of the top AIDS specialists. Hudson asked: 'Is it definitely fatal?' After what seemed an interminable pause Gottlieb replied: 'I would get my affairs in order if I were you.'

Miller says that he specifically asked Hudson whether he had anal sex with Marc Christian. Hudson denied that he had.

At the consultation on 7 June, Dr Gottlieb had informed Hudson that the main method of transmission of the AIDS virus was via anal intercourse. Hudson was thus able to say to Miller with some confidence, 'If it's anal, Christian doesn't have the virus.' However, Hudson managed to arrange a medical check-up for Christian without telling him the reason. The doctor performed a full medical and gave Christian a clean bill of health.

reputation on the line by raising funds, now had armies of allies.

Towards the end of September, Hudson decided to return to the familiar surroundings of the Castle, to be close to those whom he knew and trusted. In the last three weeks of his life, Hudson weighed less than seven stone and was seldom conscious. By this stage he was clearly in no condition to give Marc Christian any answers.

LAST WORDS

On Wednesday morning, 2 October 1985, Tom Clark came to visit Rock at The Castle. Rock was propped up in bed with pillows and attended by two nurses. They had coffee and talked about the day's news. At 8.30 am, Tom said, 'I'm out of coffee. Do you want some more?' Rock said, 'No, not now'. Tom went to the kitchen to fetch himself another cup of coffee. By he time he returned, Rock was dead.

A DOUBLE LIFE

LIKE SO MANY OTHER CELEBRITIES, ROCK HUDSON WAS CAUGHT IN THE DILEMMA OF COURTING FAME AND POPULARITY, WHILE AT THE SAME TIME JEALOUSLY TRYING TO GUARD HIS PRIVATE LIFE

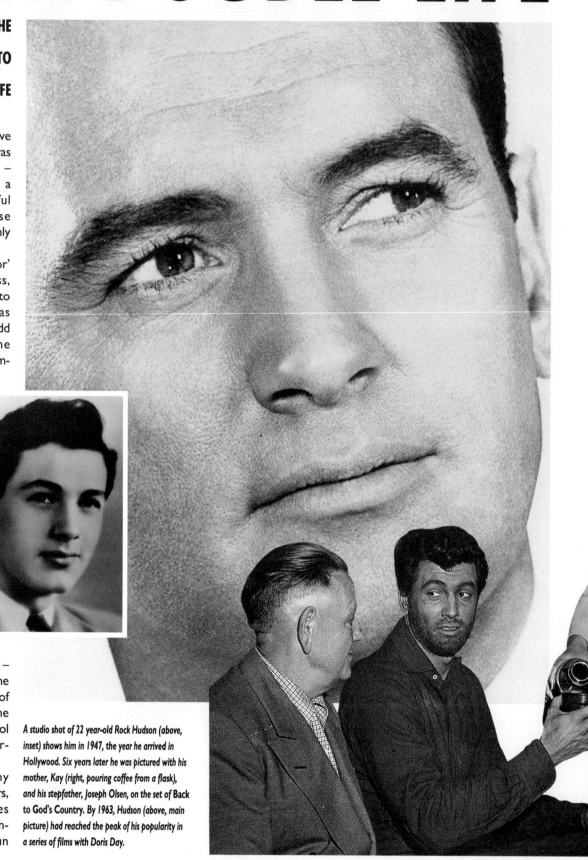

The longest and truest love in Rock Hudson's life was his mother Kay – Katherine Wood. Kay was a tall, hard-working, unfanciful Midwestern woman whose marital troubles drew her only child particularly close to her.

As a small boy, her 'Junior' was weedy, prone to illness, bashful and reluctant to go to school. Yet when he was as young as 10 he had to find odd part-time jobs around the town, not only to provide himself with a bit of pocket money, but to contribute something to the family's slender finances.

Abandoned by his own father, and relentlessly bullied well into his teens by his stepfather, he had only his mother as a constant in his life; a figure who was, he said 'mother, father, and big sister to me.' Until her death in 1972 – which left him devastated – he was no doubt ever mindful of her constant admonition: 'She always said "never make a fool of yourself, and more importantly, never embarrass me".'

As was true for so many people in the Depression years, Roy was hooked on movies from childhood – an inexpensive escape into glamour, fun

A studio shot of 22 year-old Rock Hudson (above, inset) shows him in 1947, the year he arrived in Hollywood. Six years later he was pictured with his mother, Kay (right, pouring coffee from a flask), and his stepfather, Joseph Olsen, on the set of Back to God's Country. By 1963, Hudson (above, main picture) had reached the peak of his popularity in a series of films with Doris Day.

and excitement. 'I always wanted to become an actor,' he said. 'It has always hypnotised me. I saw every film.' As an actor he could be someone else. And he could be loved by many.

George Nader, Hudson's closest friend and the principal beneficiary in his will, observed: 'There is no Rock Hudson. There are many Rock Hudsons. He projects what will appeal to the person he's with.'

SELF-CONTAINED

Rock Hudson was not a deep or deeply introspective man. He was not much of a reader and cared little for politics, religion or social issues. He did not display the modern American compulsion to 'share one's experiences' or 'get in touch with one's feelings'. Nor did he wish to discuss his hopes, dreams and relationships with everyone else.

When he was approaching death, Hudson admitted to his biographer Sara Davidson: 'I've always been a private person. I've never wanted to write a book, I've never let my house be photographed, and I've never let the public know what I really think.'

His pleasures for much of his life were simple ones that reflect the boyish, even childish, quality he exuded: dancing, water sports, silly jokes, trivial games, noisy parties, Christmas celebrations, making ice cream, watching American football, card games, and drinking with male buddies both gay and heterosexual.

NEED FOR STARDOM

The driving force in his life was to be a star, to be secure, comfortable – and loved, preferably by multitudes. While that dream is common, once he learned what was required to achieve it, Hudson worked hard to make it a reality. Certainly he was blessed with luck – his good looks, his 'discovery', his early breaks in the business. But he went after the luck, seizing every possible chance he could, whether it was something as routine as a speech class to lower his voice or the cultivation of a person who could help him.

Once Hudson had become established as a star, he loved the fame and the rewards it brought, from the first flashy convertible car and the first home he could own, to the attractive young men he could have whenever he wanted. To get, and then to keep everything he had worked for, Rock Hudson, like millions of other people, had to live a lie.

George Nader, seen at right in a 1956 Universal publicity shot, was an actor who met Hudson in 1951. Both men kept their homosexuality secret – exposure would have destroyed their careers.

TALL BLONDE AND HANDSOME

Marc Christian (below, right), the one-time lover whose lawsuit exploded the Hudson image four years after the film star's death, exemplifies the type of man Rock Hudson went for. Tall, blonde and well built, Christian was merely one of the last in a line of similar looking lovers who became collectively known as 'The Hudson Gay Company', a group as invariably handsome and virile looking as Rock Hudson was himself.

Hudson liked women and enjoyed their company, and did not care at all for effeminate or 'camp' homosexuals. It was said he preferred bisexual men; if a potential lover was married or something of a ladies' man, he

apparently took that as a particularly appealing challenge. His heterosexual men friends - and there were many - were out of the same mould: boisterous, 'joking guys' who liked sports, drinking and sex.

By all accounts he was naturally a good-hearted, generous and open man. But he was also a practical and expedient man. He knew the rules of the fame game and played it masterfully. 'The Great Unattainables' had to be pure and straight. To maintain the illusion of 'Charlie Movie Star', as Hudson called himself, he developed – out of necessity – a devious, selfish and self-preserving streak which could manifest itself in unexpected cruelty and deceit.

Some of his strongest and happiest gay relationships came to grief because he could not stand to feel possessed, nor could he bear demands on him that compromised his wants, or threatened to 'blow the whistle' on his private proclivities.

To have 'created' himself as he did, and to have preserved the image for 35 years, was the most demanding role Hudson ever undertook. That he was, almost to the end, successful at this, was a kind of triumph.

VIRGIN ISLE HOTEL

THE COST OF

HUDSON'S ILLNESS CAME AS A MASSIVE SHOCK TO MARC CHRISTIAN. HE HAD BEEN HUDSON'S LOVER FOR TWO YEARS, WITHOUT EVER HAVING BEEN TOLD THE STAR CARRIED THE VIRUS. IN 1989 HE WENT TO COURT FOR COMPENSATION

M arc Christian had twice been tested for AIDS and twice the results had been negative, but he now began to take a long hard look at his situation. He had been warned that the tests did not mean that he was definitely in the clear. On top of that, Mark Miller had made it extremely apparent during the last few weeks of Rock Hudson's life that he wanted Christian to move out of The Castle.

Christian had refused. He remembered Hudson had told him that Miller and George Nader were to be the main beneficiaries in his will, but that he, Christian would be 'looked after'. Christian was now concerned Miller was trying to ensure that he was not looked after too well.

HIGH PROFILE

Having decided to take counsel, Christian selected Marvin Mitchelson, the highest-profile lawyer in America. Mitchelson had become a household name with the Lee Marvin 'palimony' case, and the Joan Collins-Peter Holm divorce. He liked nothing better than setting a legal precedent, par-

ticularly in a case involving celebrities, which would result in a potentially lucrative pay-off.

Two weeks after Rock Hudson's death, Mitchelson filed a suit on behalf of Marc Christian against the late movie star's Estate, and Mark Miller. The suit claimed that Hudson and Miller had conspired to endanger Marc Christian's life by not revealing that Hudson was suffering from AIDS for more than a year after it was diagnosed on 7 June 1984.

The press had a field day. The *National Enquirer's* headlines announced: 'Rock's boyfriend. Why I am suing for $10 million'. Rather than telling Christian to keep silent, Mitchelson actually encouraged his client to talk to the media. He even organised a coast-to-coast tour,

as if he was promoting some newly published author. Mitchelson and Christian appeared on every major talk show, including the heavyweights such as Phil Donahue and Larry King. Mitchelson insisted that the idea behind the publicity was to establish that AIDS sufferers had a legal obligation to inform their partners.

FORCED WITHDRAWL

However, Mitchelson was forced to withdraw from the case, due to his own legal problems. His place was taken by the lesser-known but equally able Los Angeles attorney, Harold Rhoden.

More than three years after the death of Rock Hudson, the case finally came before the Superior

DATEFILE

JANUARY 6 1989

Court case begins against Hudson Estate

FEBRUARY 15 1989

Verdict delivered in Christian's favour

APRIL 21 1989

Judge revises award downwards

JAN '89-APR '89

DECEPTION

Marc Christian in court (left, and in main picture, third from right). His sensational legal action against his former lover's estate established new precedents concerning what information can be witheld from a sexual partner.

Court of the State of California for the County of Los Angeles on 6 January 1989, his Honour Judge Bruce R. Geernaert presiding. It was to last almost two months, utterly destroying Rock Hudson's screen image. The court papers named the Hudson Estate and Miller as the defendants, but in reality it was Rock Hudson himself who stood accused.

Harold Rhoden was brusque and business-like. He would prove, he said, that Hudson and Miller had conspired to conceal from Marc Christian the fact that Hudson had AIDS, thereby placing his life

in jeopardy. Rock Hudson's motive, Rhoden maintained, was that he wanted to carry on having sexual relations with Christian. The motive of Miller was to please his boss and to maximise his financial gain from Hudson's Estate. He insisted that the fact that Marc Christian had not yet been diagnosed as having AIDS was immaterial to his case. He might well develop the disease in the future and, even if he did not, the emotional trauma he had suffered warranted compensation.

Robert Mills, for the Estate, and Andrew Banks for Miller, promised to show that Christian's relationship with Hudson had ended some months before Hudson knew he had AIDS. They claimed that Christian was promiscuous and a prostitute. They also accused him of attempting to blackmail

Hudson by threatening to publish their love letters. Finally, they maintained that there was no evidence that Christian had AIDS, or would ever get AIDS.

Rhoden called Marc Christian to the stand. Christian came across as a confident and credible witness who stood up well to cross-examination. To the allegation that the whole case was about money, Christian stated that he had already been offered and refused $300,000 for his story by the *National Enquirer*.

> *I began to sweat and then I blacked out. I thought "Oh my god, I'm a dead man"*
>
> Marc Christian on hearing that Rock Hudson had AIDS

To the suggestion that his affair with Hudson had ended the February before his AIDS diagnosis and that he had in fact moved out of Rock Hudson's bedroom as early as the middle of 1984, Christian produced convincing evidence to the contrary. He claimed that he and Hudson had had a constant sexual relationship until February 1985 and that, to the best of his knowledge, the pair had been faithful to one another. Allegations that he was a male prostitute and/or promiscuous were likewise picked apart.

Miller's claim that the Christian-Hudson affair had ended in February 1984, and that Hudson had transferred his affections, were quashed as Rhoden read out Hudson's love letters to Christian.The letters were still being written as late as January 1984, at a time when the defence claimed that Rock Hudson was establishing a close friendship with Ron Channell, his masseur and trainer. The intimate and affectionate nature of the letters could not be questioned. 'I love you so much, baby,' ran one, written by Rock in either December 1983 or January 1984 when he was filming on location in Israel: 'The countdown is now twenty more days to go and they are dragging like you can't believe. I love you, love you, love you.'

BLACKMAIL ALLEGATIONS

Blackmail allegations were also dismissed. Months after his supposed attempt to blackmail Hudson by threatening to publish their love letters, Christian had still been sharing Hudson's bed. At the time, Hudson had even paid for his lover's teeth to be fixed.

The defence then called a succession of witnesses to discredit Christian, or to prove that he and Hudson were no longer intimate at the time of the ended in the February before his AIDS diagnosis, Christian produced convincing evidence to the contrary. Allegations that he was a male prostitute and, or, promiscuous were likewise picked apart.

Miller's claim that the Christian-Hudson affair had ended in February, and that Hudson had transferred his affections, were quashed as Rhoden read out Hudson's love letters. Blackmail allegations were also dismissed. Months after the supposed blackmail attempt, Christian had still been sharing Hudson's bed. Hudson had even paid for his lover's teeth to be fixed.

The defence then called a succession of witnesses to discredit Christian, or to prove that he and Hudson were no longer intimate at the time of the diagnosis. First came the butler, James Wright, who Rhoden proved had recently received an ex-gratia payment of $50,000 from the estate. Next was

CLOSE-UP

STRIKING IT RICH

To assist the jury in reaching their verdict, a questionnaire had been drawn up by the defence and agreed to by Judge Geernaert and Harold Rhoden. Known as a special verdict form, it comprised a list of 37 questions which would decide the outcome of the case.

The show stopper was question number 37: 'What is the total amount of damages suffered by the plaintiff for increased emotional distress caused by the conduct of Rock Hudson or Mark Miller'. Answer: '$14,500,000'. On the following day, the jury awarded a further $7,250,000 in punitive damages against Mark Miller.

Clarence Miromoto, the gardener – whose claim to have seen Christian in bed with another man – was shown to be false.

Finally, the defence produced two 'experts' who claimed that there was no chance that Christian was suffering from AIDS. Rhoden revealed that they were both paid witnesses – at $300 per hour – and that everything they said flew in the face of accepted knowledge.

Summing up on behalf of Miller, Banks said: 'If you find against my client, you will be sending a message to the world that a man could never keep a secret for a friend. 'Wrong,' replied Rhoden. A verdict against Miller would say: 'If you think someone has AIDS and has a lover, you dare not agree to conceal that fact from the lover.'

The jury retired on the afternoon of 9 February, and returned on 15 February.

In every instance, the jury's judgement was in favour of the plaintiff, Marc Christian.

Public reaction to the award was a mixture of disbelief and outrage. The total sum – in excess of $21 million – was deemed to be preposterous. Paradoxically, the outrage came mainly from gay circles who saw the verdict as yet further proof that AIDS sufferers were to be despised and pilloried.

> **If you think someone has AIDS and has a lover, you dare not agree to conceal that fact from the lover**
>
> Marc Christian's lawyer in court

In fact, by 21 April, the compensatory award was reduced to $5 million, and punitive damages against Mark Miller were heavily cut back to $500,000. This still left Christian with a handy $5.5 million, which in most people's view, was a great deal more than adequate.

The 'Rock Hudson trial' did a public service in establishing that those with life threatening infectious or contagious diseases have an obligation to be frank with their intimate associates. But it had also turned into a painful and highly intrusive examination of the late movie star's life. Allowing the law into yet another area of private life may come to be seen as a cause for regret.

Marvin Mitchelson, California's toughest divorce lawyer (left) announcing a multi-million dollar lawsuit on behalf of Marc Christian. The flamboyant attorney made sure that the case received maximum publicity before handing over to another lawyer.

THE DINGO BABY CASE

When baby Azaria Chamberlain was apparently snatched by a dingo from her parents' tent at a camp site some distance from Ayers Rock in Australia, the world fell apart for Lindy and her husband, Pastor Michael Chamberlain. But that was only the beginning. They were to be accused of murdering Azaria. Could the wife of a church minister have committed the horrific crime of killing her own child?

Lindy Chamberlain – a devout woman, but disliked by many for her toughness and apparent lack of emotion.

A BABY

WHEN NINE-WEEK OLD
AZARIA CHAMBERLAIN MYSTERIOUSLY
DISAPPEARED FROM A CAMP SITE AT THE
BASE OF AYERS ROCK, HER DISTRAUGHT
PARENTS WERE JUST AT THE START
OF A LONG AND DREADFUL SAGA THAT
WOULD SHATTER THEIR LIVES

DATEFILE

AUGUST 17 1980

Azaria Chamberlain disappears from her parents' tent. Her mother, Lindy, believes she has been taken by a dingo.

AUGUST 19 1980

The Chamberlains decide to go home after searchers fail to find the baby or its remains.

AUGUST 24 1980

Wally Goodwin, a tourist from Victoria, discovers some of Azaria's bloodstained clothing.

AUGUST '80

The whole family was looking forward to a holiday in the heart of the Australian Outback. The two boys, Aidan, aged six, and Reagan, four, could hardly contain their excitement as they helped their father, Pastor Michael Chamberlain, pack the car in preparation for the 900 kilometre journey to the legendary Ayers Rock.

Watching proudly was Michael's dark-haired wife Lindy who, only nine weeks earlier, had given birth to their third child – a daughter they had named Azaria, which meant 'Blessed of God'. The couple knew that it would be cold at night camping in the desert, as the moment the sun goes down the temperature falls rapidly; but they were well prepared, and had taken plenty of warm clothes for the two boys and the baby.

After stopping to camp twice on the way, they finally saw the Rock loom up on the horizon. It was the evening of 16 August 1980, a Saturday, which is the Sabbath day for Pastor Chamberlain's Seventh Day Adventist Church. The family reached their destination at the ranger check post near the 500 million-year-old monolith. Although it was Australian winter, the camping ground was quite full, but they managed to find a good spot near the barbecue area to put up their green and orange tent.

A DAY OF ADVENTURE

The following morning they had their first clear view of the Rock, which was a major attraction for visitors from around the world. Dingoes – a type of desert wolf – roamed around it, tourists clambered over it taking photographs, and Aborigines worshipped it.

The dingoes were a topic of conversation over breakfast. The Chamberlains heard from the Wests, another family on holiday in the area, that their 12-year-old daughter had been given a bad fright when a dingo, scrounging around the camp site for food, had grabbed her by the elbow.

The Chamberlains soon forgot about this as they set off to explore the Rock under a bright blue sky. They scrambled around its lower slopes and

VANISHES

Tourists make their ant-like ascent of Ayers Rock. Each year thousands of people from all over the world undertake the one kilometre trek to the summit of the Rock, from where they have a tremendous panorama of the Australian Outback.

This photograph (below), taken the day after Azaria disappeared, is one of the earliest the public were shown of the Chamberlains.

although she believed it to be shaking its head. 'Get out!' she yelled. 'Go on – get out!' She called out to Michael: 'A dingo's in the tent!'

THE BABY DISAPPEARS

Then she ran to check the baby. Azaria's blankets were scattered throughout the tent. Lindy felt sick, feeling certain that something terrible had happened. Even though she could see the baby was no longer in her cot, she felt around in a panic, just to make sure. In his sleeping bag, with the hood

ROCK OF MYSTERY

Ayers Rock, Australia's most well-known natural landmark, has been a place of worship for Aboriginal tribes for over 30,000 years, since they first made their way to the continent from the islands of south east Asia. They saw it as the creation of their mythological ancestors, and called it Uluru. Surrounded by wildlife, the Rock provided the Aborigines with a bountiful source of food and water, and they used its caves for ceremonies, sharing them with eagles which nested in the nooks and crannies. The Aborigines painted their legends on the walls of the caves, revealing their belief that the landmark was formed by the movements of their forebears. The mythical predecessors of the Aborigines were giant beings, although they behaved like humans. When these huge creatures – carpet snakes, sand lizards, marsupial moles among them – fought, made a fire, or performed a ceremony, there arose after their departure a mountain range, a hill or a valley. Among the many legendary creatures that roamed the desert was the Kurrpan, an evil creature that looked like a giant dingo.

slopes and Michael, a keen photographer, took pictures for the family album. Lindy laughed happily as she held Azaria by the arms, balancing her baby's feet on the lower slopes of the rock. By the time they returned late in the afternoon, Reagan was tired and soon went to bed.

Lindy, Michael and the older boy, Aidan, stayed around the barbecue area. Having soothed Azaria to sleep in her arms, Lindy then took her to the tent, accompanied by Aidan, who was talking about wanting more to eat, even though he had already been given his tea.

Lindy unzipped the tent flap and placed the baby in the carry cot on the right hand side, near the back of the tent. She tucked her in and made sure Azaria was warm, and she saw that Reagan was by now fast asleep. Then she went to the car to get out a can of baked beans to cook for Aidan. It was close to 8pm when she and Aidan returned to the barbecue area. Now, as she stood at the barbecue holding the tin opener, some of those with her were to say later that a sound penetrated the chilly night air. Aidan instantly said he had heard 'Bubby', as the family called Azaria, cry out.

Lindy said she would go and check the baby. As she was to relate time and again, while walking back towards the tent, which was some 20 to 25 metres away, she saw a dingo come out between the flaps. By her account, it was a youngish dog. But because fence posts and bushes partly obscured her view, she could not see it clearly,

BABY'S CLOTHING FOUND NEAR HERE — S-W CORNER OF ROCK

ROAD AROU
ROCK

CLOSE-UP

THE SEVENTH DAY ADVENTIST CHURCH

Seventh Day Adventists set aside Saturday as their Sabbath and follow a régime of strict temperance – no alcohol or tobacco, and abstinence, whenever possible, from tea, coffee and meat. Emerging from mid-19th century America, the staunch Protestant body preaches that the Scriptures provide the unerring rule of faith and that Christ's return is imminent.

Adventists believe that the 'end of age' is coming and that they have a responsibility to proclaim their message to the world. When the end comes, the righteous dead will be raised and, along with the righteous living, will be ushered into Heaven, where they will spend the next 1000 years. Satan will remain on Earth for that time and, when it is over, Christ will descend with His saints to destroy the wicked with fire. Death, say Adventists, is really like a deep sleep. When those who sleep wake up, the time will be as but a moment.

It was because Michael and Lindy Chamberlain firmly believed they would see Azaria again that they were able to remain so composed, often to the amazement of those around them who expected them to be more deeply anguished.

This aerial view of Ayers Rock (right) shows all of the important sites associated with the Dingo Baby Case, including the camp site where the family stayed. Because of the distance between this site and the spot where Azaria's clothes were found (see replica below), many people immediately dismissed the theory that a dingo could have carried a baby that far.

pulled up and his face in the pillow, Reagan was still sleeping peacefully.

Lindy backed out of the tent. Then she screamed that a dingo had taken her baby. Hearing the cry, Michael ran straight off into the scrub to look, although he didn't have a torch. 'It's no good,' cried Lindy. 'You can't see...Has anybody got a torch?'

> ' *My God, my God! The dingo's got my baby.* '
>
> Lindy Chamberlain on finding Azaria's cot empty.

As the alarm went up, campers ran in all directions to help in the search. Michael went to the tent and saw the 'horrible, lonely whiteness' of the carry cot. Out in the desert surrounding the camp site, the searchers' torches danced like fireflies.

But there was no sign of the dingo or the baby. As the hours went by, the couple seemed resigned to never seeing Azaria alive. Michael told a ranger: 'Our baby girl has been taken by a dingo and we are fully reconciled to the fact that we will never see our baby alive again. The dingo would have killed the child immediately, would it not?' At Michael's request, people prayed for the safe return of his daughter.

Meanwhile, Sally Lowe, a camper who had come to the aid of the Chamberlains, took Aidan back to the tent. The little boy was clearly disturbed, and begged her: 'Don't let the dingo eat our baby.'

At some point after midnight, the family was encouraged by a local nurse, Bobbie Downs, to spend the rest of the night at a nearby motel. In the morning, as news of the story that a clergyman's daughter had been taken by a dingo first broke, Michael told journalists: 'We've given up hope that we'll see our baby on this earth again, but we know we'll see her in the resurrection.'

INVESTIGATIONS BEGIN

In between Michael talking to the press and arranging to send pictures of the tent to a newspaper, they were interviewed by Inspector Michael Gilroy, who had travelled from Alice Springs.

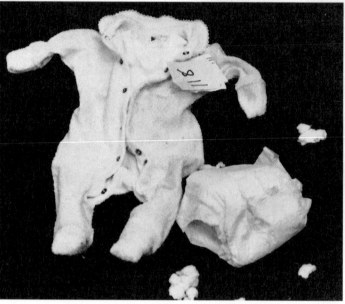

Lindy claimed that the dingo she saw emerging from the tent had been shaking its head, and she suggested that it might have been because it could have been carrying the baby by the back of her clothes. Azaria had been wearing a singlet, a nappy, a jump suit, a matinée jacket and booties.

Shortly afterwards, police and rangers started shooting dingoes around the Rock in order to examine the contents of their stomachs in the grisly hunt for Azaria's remains. Nurse Bobbie Downs decided on Tuesday that the Chamberlains should leave Ayers Rock and head for home, so they packed their belongings, bought mementoes – not souvenirs, Lindy later insisted – from the local store and returned home. Although only two days had passed since Azaria had vanished, Michael was to ask later: 'What more could we do?' They had found strength from a passage in the Seventh Day Adventists' handbook: 'Little children are borne by holy angels to their mothers' arms.'

As the Chamberlains tried to resume a normal life back in Mount Isa, various rumours started circulating, and these soon turned into malicious gos-

Above: the Chamberlains' home was in the tough mining town of Mount Isa, in a remote part of Queensland. Right: the Australian press seemed to be sceptical of the dingo story in their editorials.

ABORIGINAL CAMP

GENERAL STORE

BARBEQUE AREA

BABY DRAGGED INTO SCRUB

CHAMBERLAINS' TENT

PROBLEMS WITH DINGOES

The dingo, believed to have evolved from a domesticated version of the Asiatic wolf or the Indian wild dog, has never been far from Man, having accompanied ancestral Aborigines to Australia. Although usually shy, those living near Ayers Rock around the time when the Chamberlain family arrived had become bold, and were accustomed to being fed. Tourists at the Rock had come to regard them as rather tame creatures, always in need of food. This attitude inevitably created problems, with dingoes sneaking into tents to steal food, and sometimes grabbing hold of hands and arms, although there have been no reports of anyone being savaged.

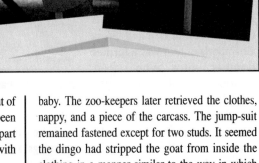

sip. Lindy had not loved the child, it was said. The Seventh Day Adventist Church practised ritual sacrifices. Sorcery was afoot.

THE CLOTHES ARE FOUND

A week after Azaria's disappearance, Wally Goodwin and his family were exploring the Ayers Rock region. Margot, Wally's wife, was keeping to the high ground near a gully at the bottom of the Rock, while her husband walked through denser foliage lower down. Suddenly, she spotted something on the ground and, on closer inspection, Wally realised that they had discovered some of the missing baby's clothes. Because everyone around Ayers Rock was still talking about Azaria's disappearance, he knew immediately whose clothes they were. His first impression was that the child had been eaten out of them, as only four studs on the jump-suit had been opened. But there was no sign of the baby, apart from the bloodstains. Police combed the area with no further success.

The investigators who examined the bracken found on the child's clothing were certainly puzzled. It did not match the vegetation a dingo would have passed through on its way back to the Rock. Meanwhile, at a zoo in Adelaide, a young goat was humanely killed, dressed up in baby clothes, and then thrown into a dingo's pen to establish how one of these animals might have devoured the missing baby. The zoo-keepers later retrieved the clothes, nappy, and a piece of the carcass. The jump-suit remained fastened except for two studs. It seemed the dingo had stripped the goat from inside the clothing in a manner similar to the way in which Azaria's clothing had been found at the Rock.

Detective-Sergeant Graeme Charlwood interviewed the Chamberlains at their home and also at Mount Isa police station, where the conversation was secretly taped. He took them over their story in fine detail. He gave the distinct impression that there were aspects about which he had serious misgivings, including the seeming lack of dingo saliva or hairs on the baby's clothing – an absence as yet unexplained. He asked them outright: 'Do you know what happened to Azaria?' They replied they did not.

Meanwhile, a date for the inquest had been set. Lindy and Michael hoped it would stop the ugly rumours and lay all the suspicions to rest.

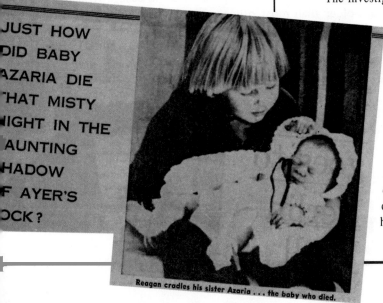

JUST HOW DID BABY AZARIA DIE THAT MISTY NIGHT IN THE HAUNTING SHADOW OF AYER'S ROCK?

Reagan cradles his sister Azaria . . . the baby who died.

FOR LINDY AND MICHAEL CHAMBERLAIN, THE SEVENTH DAY ADVENTIST CHURCH WAS THE ROCK ON WHICH THEIR LIVES WERE BUILT. IT HAD BROUGHT THEM TOGETHER, WOULD HOLD THEM TOGETHER, AND PROVIDE THE WALL OF PROTECTION THEY STILL NEEDED WHEN THEIR CRISIS WAS ALL OVER

LIFE ON THE MOVE

Neither Michael nor Lindy Chamberlain had led remarkable lives before they met, and if it had not been for the dramatic events at Ayers Rock in 1980, they would possibly have continued as two peacable, God-fearing parents propagating the gospel of the Seventh Day Adventist Church.

RELIGIOUS ROOTS

Michael, a New Zealander, is the elder son of Ivan and Greta Chamberlain. Ivan was a former bomber pilot who, after returning from the war, ran the family's 600-acre sheep station and flower farm; Greta was a shop assistant. Michael's parents were a devout religious couple – his father a Methodist, his mother a Baptist – and they expected that Michael would probably take over the farm.

But Greta Chamberlain became converted to Seventh Day Adventism. Michael discovered that he liked the church's teachings and so, aged 21, he was baptised into the church.

Michael decided he would like to enter the church as a pastor and applied for a place at Avondale, the Seventh Day Adventist Training College at Cooranbong in New South Wales. He was accepted and commenced a four-year course, studying for an arts and theology degree. Some five years older than most other students there, Michael was nevertheless readily accepted, partly because he was as fit as the fittest. Taking to heart the teachings of founder Ellen White, who advocated health in religion, Michael ran regularly around the college grounds. It was during his studies that he met Lindy, herself a Seventh Day Adventist. Her father, Cliff Murchison, was a long-standing pastor of the faith.

Lindy's early childhood was spent in Whakatane, on New Zealand's North Island. However, her parents decided to emigrate to Australia, where they spent the first few years

CAMPAIGNING FOR A HEALTHY LIFE

A former smoker, Michael was particularly keen to encourage the community he served to give up the habit. Sometimes at his health meetings in the church hall, he would show films of the damage smoking can do to the body. It was his idea to have two pall-bearers carry a small coffin along the aisle, into which those who had decided to give up the habit could throw their lighters, matches and cigarettes.

Michael kept the coffin in the house he and Lindy had been provided with in the grounds of the Avondale theological college, at Cooranbong (right).

moving from town to town in the State of Victoria, where Pastor Murchison went about the Lord's work. Lindy's mother, Avis, encouraged her daughter to take up dressmaking, and within a few years of leaving school she was a qualified tailoress with a high reputation. For her marriage in 1969, when she was 23 and Michael 27, Lindy made her own white wedding gown .

The couple could not have been more excited as they looked forward to their future together in what they knew would be a variety of towns. The church would regularly move Michael and his family from one parish to another.

First they lived in the small community of Burnie, Tasmania; then they were moved to the sugar-growing town of Innisfail, Queensland.

This was followed by a transfer to the 'company' town of Mount Isa, an oasis of

The Murchison house was situated right next to the Seventh Day Adventist Church where Pastor Murchison regularly held his services.

Five months after moving to the area, Lindy gave birth to their daughter Azaria at the Mount Isa Maternity Hospital on 11 June 1980. Michael, in particular, was delighted that the child was a girl. His family had been predominantly male and with two sons already in his own family, he had all but lost hope that they would have a female child.

A WISH IS GRANTED

'You're kidding!' he exclaimed when told he was the father of a little girl. Lindy, too, was over the moon. 'It was the one she had always wanted, waited for,' a friend was to recall later. Lindy, her friends noticed, put her whole heart into mothering the girl whose name, Azaria, meant 'Blessed of God', or 'Whom Jehova Aids'.

Lindy wrote to many of her close friends about the birth of her youngest child, enthusiastically describing to them everything about Azaria: she had fine brown hair, weighed nearly 3 kg at birth, and was exactly 47cm long. Well aware that Azaria wouldn't remain that small for long, Lindy had already paid

Lindy Murchison grew up in 55 James Street in Whakatane, New Zealand. Like her husband-to-be, Lindy emigrated to Australia, where her pastor father moved from parish to parish.

civilisation in the desert country surrounding it. Here, with two planned children having already swelled the size of their family and another on the way, Michael settled into his regular services at the rather plain, but modern church.

A COMMUNITY STRIKES BACK

It was after Azaria's bizarre disappearance that the rumour-mongers started recalling various details about the Chamberlains. They remembered Michael having that 'weird idea' with the coffin, and then someone put around the story that Azaria had received brain damage after she fell from the supermarket trolley. One rumour fuelled another. Someone looked up the meaning of the name Azaria, but mistakenly confused it with another, Azazel, which meant 'bearer of sins'. The Chamberlains, in many eyes, had been proven guilty on the strength of gossip alone.

in part for some clothes which she would collect when Azaria was six months old.

SEEDS OF SCANDAL

But then an event was to occur that would lead to later trouble. Azaria was sitting in a supermarket trolley one day when her brother Reagan accidently tipped it up as Lindy was going through the checkout. A woman shopper yelled 'Look out!' and, although Lindy dived for the trolley, Azaria hit the floor and the trolley spun around and struck her across the top of the head. She was taken straight to a baby clinic, but nothing was found to be wrong with her – her sight, coordination and hearing were all normal, or even above.

Their friends were rather surprised when, only nine weeks after Azaria's birth, the Chamberlains announced, that they were going on holiday to Ayers Rock. Some thought it was a long way to drive with such a tiny baby. But Michael was keen to go and the family needed a holiday.

Although Michael had never been to the Rock, Lindy had visited the area 16 years earlier with her father, when the drought was at its height. Before they set off, Lindy told Michael all about the dingoes that roam around the Rock.

Whakatane (right) is situated on the North Island of New Zealand. It lies on the coast (below), and faces Whale Island, a popular tourist resort.

A SEARCH FOR

THE CHAMBERLAINS NOW HAD TO FACE THE ORDEAL OF AN INQUEST. THEIR DINGO STORY HAD BECOME THE SUBJECT OF RUMOUR AND SPECULATION THROUGHOUT THE COUNTRY. UNDETERRED, CORONER DENIS BARRITT THREADED HIS PATH THROUGH A MOUND OF EVIDENCE BEFORE COMING TO HIS CONCLUSION

The inquest into the presumed death of nine-week-old Azaria Chamberlain was set for 16 December 1980 – four months after she vanished from the tent at Ayers Rock. Police had been carrying out lengthy investigations and numerous interviews, and now the whole affair was to be examined by a former detective, 54-year-old Denis Barritt, who was currently serving as the Alice Springs Coroner.

HUMAN INTERVENTION

The inquest began in the most sensational manner. Deputy Crown Solicitor Ashley Macknay, assisting the coroner, said that tests on the bloodstained clothing had shown the child had lost at least 20 per cent of its blood, then added that the tests had also suggested that the baby had been removed

The first inquest took place at both Alice Springs, and Uluru Ranger Station, Ayers Rock (right), where on-the-spot investigations were held. The press, meanwhile, constantly hounded the Chamberlains in and out of court.

DATEFILE

DECEMBER 16 1980
The inquest into Azaria's death begins, but Coroner Barritt adjourns the hearing for the Christmas recess

FEBRUARY 9 1981
The hearing resumes at Ayers Rock, and returns to Alice Springs in its tenth day.

FEBRUARY 20 1981
On TV, Coroner Denis Barritt acquits the Chamberlains in his summary

DEC '80-FEB '81

ANSWERS

The Chamberlains returned to the
Rock for the hearing in a private
aircraft they had hired. The press
were there, in position to follow
their every move, providing visual
material for headlines such as:
'RUMOURS HARASS FAMILY OF
AYERS ROCK BABY' and 'IT'S
TRIAL BY SATAN, SAYS WIFE.'

BACK TO THE ROCK

Azaria's father in tears

from her clothing by a
person, rather than by a
dog or dingo. The dam-
age to the clothing, he
told the court, was more
consistent with being
done by a human, and it
appeared the clothing
had been placed where
it was found, rather
than being dragged
there by a dingo.

It was a sensa-
tional start to the
proceedings, fuelled
even further by
Barritt's comment that the indica-
tions were that there had indeed been human intervention in the disposal of the body.

The case was continuing to receive widespread
publicity, and with it came a number of crank
phone messages. One caller to the Alice Springs
courthouse switchboard said he was going to
'blow that bitch (Lindy) away.' The result was a
police escort for the couple when they went to the
courthouse the following day. Then an intriguing
question was raised. Could Michael explain a hole,
about the circumference of a knitting needle, that
had been found in the baby's clothing? No, he
said, he could not.

LEAVING TRACKS

Derek Roff, the chief ranger in the Ayers Rock
region, described the number of dingo tracks and
drag marks that had been found leading away from
the camp site on the night of 17 August. When he
was asked whether he thought it
was possible that a dingo had taken the child, he
replied: 'Yes, it's possible.' Another witness was
an elderly Aborigine, Nipper Winmarti. Through
an interpreter he told the court of the legend of the
Dingo spirit who takes children who dare to leave
the camp at night. But he had never heard of dingoes or other dogs taking Aboriginal children from
his people's camp near the Rock.

When Senior Constable Frank Morris, the first
police officer to examine the baby's clothing, was
called, he described how he approached the jum-
bled clothes at the base of the Rock with apprehension because he thought they might contain
remains. Some 10 metres from the clothes he had
found animal tracks, some of which led into and
out of a dingo lair. The animals that lived there had
all been shot and their stomachs examined. There
were no traces of the child's remains, however.

PERSPECTIVE

NATIONAL PARKS

More than 12 million hectares of land
have been set aside as national parks in
Australia, encompassing a variety of
geographical regions ranging from desert
areas to tropical rainforests. All are
patrolled by rangers, whose job is to
protect flora and fauna. They are normally
on hand to give advice to tourists and, in
some areas, they distribute pamphlets
about the land under their control. In the
Northern Territory, where Ayers Rock lies,
the task of looking after the parks is shared
by Aborigines and whites.

The movements of tourists in the Ayers
Rock national park have been monitored
since 1979 by the Yankuntjatjara tribe, who
claimed the area from the whites who had
been administering it . The Aboriginal Land
Commission granted them full rights in
1980, but the Aborigines continued to
welcome tourists as much as the white
administrators who still worked alongside
them. Until Azaria disappeared, dingoes in
the park were allowed to roam freely.
However, signs have since been erected
warning tourists not to feed the animals.

Christmas arrived, and so the coroner, adjourning the inquest until 9 February 1981, announced that he planned to continue the hearing in the New Year at the Ayers Rock ranger station. The Chamberlains were not to know as they left the courtroom that the months ahead were to be as traumatic as the night Azaria vanished.

QUESTIONS AND REVELATIONS

Over the following weeks the entire country discussed the case. The inquest had so far only deepened the mystery. Prominent on the list of unanswered questions was whether a dingo was actually capable of entering a tent, pushing or pulling aside several layers of blankets, picking up a four-kilogramme baby in its mouth, and running off for several kilometres into the desert. If this was possible, what had happened to the child's remains? And who was the human or humans who had intervened in the disposal of the baby? Where was the matinée jacket Lindy said Azaria had been wearing? It had not been among the other discovered clothes, or nearby. If it could be found, the garment would possibly explain the absence of saliva on the jumpsuit, as the jacket would have covered the suit. The missing matinée jacket was certainly a mystery – and it was to remain a key element in this case.

The inquest resumed at the National Park visitors' centre at the Rock and it was not long before a number of sensational revelations emerged. Dr Rex Kuchel, a consultant botanist to the South Australian police, believed there was a 'distinct possibility' that Azaria's clothes had been buried

> *There's an old adage in forensic science – 'Failure to find is failure to look'.*
>
> Coroner Barritt to Policewoman Myra Fogarty

and then dug up before being placed where they were found. He based this opinion on 'considerable quantities' of reddish sand in the clothing. He also pointed out that, while threads on the garment that had been run through the undergrowth by a policeman during a test had been pulled, there were no pulled threads on Azaria's clothes.

Now it was time for the coroner to inspect the place where the baby's clothing had been found. With the temperature touching 40°C, Mr Barritt, lawyers and other interested parties travelled in a convoy of vehicles to the south-west face of the Rock and climbed over stones and through bushes. The exact spot lay between two large boulders some two metres apart. The coroner took in the general scene, then resumed the hearing at the makeshift courtroom. Witnesses disagreed on various conclusions and the confused state of affairs was not helped by Inspector Michael Gilroy who, when asked whether he thought a dingo had taken the baby, replied: 'I have changed my view several times.'

One by one the witnesses were called, but there was still no real hard evidence to lead the investigation in any specific direction. A statement from Aidan, who had been interviewed by police, confirmed his parents' story about the night – how he had gone to the tent with his mother, followed her to the car to get some baked beans and then returned with her to the barbecue area where his father had asked 'Is that Bubby crying?'

The coroner then called upon Dr Andrew Scott, a veterinary expert who had conducted the Adelaide zoo experiment with the dead goat dressed in baby clothes. He told the court that he

Lindy Chamberlain looks on (below) as a member of the coroner's team examines soil from the spot where Azaria's clothing was found between two large boulders at the base of the Rock.

had found dingo saliva on the test clothes. But he said it was possible that a matinee jacket could have prevented saliva reaching Azaria's jumpsuit and singlet. He also said bloodstains on the baby's jumpsuit were heaviest around the collar, where the blood appeared to have flowed down to the left shoulder straps and the back of the right shoulder.

CUTS AND MARKS

The hearing, by now into its tenth day, returned to Alice Springs. Meanwhile, Sergeant Frank Cocks had been experimenting with scissors. In court he brought out the sensational evidence that holes in the right collar and left sleeve of the jumpsuit appeared to have been made with some sort of blade, possibly scissors. Under a microscope, the fibres of the material showed up as being cleanly sliced, rather than being frayed, he explained, and he showed how scissors could have made the cut.

Another witness, Dr Kenneth Brown of the University of Adelaide, cast further doubt on the Chamberlains' account when he said that two holes in the singlet were inconsistent with the teeth

AUSTRALIA'S TOURISTS

When the Chamberlain family arrived at Ayers Rock, they were among thousands of tourists from around the world who travel to the monolith, the colours of which change according to the weather and the time of day. One of the tourist's favourite occupations is to walk up the steep incline to the top of the Rock, a one-kilometre haul along an anchored chain that provides a good hand-hold. For the average tourist it takes 40 minutes to get to the top, but a New Zealand athlete once baffled the locals by managing the distance in just 10 minutes.

The first white 'tourist' to arrive at the Rock was the explorer W.C.Goss, who was probing inland Australia with his camels, billy-cans and salt beef in 1873. After seeing the enormous shape on the horizon, his excitement flowed from his diary: '...what was my astonishment, when, two miles distant, to find it was an immense pebble rising abruptly from the plain...it is certainly the most wonderful natural feature I have ever seen.' Goss named the Rock in honour of Sir Henry Ayers, the then Premier of South Australia.

INSIDE VIEW

SCIENCE UNDER SCRUTINY

From the start of the inquest, Coroner Barritt (above left) was quick to dismiss evidence that he believed did not fit in with the way he saw the case.. Being a former detective, he was ready to criticise anyone who had failed to act professionally or objectively.

His most severe criticisms were of 25-year-old Myra Fogarty, an inexperienced member of the forensic team of the Northern Territory Police. She told Barritt that there had been a noticeable lack of blood on items in the tent, whereas evidence had been given that blood had been found. Angry that she had missed the blood, Mr Barritt asked her: 'Were you taught anything about the objectivity that a forensic technician should adopt?'...'I will tell you for the future that it is utterly vital for a forensic scientist not to go outside observation and to be totally objective when making examinations. There's an old adage in forensic science – 'Failure to find is failure to look.' His words proved prophetic.

Above: Coroner Barritt was tired of the vicious rumour-mongering that had surrounded his inquest into the case of missing baby Azaria. At the end of the hearing, Barritt took the unprecedented step of televising his summing up to the nation, in order to dispel the gossip surrounding the Chamberlains.

marks of a dingo. Yet Les Harris, a dingo expert, said that, based on his knowledge of the animals' feeding habits, it was a distinct possibility that a dingo could have taken away the baby and consumed the corpse.

CAMERAS MOVE IN

After two weeks of evidence, Coroner Barritt announced his findings. The way he did this caused a sensation – he allowed a television camera into the courtroom so that the delivery of his verdict could be shown to the entire nation. This decision was as unprecedented as cameras being allowed into a court in the UK. In 24 hours the opinions of this softly-spoken man would, he hoped, put to rest one of Australia's most baffling mysteries.

After going carefully and methodically over the background, and recounting the scientific evidence, Mr Barritt commented that bloodstaining to the neck and back of the jumpsuit coincided with the theory that Azaria was taken away by her head and neck in the mouth of a dingo, although he agreed there were inconsistencies in the evidence. He also put forward the suggestion that there were some people living around the rock who might be inclined to conceal Azaria's body to protect the reputation of dingoes, which were a tourist attraction. Of one thing he was certain – that the accounts given by Pastor and Mrs Chamberlain were truthful. And now he gave his conclusions.

Delighted by the result of the first inquest, in which Coroner Barritt exonerated them from any responsibilty for Azaria's death , the Chamberlains relax by the poolside at a friend's house. Their happiness , and that of their family, would last only briefly.

When Lindy saw the dingo at the entrance to the tent, it was holding her baby by the neck or head, causing fatal injuries. But Barritt accepted the evidence, too, that cuts to the sleeve and neck of the jumpsuit could have been caused by scissors. The absence of dingo saliva and hairs suggested the animal's possession of the child was interrupted by a human, or humans.

He was satisfied that at some stage the child's clothing was removed and buried, to be later dug up, rubbed on undergrowth near the base of the Rock, and placed at the spot where it was later found. He again reinforced his belief that these actions had been carried out to protect the reputation of the dingo.

BARRITT'S CONCLUSION

The Chamberlain family, he said, were in no way responsible for the baby's death. His conclusion was that after the child had been killed by the dingo, and after her clothing had been removed from the body, buried and then dug up again, the baby's body had been disposed of by a person or persons unknown.

So the inquest was over. The Chamberlains walked out into the sunlight, free of all blame. Their happiness was not to last.

DAWN OF A

DESPITE THE OPTIMISM OF THE NEW DECADE, THE YEAR 1980 BROUGHT TO AUSTRALIA A HIGH INCIDENCE OF CRIME, TOP-LEVEL CORRUPTION AND MISDIRECTED JUSTICE

The 1970s had ended with the Vietnamese invasion of Cambodia, the exile of the Shah of Iran and the rise to power of Ayatollah Khomeini. A nuclear accident at Three Mile Island in Pennsylvania caused panic on the USA's east coast, and Margaret Thatcher became Britain's first woman Prime Minister.

GLUT OF CRIME

The first year of the new decade was an optimistic one for Australians, with the birth of the world's fourth test tube baby in Melbourne and the emergence of the country as a leader in in-vitro fertilisation research. The Australian racing driver Alan Jones won the Formula One World Championship and Australian Evonne Cawley became only the second mother in history to win the Women's Championship at Wimbledon.

In April 1983, while the superb beaches around Sydney were packed with the usual contingent of surfers and sunbathers (above), several Australian peace organisations took to the city's streets (right) to demonstrate their opposition to the nuclear arms race and nuclear test explosions in the Southern hemisphere.

Crime appeared to be on the increase, however. In the week leading up to Azaria's disappearance, the Australian media carried more than the usual number of 'heavy' crime stories. Alleged crime boss Robert Trimbole, who was to gain international infamy when he was eventually arrested in Ireland, was excused from giving evidence at a Melbourne inquest even though police said there was evidence linking him to drug-related murders in New Zealand.

Australian Labour leader Bob Hawke (seen left with his wife and the Prince and Princess of Wales) succeeded Malcolm Fraser (inset) as Prime Minister in 1983.

In Sydney, former Cabinet minister Ian Sinclair was found not guilty of forging the annual reports of a funeral company while he was a director. On the same day, 14 August, the Mayor of a New South Wales community was charged with conspiracy, forgery and making false statements. The following day, Federal Police seized counterfeit US bank notes totalling more than $1million, along with a printing press and counterfeiting plates.

By a strange coincidence, just two days before Lindy Chamberlain was to become

THE MEDIA

While much of the reporting was accurate, there were cases of blatant inaccuracy or stories written on the basis of rumour.

In fact, there are only about five reporters who actually write exactly what you say .The rest of them use a little bit of licence.

Lindy Chamberlain

DECADE

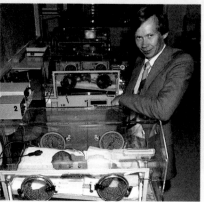

In-vitro fertilisation expert Dr Andrew Speirs poses with Australia's first test-tube quadruplets.

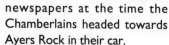

In 1983, Australia became the first nation other than the United States to win the America's Cup yacht race. Initially seen as the underdog, the yacht Australia II beat the much-favoured Americans and took home the most coveted of all yachting trophies. The Australian public – to say nothing of the boat's crew (inset) – were ecstatic.

newspapers at the time the Chamberlains headed towards Ayers Rock in their car.

As if the Australian public had not had more than its fair share of crime stories in the media, some front pages on Sunday 17 August gave prominence to the murder of Playmate of the Year Dorothy Stratten in Los Angeles. She was killed by a shotgun blast to the head from her estranged husband Paul Snyder, who had then turned the gun on himself.

It was perhaps not so surprising then, that after reporting on crime for a month, the Sydney media were almost at the shoulder-shrugging stage when news reached them of Azaria's disappearance. The story made it on page three of the widely-read *Sydney Morning Herald* under the heading 'Little Hope for Baby Girl Taken by Wild Dog'. However, it received less prominence than a story reminding readers that 50 years had passed since the two arms

of the arch of the Sydney Harbour Bridge had first been brought together.

SMALL NEWS

Over the following weeks, the child's disappearance became lost among a flood of other events. The US presidential election was looming and protests against the Soviet invasion of Afghanistan were gaining momentum. And John Lennon was shot dead. In contrast, the case of a missing baby seemed relatively minor.

The Aborigines fought a hard legal battle to win back their traditional lands. Heralding a positive change in white Australian consciousness, this sign at Ayers Rock openly acknowledges Aboriginal land rights.

named Arthur Thomas who had been convicted of the murder of his neighbours Harvey and Jeanette Crowe in 1970. After two unsuccessful appeals in 1973 and 1975, the then Prime Minister, Robert Muldoon, ordered an inquiry into the case in 1978.

WARPED JUSTICE

Thomas was pardoned just before Christmas 1979, and the government set up a commission of inquiry to examine the misconduct of the police and to assess the financial damages due to Thomas. Details of the police force's hostile attitude to the inquiry were published in Australian

embroiled in a mystery that was to put justice itself under the microscope, developments were taking place in a fascinating case in New Zealand. It involved a farmer

Pukulpa pitjama aṉanguku ngurakutu.....

Welcome to Aboriginal Land!!

MANTA DAY 1985

THREE

A QUESTION OF

THE CHAMBERLAINS' HAPPINESS WAS SHORT-LIVED. ALMOST A YEAR AFTER THEIR NAMES HAD BEEN CLEARED AT ALICE SPRINGS, THEY FOUND THEMSELVES AT THE CENTRE OF A SECOND INQUEST – ONE WHICH HAD ALL THE ATMOSPHERE OF A MURDER TRIAL

After the coroner had handed down a verdict exonerating Lindy and Michael, they walked out onto the steps of the court building. There, before a large crowd, they held up a poster-size photograph showing Lindy with Azaria in her arms. The photo, they said, was their greatest treasure, and those who had spread rumours about them would have to make peace with their God.

INTERNATIONAL INQUIRIES

As the Chamberlains headed back to Mount Isa to restart their life, new investigations began. With the coroner's finding of 'human intervention', police agreed that they could not close the case. One month later, in February 1981, they launched a highly secret investigation codenamed Operation Ochre. It was named after the yellowish clay Aborigines use for their rock paintings.

The investigation spread its tentacles across Australia and also overseas, to London. The

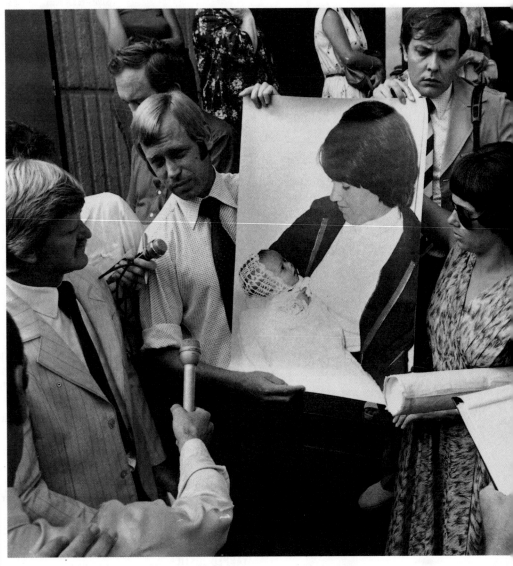

DATEFILE

NOVEMBER 20 1981

The findings of the first inquest are superseded by new evidence.

DECEMBER 14 1981

The second inquest begins.

FEBRUARY 1 1982

The inquest resumes after the Christmas adjournment. Des Sturgess, representing the coroner, suggests that Azaria was murdered in the Chamberlain family car.

NOV '81-FEB '82

Adelaide police scientist, Dr Kenneth Brown, had been disappointed that much of his evidence had been dismissed by Coroner Barritt on the grounds that he was not a dingo expert. Reluctant to stand down, he obtained permission to take Azaria's clothing to England for examination by one of the world's top forensic scientists, Professor James Cameron of the London Hospital Medical College.

Applying the latest scientific techniques, the 51-year-old professor built up his own theory as to what had happened to Azaria. His experiments set

into motion a new chain of events. First, Cameron flew to Australia for a secret meeting with the Northern Territory Chief Minister and the Solicitor General, where he presented a report of his findings.

The result was another visit to the Chamberlains by Detective Sergeant Graeme Charlwood – the man who had questioned them so thoroughly before. It was a tense meeting, details of which were to emerge later. The police then seized the Chamberlain's yellow car as rumours spread that Azaria had been decapitated and that a

MURDER

The Alice Springs law courts (above) were the scene of the first and second inquests into the death of Azaria Chamberlain. Detective-Sergeant Graeme Charlwood (right), who collected evidence for both hearings, was closer to the Chamberlain case than any other police officer. Charlwood's easy-going, yet courteous manner, gave Lindy the confidence to give interviews which – unbeknown to her – were being taped.

Vindicated by Coroner Denis Barrit, the Chamberlains walked out onto the steps of the Alice Springs Law Courts. They smiled at the 100 or so waiting people and unrolled a poster-sized photograph of Azaria, aged six weeks, lying contentedly in Lindy's arms.

bloody human palm-print had been discovered on her clothing.

Yet another scientist was called in. Mrs Joy Kuhl, a forensic biologist from New South Wales, spent three days going over every inch of the vehicle's interior in a chemical search for traces of baby's blood.

On 20 November, a second blow was delivered to the Chamberlains. There was to be another inquest, since the findings of the first had been superseded by new evidence. At Ayers Rock, a team of police started digging, without saying what they were looking for. Michael and Lindy's nightmare had started all over again.

TRIAL BY INQUEST

The second inquest began at Alice Springs on 14 December 1981, almost a year to the day since the first. It had all the atmosphere of a criminal trial, the legal benches being filled with lawyers, including a QC and a Queensland barrister named Des Sturgess, who was appointed to assist the coroner, Gerry Galvin. When Galvin opened the proceedings, relevant items of clothing, including those worn by the baby and by Lindy on 17 August 1980, were brought before the court.

Michael was called to give evidence before Lindy. When questioned by Sturgess, he admitted that he had been under stress and could not recall things – but he did think, when questioned about accidents involving the family car and about people who might have bled in the vehicle, that there had been three. There was also a man they had picked up after a road accident and taken to hospital.

When Sturgess pointed out that Michael had kept his camera bag under his legs in the car on the night Azaria vanished, the pastor explained that he always kept it there to allow him fast access to his cameras. The explanation seemed simple enough at the time, but as it turned out, the camera bag was to be a vital exhibit.

It was then Lindy's turn to sit in the witness box. She too was questioned about people who might have bled in the car, and replied that, on more than one occasion, both her sons had had nose bleeds and once, Reagan had hit the dashboard, bitten his lip, and bled onto the door handle. Furthermore, members of a young people's group in the church had sat in the car with cut feet, cut fingers and nose bleeds, because the car had been used as a first aid station.

Lindy was then questioned about the visit Detective-Sergeant Charlwood had made to her and she agreed they had discussed Professor Cameron's alleged new findings – findings that supposedly showed the baby had been decapitated and that a bloodstained hand-print had been found on the clothes.

Lindy was asked if she would be prepared to give a sample of her palm-print. She would, she said, if her lawyers gave her the go ahead. The

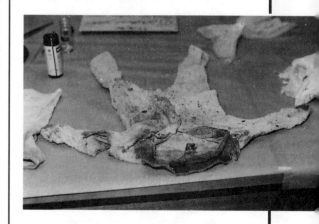

Azaria's blood-stained jumpsuit is displayed as evidence during the second inquest. Many forensic experts suggested that the almost uniform bleeding around the neck did not indicate a dingo attack, but rather decapitation by human hand.

151

a child could be grasped by the neck and bleed to the extent Azaria had bled without causing damage to the neck of the clothing. The damage to Azaria's clothes, he said, had been caused by a cutting instrument such as a pair of scissors.

THE VOICE OF SCIENCE

With the aid of ultraviolet fluorescent photography, which helped distinguish blood marks, Cameron had been able to create a clear picture of staining on the clothing because blood showed up darker than other marks. It was clear to him that Azaria had not bled from two areas of the neck, as would occur if an animal's jaws had held her, but from all around the neck.

Cameron believed that, at some point, Azaria had been buried while fully clothed. If the clothes had been buried without the baby, he said, there would be folded or 'pinched' areas that did not have sand and earth on them. However, Cameron claimed he had found staining all over the clothes, suggesting that the baby was wearing them for some time after its death.

BLOODY HAND-PRINT

Further tests had identified what Cameron believed to be four fingerprints of a young adult right hand on the left shoulder blade – he dismissed any suggestion that it could have been made by a child of four or six. The mark, he said, had been produced by an 'adult human hand that was bloodstained and of the same blood group as the rest'. Cameron had also found what he said was a thumb mark on the front of the right shoulder. To demonstrate the way he believed Azaria

Professor James Cameron (seen right) at Ayers Rock during the second inquest. He travelled from England on three separate occasions to answer questions about the Chamberlain affair.

THE COLOUR OF BLOOD

In her preliminary search for blood in the Chamberlains' car, biologist Joy Kuhl used what is known as the ortho-tolidine test. Under this system, a dry filter paper is rubbed on the surface being tested and a drop of reagent, or ortho-tolidine fluid, is then added to the paper. If there is no change in colour, a drop of hydrogen peroxide solution is added to the same area on the paper and the presence of blood – and sometimes other substances – is shown by the appearance of a bright blue colour.

Mrs Kuhl's experiments produced a number of colour changes when she ran tests in the car, so to confirm her belief that blood might be present, she then scraped areas of the car and tested these samples by using an anti-serum (a fluid constituent of blood with antibodies in it). An anti-serum is designed to show a reaction to blood or a component of blood. When these anti-bodies are brought together with antigens (enzymes and toxins) present in particular types of blood, the resulting reaction produces a visible band of colour.

A disdainful Lindy Chamberlain looks on as biologist Joy Kuhl, Barrister Des Sturgess and others prepare to examine the Chamberlain's car. Kuhl was called to offer a scientific opinion, but her laboratory techniques had an aura of infallibility about them, which made her testimony seem more like fact than opinion.

court then moved to a police vehicle compound where the Chamberlain car was stored. There, biologist Joy Kuhl made her claims. She had found blood in several areas of the car, she said, and after testing some of the larger stains, had discovered the presence of foetal haemoglobin, a blood constituent only found in babies of six months and under.

FORENSIC INFALLIBILITY

Back in the court-room, with scientific evidence dominating the proceedings, pathologist Anthony Jones from Darwin told how he had examined the car and found tiny drops of blood with 'tails'. According to Jones, they were the result of 'arterial spray', an effect produced by the vigorous flow of blood from a small artery while the heart was still beating.

After Coroner Galvin and the team of lawyers, along with Lindy and Michael, visited Ayers Rock again to inspect the camping area and the place where the clothes were found, it was time to call the man whose findings were said to have changed the whole course of the investigation – Professor James Cameron. Professor Cameron told how, using a dingo skull, he had been unable to find how

INSIDE VIEW

FOETAL BLOOD

One of the damaging earlier findings, later to be disputed, was the discovery of what was described as foetal blood in the Chamberlains' car. This is also known as baby's blood, or foetal haemoglobin, and is present in infants up to the age of about six months.

Haemoglobin is the red colouring matter of the red blood corpuscles. The level of the foetal variety starts to decrease from the time of birth and is gradually replaced by adult haemoglobin, so that by the time a child is past six months old, less than one per cent of foetal haemoglobin is present in its blood. Azaria's blood contained about 25 per cent foetal haemoglobin and 75 per cent adult.

There have been cases where foetal haemoglobin persisted through life as a result of an abnormal genetic condition, particularly in some Mediterranean countries, but such cases are extremely rare in Australia and New Zealand. Forensic biologist Joy Kuhl, who carried out tests in the car to search for foetal haemoglobin, had come across only one case where it was still detectable in a girl of 12 – and she had emigrated from Greece to Australia with her parents.

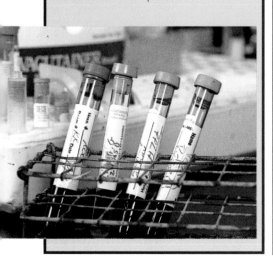

had been held, he raised a doll in front of the Coroner, his thumbs at the front, fingers at the back. Someone, he concluded, had held the baby while the blood was flowing, or had hands that were 'damp with blood' when the child was picked up.

Professor Cameron said he thought that the baby's jumpsuit had been fastened at the neck at the time bleeding occurred, but that the two top studs had been undone before the jumpsuit came

The Chamberlains had to suffer the trauma of two return trips to Ayers Rock – one for each inquest. They are shown here at the base of the Rock with their lawyer, Stuart Tipple, in the foreground.

into contact with the reddish sand of the Ayers Rock area. It would be reasonable to assume that Azaria 'met her death by unnatural causes and that the mode of death had been caused by a cutting instrument, possibly encircling the neck or certainly cutting the vital blood vessels and structures of the neck'.

The words of the remaining witnesses seemed almost incidental to the mound of evidence that had been presented to discredit the dingo story.

Michael and Lindy Chamberlain leave court after a day's proceedings at the second inquest. The attentions of the media showed no sign of abating throughout the hearing.

But Detective Sergeant Charlwood raised further doubts when he told how he and six other police officers searched the Ayers Rock area for three–and–a–half days without finding a shred of new evidence that could be linked with Azaria's disappearance. He said that during a visit to the Chamberlain home, he had seized a variety of items the family had taken with them on their holiday, but when he asked for the tent pegs, Michael said he did not know where they were.

> *You're crediting me with the brains to commit the perfect murder and get away with it.*
>
> Lindy Chamberlain to Detective Charlwood

When the inquest resumed on 1 February, after the Christmas adjournment, Des Sturgess caused a sensation by suggesting that Azaria had been killed in the family car and that Lindy had later told her husband a dingo was not involved. He pointed out that there was ample opportunity for the baby to have been buried in her clothes, dug up later, undressed and for the clothing to be taken to the base of the Rock. The camera bag, he suggested, had been used for a time to hide the body.

Lindy was committed for trial on a charge of murder, Michael on a charge of being an accessory after the fact of murder.

FACE TO FACE WITH *Lindy Chamberlain*

LINDY CHAMBERLAIN SURVIVED A DECADE OF MENTAL TORTURE AND EMERGED FROM THE EXPERIENCE A STRONGER, MORE INDEPENDENT PERSON. HERE, SHE TALKS ABOUT HER LIFE BOTH DURING AND AFTER HER ORDEAL

Lindy Chamberlain sees herself as the victim of a huge miscarriage of justice. Although she continues to feel angry about it, she is thankful that her family have remained together and are able to live like normal human beings. But she knows that Australia will not forget the case.

ON MICHAEL

When Lindy was sent to prison, she asked Michael if he wanted to divorce her. She knew that her family needed a mother, a role she could

not fulfil while she was in prison. However, Michael emphatically refused to divorce her, convinced of her innocence and determined that, eventually, Lindy would be able to

❚❚ It's going to take another tragedy for all the doubts to be dispelled. ❚❚

resume her normal roles of mother and wife. She says: 'Our relationship is much deeper than one which has been held together by the fight to prove our innocence. What attracts you in the first place, keeps you together. If you don't lose that, then you stay together. Yes, Michael and I had to re-learn being married after I came home from jail, but we did it. The kids settled into having me back straight off. There were no problems – except telling them to have a bath every night. Oh, and making their bed every morning.'

ON STRESS

Lindy's emotions often deceived the public. 'People tend to think that you've got to be in buckets of tears every time they see you. I suppose there was antagonism because, under stress, I reacted a little differently from the expected norm and from what you usually see in the movies. Women are supposed to be stupid, lose their heads and scream and panic, and I don't do it. In human nature, there's a blink between laughter and crying. There's no middle road – you have either got to learn to laugh at yourself, to live with yourself, or you cry.

'If you howl all the time, nobody wants to know you, or you try to see whatever is reasonable in a situation and you laugh at yourself. If you can't take any more, well, I guess you are knocked around a bit. You cannot take any more, so it all goes over your head and you've got to make the best of what is around you, otherwise you will have a complete, total mental and physical breakdown. But we're no longer in battledress. We're free now and prepared to talk much more.'

ON PRISON

'Every time I see a policeman, I cringe. They tried to break me, but they couldn't. The police who pursued me have got to live with themselves, which is the hardest thing to do. With that type of nature, you become so suspicious of everyone and everything that the best friend you have is yourself. People with that sort of personality only have friends with a similar personality, be they police or prison officers.

'You know, I really am just an ordinary woman. There are hundreds of people around like me. I saw girls day after day coming to jail, with their kids ripped off them, and they knew how to handle that. There were only two ways – you grin and bear it, despite what you feel inside and you don't let others know what you feel inside, or you take it hard and make it worse on yourself. What got me through was my determination.

'You could go to any average street in any average town and pick one person out of each street and throw them into jail for ever and ever. There are some really lovely people in jail, there are some really nasty ones and there are a lot in between. You have the whole range of human behaviour.'

ON GOD

Lindy says she found her strength in her faith. 'I found I had to rely totally on God and very early on I had to say "I don't know why this is happening, but You (God) know the end from the beginning, so just hold on there and see me through this." I thought there would be stages where I wouldn't have the strength to hold to God, so I asked Him to hold to me and we'd get through this together.

'There was a tremendous amount of trauma at being parted from the family, but I knew that somewhere along the line it would be realised that a mistake had been made, and I just trusted God to work that out because

❚❚ Every time I see a policeman, I cringe. They tried to break me, but they couldn't. ❚❚

there was nothing that I could physically do.'

ON PUBLICITY

'People get an idea in their head of what they want you to be like. They see you on TV, they write to you and from your letters and your looks they have a mental picture of you. When they meet you, it's not necessarily you, but they have sat you on a pedestal and if you do anything that takes you off it, then they can't handle the difference, so they go back to what they think you ought to be.

'Out of it, I've become a much more forthright, more forceful and independent person than I once was. I've learned, perhaps, to be self-sufficient. People automatically think you are rich and powerful because they see you on telly and think you're a superstar. Now I hear people saying we don't need compensation because we're rich. They don't stop to think about our legal and personal debt. If you don't work – and Michael has had his living taken away from him; he can never work as a pastor again – you're in debt. Some of the legal debt has been paid off by public contribution, but there is still a lot of pay-off and we still have to live.'

ON DINGOES

'It's going to take another tragedy for all the doubts to be dispelled forever from the mind of the public. One day it will happen again. The dingoes come up to the outskirts of Alice Springs now. One day, one will take a kid out of a bed. It's only a matter of time. And then, will someone go for murder for something they didn't do, like me?'

Lindy Chamberlain remains an optimist, despite the continuing pressure of hostile public opinion.

FOUR
THE TRIAL

ON 13 SEPTEMBER 1982, THE CHAMBERLAINS
PLEADED 'NOT GUILTY' TO A CHARGE OF
MURDER. DURING A TRIAL WHICH WOULD LAST
ALMOST SIX WEEKS, THEY WERE TO FACE A
BARRAGE OF CROSS-QUESTIONING AND THE
ACCUSING VOICE OF FORENSIC SCIENCE

It was billed as 'The Trial of the Century'. On the morning of 13 September 1982, Ian Barker QC, for the Crown, told the Darwin Supreme Court that baby Azaria Chamberlain died very quickly 'because somebody had cut her throat.' In the dock, Lindy and Michael sat side by side. They had pleaded not guilty.

Mr Barker said the Crown did not venture to suggest any reason or motive for the killing. 'We simply say to you that the evidence... will prove beyond reasonable doubt that, for whatever reason, the baby was murdered by her mother.' The dingo story, he told the Supreme Court judge, James Muirhead, was a fanciful lie, designed to conceal the truth that Azaria had died by her mother's hand. 'When the mother commenced to walk to the tent, the child Azaria had not long to live.'

The Crown alleged that Lindy sat in the front of the car and cut the baby's throat. The blood in

A MOTHER ON

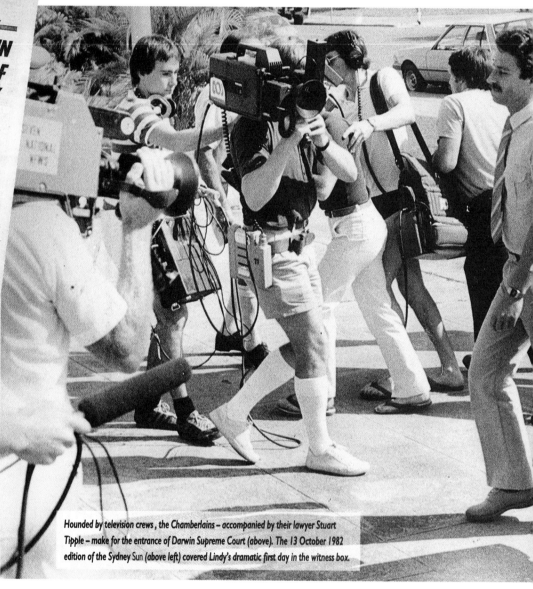

Hounded by television crews, the Chamberlains – accompanied by their lawyer Stuart Tipple – make for the entrance of Darwin Supreme Court (above). The 13 October 1982 edition of the Sydney Sun (above left) covered Lindy's dramatic first day in the witness box.

DATEFILE

SEPT 13 1982
The trial begins. The Chamberlain's enter a plea of 'not guilty'

OCT 29 1982
Lindy Chamberlain is convicted of murder. Judge Muirhead passes a sentence of life imprisonment with hard labour

SEPT '82 – OCT '82

The strain of her long trial showing clearly on her face, Lindy leaves Darwin Supreme Court after a day of cross-questioning.

TRIAL

the car, said Mr Barker, was critical to the Crown's case. It would be preposterous to believe that a dingo carried the baby into the car. The likelihood was that the child's body was in Michael Chamberlain's camera bag in the car when Lindy returned to the barbecue area, because foetal blood had been found on the camera bag.

Mr Barker then went on to suggest that, during the night of 17 August 1980, somebody buried the baby's body, still in its clothes, near the camp-site. The body was later recovered from the shallow grave, the clothes removed and the body reburied.

DAMNING EVIDENCE

The Crown witnesses were called, many repeating what they had already told the Coroner at the second inquest. For the Chamberlains, it was looking bleaker by the day. Having already told the inquest he believed the jumpsuit had been cut by scissors and not dingo's teeth, textile expert Malcolm Chaikin revealed that he had found six baby hairs in Michael's camera bag.

As expected, Professor Cameron, who had flown back to Australia for the trial, came under critical questioning by the Chamberlains' lawyer, John Phillips QC, who suggested he had made a number of false assumptions.

The next witness was Lindy Chamberlain herself, now heavily pregnant with her fourth child. Guiding her through her evidence of seeing the dingo coming from the tent, Mr Phillips then reminded her that the Crown claimed 'you did not put your baby to bed but you took her to the car and, in the front seat of the car, you cut that child's throat. What do you say to that?' For a moment, Lindy looked directly at her lawyer. Then she threw her hands to her face and cried: 'It's just not true!'

DENIAL

Mr Barker, cross-examining Lindy, said: 'I put it to you that you sat in the front passenger seat... that you held the baby in front of you and that you cut its throat.' She denied this and angrily told him: 'We are talking about my baby daughter – not some object.' Lindy denied that blood from the child splattered the front of her tracksuit pants and fell onto her shoes or that a spray of blood went up under the dashboard, or that blood flowed down the offside of the seat in which she was sitting and

ran under the hinge. She denied removing her bloodstained tracksuit pants before going back to the barbecue area.

Michael was then called to give evidence, and within half an hour, he was slumped forward with his hands to his face, tears pouring down his cheeks. Mr Phillips said to him: 'The prosecution case is that at some stage during the evening you became aware that your baby had been murdered by your wife. What do you say to that?'

'False.'

'It is suggested that at some stage during the evening you buried the child somewhere near the area of the tent.'

'Quite false.'

'And it is suggested either you or your wife then took the baby's clothes off and put them near the Rock, where they were found on 24 August. What do you say to that?'

'That is clearly false.'

When asked about the cuts in the sleeve of the jump suit, Michael denied that he had made them.

'Did you cut the collar?'

'No.'

'Did your wife cut the sleeve?'

'I don't think so.'

'Did she cut the collar?'

'I don't think so.'

Asked whether he knew if his wife had gone to the base of the Rock after they had checked in at the motel on the night of the disappearance, Michael said: 'Well, I was asleep most of the night; at least, I was asleep some parts of the night, fitfully. But to my knowledge, she didn't.'

Michael was then asked whether he and his wife had ever discussed the possibility that some-

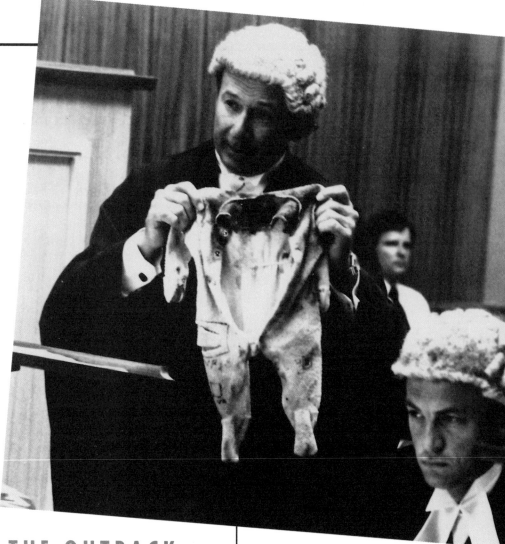

Above: Prosecuting barrister Ian Barker, played here by an actor, presents Azaria's jumpsuit as evidence during the trial (taken from the 1988 film A Cry in the Dark). *Right: Michael enters Darwin Supreme Court in the company of Stuart Tipple and a sheriff.*

thing other than a dingo caused the death of their child. Yes, they had. 'One was a theory that an Aboriginal person looking like a dingo or dressed in feathers might have tried to simulate an attack.'

'And most of the others have been as fanciful as that?'

'Yes.'

The questioning was over. The trial had been running for 28 days, the prosecution had called 45 witnesses, the defence 28, and their evidence had filled 2800 pages of transcript. Now all that remained was the summing up – and the verdict.

THE ABSENCE OF MOTIVE

Mr Phillips spent over a day addressing the jury, giving an eloquent speech charged with emotional phrases and packed with as many facts that contradicted the prosecution's arguments as he could draw from his briefcase.

As far as motive was concerned, he said, the prosecution was 'stone motherless broke.' Whereas the defence, he added, had been able to

THE ABORIGINES OF THE OUTBACK

In Alice Springs and at Ayers Rock, a number of Aborigines live in what most white people consider to be primitive conditions — sheltering under canvas and cooking their food over open fires. Because of the widely differing cultural backgrounds of the two races, there have been occasional clashes, with the whites claiming the Aborigines are frequently drunk, and the Aborigines accusing the whites of destroying their culture.

However, both Aborigines and white Australians are united when emergencies, such as lost people, arise in the Outback. Police frequently call in Aboriginal trackers to help them with searches, due to their ability to find tracks that the whites would miss.

When the cry went up that Azaria was missing, a number of Aboriginal trackers from the Pitjantjatjara tribe who lived around the Rock joined in the search. They told police of finding

drag marks in the sand, and a depression where a dingo had laid down something it was carrying. There was also a furrow in the sand, they said, that could have been made by the dragging of an arm or a leg. After following numerous tracks, the Aborigines pointed out that the changes of direction revealed the cunning of a dingo. They finally lost the tracks, however, finding that they had been blown away by the wind.

DID THIS MOTHER KILL THE DINGO CASE BABY?

Mystery of the outback

The Daily Mirror helped keep British interest in Lindy's case alive. This article, published on 14 September 1982, discusses the proceedings of her trial.

provide 'proof after proof of this mother's love and affection for her baby.' The prosecution had had two years and three months to think of a reason, any reason, why Lindy should have cut her baby's throat, but had failed to find even one.

Mr Barker, in his summing-up for the Crown, conceded there were no eye-witnesses who had seen the child killed and that the case was based on inferences drawn from established facts. While the Crown could not provide a motive for the killing, the prosecution was able to say that it did happen. Lindy Chamberlain's story, he said, was an affront to the intelligence of the jury. Having told the lie Lindy had stuck with it.

DEXTEROUS DINGO

On the defence account, said Mr Barker, the dingo went to the tent, pulled the child from its cot, ran from the tent, buried the child, disinterred it, then carried it across 14 kilometres of desert. It then took the child from the clothing, causing relatively little damage, turned the singlet inside out and left the booties inside the jumpsuit. If the Chamberlains were to be believed, he said, the court was dealing with not only a dextrous dingo, but a very tidy dingo.

At 2pm on Friday 29 October, the jury filed out of the courtroom. At 8.30pm the nine men and three women returned to their places in the jury box. The foreman was asked: 'Do you find the accused, Alice Lynne Chamberlain, guilty or not guilty of murder?'

'Guilty.'

With that word, a stunned hush fell over the court. Even the judge seemed taken aback, having directed the jury that they had to be sure beyond reasonable doubt that Lindy had murdered Azaria

PROFESSIONAL PRIDE

What became abundantly clear during the two inquests and the trial was the professional pride that various experts place in their work – and how much they dislike being challenged. It was because dental expert Dr Kenneth Brown from Adelaide had been disappointed by the rejection of his evidence in the first inquest, that he applied to Professor Cameron in London in the hope of having his findings confirmed.

When biologist Richard Nairn, Professor of Pathology and Immunology at Melbourne's Monash University medical school said he disagreed with the prosecution's forensic evidence, including that of Professor Cameron, he was asked if he was suggesting that methods employed by police forensic experts in London were in some way inferior to those used by research biologists. Professor Nairn replied testily: 'Some of them are, because they haven't the advanced equipment and they haven't got the very advanced training. Since forensic science laboratories were established, immunological courses were set up. Mine was the first in Australia, and indeed one of the first in the world, in which we actually train young scientists as immunologists. One day those people will filter into forensic science laboratories and then the problem will be solved.'

Michael was convicted of being an accessory after the fact of murder, but his sentence was to be determined the following morning. For Lindy Chamberlain, there was only one punishment. 'You', said Judge Muirhead, 'will be imprisoned with hard labour for life.' Outside it was dusk. Lindy's sabbath had just begun.

> *So the case ends as it began, with a cry in the dark.*
> Malcolm Brown, journalist
> — *Sydney Morning Herald*

MISUNDERSTOOD

LINDY CHAMBERLAIN REPRESENTED A DISTURBING AND UNACCEPTABLE CONTRADICTION. SEEN AS BOTH A DEVOTED MOTHER AND A CALLOUS MURDERESS, SHE ATTRACTED LITTLE SYMPATHY FROM THE AUSTRALIAN PUBLIC

Alice Lynne Chamberlain was convicted partly because of the way she conducted herself after the disappearance of Azaria at Ayers Rock. A short, dark-haired woman who belonged to a little-known church, the Australian public found her difficult to understand. And by failing to understand her, some saw her as a mysterious figure capable of evil. She was condemned not for murder as such, but because of a public belief that she had violated the sanctity of motherhood.

PUBLIC DISGUST

Lindy was considered guilty from the time she and her husband announced, only a few hours after Azaria's dramatic disappearance, that they were convinced their baby was dead. What mother, the public asked, would give up hope so easily? Why did they not frantically search through the night for their new-born child who, for all they knew, could still be alive out there in the darkness?

As time was to prove, Lindy is a strong-willed woman with deep-seated beliefs in her religion. She accepted that a nine-and-a-half-week-old baby could not survive for long in the freezing hours of a desert winter night and believed that

Lindy and Michael pose with 'their greatest treasure' – the poster of Lindy holding Azaria – shortly after the first inquest. Many felt that such publicity exercises were in bad taste.

she and Azaria would be reunited in heaven.

In her mind, having accepted that Azaria was dead but that she would meet her again, Lindy saw no harm in purchasing mementoes from the Ayers Rock store before she and Michael headed back to Mount Isa. In the public's mind, it was at best the act of a tasteless,

bad mother; at worst, the actions of a callous murderess who wanted to leave the scene of the crime, along with a few spoils, as quickly as possible.

For the first inquest, Lindy appeared to be a rather plain woman who made almost no effort to make herself look attractive – a practice in keeping with the teachings of

her church. Yet for the second inquest, after she and Michael had been warned that some allegedly damaging evidence would be presented against them, her appearance changed considerably. She rarely wore the same dress more than twice and made little attempt to cover up her tanned shoulders. This had a negative

THE GOOD MOTHER

In his examination of the Chamberlain affair, Royal Commissioner Mr Justice Trevor Morling summed up Lindy's character as a mother. 'The undisputed evidence,' he said, 'is that Mrs Chamberlain was an exemplary mother and was delighted at Azaria's birth. She did not suffer from any form of mental illness nor had she ever been violent to any of her children. She had spent the day with her family on 17 August and had not exhibited any sign of abnormal behaviour or irritation with Azaria.'

The Judge believed that any inconsistencies in Lindy's evidence might have been caused by her confusion of mind. 'The belief that people might unjustly accuse her of making up the dingo story might have led her, even subconsciously, to embellish her account of what happened, and this may explain some of its improbabilities,' he said.

impact on many Australian women, who had become convinced of Lindy's guilt simply because she seemed to be more interested in making herself look attractive than in the death of her baby.

What few saw as Lindy sat through the daily routine of the second inquest was what she was sketching in a notebook. In

Below: A free Lindy Chamberlain thinks back over a decade of trauma.

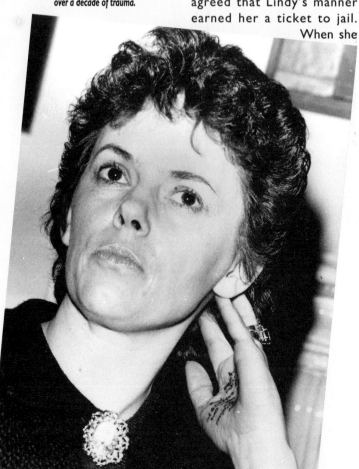

between the recorded comments of the various witnesses, Lindy was drawing tombstones – row upon row of graves. Those who saw this wondered whether her outward appearance belied her inner thoughts.

TICKET TO JAIL

Nevertheless, members of the legal profession have since agreed that Lindy's manner earned her a ticket to jail. When she finally appeared before a criminal trial looking very plain and very pregnant it was too late to change public opinion of her. Kerryn Goldsworthy, a lecturer in English at Melbourne University comments:

'I think it might well have been her pregnancy, more than her determined attempts to speak for herself – to construct her own image in her own words – which turned the scales against her, simply because she represented for Australian society a disturbing and unresolvable contradiction and therefore a threat to complacently held beliefs.'

While the public had its views about Lindy, she had her own perceptions about the public. As her trial approached, she knew that the majority of

Lindy holds Reagan to her during the first inquest in 1980 (top). Her appearance was greatly changed by the time of her trial in 1982 (above).

people held her to be guilty because of her behaviour and because of the belief that it was impossible for a dingo to have taken the child. And even after her conviction was finally quashed, she was prepared to accept there were many who still considered her guilty.

SENTENCED TO LIFE IMPRISONMENT, IT SEEMED

THAT LINDY CHAMBERLAIN WOULD NEVER BE

REUNITED WITH HER FAMILY. FOUR YEARS

LATER, NEW EVIDENCE CAME TO LIGHT WHICH

THREW DOUBT ON THE PROSECUTION CASE AND

LED TO HER EVENTUAL RELEASE

PICKING UP THE PIECES

Above: The High Court of Australia
in Canberra, where Lindy's second appeal
was rejected in February 1984.

DATEFILE

NOV 14 1982

Lindy is released on bail, pending an
appeal to the Federal court in
Sydney

APRIL 30 1983

The Federal court rejects Lindy's
appeal and she returns to Berrimah
Prison

FEB 22 1984

A second appeal, this time to the
High Court, is rejected by a three-
to-two majority

NOV'82-FEB'84

After her conviction for murder in October 1982, Lindy Chamberlain was taken to Darwin's Berrimah jail. Michael was put on a suspended sentence of 18 months and a good behaviour bond. Less than three weeks later, Lindy was transferred to a local hospital where, under guard, she gave birth to her second daughter, Kahlia. The authorities allowed Lindy to spend four hours with the baby, before taking Kahlia from her; they believed a woman found guilty of murdering a child might be capable of doing it again. Released on bail in November, pending an appeal to the Federal Court, Lindy was briefly reunited with her family. The court rejected her appeal, however, and she returned to jail in April 1983, where she would spend the greater part of three years.

Lindy and Michael appealed again, but the case was rejected once more. By that time, many Australians had started to take Lindy's claims of innocence seriously, and public meetings were held to discuss action to secure her release.

Towards the end of 1985, with Michael looking after the three children, the campaign really

Michael Chamberlain (left) studied at Avondale College for his Masters degree while Lindy, shown cradling Azaria in her arms, served time in prison.

gained momentum. Lawyers were hired by a syndicate of Seventh Day Adventist businessmen who pressed the Northern Territory Government for an inquiry into the case. The response was that there would be no inquiry without new evidence. The Chamberlain's long-term solicitor, Stuart Tipple, agreed that any new evidence had to be 'genuinely new... it has got to be completely new and something of sufficient cogency.' When the new evidence they had all been hoping for came, it turned up in the most dramatic manner.

THE 'POSSESSED' ENGLISHMAN

Thirty-one year-old English tourist David Brett was walking through the scrub towards the southwest corner of Ayers Rock where, five-and-a-half years earlier, Azaria's jumpsuit had been found.

Originally from Kent, David Brett decided in his early twenties that he wanted to travel around the world, and in the late 1970s he arrived in Australia for the first time, and found work in an

Below: After Lindy's sentence was passed, a group convinced of her innocence founded the 'Free Lindy Campaign'. Sally Lowe (right), one of the Chamberlains' fellow campers at Ayers Rock, was an active campaigner.

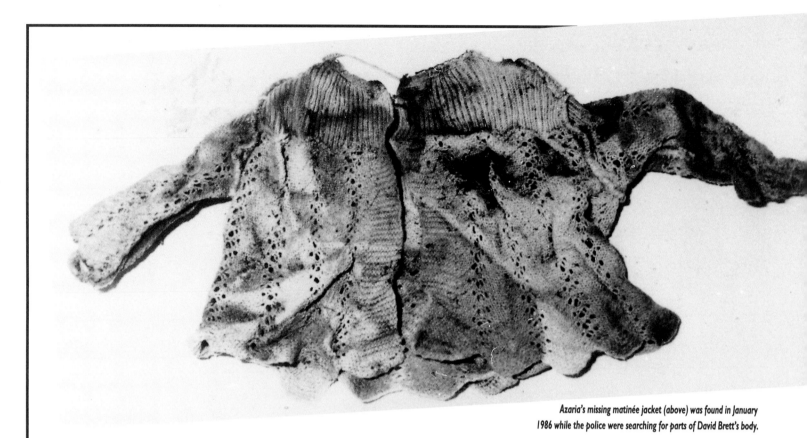

Azaria's missing matinée jacket (above) was found in January 1986 while the police were searching for parts of David Brett's body.

INSIDE VIEW

LINDY'S LIFE IN JAIL

The authorities at Darwin's Berrimah Prison placed Lindy in a cell on her own, as they were concerned that other prisoners would, on their release, boast that they had shared a cell with the 'notorious' Lindy Chamberlain. Some inmates regarded Lindy as the Queen Bee first because of her infamy; secondly, she was the oldest prisoner in Berrimah; and thirdly, she was serving a life sentence for murder.

Life with hard labour did not mean breaking up rocks, but it certainly meant toeing the line and doing a variety of menial chores around the jail complex. After her release, Lindy said that rock-cracking might have been preferable to scrubbing out the male warders' toilets. She also had to scrub out the medical centre and the warders'

recreation room, picking up their discarded cigarettes and litter.

Lindy soon learned the individual whims of women warders: one would allow her to take her shoes off to give her feet a rest, while another would insist she kept them on. Some prison officers were particularly harsh. After having her new baby daughter taken from her, Lindy was in agony as her milk continued and her breasts swelled. When she asked one officer for a breast pump, the request was refused, and it was only when she almost fainted that a different officer brought a pump to her. Lindy shed the extra kilograms from her pregnancy by jogging around the compound and following a strict diet and exercise routine.

iron ore mine. The next few years saw him drifting from place to place, playing his guitar and finding work to pay his way.

David Brett dabbled in the occult, and many of his friends engaged in mystic practices. Until May 1985, his mother, Mrs Doreen Brett, assumed all was well with her son, but then he started sending her cryptic messages indicating something was wrong. Greatly disturbed, he told his friends in Perth that he was possessed by a demon, saying, 'it's living in my stomach'.

Brett was put in touch with a Congregational clergyman, Pastor Milton Gabrielson, who believed the young man to be possessed. The pastor tried to exorcise the evil spirit, but realised his attempt was unsuccessful. 'I know I'm going to be killed. They want me to die,' David told the Pastor, without being specific. He visited his family in England, and told them that the exorcism had only made matters worse, that it had taken all the good from him.

A FALL WITH CONSEQUENCES

Back in Australia once more, Brett started reading the Bible avidly. Then, without telling friends where he was going, he suddenly headed out to Alice Springs, where he got into conversation with a farmer about exorcism. He was next seen walking along the road towards Ayers Rock. It was Australia Day, 26 January 1986. On reaching the base of the Rock, Brett started climbing. He began his ascent a little after 8pm – about the same time

BACKDROP

DAVID BRETT'S INQUEST

It may have seemed a strange twist of fate that Denis Barritt, the Coroner who had presided over the first inquest into Azaria's death, found himself conducting another bizarre inquiry connected with the case – the inquest into the death of Englishman David Brett.

Brett, who fell off Ayers Rock and landed close to Azaria's missing matinée jacket, had claimed earlier that he was possessed by the devil. But Coroner Barritt had his own opinions: 'I take the view that all this stuff about witchcraft and stuff like that is just an irrelevancy,' he said. In his official finding, he said: 'The deceased was apparently observed attempting to climb the Rock from an unauthorised locality late on 26 January 1986. His actions were reported to rangers who went to the area but could not see the deceased on the Rock. The Rock was not unclimbable in the area where the deceased was observed. It appeared the deceased left scuff marks on lichen (moss) on the side of the Rock above

Continued on page 2

where his body was discovered. It appears the deceased had been suffering from mental illness during the latter years of his life but there is no evidence to indicate his fall was a deliberate act on his part. Accordingly, I find the deceased died by accident.'

David Brett (left) believed that he was hunted by members of an occult group bent on doing evil to him. After his death, Brett's mother claimed her son had told her that he might be the victim of a ritual human sacrifice.

PROFESSOR JAMES CAMERON

Dingo case professor defends findings

By Christopher Zinn in Sydney

ONE OF Britain's leading forensic pathologists yesterday defended his key findings to an official inquiry into the controversial Australian dingo baby case.

Prof James Cameron of the London Hospital's Department of Forensic Medicine, has been recalled to testify to the Royal Commission inquiring into the conviction of Mrs Lindy Chamberlain for the 1980 murder of her daughter, Azaria.

It was Prof Cameron's evidence in 1982 that helped jail Mrs Chamberlain for life for the murder of nine-week-old Azaria, who vanished from her parents' tent at Ayers Rock.

After two inquests, a trial, and two appeals a Royal Commission is examining the case in which Mrs Chamberlain claims a dingo took her baby.

In Sydney yesterday Prof Cameron said he stood by his evidence that a human hand, and not a dingo, was behind the death.

He said the blood staining on the baby's jumpsuit, the

Prof. James Cameron

only trace of Azaria that was ever found, indicated her throat had been cut with a sharp object.

"The incisive wound to the neck would not have been any form of attack I know from the canine family," he continued.

The professor, who suffers from a serious heart complaint and flew in for only two days to give evidence, denied claims from the Chamberlains' lawyers that he was sticking to his story to defend the reputation his forensic work in the case had made.

He also defended his claim that special photography revealed the imprint of a blood-stained human hand on the jumpsuit, despite being told the "blood" was probably the mark of red iron oxide from the desert sands.

Prof. Cameron was the last important witness to be called before the Commission which has heard testimony from 150 people and cost more than £3 million.

It is expected to hand down a decision on the case, which has polarised Australian public opinion for nearly seven years, by July.

The man who changed the course of the Chamberlain inquiry enjoyed a high reputation in Britain for over two decades. Professor James Cameron – whose credentials include Doctor of Medicine and Doctor of Philosophy at Glasgow University and Professor of Forensic Medicine at the London Hospital Medical College – successfully helped the British police with their inquiries for several years.

Cameron told the Chamberlain inquest that since 1957 he had conducted some 1500 to 2000 post-mortem examinations a year. A consultant to the Home Office and Scotland Yard's detective training school, Cameron had been involved in a range of cases, including a blaze in which 10 people died when a fire bomb was thrown into their south-London house in 1980.

Some of Cameron's findings have been contradicted by other pathologists, however, most notably in the case of Maxwell Confait, a transvestite who was murdered in Catford, near London, in 1972. Three teenage boys were convicted on the weight of Cameron's forensic evidence. They spent three years in prison before it was discovered that the professor – who concurred with this – had based his investigation upon an incomplete knowledge of the facts of the case.

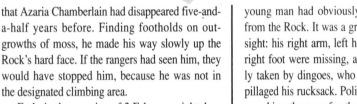

that Azaria Chamberlain had disappeared five-and-a-half years before. Finding footholds on outgrowths of moss, he made his way slowly up the Rock's hard face. If the rangers had seen him, they would have stopped him, because he was not in the designated climbing area.

Early in the morning of 2 February, eight days after David Brett had started his climb on the Rock, a tourist stumbled across his body. The young man had obviously fallen from the Rock. It was a gruesome sight: his right arm, left hand and right foot were missing, apparently taken by dingoes, who had also pillaged his rucksack. Police started searching the area for the lost human limbs. Just 150 metres from the body, one of the officers found clothing, soiled, stained and partly buried – it looked as though it could be Azaria Chamberlain's missing matinée jacket.

This was a devastating blow for the prosecution evidence. The Crown had earlier dismissed her frequent claims that Azaria had been wearing a matinée jacket, which would have explained why no dingo saliva or hairs had been found on the jumpsuit. The prosecution had also said that patterns of blood on the jumpsuit were not consistent with the child wearing a matinée jacket at the time.

SHIFTS IN PUBLIC OPINION

With the discovery of the jacket, the authorities had no alternative but to release Lindy from jail. The authorities went back through her evidence, checking all references to the matinée jacket. One comment, made to Detective Sergeant Charlwood before the first inquest, now seemed particularly significant. All relevant clothing had been collected by police, she had said, 'except that matinée jacket... there is as much chance of it being off on

Above: Lindy Chamberlain flew home to Avondale immediately after her release from prison in 1986. Although she was free, her conviction was to stand until the following year.

a bush, on the way from the Rock somewhere, as there would be down a den (dingo lair), and left away from the other clothes, I should think.'

Police could not explain why the jacket had been missed during meticulous searches of the Rock area. Concentration was shifted to an official inquiry into a re-examination of the entire evidence. With Lindy, now aged 38, out of jail after serving close to three years, she was free to give interviews, and told a nationwide audience that she loved 'that little girl.' She had not wiped that night from her mind. 'I've got a very good memory. I can shut my eyes and see it all over again.' In a television poll, viewers were asked whether they thought Lindy was innocent. A total of 52,250 said yes; 48,242 said no.

ROYAL COMMISSION

A Royal Commission of Inquiry into the Azaria Chamberlain affair began in October 1986, before Mr Justice Trevor Morling. One by one, the wit-

DATEFILE

FEBRUARY 2 1986

Azaria's matinée jacket is found near the body of David Brett, who fell from Ayers Rock

FEBRUARY 7 1986

Lindy is released from jail, but her conviction stands

JUNE 2 1987

The Royal Commission of inquiry concludes that the evidence could not justify a conviction of the Chamberlains

JUNE 2 1987

Three judges in the Northern Territory Court of Criminal Appeal quash Michael and Lindy's convictions and they are acquitted

FEB'86-JUN'87

nesses, many of them already familiar with the questions from previous inquiries, were called to give their evidence. The hearing, which was costing over £90,000 a week, became weighed down with the vital, but complicated issue of whether there was baby's blood in the Chamberlains' car. Opinions on this were diverse, but what became abundantly clear was that the 'routine' tests carried out by forensic scientist Joy Kuhl were questionable. Under question was the age of the blood (which would go through a deterioration process during which its make-up could alter), the various temperatures to which it had been exposed in the car, and the suitability of the flu-

ids Joy Kuhl had used to test whether it was baby's blood, or in fact blood at all.

When Lindy, by now more confident than she had been during the trial, was called to give her evidence, she told Ian Barker, the QC who had led

> ' *I don't like you, Mr Barker.*
> *I never have liked you.*
> *If you expect me to be polite*
> *to you, don't.* '
>
> Lindy to the Prosecution lawyer,
> Ian Barker QC

the Crown case against her and who was now representing the Northern Territory Government: 'I don't like your form of law and I don't adhere to it. It's the reason for these courts in Australia being in such a mess.'

After 92 days of evidence from 145 witnesses, with a further nine days taken up with submission from counsel, Judge Morling could now begin writing his report and adjudicatewhether or not Lindy Chamberlain murdered her baby and whether her husband helped her in a cover-up. The judge could reach only one of two simple conclusions: either the evidence would persuade him beyond reasonable doubt that the Chamberlains were guilty, or he would decide that it was insufficient grounds for a murder conviction.

In 1987, three Northern Territory judges quashed the Chamberlains' convictions. Michael and Lindy leave court (left), ecstatic at having their names finally cleared.

PERSPECTIVE

LETTER TO A PRINCESS

Among those who joined in the long campaign to free Lindy Chamberlain were her two sons, Aidan and Reagan. They penned letters to a number of personalities, including the Northern Territory's Chief Minister, Mr Ian Tuxworth, Prime Minister Bob Hawke, and the Prince and Princess of Wales. Aidan wrote: 'Dear Mr Tuxworth and Mr Hawke, I cannot understand why you are keeping my mummy in jail when I know she did not kill my baby sister Azaria.

My mummy loved bubby just as we all did and I was with mummy and talking to her the hole (sic) time. I miss my mum and Kahlia, Reagan and Dad do to (sic). Is there nothing you can do to help me?' Reagan wrote: 'Dear Mister Tuxworth, Mr Hawke, Prince Charles and Princess Diana, I can still remember the dingo walk on my chest. I loved my bubby Azaria and so did mumy (sic). We need mummy at home so does kahlia need a mumy. Can you make them let my mum come home to me? From Reagan.'

One area Judge Morling examined very carefully was the question of blood in the car. He felt he would not be able to conclude beyond any reasonable doubt that blood was present in the car, but he considered that the number of positive results from the various tests obtained by Mrs Kuhl in the area of the hinge of the passenger seat and the floor beneath showed it was more probable than not that some blood was present in those areas.

Whose blood was it? Mr Justice Morling decided that none of Mrs Kuhl's tests established clearly that any such blood in the car was Azaria's.

He further decided that he was 'far from persuaded that Mrs Chamberlain's account of having seen a dingo near the tent was false, or that Mr Chamberlain falsely denied that he knew his wife had murdered his daughter. That is not to say that I accept that all their evidence is accurate. Some of it plainly is not, since parts of it are inconsistent

with other parts.' But he went on: 'In my opinion, if the evidence before the Commission had been given at the trial, the trial judge would have been obliged to direct the jury to acquit the Chamberlains on the ground that the evidence could not justify their conviction.'

The Crown's case against the couple had completely collapsed. Science had gone under the microscope and had been found wanting. Without hard scientific fact to back up the supposed sequence of events at the camp site, that was the end of the case against the Chamberlains.

QUASHED CONVICTIONS

The couple still had two more fights on their hands – to clear their names completely (because their convictions still stood), and to win compensation for Lindy's imprisonment and for the money spent on legal fees, estimated to be at least £500,000.

It was 15 months before their prayers were answered when, on 15 September 1988, three judges in the Northern Territory Court of Criminal Appeal quashed their convictions and entered verdicts of acquittal. Wrangles about compensation were to drag on until 1990.

Lindy concedes that some people will, in spite of the new evidence and judge's decisions, always believe that she and Michael were responsible for Azaria's death. 'They will die maintaining we are guilty and we will just have to live with that,' she said. Knowing that some still saw her as a murderess – could she really live with that? Yes, she said, quite easily, 'because I know they are wrong and it's what you know yourself that counts. Because the person you have to live with is yourself.'

Top: After Lindy's release, the Chamberlains resumed a relatively normal family life at their home in Avondale (inset).

THE BIRD FACTOR

One fascinating question raised by the Chamberlains after the inquest that cleared their names was why police had not investigated bird involvement in disturbing or damaging Azaria's clothing.

The Outback is alive with birds of prey ranging from soaring eagles to flesh-eating crows. En masse, they have the ability to strip a kangaroo carcase to the bones within hours. Lindy, who was keenly interested in the Outback and the creatures that inhabit it, suggested during the initial police investigation that the habits of certain birds might hold an answer to at least part of the mystery. She complained publicly that nobody had investigated the possibility that birds such as crows or eagles could have dropped Azaria's clothing at the spot it was found. Since the inquest, she said she and Michael had received information that a bird's beak or talons were capable of inflicting the scissor-like marks on a jumpsuit.

PERSPECTIVE

THE BEHRINGWERKE REPORT

Apart from the discovery of the matinée jacket, which considerably weakened the Crown's case against Lindy, there was one other factor which resulted in her release. This was a letter sent to the Northern Territory Solicitor General by the German chemical company Behringwerke – the firm which supplied the chemical reagent used by biologist Joy Kuhl to test stains found in the Chamberlains' car. The letter said the stains found in the car were not suitable for detection and determination of foetal or adult blood, and the company could not guarantee that the anti-serum would react only with HbF – a factor in foetal blood – in all test conditions. 'Referring to the HbF detection in the Chamberlain case, the results obtained in our view remain doubtful,' said the letter. The fact that the Press had got its hands on the letter put the government in a spin, and to lessen its impact, Lindy was released.

BACKDROP

THE DOWNFALL OF JEREMY THORPE

The saga of Jeremy Thorpe began in 1961 when he received an unexpected visit from a young man at the House of Commons. Eighteen years later, after allegations of a homosexual affair, the bizarre shooting of a dog on Exmoor and the revelations of a self-styled 'hit man', the results of that visit reached an extraordinary climax. Jeremy Thorpe, Privy Councillor and ex-leader of the Liberal Party, went on trial along with three others faced with charges of conspiracy to murder.

The four men were cleared of all charges.

Jeremy Thorpe, *MP for North Devon and Leader of the Liberal Party from 1967. He quickly became one of the most well-known and popular characters in British politics.*

Norman Scott, *the stable boy and unsuccessful male model with a fatal inability to look after his own life.*

Peter Bessell, *Liberal MP for Bodmin and Thorpe's closest political friend. Unknown to most, his finances were constantly on the brink of collapse.*

Andrew Newton, *the airline pilot with an appetite for taking risks, who was said to be prepared to do 'anything for a laugh'.*

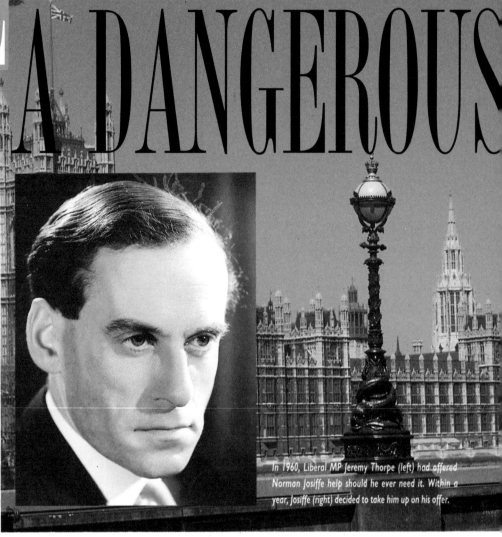

A DANGEROUS

JEREMY THORPE WAS 32 YEARS OLD AND EMBARKING ON A POLITICAL CAREER OF OUTSTANDING PROMISE, WHEN HE BEFRIENDED A YOUNG STABLE BOY MORE THAN 10 YEARS HIS JUNIOR. IT WAS AN INVOLVEMENT HE WOULD NEVER BE ALLOWED TO FORGET

A t the Houses of Parliament, on the winter afternoon of 8 November, 1961, a young man named Norman Josiffe turned up looking for help, and was turned away. There was nothing malicious in the act. It was just that he was accompanied by his Jack Russell terrier, 'Mrs Tish', and dogs are not allowed into the Palace of Westminster. A policeman directed him round the corner to the Whitehall office of the Anti-Vivisection League, where he was able to leave the dog before coming back.

This time, he entered the visitors' lobby without trouble and filled in a green card asking to see Mr Jeremy Thorpe, member of Parliament for North Devon, and one of the Liberal party's rising stars. Josiffe was neither a Liberal nor from Devon. He had met Thorpe the year before at the riding stables at which he had then been employed and had found the MP to be a sympathetic listener.

Thorpe remembered the good-looking young man, and asked that he be shown to his office. There, Josiffe poured out his story concerning troubles he had had with Brecht Van de Vater, his ex-employer at the stables. Thorpe was as

In 1960, Liberal MP Jeremy Thorpe (left) had offered Norman Josiffe help should he ever need it. Within a year, Josiffe (right) decided to take him up on his offer.

sympathetic as Josiffe remembered him to be. Josiffe explained that he had walked out of the job and had shortly afterwards suffered a nervous breakdown which had led him to the Ashurst Clinic, an Oxfordshire psychiatric unit. He had left the clinic a few days before with no money, no job, and nowhere to live. Most importantly, because of his abrupt departure from de Vater's Kingham riding stables, he did not have a National Insurance card, making it difficult for him to get a job.

THE FIRST NIGHT

Jeremy Thorpe was kindness itself. He would do all he could to help, and in the meantime would solve Josiffe's immediate problems of accommodation. He told the young man to collect his dog and meet him that evening. As dusk descended, Josiffe, 'Mrs Tish' and Jeremy Thorpe drove out of central London together. First they went to a house in Dulwich, where Josiffe was introduced to two friends of the MP and then on to Thorpe's mother's house in Surrey. Mrs Ursula Thorpe lived at 'Stonewalls' in Oxted, an area

familiar to Josiffe from the fact that he had learned to ride at the Westerham stables nearby. On the way, Thorpe suggested to him that it might be easier if he introduced him to Ursula as a member of the TV crew which was to follow Thorpe abroad the next day.

That night, according to the evidence that Norman Josiffe was to give at the Old Bailey 17 years later, Jeremy Thorpe came to his bedroom. Josiffe's vivid account of their love-making was to be steadfastly denied by Thorpe. According to Josiffe, it was the beginning of a long homosexual affair, while Thorpe consistently maintained that the connection between the two men was nothing more than a warm friendship.

Over Christmas 1961, Thorpe arranged accommodation for his new friend at the home of old friends, James and Mary Collier of Culmstock, Devon. Mr Collier was prospective Liberal candidate for Tiverton. According to Josiffe, Thorpe and his mother came down over the holiday and stayed at the Broom Hill Hotel near Barnstaple. Josiffe was to claim at the Old Bailey that the two men had continued their sexual

DATEFILE

NOVEMBER 8 1961
Josiffe visits Thorpe at the Houses of Parliament

FEBRUARY 8 1962
Police interview Josiffe at Thorpe's Westminster office

FEBRUARY 13 1962
Thorpe writes 'Bunnies' letter to Josiffe

NOV '61 – FEB '62

FRIENDSHIP

PERSPECTIVE
THE BUNNIES LETTER

Thorpe's 1962 letter to Norman Josiffe became one of the most talked about pieces of evidence in the lead-up to the Liberal Party leader's trial 17 years later. It was one of the few surviving letters between the two and was relied upon by the prosecution as strong evidence to counter Thorpe's claim that there was no more to the relationship than simple friendship. 'My Dear Norman,' it began,

'Since my letters normally go to the House, yours arrived all by itself at my Breakfast table at the Reform, and gave me tremendous pleasure.

I cannot tell you just how happy I am to feel that you are really settling down and feeling that life has something to offer.

This is really wonderful and you can always feel that whatever happens Jimmy and Mary and I are right behind you. The next thing is to solve your financial problems and this James Walters and I are on to. The really important point is that you are now a member of a *family* doing a useful job of work – with Tish – which you enjoy. Hooray!! Faced with all that no more bloody clinics.

I think you can now take the Ann Gray incident as over and done with.

Enclosed another letter!! I suggest you keep them all – just in case – but will you send back the photo? Thank the guy but say you are fixed up. Bunnies *can* (and *will*) go to France. In haste.

Yours affectionately, Jeremy
I miss you'

relations both at the Barnstaple hotel and at the Colliers' home.

Back in London, Jeremy Thorpe helped Josiffe to find a small flat in Chelsea. Gradually, Thorpe built up what he thought was a picture of the personable, sensitive young man. Josiffe told him how his father, an architect, had been killed in an aircraft accident in South America, and that his mother had disappeared. Thorpe, who had a genuine desire to help the underdog, took Norman with him to the Reform Club and to dine at Chelsea restaurants. He also got him a temporary job helping Len Smith, a Liberal Party official who was organising an appeal for victims of a hurricane disaster in British Honduras.

Then, at the end of January 1962, came the first inkling of trouble. When Josiffe left at the end of the appeal job, he took Len Smith's briefcase with him. He had, he told Thorpe, taken it 'inadvertently' and Thorpe smoothed out the ripples caused. Almost simultaneously, a Mrs Ann Gray, whom Josiffe had known at the Ashurst Clinic, complained to police that Josiffe had stolen her suede coat. When the police came to interview Josiffe, Thorpe insisted that they question him at Thorpe's own office near the House of Commons.

The MP told the investigating officer that Norman's father had been killed in an air crash, and that since his mother had also disappeared, Thorpe was 'more or less guardian to him'. The policeman formed the opinion that Norman Josiffe was a weak personality, nervous and completely dominated by his 'guardian'.

LETTERS TO JOSIFFE

After the police interview, Josiffe went to a farm at Withypool, Somerset, where Thorpe had found him a job in the stables. There, on 13 February 1962, Jeremy Thorpe wrote to him. It was one of several affectionate letters Norman Josiffe was to claim at the Old Bailey he had received from Thorpe. The letter concluded: 'Bunnies *can* (and *will*) go to France.' There was a postscript; 'I miss you'. 'Bunny' was Thorpe's pet name for Josiffe, and the reference to France was an allusion to Josiffe's ambition to go there and study dressage.

In the months that followed, Thorpe's mood was to change dramatically as it became more and more evident that his enthusiasm for Josiffe was cooling. But the politician's attempts to disentangle himself from his involvement were hampered by a severe problem. Norman Josiffe was not going to accept rejection with good grace.

MAKINGS OF A

JEREMY THORPE WAS A BORN POLITICIAN. HE WAS A SUPERB ORATOR WITH THE CHARISMA AND ORIGINALITY TO WIN A PERSONAL FOLLOWING, AS WELL AS THE PERSUASIVE CHARM TO CARRY FORWARD HIS POLITICAL CAREER

The Oxford Union – Oxford University's most prestigious debating society – boasted some famous faces in 1951. Most notable are William Rees-Mogg, later to edit The Times newspaper (back row, fourth from right); Asa Briggs, historian (front row, second from right); Jeremy Thorpe, President (fourth from left) and a youthful Robin Day (front row, far left).

Although identifying himself as 'middle-class', Jeremy Thorpe had distinguished ancestors of whom he was very proud. These included a John Thorpe, Speaker of the House of Commons during the Peasants' Revolt of 1381, who was butchered by the mob at Westminster. His maternal grandfather was Sir John Norton-Griffiths – known as 'Empire Jack' because of his colonial exploits.

Thorpe was born on 29 April 1929, into a family he was to describe as 'warm, emotional, neurotic, close.' It was also staunchly conservative. His affable Anglo-Irish father, John Thorpe, was born in Cork but raised in England. Thorpe senior had a distinguished career as a barrister, becoming a King's Counsel before being elected Conservative MP for Rusholme (Manchester).

Thorpe's mother Ursula (daughter of 'Empire Jack'), was a formidable figure in her local Surrey Conservative constituency, sporting a monocle and an 'Eton Crop' hairstyle. Jeremy had two elder sisters, Lavinia and Camillia. Camillia, who was seven years older than Jeremy, was to commit suicide in 1974.

FAMILY SERVANTS

The Thorpe family home was a Georgian town house in Kensington with a staff of servants. At the age of five, Jeremy's precocious libertarian instincts led him to question why the parlour maid, rather than his mother, had to bring in coal for the fire.

When he was six years old, Thorpe developed tubercular glands which affected his spine, obliging him to lie flat in a spinal carriage. Apart from causing a life-long back problem, this meant that he was never able to take part in sport at school. Instead, he specialised in music and drama, becoming an excellent violinist and a brilliant mimic.

In 1940, Jeremy, like many other middle-class children, was shipped off to the United States to avoid the Blitz. He stayed with an aunt in Connecticut, and attended the Rectory School, a stronghold of budding Republicans. It was here, he claimed, that his radical leanings began to become pronounced.

Returning to England in 1943, he immediately went to Eton, where he excelled at French, drama and public speaking. He won a prize for his violin playing, shunned sports and annoyed his contemporaries by boasting of being 'middle-class' and an American-style Democrat.

ARMY CALL-UP

At 18, Thorpe, like all other young men of the time, was called up for two years' National Service. He was conscripted into the Rifle Brigade as a private, but served only six weeks before being discharged. He was, he later explained, judged 'psychologically unsuitable.'

STRENGTH THROUGH BEREAVEMENT

Unknown to his fellow Etonians, Jeremy Thorpe had been facing domestic tragedy with great courage. Shortly after Jeremy's return from America, his beloved father suffered a massive stroke which deprived him of speech. Jeremy, aged six, is pictured (left) with his father at centre, outside Westminster Abbey. When John Thorpe died, Jeremy was grief-stricken. He grew closer to his mother and to her old friend Lady Megan Lloyd George, Jeremy's godmother and daughter of former Liberal Prime Minister, David Lloyd George.

STATESMAN

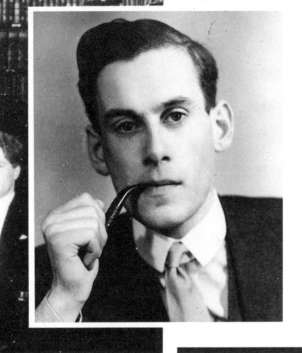

Living in elegant style during his student days at Oxford, Thorpe's flamboyant Edwardian clothes, which he was to sport throughout his career, soon made him a familiar figure. Law studies took second place to socialising and politics, tastes which he shared with such contemporaries as William Rees-Mogg, later to edit *The Times*, and Robin Day. He joined the University Liberal Party with men such as Timothy Beaumont, later a prominent Liberal peer; David Holmes, who was to stand alongside Thorpe in the dock of the Old Bailey; and George Carman, who was to defend Thorpe.

Lady Megan Lloyd George (above) had a vital influence on Thorpe. Later, he claimed that she, more than anyone, drew him to Liberalism.

After his discharge, Thorpe went straight to Trinity College Oxford to read law. His undergraduate career was characterised by an undisguised ambition to gain office in influential and fashionable student clubs. Thorpe's enormous charm probably saved him from the worst consequences of an emergent streak of ruthlessness.

In quick succession, he was elected President of the Oxford Liberal Club and then the Law Society. He then pursued the biggest prize of all, the presidency of the Oxford Union. It was a post which guaranteed safe entry to any chosen career for a reasonable applicant.

In pursuit of his election to the post, he was alleged to have used tactics which included orchestrating an underhand campaign against another candidate, and usurping the sitting president's privilege in personally inviting guest speakers to take part in Oxford Union debates.

UNION PRESIDENT

Regardless, in 1951, he joined the distinguished list of people who have been president of the Oxford Union. But all this was at the expense of his studies. 'Jeremy,' said his mother, 'carried all before him except his degree.'

He managed, in fact, a third class degree, which was sufficient to get him into the Inner Temple, where he was eventually called to the Bar. A year later, in 1952, he was adopted as Liberal candidate for North Devon. The constituency had once been a stronghold of his party, but was by then Tory. For seven years he was to use all his charms on his potential constituents – addressing the older folk in a perfect North Devon accent.

While campaigning for the Liberal party, Thorpe pursued a career as a barrister on the Western Circuit and became familiar as an early television personality on ITV political programmes. He also took a pioneering stand against South African apartheid.

The people of North Devon finally voted him into the House of Commons on 10 October, 1959.

Thorpe's grandfather (below), Sir John Norton-Griffiths, better known as 'Empire Jack'.

KEEPING THE PAST AT BAY

THORPE WAS RISING RAPIDLY THROUGH THE LIBERAL PARTY RANKS, BUT THE SECRET OF NORMAN JOSIFFE REFUSED TO GO AWAY. FIRST, FRIENDS WERE CONFIDED IN, THEN A GOVERNMENT MINISTER WAS APPROACHED. FINALLY, MONEY BEGAN TO CHANGE HANDS

T he first sign that Thorpe was trying to find a way to end his involvement with Norman Josiffe came at the beginning of 1962, when he engaged a solicitor friend named James Walters to dig into Josiffe's background. If, as Josiffe had said, his 'architect' father had been rich, the young man might have expectations from the estate. By May 1962, Walters had discovered the truth. Mrs Ena Josiffe, Josiffe's mother, was alive and well and living in Bexleyheath, Kent, in his boyhood home. Her divorced husband, Albert, an accountant, was also alive and living a few miles away in Orpington.

Walters contacted Ena Josiffe by telephone and reported back to Thorpe by letter: 'She is vicious about you...as being largely responsible for the rift between her son and herself.'

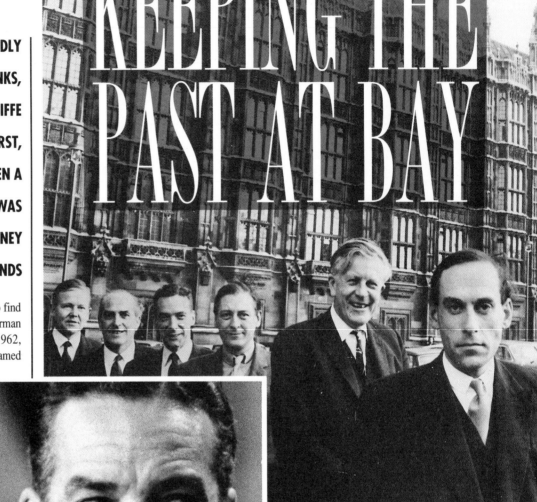

Thorpe's political career began to snowball. He is shown (above) outside Parliament in January 1967 as newly elected leader with 10 of the other 11 Liberal MPs – nearly a full house. Peter Bessell, third from left (and inset) was to become his most significant ally in and out of political life.

The solicitor's discoveries seem to have marked the abrupt cooling of Thorpe's affection for Josiffe. The young man had moved again, this time to the household of Dr Keith Lister of Porlock Weir, Somerset. When Dr Lister wrote to Thorpe requesting references for his new lodger, Thorpe sent him a terse note with the addresses of Josiffe's parents. In the meantime, however, Thorpe had sorted out the problem of the National Insurance card. Records of the Ministry of Pensions and National Insurance showed that they had sent a new card to Josiffe in April. Josiffe was to claim that this card was retained by Thorpe, that Thorpe had promised to pay his contributions, and that 'if he'd only sent me the card, none of this would have happened.' Thorpe denied all of this.

In September 1962, 'Mrs Tish', Josiffe's dog, killed Dr Lister's ducks and had to be put down.

> *He [Josiffe] can be such a charming boy and just as quickly he can be very nasty*

Mrs Quirke writing to Jeremy Thorpe

By 1964, when this picture was taken, Norman Scott had taken to calling himself the Honourable Norman Lianche-Josiffe, upgrading his imaginary architect father to the rank of peer of the realm. As his fortunes began to deteriorate still further, he turned to Jeremy Thorpe for help once more.

INSIDE VIEW

POLICE INTERVIEW

In December 1962, Norman Josiffe, still brooding about the injustice he felt he had suffered at Thorpe's hands, told a young woman acquaintance that he was going to kill Thorpe and then commit suicide. She reported the conversation to Chelsea police and, on 19 December 1962, Josiffe was interviewed at Chelsea police station. 'I have come to the police,' his statement ran, 'to tell you about my homosexual relations with Jeremy Thorpe, who is a Liberal MP, because these relations have caused me so much purgatory and I am afraid it might happen to someone else...'

He was subsequently examined by a police doctor who confirmed that he was a practising homosexual, and two 'My dear Norman' letters were put on file by the Chelsea officers, eventually finding their way to the confidential safe of Assistant Commissioner (Crime) Richard Jackson. Thorpe was not interviewed in connection with Josiffe's statement.

The bereaved dog owner wrote to Thorpe, and received another 'My dear Norman' letter, though distinctly cooler than the February one. Josiffe left the Listers and travelled back to London, where, according to his Old Bailey evidence, he and Thorpe had further sexual encounters. Josiffe's mother pleaded with him, as did a Catholic priest to whom he confessed, to end the friendship, but it is likely that Thorpe had already done so.

TAKING LIBERTIES

Four months later, in February 1963, Thorpe received a bill from the Bond Street tailors, Gieves Ltd, for a pair of silk pyjamas, which Josiffe had ordered at about the time of the Chelsea interview. The MP wrote back indignantly that Norman Josiffe had no right to charge on his account. He refused to pay for the purchase, and said that he had no idea of Josiffe's whereabouts. For the next

two years, there seems to have been no contact between the ill-starred pair.

Norman Josiffe's fortunes were in fact going from bad to worse. For a while he had held a job in a racing stables near Wolverhampton and had become engaged. When he lost both the job and his fiancée, he made a half-hearted attempt at suicide. In autumn, 1964, he again turned to Jeremy Thorpe for help.

Josiffe had been offered a job in a riding stables in Porrentruy, Switzerland and asked Thorpe for money for the fare. Thorpe funded him, but Josiffe took an instant dislike to the place and the job, and returned home almost immediately, leaving his luggage behind. With amazing patience, Thorpe agreed to try and find the luggage and have it sent back to England.

LOOKING FOR SYMPATHY

By now, the itinerant horse-handler had taken to calling himself 'The Honourable Norman Lianche-Josiffe', and invented a young wife who had died in a car crash.

In January 1965 he went to Ireland and in Dublin met a sympathetic Jesuit priest, Father Michael Sweetman, who agreed to try and sort out his affairs. Meanwhile, he obtained a job at Redcross, County Wicklow, about 40 miles from Dublin, on a stud farm owned by a Mr and Mrs Quirke. On 6 March 1965, Mrs Quirke was driven to write to Norman's 'guardian' Jeremy Thorpe. Her letter told a familiar tale of chances given and

money forwarded to Josiffe. Thorpe wrote back to Mrs Quirke, denying guardianship and adding 'I fear I have no responsibility for his actions'.

Norman Josiffe obviously thought otherwise. Back in Dublin with Father Sweetman, he began to agonise again over the missing Swiss luggage and various unpaid bills, and finally decided on what, even for him, was a disgraceful course of action. He wrote a long and lurid letter, detailing his alleged homosexual affair with the Liberal MP and sent it to Thorpe's mother, Mrs Ursula Thorpe. She, in turn, passed it straight on to her son.

Thorpe had been dealing with Josiffe's unpredictable demands for nearly four years without outside advice. But far from fading away, the problem had been growing. With the arrival of this latest letter, it was beginning to dawn on Thorpe that what had been a nagging worry was rapidly turning into a serious threat to his career. The time had come to share his secret with someone.

Thorpe's closest friend in the House of Commons in 1965 was the 43-year-old Liberal MP for Bodmin, Peter Bessell. They had met on the political campaign trail 10 years before and, although Thorpe was nearly 10 years younger than Bessell, he had the advantage of five years more experience in Parliament. In the aftermath of Josiffe's letter, it was to Bessell that Thorpe turned.

There was another reason why Bessell seemed appropriate. A few weeks earlier, at a relaxed lunch, the two MPs had exchanged sexual confidences. Bessell admitted that, as a schoolboy, he had had homosexual tendencies. In return, Thorpe confessed his own leanings in that direction as a youth.

The two met, at Thorpe's invitation, for lunch at the Ritz Hotel, and Bessell read Josiffe's letter. After a discussion, it was decided that Bessell should go to Dublin, meet Josiffe and the priest, Father Sweetman, with whom Josiffe had stayed for a time, and assess the situation at first hand.

DUBLIN RENDEZVOUS

In March 1965, Bessell booked in at the Dublin Intercontinental Hotel. He first called on Father Sweetman and tried to persuade him that there was no truth in Josiffe's homosexual allegations, but the priest was sceptical. At 3 am the following morning, Josiffe rang Bessell at the Intercontinental, and they arranged to meet after breakfast.

When Josiffe arrived, Peter Bessell attempted to pressurise him into silence by saying that, if he persisted with his 'damaging and groundless

> ‘ *I think honestly that he [Josiffe] has a split personality and does not seem capable of standing on his own feet for long* ’
>
> Thorpe writing to Mrs Quirke

PERSPECTIVE

MEETING THE HOME SECRETARY

Towards the middle of 1965, worrying rumours began to reach Thorpe that he was the subject of police inquiries being carried out in North Devon. Anxious to find out about them, Thorpe persuaded Peter Bessell to arrange a meeting on his behalf with the Labour Home Secretary, Sir Frank Soskice, (shown below), to discuss the matter.

In May 1965, Bessell met Soskice at the Minister's office in the House of Commons. The Home Secretary had some knowledge of the

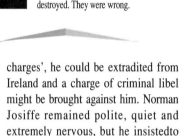

Josiffe connection, and he appeared to be under the impression that the friendship was still going on. However, his attitude seemed to suggest he was on Thorpe's side. Referring to 'that creature Josiffe', he went on to say that 'it's a pity about the letters' and concluded: 'Keep them apart. Don't allow him to get a hold over Jeremy...tell him to go to hell.' Some months later, both Thorpe and Bessell were relieved when Bessell accidently met Soskice in the House and thanked him for his assistance. 'That's all right,' said Soskice, 'it's over.' They took this to mean that the police file on the matter had been destroyed. They were wrong.

charges', he could be extradited from Ireland and a charge of criminal libel might be brought against him. Norman Josiffe remained polite, quiet and extremely nervous, but he insistedto Bessell the truth of his alleged relationship with Thorpe.

Bessell was booked on a flight back to London, and invited Josiffe to come to the airport with him in the taxi. On the way, Bessell asked his companion if he had any proof of a relationship with Thorpe. Josiffe told him that the missing luggage from his brief stay in Switzerland contained letters which would provide proof. Bessell promised to try and recover the luggage for Josiffe, and meanwhile said that he would look out for job opportunities for him, perhaps in America, where Bessell had business dealings.

Back in London, Bessell reported his findings to Thorpe. Josiffe did not seem to pose any immediate threat, though the 'letters in the luggage' might prove to be a risk. A few days later a long, calm letter from Josiffe in Dublin assured Bessell that he was terribly sorry with 'regard to all this mess'. But shortly after that, Bessell received a bill run up by Josiffe at a Dublin hotel. Bessell sent it back to Father Sweetman with an angry letter. 'Frankly,' he wrote, 'I have lost patience (with Josiffe)

and if you are managing to retain yours then I think you should be canonised.'

MISSING LUGGAGE

In the summer of 1965, Peter Bessell was out of the country for a fortnight in order to attend a series of meetings with various business connections. While he was away, his secretary, Diana Stainton, was left to retrieve Josiffe's missing luggage from Switzerland. When it finally arrived at Victoria Station, she took it to Bessell's office and left it there. That evening, she received a telephone call at her Islington flat from Thorpe. Chatting casually, he asked for news of the trunk – and Miss Stainton told him where it was. The luggage was subsequently sent on to Dublin, but when it arrived, Josiffe made a furious

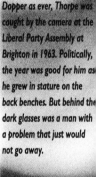

Dapper as ever, Thorpe was caught by the camera at the Liberal Party Assembly at Brighton in 1963. Politically, the year was good for him as he grew in stature on the back benches. But behind the dark glasses was a man with a problem that just would not go away.

front runner to replace him as party leader.

On 18 January 1967, at the age of 37, Thorpe was elected leader of the Liberal Party. Two months later, Labour Prime Minister Harold Wilson – who almost certainly knew of the Josiffe allegations from his Home Secretary Frank Soskice – made him a Privy Councillor – one of the top inter-party elite who advise the Queen and have access to state secrets at the highest level.

The Right Honourable Jeremy Thorpe, as he was now entitled to call himself, had still not learned his lesson. In April, he received a letter from a man he had met in the King's Road, Chelsea, thanking him for 'the two very pleasant nights' they had allegedly spent together, and asking for money. Thorpe passed the letter to Bessell and asked him to deal with the matter. Bessell met the man and threatened him with a blackmail charge. No more was heard.

> *Frankly I have lost patience [with Josiffe] and if you are managing to retain yours then I think you should be canonised*

Peter Bessell writing to Father Sweetman

But Norman Josiffe was much less easily turned away. On 20 April 1967, after a two year silence, Bessell received a letter from Dublin. It opened ominously: 'It is with regret that I write to you, for I know you don't want to remember me...' It went on to say that Josiffe had now taken the name of Norman Scott, and had been working as a male model. He had done some TV commercial and magazine work, and wanted to try his luck in

Thorpe fought an arduous campaign during the 1964 election. He retained North Devon and there was one Liberal gain. Bessell was the new member for Bodmin, where the two MPs are shown .

telephone call to Bessell's office. The letters and various other things, he said, were missing.

Thorpe himself was making swift progress in the Liberal Party. Three years earlier, he had set up a 'marginal seats fund' to help party strategy. In 1965, he became party treasurer proper, and set about tapping private industry for financial backing. To help him he appointed four honorary deputy treasurers. One of these was his old Oxford friend David Holmes, now a merchant banker in the Manchester area.

RIGHT HONOURABLE

In April 1966, Labour leader Harold Wilson won an overall majority in the General Election, dashing Liberal hopes of forming a Government alliance with the Labour Party. For Jo Grimond, the leader of the Liberal Party, this had been a political ambition he had long cherished and now that the opportunity had gone, he decided it would soon be time for him to step down, leaving Thorpe as a

CLOSE-UP **PETER BESSELL MP**

Thorpe's friend and fellow Liberal MP, Peter Bessell (above), was not acting entirely out of friendship when he agreed to help Thorpe with his problem over Norman Josiffe. He was a businessman whose schemes and ventures had an uncanny habit of going wrong or coming to nothing. By the time Thorpe confided in him

in March 1965, he was running into increasing debt. And Thorpe had access to financiers.

By August 1965, Bessell owed at least £20,000 to pressing creditors. Thorpe secured him £15,000 and Bessell managed to borrow a further £15,000 from an 80-year-old Cornishwoman, a Liberal supporter. Five years later, no wiser and no more cautious, he embarked on a disastrous scheme to set up a factory for an American corporation in Britain. The corporation went bankrupt, Bessell's creditors were left unpaid, and the Liberal MP was so desperate that he considered suicide. And yet, armed with new funds from the Liberal Party benefactor, Jack Hayward – whom Bessell later tried to swindle – he quickly recovered to set up a new company, Peter Bessell Inc.

In 1968, Thorpe married 29-year-old Caroline Allpass. A lavish reception followed a private wedding ceremony and the couple spent their honeymoon on the Mediterranean island of Elba. The photograph (right) was taken at Westminster when the couple had announced their engagement.

the United States. Unfortunately, he had burned his passport over his 'upset' with Thorpe. Could Bessell help?

Bessell ignored the letter. On 14 July, however, Josiffe-Scott wrote again, this time from Maidstone. Filled with implied threats, the letter told how Scott had spent his savings for his American trip on psychiatric help, and had told the psychiatrist, Dr Brian O'Connell, all about his alleged relationship with Thorpe.

THE PAY-OFF

On 2 August 1967, at Bessell's invitation, Scott came up to London to discuss his problems. He needed, he said, money to keep him going without having to apply for unemployment benefit. He also needed an insurance card and a passport. Bessell surmised that if Scott applied for either benefit or cards he would blurt out the saga to any official who would listen. Therefore, he arranged to pay Scott a 'retainer' of between £5 and £10 a week until he could find either a job or obtain another passport. The payments, which were to go on until May 1968, were to amount to between £600 and £700, of which Bessell claimed he received about £400 back from Thorpe. Meanwhile, Bessell was not at all keen for Scott to go to the United States.

Although the previous month – July 1967 – had seen the legalising of homosexual acts between consenting adults, such practices were still not accepted with tolerance. If Scott accused Thorpe openly in Britain now, Thorpe could sue him for libel and, in the absence of real proof, would win his case. In America, however, Scott could say what he liked and the results could damage everyone concerned – including Bessell,

with his troubled business interests there.

On 30 May 1968, after a few months' courtship, Thorpe surprised many of his friends by marrying Caroline Allpass, a 29-year-old who worked at Sotheby's fine art auctioneers. Thorpe had met her through his old University friend David Holmes, who was his best man at their private wedding. Afterwards, Thorpe and his bride flew off to their honeymoon in the Mediterranean island of Elba, and during his absence a group of 'rebel' Liberals tried to oust him from the leadership. Thorpe flew back and rallied the Party Executive behind him to defeat the attempt.

All that summer, the Scott problem continued to loom. Shortly after Thorpe's wedding, Bessell gave Scott £75 to kit himself out with items needed for his modelling, but Scott continued to

Scott worked on and off as a model (right) from 1967 until 1969. He attributed his inability to cope to his mental state and the quantities of drugs he was taking. His career ended shortly after his marriage when he and his bride, Sue Myers, moved away from London to Dorset.

nag Bessell about his passport and insurance card. It seemed that nothing would satisfy the young man. He responded to helpfulness by taking advantage of it. He seemed incapable of holding down any job that was offered to him. If he was given money he simply spent it and then expected more. Even implied threats, such as Bessell had tried when he first met him in Dublin, had no effect. The number of options available to the two Liberal MPs, nearly seven years after the problem had first arisen, were diminishing rapidly.

INSIDE VIEW

A NEW PARTY LEADER

DAVID HOLMES

David Holmes (right), who began to take over the 'monitoring' of Scott in about 1968, was an even older friend of Thorpe than Bessell, and certainly more devoted. He met Thorpe at Oxford, where his elegance and style brought him acceptance into Thorpe's social circle. Like Thorpe, he seems to have spent more time socialising and playing politics than at academic matters. After spending two years of National Service with the army, he went back north to Manchester, where he went into business. He was a tall, good looking man, invariably well dressed, with dark hair, short side-burns, and heavy black-framed spectacles.

Holmes lived in a converted coach-house in Salford, outside Manchester. In London he was a member of the Reform Club, and holidayed in Greece occasionally with Thorpe. After his appointment, by Thorpe, as honorary deputy party treasurer, Holmes' main efforts on behalf of the party were ostensibly to wheedle money from business and commerce for Liberal party funds. He attended Liberal Party conferences as assistant and right hand man to Thorpe, although one party official described him as 'a willing pair of legs' in reference to all the running around he did after the leader.

> *I have no money left now. I cannot model because my nerves are so shot to shreds...I have no real qualifications, I am still on a vast amount of drugs...so I beg you Mr Bessell to help somehow*
>
> Norman Scott writing to Peter Bessell

Finally, according to the prosecution evidence that Peter Bessell was to give at the Old Bailey over 10 years later, he and Thorpe had a fateful conversation. Late one night in the Liberal leader's office, in November or December 1968, they were discussing the threat Scott posed, when Thorpe asked if it was impossible to find Scott a job in America. Bessell told him that it was.

'In that case,' said Thorpe, 'we have got to get rid of him.' Bessell asked lightly, 'Are you suggesting killing him off?' Thorpe turned to Bessell and replied 'Yes.'

The discussion which followed – on what Bessell claimed Thorpe called his 'ultimate solution' – was to form one of the most fiercely contested highlights of the later trial.

Jeremy Thorpe's succession to the leadership of the Liberal party was not a smooth one. Although Jo Grimond, who formally announced that he would be standing down in January 1967, made it clear that he favoured Thorpe as his successor, there were a number of reservations about the 37-year-old MP.

Many Liberals felt that he was a political light-weight by comparison, who spent much of his time socialising and relied too heavily on his personal charm and wit for his success. Even more worrying for Thorpe were the rumours that had been circulating among the Liberals at Westminster about his private life. MP Richard Wainwright had been told about Norman Scott by Bessell himself, while Alisdair Mackenzie had come to hear about it through one of his constituents. These reservations were sufficient for a 'Stop Jeremy' campaign to be mounted. At the first ballot between the 12 Liberal MPs, Thorpe polled only half the votes. Only after that did the two rival candidates, Emlyn Hoosen and Eric Lubbock, withdraw and provide Thorpe with a unanimous victory.

The picture (left) of a youthful Thorpe and his leader was taken in 1959.

HOMOSEXUALITY HAS A LONG HISTORY OF PERSECUTION IN BRITAIN, AND HAS EVEN BEEN THOUGHT A THREAT TO NATIONAL SECURITY – DESPITE TACIT CONDONEMENT AT THE HIGHEST LEVELS OF SOCIETY. THE ROAD TO REFORM HAS BEEN LONG AND DIFFICULT.

VICTIMS OF MORALITY

Male homosexuality was a serious offence in English law for almost nine hundred years, and until the early part of the 19th century its ultimate act, anal intercourse – described on the Statute Books as 'The Abominable Crime of Buggery' – was a capital offence.

DEATH SENTENCE

It was, of course, difficult to prove, though in 1808, the year in which the poet Lord Byron sailed from England amidst rumours of incest and homosexuality, two men were hanged for the crime.

In 1861, the homosexual laws were reformed, life imprisonment being substituted for the death penalty. Homosexuality

In 1954, Lord Montagu of Beaulieu (seen right with his wife in 1959) was jailed with two other men – Michael Pitt-Rivers and Peter Wildeblood – for his involvement in 'an upper-class homosexual circle'. But almost more frightening than jail was the prospect of blackmail, memorably portrayed in the 1961 film Victim (above, with Dirk Bogarde in the leading role) in which a happily married barrister is confronted by blackmailers. Pressures eased during the 1960s and towards the end of the decade playwright Joe Orton (above right) was openly affirming his homosexuality.

among members of the literary and society set continued to thrive quietly.

Then, in 1895, came sensation. Oscar Wilde, poet, playwright and the major celebrity of his day, was accused of being a 'sodomite' by the Marquess of Queensbury, with whose son, Lord Alfred Douglas, Wilde had

pers, but the victims were almost exclusively lower middle class – vicars, schoolteachers, and servicemen. Memoirs of the era have shown that homosexuality was practised more or less blatantly by the upper echelons of society, leaders of the arts, and in Oxbridge and Parliamentary circles.

Then sensation stirred again. In 1954, three members of a so-called 'upper class homosexual circle' – Lord Montagu of Beaulieu, Michael Pitt-Rivers, and Peter Wildeblood – were prosecuted and jailed. But ordinary public attitudes were slowly changing; when Lord Montagu was finally freed from

ality. The report recommended radical reforms in the laws against homosexuality, in particular that sexual acts between consenting males of over 21 should no longer constitute a legal offence.

TREACHERY AND DEBAUCHERY

One reason for the Tory Party's reluctance to act upon the Wolfenden Report was that homosexuality had come to be regarded as prejudicial to state security, due in part to the potential for blackmail.

Guy Burgess, the Foreign Office official who defected to the Soviet Union in 1952, had

been a blatant homosexual, while his colleague Donald Maclean had been an alcoholic with bisexual tendencies. After examining the Burgess and Maclean affair, the Conference of Privy Councillors reported in 1956 that as well as communist sympathies, 'character defects' such as 'drunkenness, addiction to drugs, homosexuality or any loose living' should be grounds for 'exclusion from state posts.'

It was not until 1967 that the Sexual Offences Act made all consenting acts of homosexuality legal. Whether this has softened the view of homosexuality as a security risk is still an open question.

Labour MP Tom Driberg (seen above with politician Barbara Castle) managed to survive politically because he made no secret of his homosexuality. For Admiralty clerk William Vassall (right) concealment spelled disaster when he was blackmailed by the KGB and spent six years spying for the Russians. When found out, he was sentenced to 18 years imprisonment.

an open friendship.

Foolishly, Wilde launched an action for criminal libel against Queensbury, and lost his case. He was immediately prosecuted on charges of gross indecency, convicted, and sentenced to two years' hard labour. Wilde died penniless in Paris two years after his release. Sir Frank Lockwood, the Solicitor-General at the time, spoke for 'respectable' Victorian values when he called Wilde's offences 'vice in its most hideous and detestable form.'

The flamboyant actress Mrs Patrick Campbell gave the pragmatic view when she declared: 'I don't care what they get up to as long as they don't do it in the street and frighten the horses.'

SELECTIVE PROSECUTIONS

For the next half century, occasional prosecutions for homosexuality provided fodder for the more lurid Sunday newspa-

Wakefield Gaol, a large crowd gathered at the gates. Some elements catcalled and jeered, but the majority had come to cheer and applaud. Undoubtedly they were influenced by a moving book, prepared in prison by Peter Wildeblood. Entitled *Against the Law*, the book made a plea for moderation.

In 1957, Sir John Wolfenden published his influential report on prostitution and homosexu-

CHAPTER THREE

ON PORLOCK HILL

THE MYSTERIOUS ARRIVAL ON THE SCENE OF 'MR KEENE', FOLLOWED BY THE DEATH OF RINKA ON PORLOCK HILL, CAST A SINISTER SHADOW ON EVENTS. MATTERS WERE NOW GETTING OUT OF HAND AND, WITH ATTEMPTED MURDER AS THE NEW INGREDIENT, THORPE'S PROBLEMS SEEMED TO BE MULTIPLYING RATHER THAN RECEDING

At the end of 1968, pressure on all parties seemed to ease with a change in Norman Scott's fortunes. Scott began to pick up modelling work and moved to the King's Road, Chelsea with a boyfriend. There he met a girl named Sue Myers, whom he married on 13 May 1969. When Sue became pregnant, they moved to a rented cottage near Milton Abbas, Dorset.

During the summer of 1969, Scott sold second-hand jeans from a Bridport market stall, regaling locals with his tales of Thorpe – and taking to drink. He finally obtained an emergency insurance card from the Weymouth Department of Health, but by this stage, he was becoming frustrated and hysterical again.

One evening, he rang Thorpe's house in Devon and poured out his version of events to Caroline Thorpe. He also rang Bessell, threatening to give his story to the Sunday newspapers. On 18 November 1969, Sue gave birth to a boy named Diggory Benjamin Scott, but this did not prevent her from leaving Scott shortly afterwards, when he confessed to sleeping with a boyfriend.

PERSONAL TRAGEDY

On 13 June 1970, Harold Wilson called a summer election in which he lost to the Conservatives. The Liberal seats dropped from 13 to 6, and Thorpe's majority in North Devon fell to a slender 396. But the greatest tragedy befell Thorpe a fortnight later when, on 29 June, his wife Caroline was killed in a car crash, while travelling to London. Rumour had it that Scott had visited her the day before and that the meeting had therefore been preying on her mind. Scott denied this and, in any case, it appears that he was in London at the time in question. Undeterred by Thorpe's tragedy, Scott approached the beleaguered MP for a final time, thus bringing matters out into the open.

In February 1971, with a small financial advance from Bessell – who was himself in deep water with creditors – Scott rented a cottage in Talybont, Caernarvon, with a view to training horses. He continued to talk of his relationship with Thorpe and, when his money began to run out, he rang Bessell again. This time, however, he received

DATEFILE

JUNE 29 1970
Caroline Thorpe killed in a car crash

MAY 27 1971
Emlyn Hooson and David Steel interview Norman Scott

MARCH 14 1973
Thorpe marries Marion, Countess of Harewood

OCT 24 1975
Andrew Newton shoots Rinka on Porlock Hill

JUNE '70-OCT '75

While Norman Scott (far left)) lived his solitary life in Dorset, Jeremy Thorpe was quickly becoming one of the most popular characters in politics. He travelled the country in his private helicopter, tirelessly campaigning for the General Election in 1974. He is seen (left) with megaphone in hand, addressing factory workers at Chelmsford, Essex.

young man of her acquaintance and, in concealing the affair, had damaged the reputation of the Liberal Party itself.

Hooson invited Mrs Parry-Jones and Norman Scott to the House of Commons on 29 May, where they were interviewed by Liberal MP David Steel, a firm supporter of Thorpe. Steel considered Scott highly-strung, but he was impressed by Mrs Parry-Jones: indeed, he felt that their story seemed to carry substance, particularly in view of the rumours he had heard about Thorpe. The following day, four Liberal MPs interviewed Scott, and when one of them openly accused him of blackmail, he walked out indignantly.

COURT ALLEGATIONS

Scott tried to sell his story to the newspapers, but they declined to touch it. His next opportunity came nine months later, when Gwen Parry-Jones died of alcoholic poisoning, and the case was referred to the coroner's court. At the inquest, Scott made his allegations to the astonished coroner. Local reporters filed the story to Fleet Street, but again it was spiked.

After the death of Mrs Parry-Jones in March 1972, Scott rented a cottage on Exmoor, where he lived in a state of drunken squalor. Suffering from growing anxiety, he had become a patient of Dr Ronald Gleadle, who prescribed him doses of Librium and other sleeping pills. During his treatment, Scott related the Thorpe story to Dr Gleadle who, in turn, passed it on to a Liberal friend, from whom it eventually reached Jeremy Thorpe. Once again, Thorpe denied everything, although he decided to inform his friend, David Holmes, of the latest development.

THE BESSELL FILE

In February 1974, a General Election was called. Holmes was well aware of the danger that Scott could pose if he were to spread rumours in Thorpe's constituency. Therefore, on 27 February, he managed to obtain letters from Scott relating to the payments Scott had received from Bessell. In exchange for what was to become known as the Bessell File, Holmes deposited £2500 in a bank account for Scott. The file was promptly burned.

The money merely granted Scott a reprieve

BACKDROP
PUBLIC MEMORIAL

The death of his first wife, Caroline, had a profound effect on Jeremy Thorpe. For more than a year he was unable to speak for any length of time without mentioning her. He forgot about the electoral disaster – 'it just blurred' – and went about his duties mechanically.

To commemorate Caroline, he asked the Welsh architect, Clough Williams-Ellis, to design a tall column of Portland stone, which would stand 600 feet up on Codden Hills, a wild area of Exmoor overlooking the Taw Valley near Barnstaple. It was dedicated by the Archbishop of Canterbury, who flew down for the ceremony by helicopter. 'When people see it rising into the sky,' said Thorpe, 'they will think of Caroline Thorpe and the sunshine she brought with her during her tragically short stay in North Devon.' It remains a very public memorial, however, and at the time of its erection there was strong local feeling that it damaged an area of outstanding natural beauty. Today, many people still feel the same way.

---

a firm brush off. One of Scott's friends, who had been listening in to the telephone conversation, indignantly wrote to Thorpe at the House of Commons on Scott's behalf, relating what Bessell had said. The following terse response was signed by Thorpe's assistant:

'As far as [Mr Thorpe] is aware, he does not know Mr Norman Scott. However, he believes that

> *I pointed the gun towards him [Scott], but not directly at him. I wanted to frighten him but the gun wouldn't go off.*
>
> Newton's initial statement to DI Braund on 18 November 1977.

Mr Van de Brecht de Vater knew a Mr Norman Josiffe who may be the same person. Mr Thorpe asks me to say that he is under no obligation to this gentleman.'

In effect, Thorpe was following the advice of the ex-Home Secretary, Sir Frank Soskice, by telling Scott to go to hell. The reply caused outrage in Talybont. Mrs Gwen Parry-Jones, a widow and retired village postmistress, took matters into her own hands. She wrote a letter to the Liberal MP, Emlyn Hooson, saying that a certain Liberal MP had shamefully wronged a

On 13 May 1969, Norman Scott married Sue Myers who, shortly afterwards, gave birth to Diggory Benjamin Scott (below, seen with his mother). Divorce soon followed, however, when Sue discovered that Norman had been sleeping with a boyfriend.

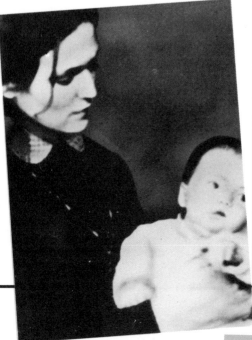

GORDON WINTER

On 16 June 1971, one week after he had walked out of the internal Liberal inquiry into the Scott/Thorpe allegations, Norman Scott agreed to spend two weeks being interviewed by a British-born, South African journalist named Gordon Winter (left). Scott had been put in touch with Winter through a reporter on the *Daily Mirror*, and it was the first time he had spoken directly to the press.

It later emerged that Winter's motives for finding out about Scott's allegations seemed to have been more than purely journalistic. In 1966, he had been deported from South Africa, after his involvement in a scandal involving the death of a mine-owner from Johannesburg. Wanting to climb back into favour with the South African authorities, and aware of the Liberal Party's strong stance against the apartheid regime there, he may well have been using Scott's allegations to damage Thorpe and his Party.

John Le Mesurier (below), a Welsh businessman who ran a carpet discount business in Port Talbot, was the second link in the chain between David Holmes and Andrew Newton. It was Le Mesurier who arranged for Scott's briefcase to be stolen.

from his anxiety. In February 1975, Scott was telephoned by a man calling himself Steiner and claiming to be from the German magazine, *Stern*. They arranged to meet at the Imperial Hotel, Barnstaple, and Scott took with him a briefcase containing photocopies relating to the sale of the Bessell File. Once in the hotel, however, his briefcase was stolen – presumably by two men he had seen arrive shortly after him. A week later, he was set upon and beaten up by two men, as he was leaving a pub in Barnstaple.

STRANGE PHONE CALLS

By now, understandably, Norman Scott was suspicious of everyone. During the summer, he received a telephone call from a man calling himself Ian Wright claiming to work for an Italian fashion house. The man asked Scott to go to the Royal Garden Hotel, Kensington, to model some clothes. At first, Scott was delighted. But when the caller quoted a fee of £400 for the session, which was well over the rate for a model of Scott's experience, Scott declined the offer.

In mid-September 1975, Scott moved to the Market Inn in Barnstaple

where he had become something of a favourite with the landlady, an elderly and motherly woman named Edna Friendship. While he was there, a man introducing himself as a journalist called Masterson asked him to go for an interview in Bristol, but Scott refused. Then a man giving the name Peter Keene rang several times, and Mrs Friendship took the calls. On the afternoon of Sunday 12 October, Keene turned up in person.

Keene told Scott that he was in great danger from a man who was travelling over from Canada to kill him. Keene claimed he had been hired by an unnamed benefactor to protect Scott from the killer. When he asked Scott to drive with him to the village of Knowstone, near South Molton, where someone wished to speak to him, Scott's fears were aroused again. Refusing to go with Keene, he instead offered to have a drink with him at the Imperial Hotel later that day. When Scott informed Mrs Friendship of the encounter, she prudently took the number of the yellow Mazda that Keene was driving.

MYSTERY TOUR

By Thursday 23 October, Scott had moved to the village of Combe Martin to look after a friend's cats, when Keene again telephoned. At first the man announced himself as 'Andy' and then, realising his mistake, suddenly changed this to 'Peter'. The caller informed Scott that the killer from Canada had finally arrived. He then arranged to meet Scott at 6 pm the next day outside the Delves Hotel in Combe Martin. Scott arrived at the hotel with his recently acquired Great Dane bitch, Rinka, whom he insisted travelled with him.

It was beginning to rain, and the pair got into Keene's car, a blue Ford Escort this time. Keene explained that he had to see someone on business in Porlock, about 25 miles across the moors, and that Scott and the dog could wait for him in the Castle Hotel there. By now, Scott had become more relaxed and agreed to Keene's plan.

At 8 pm, as arranged, Scott emerged from the Castle Hotel and peered out into the dark, rain-lashed street. It was deserted. As time passed, he began to get nervous. When he noticed the blinking of headlights, Scott and the dog hurried across and scrambled in beside Keene, who began to drive back up Porlock Hill towards Combe Martin. As they reached the top of the hill and levelled out to cross the pitch-black moor, Keene's driving became erratic, and Scott asked if he was tired. Keene admitted that he was 'knackered' and,

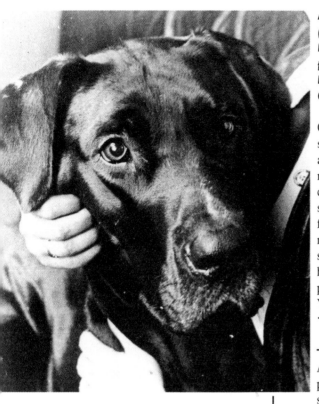

An innocent victim – when Scott's pet Great Dane, Rinka (left), was shot dead by Andrew Newton (alias Peter Keene) on Porlock Hill, both the local newspapers and the police were initially unable to make sense of what lay behind the incident. Headlines, such as 'Dog-in-a Fog Case Baffles Police' aptly reflected the confusion.

On looking up, however, he noticed Keene standing by the car, with Rinka bounding and splashing about beside him. Scott reached for the dog's collar, but before he could grab it, Keene pulled out a pistol and shot Rinka through the head. Scott saw the flash, but the sound of the wind and rain muffled the gun's crack. For several seconds, Scott remained confused, and then he dropped on his knees beside his dead pet, shouting: 'You can't involve Rinka. You can't involve the dog.'

JAMMED PISTOL

According to Scott, Keene then placed the pistol's muzzle next to Scott's head and said: 'It's your turn now.' Scott froze, but there was no second shot. Instead, Keene began to shake the weapon as if trying to free it. Seizing his chance, Scott began to run across the moor. Turning round, he saw Keene leap back into the car and heard him yell: 'I'll get you'. Keene then roared off back towards Porlock, leaving Scott sobbing hysterically and trying to give the kiss of life to Rinka. After a while, Scott became aware of headlights approaching from the direction of Lynton, and ran into the road, waving his arms.

accepting Scott's offer to take over the driving, he pulled over on the right hand side of the road. By now, the rain was pelting down.

THE DEATH OF RINKA

'If you just move over,' said Scott, 'it'll stop Rinka jumping out and jumping back in and making the car all wet.' He opened the passenger door and, crouching down, ran around the front of the car.

PERSPECTIVE

CRISIS AVERTED

The 1971 internal party inquiry into the Scott/Thorpe allegations was an unhappy compromise forced on Jeremy Thorpe by Liberal MP Emlyn Hooson (right). Hooson, who was on the right wing of the party and whose views on homosexuality were less open-minded than many of his colleagues, had first heard of the allegations via a letter from Mrs Parry-Jones, a friend and neighbour of Norman Scott.

Hooson insisted that both Scott and Mrs Parry-Jones come to Westminster to give substance to their claims. He then spoke to Peter Bessell who, with very nearly disastrous results, confessed to the retainers he had been paying Scott. Hooson's immediate reaction was that Thorpe would have to resign as leader of the Liberal Party. Bessell was horrified, and after Hooson had confronted Thorpe and the two had had a blazing row, it was decided that an inquiry should be set up, with Lord Byers, a respected Liberal dignitary, chairing it. The inquiry came to no satisfactory conclusion. Hooson remained suspicious and Norman Scott, after being cross-examined by Lord Byers, walked out of the interview. When it came down to believing the word of the Liberal Party leader against that of Scott, the result was not in question.

Jeremy Thorpe takes centre stage with his two rival political leaders, Edward Heath (left) and Harold Wilson (right) in 1974, to celebrate the 89th birthday of Lady Spencer-Churchill.

CLOSE-UP

NEWTON'S ALIBI

When DI Braund questioned Newton (right) on 18 November 1977, Newton gave an 'explanation' that was tailored to the belief that he might still make some money out of his part in the Rinka affair.

Newton's story was that Scott had been blackmailing him over a photograph showing the naked Newton in a compromising pose. Newton said that he had replied to an advertisement in a 'contact' magazine catering for people looking for sexual partners, and had enclosed the picture. He was amazed, he said, when instead of a willing young woman, a strange young man named Norman Scott had turned up at his Blackpool flat, threatening to show the photo to Newton's employers unless he paid him £4 a month.

At first, Newton had paid up, but then had driven down to Barnstaple in an attempt to frighten off his blackmailer. Unfortunately, Scott had only wanted to talk about his involvement with Jeremy Thorpe, and how badly he had been treated. Frustrated in his efforts, Newton had therefore returned home.

It was during his second visit and attempt to 'frighten' his alleged blackmailer, Scott, that he shot the dog. He claimed that he had 'pointed the gun towards [Scott] but not directly at him', but this time 'the gun wouldn't go off'.

The car, driven by an off-duty Automobile Association scout named Edward Lethaby, pulled up, and Lethaby and three passengers got out.

As they attended the stricken Scott and checked the dog for signs of life, Lethaby's wife saw a car coming rapidly towards them from Porlock. But as the beam of its headlights touched their group, it suddenly spun around and returned the way it had come. After Scott had given a garbled account of what had happened, Lethaby drove him to Bridgwater police station.

By this time, almost every policeman in the West Country knew of Norman Scott and his allegations – thanks to Scott's self-publicising. The CID man on duty at Bridgwater was no exception, and with the body of Rinka providing firm evidence to Scott's story, he contacted his headquarters in Bristol. Detective Chief Superintendent Michael Challes, head of Somerset and Avon CID, immediately contacted his opposite number in Devon and Cornwall,

Detective Chief Superintendent Proven Sharpe.

Finding 'Keene' proved fairly straightforward. Armed with the registration number of the yellow Mazda taken by Mrs Friendship in Barnstaple, the police traced the vehicle to a car-hire firm in Blackpool, Lancashire, where it had been hired by Andrew 'Gino' Newton, a 29-year-old airline pilot. The police decided not to arrest him immediately, but to watch his movements instead.

SHADOWING NEWTON

Newton was finally arrested on 18 November, after returning from a holiday in India with a girlfriend and another man named David Miller. His explanation for the events on Porlock Hill was that Scott had been blackmailing him with a compromising photograph. His intention that night had been to frighten Scott sufficiently to force him to drop his demands for money. The police, at any rate, seemed satisfied. The gun, an ancient 1910

model, was recovered from a shed in Newton's mother's house at Chiswick, and firearms examiners found that it did have a tendency to jam. On 20 November, Andrew Newton was charged with possession of a firearm with intent to

INSIDE VIEW

BESSELL'S DISAPPEARANCE

Detective Chief Superintendents Michael Challes (left) and Proven Sharpe (below), who headed the inquiry into the shooting of Rinka. Sharpe's first reaction was that Scott had shot Rinka himself for publicity. But both agreed that an overall press blackout should be maintained during the investigation.

After several meetings, Deakin was told that Holmes had a friend who was being troubled by a blackmailer. Holmes asked Deakin if he knew of anyone who could frighten the blackmailer off – 'someone who could break arms and legs'. Deakin promised to see what he could do, and in his search for a 'strong man', eventually contacted his friend, David Miller, a printer from Cardiff, who in turn recommended Andrew 'Gino' Newton.

HIRING NEWTON

At first glance, the airline pilot seemed an unlikely choice, but as Miller told Deakin: 'He would do anything for a laugh.' Through Deakin, Newton was put in touch with Holmes. First, Le Mesurier organised the theft of Scott's briefcase from the Imperial Hotel, and then he had him beaten up in Barnstaple. When this had still failed to silence Scott, Newton was hired.

As his arrest and subsequent testimony at the Thorpe hearing at Minehead was to show, Newton was not an ideal choice. Newspapers were to dub him the 'Hit and Miss Man'. After he was freed on bail, his several meetings with Holmes in London, Manchester and Bolton were monitored from a distance by police.

PRESS INTEREST

By now, there was a new peril for Jeremy Thorpe. For the first time in over a decade, the press were beginning to smell a real story. Admittedly the first headline, published by the *West Somerset Free Press,* failed to grasp the underlying significance of the Rinka story: 'The Great Dane Death Mystery', it ran, 'Dog-in-a-Fog Case Baffles Police.' Realising that matters were beginning to get out of hand, Jeremy Thorpe now decided to turn for assistance to his old Scott-minder, Peter Bessell. This time, however, all he managed to do was dig himself in even deeper.

endanger life, and released on bail. Unknown to him, however, the police continued to keep watch over his every move.

THE TRUE STORY

It was to be over two years before Newton told his real story. During that time the police were to piece much of it together. It began almost a year prior to the death of Rinka, when David Holmes, Jeremy Thorpe's personal friend and financial assistant, visited an old acquaintance of his in South Wales, named John Le Mesurier. Le Mesurier was in his forties and an ex-regular in the RAF, who ran a carpet discount business in Port Talbot. For a while, David Holmes had flirted with the carpet import market, which is how the two men had crossed paths.

Through Le Mesurier, Holmes had met 35-year-old George Deakin, a red-headed, ex-fairground roustabout, who had entered the fruit-machine business, when it became legalised in the 1960s. By the early 1970s, Deakin had become the biggest gaming-machine operator in South Wales, as well as being the owner of a number of night clubs and pool halls.

In January 1974, Peter Bessell (left), who had run up debts of half a million dollars, fled to Mexico to escape his creditors in England. At the time of his disappearance, Bessell had been involved in two major deals: one, involving property worth millions of dollars in the wealthy New York suburb of Bronxville; the other, involving the purchase of the Grand Bahama Port Authority Ltd, a company owning most of Freeport and estimated at around $100 million. Bessell saw either deal as a gateway to making his own fortune. But when it seemed that neither transaction would come off, he attempted to raise the money for the Bronxville property himself. His plan involved an attempt to swindle half a million dollars out of the Liberal Party's chief benefactor, Jack Hayward, who had a 25 per cent holding in the company.

Thorpe had also been involved in Bessell's attempt to clinch the deal with Hayward, although in Hayward's words, he had been unwittingly 'sucked in'. In any case, Hayward was advised by a close business associate that it was all a 'confidence trick', and so eventually backed out, despite all assurances that Thorpe had given about Bessell's integrity.

Such were the circumstances surrounding the mysterious and hasty disappearance of Peter Bessell.

FACE TO FACE WITH *Peter Bessell*

IN THE MONTHS SURROUNDING THE 1979 OLD BAILEY TRIAL, PETER BESSELL – THORPE'S ONE-TIME FRIEND AND POLITICAL ALLY– COMPILED HIS PERSONAL ACCOUNT OF THE CASE, ENTITLED *COVER-UP*.

Cover-up was published privately in the United States by Peter Bessell in 1981. It was limited to a first edition of 2000 copies and never brought out in Britain. In it, Peter Bessell used his first-hand recollections of the events between 1965 and 1979 to provide valuable new insights into the most important aspects and characters in the Thorpe case. Bessell died in 1985 in California, having been largely discredited as a prosecution witness at the Old Bailey six years earlier and having broken off all contact with his former colleague, Jeremy Thorpe.

ON THORPE

Jeremy's election as leader of the Liberal Party was a prodigious advancement in his political career, and would prove to be a turning point in the Norman Josiffe affair. Jeremy always saw himself, correctly, as the idealistic politician whose ambitions were centred on the advancement of the party, rather than on mere personal achievement. Therefore, from the outset, he

thought of Josiffe as a threat to the Liberal Party, rather than to his own ambitions. Jeremy was unable to accept the fact that Josiffe could only damage the party through him. Although I readily played pawn to the king, at least I had no illusions about whose crown I was trying to save.

ON SCOTT

Norman Josiffe had a remarkable ability to enlist sympathy. At our first meeting, he gave an appearance of utter defencelessness...My meeting with Father Sweetman satisfied me that Josiffe was not the vicious character I envisaged when I set out from London and was really someone in need of care. Even if I had not talked with the priest, there is no doubt that despite the tough line I took over the letter I would have automatically responded, as others did later, to his dejection and helplessness.

As the years were to prove, however, Norman Josiffe's demeanour masked an extraordinary stubbornness and resilience. His letter to Ursula Thorpe was his first move in a plan of action upon which I am certain he did not consciously embark, but which he was to pursue to its disastrous climax 14 years later.

ON SCOTT'S MOTIVES

Jeremy lived comparatively modestly, but Scott witnessed a life-style most youngsters of his upbringing hardly knew existed. Although worn out, Jeremy's shoes were handmade. He had his hair cut at Trumpers. The only ornaments in his flat were antique ceramics. If Norman Scott tried to mirror Jeremy, as star-struck girls once aped the mannerisms and hairstyles of movie actresses, the effect

was more profound. Norman Scott did not merely see his idol reflected on a silver screen, he shared a significant part of Jeremy's life.

ON DAVID HOLMES

David Holmes was someone I never completely understood. Quiet-voiced and apparently unemotional, his personality had, for me at least, certain unfathomable characteristics...he cared deeply for Jeremy and would go to extraordinary lengths to please him. David was the antithesis of a man who would tolerate violence. His hobbies centred round music, particularly the operas of Mozart, and collecting small antiques...As far as I knew he was a modestly successful merchant banker who lived unobtrusively and contentedly. I did not mean it unkindly when I described him to Jeremy in 1968 as 'wet'. But nothing that happened subsequently caused me to alter my view that David had no more than average intelligence, in an emergency would not be reliable, and was too malleable for someone of Jeremy's impetuosity to choose as an ally.

THE COMMITTAL

My recollections of the committal proceedings will always be dominated by my memory of Jeremy. At times he had lolled on the front pew of the public gallery almost insolently. At others he appeared to be bored by the proceedings, but every now and then the mask slipped and I caught a glimpse of a man who had changed so much that I hardly knew him. Once when everyone was waiting for the court to resume sitting, I found myself within feet of him. He was talking to reporters and when he turned his head and saw me it seemed for a split second that the instinct must take over from reality and we would react to each other with the old

> **Jeremy was like a moon that had been forcibly twisted so that only the dark side was visible**

warmth. There was a flicker but the moment was stillborn. I was looking into the eyes of a stranger.

ON THE TRIAL

'My Lord, on behalf of Mr Jeremy Thorpe, I call no evidence.'

It should have been obvious to me from the outset. It did not matter that Jeremy had pledged to 'vigorously defend' himself against the charges of which he stood accused. Throughout his life he had depended on others to extricate him from every personal crisis with which he had been confronted. What could be more logical than that he should now depend on George Carman to do that which so many others had done before?... Not giving evidence appeared to be a colossal gamble.

ON THE FUTURE

The journalists who wrote off Jeremy in the days following the trial as an ambitious politician who had met his comeuppance, were blinded by the events of the preceding three years. Jeremy was like a moon that had been forcibly twisted so that only the dark side was visible, and few remembered the brilliance they once had lauded, which is unlikely to have been extinguished and which in an age of mediocrity should not be completely lost. I agree...that Jeremy will not return to Parliament, nor do I think he would be able to serve it effectively if he could. But there are other means of employment, and I believe he will only find ultimate contentment through service.

The two faces of Peter Bessell. The new MP (right) having won Bodmin in 1969 and (left) the star witness, with immunity from prosecution against his former friend.

❚❚ *Norman Josiffe had a remarkable ability to enlist sympathy... At our first meeting, he gave an appearance of utter defencelessness* **❚❚**

BETRAYAL AND

THINGS WERE CLOSING IN ON THORPE. THE PRESS NOW SENSED THEY WERE ON THE BRINK OF A MAJOR NEWS STORY: A HIT MAN WITH A STORY TO SELL, AN OLD FRIEND TURNED ENEMY, SEVERAL COMPROMISING LETTERS AND, ABOVE ALL, THE UNFORGIVING GRUDGE OF NORMAN SCOTT

When Thorpe released the letter that Bessell had specifically requested be used only in an emergency, the friendship was effectively over. It was also the decisive factor in persuading Bessell to travel from the US back to England to testify against the Liberal leader. He is shown here with one of the British detectives who interviewed him in California.

DATEFILE

FEB 8 1976

Thorpe questioned by police

MARCH 16 1976

Newton's trial begins at Exeter Crown Court

MAY 10 1976

Thorpe resigns from leadership of Liberal Party

NOV 20 1977

Committal hearings begin at Minehead, Somerset

FEB '76-NOV '77

To Jeremy Thorpe, Andrew Newton's arrest spelled disaster: Scott would be forced to appear as a witness at Newton's trial and would no doubt repeat his allegations, which the press would then print. Newton's line of defence was that Scott had blackmailed him with a compromising picture. Thorpe's only hope was that, if Newton's claim of blackmail could be made to stick, Scott would be discredited – especially as Scott's only proof seemed to be the photocopies of the letters Bessell had written him concerning his 'retainer'.

Once again, it was to Peter Bessell that Thorpe turned for help. Since his 'disappearance' from England in 1974, Bessell had moved to Oceanside,

California, where Thorpe despatched David Holmes to see him.

Holmes's plan seemed simple: Bessell was to write a letter, to be held by Thorpe's solicitor, explaining that Scott had tried to blackmail Bessell over an illicit affair he had been having. Bessell reluctantly agreed to write the letter, on condition that it would be used only in an emergency.

The emergency arrived sooner than expected. On 29 January, Norman Scott appeared in court in Barnstaple, Devon on a charge of having defrauded the Department of Social Security of £58.40p. During the proceedings, Scott informed the court of a sexual relationship he had once had with the Liberal leader, and Thorpe's worst fears

RESIGNATION

from David Steel, MP

HOUSE OF COMMONS
LONDON SW1A 0AA

10th May, 1976.

My dear Jeremy,

You told me this morning that you had decided over the weekend to give up the leadership of the Liberal Party and I thank you for your letter confirming this. Your decision will be received by your colleagues with understanding but great sadness nevertheless. Your contribution to the party has been remarkable, particularly in your nine years as our leader, for more than half of which I had the pleasure and privilege of serving as your Chief Whip. You have raised us from being a sporadic political force to one with candidates in nearly every constituency, and over five million votes in each of two general elections.

Your personal qualities of leadership, charisma and sheer perseverance, and your triumphs over adversity, are held in the highest regard by all your colleagues and admired by the public at large. Your selfless decision to stand down now in the interests of the party is characteristic.

I am glad that you are remaining with us as a parliamentary colleague. You will be greatly sustained in the months ahead by your constituents as well as your family, and we all look forward to the time when freed of your present troubles you return to a key role in the public life of our country.

Yours affectionately,

David

were realised when the press ran the story.

The Liberal Party's new Chief Whip, Cyril Smith, was shown a teletext of the story before it was printed. When he asked Thorpe about it, Thorpe gave him the Bessell 'blackmail' letter and Fleet Street began to hunt for Peter Bessell. In Oceanside, California, Bessell was appalled to hear that Thorpe had broken his promise not to use the letter except in an 'emergency'. When Thorpe rang Bessell that evening, the latter said that he intended to follow his solicitor's advice to withdraw the letter. 'Peter,' pleaded Thorpe, 'I am begging for time, that's all. Give me time.'

FACING THE PARTY

On 4 February, Thorpe attended the parliamentary party's weekly meeting and, for the first time, was asked to explain what he knew of Scott to the whole party. Under the circumstances, Thorpe handled himself well, although helped by Emlyn Hooson, who handed round a document indicating Bessell as the key to the whole affair.

David Steel's generous letter to Thorpe on his resignation as leader is shown (right). Steel had always felt that if charges were brought against Thorpe he would resign his seat as well. He was wrong. With the committal over, Thorpe obstinately contested North Devon. He lost to the Conservative candidate by over 8000 votes.

Afterwards at dinner, Hooson raised his glass to Thorpe: 'I drink your health, Jeremy,' he said, 'but I'm afraid I fear for your future.' Four days later, Thorpe was questioned by the police. He told them that he was preparing a comprehensive account of 'Mr Norman Josiffe, otherwise Norman Scott', which they would have later. He then gave them a modified account of what he knew of the £2500 payment for Scott's letters. Concerning the dog-shooting incident, however, he stated that he had never had any contact – either 'direct or indirect' – with the accused, Mr Newton.

The police were not satisfied. Equally suspicious were the press, who had by now

INSIDE VIEW

SOUTH AFRICAN LINK?

Sir Harold Wilson (right), who had resigned as Prime Minister on 16 March 1976, had long suspected that South African interests were out to discredit various British politicians, himself included. His homes in London and the Isles of Scilly had both been burgled. After his resignation, he voiced his suspicions to two BBC journalists, Barrie Penrose and Roger Courtiour (below right), suggesting that Thorpe had been vilified because of his opposition to apartheid.

From Thorpe's point of view, this well-meaning intervention was less than helpful. Penrose and Courtiour – 'Pencourt' as they became jointly dubbed – dug deeply into the background and discovered, instead, the 'South Wales Connection': Holmes's dealings with Le Mesurier, Deakin, Miller and, eventually, Newton. For a while, they even pooled information with Detective Chief Superintendent Challes, in charge of the investigations, helping him to contact Peter Bessell in California.

discovered the link between David Holmes and the payment of £2500 into Scott's bank account in 1974. In a statement issued on Friday 5 March, Holmes admitted to having paid money for Bessell's letters – but they had turned out to be worthless and so he had burned them. He also stated that his first intention had been to protect the Liberal Party on the eve of a General Election – an admission that caused a Press sensation, with headlines christening Holmes 'The Godfather'.

This story cast doubt among even loyal Thorpe followers, with Cyril Smith angrily resigning the post of Chief Whip. *The Sunday Times*, however, came out in favour of Thorpe, dubbing Scott an inveterate liar and Bessell a gullible dupe who had exposed himself to blackmail. The front page ran a prominent feature giving Thorpe's refutation of the allegations against him.

NEWTON'S TRIAL

Thorpe was delighted. In the short term, at least, the coverage helped him through the Newton trial, which opened at Exeter Crown Court two days later, on 16 March, 1976. Andrew Newton swaggered into the box, in front of a packed court room, clearly relishing the publicity he was receiving. The international press, however, were more concerned with Norman Scott – the prosecution witness. Scott began to give his evidence haltingly, frequently bursting into tears.

Gradually, however, he began to bring Thorpe into the proceedings. Denying all knowledge of Newton's concocted blackmail story, he began to relate his own version of events with unusual zeal.

Newton claimed that he had only intended to scare Scott; that he had pointed the gun away from him and then pulled the trigger, but that the gun had jammed. On Friday 19 March, Newton was found guilty and sentenced to two years – an extremely light sentence, in view of the maximum possible penalty of 20 years.

A FRIEND TURNED FOE

Peter Bessell, meanwhile, had read *The Sunday Times* article and was furious, realising that some of the information must have come from Thorpe. *The Daily Mail* published an interview with Bessell headlined 'I Told Lies to Protect Thorpe', in which Bessell not only mentioned the fake 'blackmail' letter, but also confirmed that the payments to Scott had been to prevent him talking.

With Fleet Street buzzing, Thorpe now made a fool of himself publicly. On 1 May, Scott issued a summons for the return of the two letters taken from him by the police in 1962. Thorpe's lawyers also applied for them. On 7 May, the Yard's legal department adjudicated that the letters belonged to Scott, though the wording was Thorpe's copyright. They therefore returned the letters to Scott and gave Thorpe photocopies. Thorpe decided to allow *The Sunday Times* to publish. The 'Bunnies' letter duly received

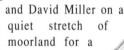

When Cyril Smith (right), the member for Rochdale, and the party's new Chief Whip, first heard Scott's allegations, his attitude was one of disbelief. Thorpe's denial only served to reinforce this view. As details of the alleged affair unfolded, however, he was to change his mind. When Holmes admitted paying money into Scott's bank account and then suggested to the press that he had been protecting the Liberal party in the process, Smith had had enough, and resigned the Whip.

full-page treatment and, within days, 'Bunnies' T-shirts were doing a roaring trade in London's busy Oxford Street. It was the last straw. Clement Freud, the urbane Liberal MP for Ely, and one of Thorpe's last loyal parliamentary friends, suggested that it was time to resign the leadership. Thorpe agreed. In his resignation letter to the acting Chief Whip, David Steel, on 10 May, he 'categorically repeated' his denials of the 'so-called Scott allegations' but concluded that effective party leadership was not possible amidst such 'allegations...continuing plots and intrigues'. There the matter appeared to rest for 18 months. Behind the scenes, however, investigations continued to make rapid progress.

In April 1977, Andrew Newton was released from Preston Prison, after serving just under half his allotted sentence. Three weeks later, he arranged to meet John Le Mesurier and David Miller on a quiet stretch of moorland for a

NEWTON'S FEES

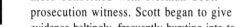

At the time of Thorpe's trials, Andrew Newton (above) had received several payments from the media for his story. Apart from the £5000 for his part in the Rinka incident, there had also been other payments: from *The Evening News*, £3000; *Der Spiegel*, £4000; *The Daily Express*, £600; *American Broadcasting Corporation*, £2000; *Columbia Broadcasting Corporation*, £500; and *Canadian Television*, £850.

Gareth Williams, QC, and counsel for Deakin, claimed that his client was there on the evidence of 'a single man – Newton... who was made and shaped by his own greed and self-delusion, finished and polished by the financial rewards he seeks... he has been paid, paid, and paid again.' Indeed, in view of the fact that, as an airline pilot, Newton received an annual salary of under £6000, he had done extremely well out of the whole incident.

BRITAIN'S BIGGEST EVENING SALE

Evening News

LONDON: WEDNESDAY, OCTOBER 19 1977 8p

LATE SPECIAL CITY PRICES

EXCLUSIVE: Gunman tells of incredible plot—a murder contract for £5,000

I WAS HIRED TO KILL SCOTT

By STUART KUTTNER and JOANNA PATYNA

A SEARCHING new police investigation has been ordered into the Norman Scott shooting affair after startling admissions from a convicted gunman that he was hired to kill Scott.

payment of £5000. As they talked, a car roared by with a man leaning out of the window snapping photographs. It later emerged that he had been hired by Miller with a view to selling the photographs to the newspapers. With his 'blood' money banked, and armed with a taped conversation with David Holmes, Newton now set out to haggle with the newspapers for the huge price of £150,000.

EXCLUSIVE

Eventually, the *London Evening News* secured the story for £3000, running it on 19 October 1977. The headlines were now quite unequivocal: 'I WAS HIRED TO KILL SCOTT. Exclusive: Gunman tells of incredible plot – a murder contract for £5000.' Calls were now coming from all over the country for Thorpe to resign his seat. On 27 October, he called a news conference in which he continued to deny everything. He even stated that Bessell should have gone to the police rather than the press, if he was in possession of any 'creditable evidence'. It was virtually a declaration of war on the man who had, for whatever reason, helped him so much. Indeed, Bessell took it as such.

Throughout that winter and the spring of 1978, the police compiled a dossier. They visited Bessell in the US, twice interviewed David Holmes, and even confronted Thorpe, who remained steadfast in his denials. Despite this, on 2 August 1978, warrants were issued for the arrest of Jeremy Thorpe, David Holmes, John Le Mesurier and George Deakin. All four were to face charges of conspiracy to murder, while Thorpe was to face the additional charge of incitement to murder.

THE MINEHEAD HEARING

On 20 November, the four men surrendered to bail at Minehead, Somerset. The town was packed with reporters and camera crews from all over the world. Thorpe sat alone, his face impassive, as Peter Taylor, QC for the prosecution, opened the case. For four weeks, the principal witnesses outlined the evidence which they would later have to give in detail, should the case go to trial. Peter Bessell, back from the US, spoke confidently. Andrew Newton's attempts at jaunty wise-cracking were less impressive, though his evidence

The committal proceedings at the Somerset seaside resort of Minehead (below) were the first stage of the media circus that was to reach its climax at the Old Bailey 18 months later. Thorpe is shown (right), arriving alone at a back entrance of the court on the second day of the hearing.

was dramatic enough. Norman Scott, on the other hand, merely caused embarrassed laughter.

Sir David Napley, Thorpe's solicitor, refused to accept that Scott had ever had a homosexual relationship with his client. But Scott indignantly pointed out that Thorpe had some warts under one arm and a curvature of the spine – alleged details he could only have known about if he had seen him naked.

After the police evidence had been read, the defence made their submissions. When it came to Thorpe's defence, Napley submitted that all three main witnesses were inveterate liars, and that Scott's evidence had 'as much to do with the case as the flowers that bloom in the spring.' The case for the prosecution, he said, 'stands or falls on the evidence of Mr Bessell and,' he continued, 'when you looked at his demeanour, mendacity was oozing out of every pore in his body.'

On 12 December, the magistrates withdrew to consider their decision overnight. The following morning they returned to commit all four of the accused to stand trial at the Old Bailey.

SEARCH FOR AN

AN UNFORTUNATE MISFIT – WHO RARELY MADE A LIVING AND BLAMED OTHER PEOPLE FOR HIS OWN SHORTCOMINGS – WAS TO BRING DOWN THE LEADER OF THE LIBERAL PARTY. BUT WHO EXACTLY WAS NORMAN SCOTT?

In almost every interview he gave on the Thorpe affair, Norman Scott was looking for ways of securing his future well-being: 'If only I could put down permanent roots...if only I knew what my real sexual feelings were...if only I could come to terms with myself.' He made it sound as if Thorpe alone had made all this self-questioning necessary. In fact, as his mother confirmed: 'Norman was always looking for some Shangri-La.'

WASTED OPPORTUNITIES

Norman Scott was an inadequate person who rarely made his own living, despite having opportunities to do so. His real ability lay in his skills as a horseman and he could in fact have made a decent living as a riding instructor. Good looking, and not without charm, he had, at one time, prospects as a male model, but failed to develop his chances.

He had aspirations, but these were dissipated into fantasies spun around a bogus family background. Apparently unable to accept responsibility for his own life, Scott blamed circumstances and other people for his own shortcomings.

His friendship with Jeremy Thorpe was brief, but it ultimately became the excuse for whatever went wrong with his own life. Thorpe was perhaps a substitute figure for the father

In 1979, Scott became one of the most photographed faces of the year. He reflected that the affair he claimed he had had with the Liberal leader had effectively ruined his life every bit as much as it had that of Thorpe.

IDENTITY

he never knew, but then again, as a self-dramatist, Scott needed a story to tell – part of the reason he clung to his Thorpe connection was because the Liberal politician was the only public figure he had ever met.

In 1968, Scott (above) was riding high. He was working as a model and had money in his pocket. Both situations were to be short-lived.

Like many self-excusers, Norman Scott could be very manipulative in his dealings with others. He was certainly a disruptive influence on other people's lives – drastically so, in Jeremy Thorpe's case.

Norman Scott was born Norman Josiffe at Sidcup, Kent, on 2 February 1940, the son of Albert Josiffe, an accountant, and his wife, Ena. Ena Josiffe worked as a switchboard operator at the London office of Pan American Airways, where she

was later to achieve supervisory rank. She had been married to Albert Merritt, a shipping executive, and had borne him three sons and a daughter before he died when Ena was barely into her twenties.

FAMILY SEPARATION

After Norman's birth, the family moved to Bexleyheath, a pleasant Kent dormitory town where Mrs Josiffe had a further son before she and her second husband separated. Albert Josiffe moved to Orpington and rarely saw his family again. Neither Norman nor his younger brother had any childhood memories of their father.

His mother was the head of the family, a strong woman whose dominance seemed to make Norman's own budding manhood unnecessary. She was still young and attractive, and her local political activities had broadened her circle of men friends, threatening, in the boy's mind, access to her affections.

LASTING OBSESSION

However, while in his early teens, it was his mother who bought him his first pony, 'Listowel', on which he went for long solitary rides.

At 15, he left school and became a trainee clerk in a

EARLY INFLUENCES

To help bring up her large family, Norman's mother Ena turned to her own Irish Catholic mother, Mrs Lynch, who lived nearby. The family were neither emotionally nor financially deprived. Albert Josiffe provided money, and Ena's own income was quite good. Mrs Lynch lavished affection on her six grandchildren, taking them to Mass every Sunday.

Norman did reasonably well at his primary school. But at his strict disciplinarian Roman Catholic secondary school, he began to have problems in keeping up, and was transferred to the local secondary modern. Even here, he was indifferent to academic studies as well as being poor at games. However, horse riding proved a partial salvation.

THE THORPE CONNECTION

At 19, Scott moved back from Cheshire to work in the Kingham Stables at Chipping Norton, Oxfordshire, and to learn the finer points of dressage. The owner of Kingham, Brecht Van de Vater, was also something of a fantasist, though a more successful one. He was certainly rich and well-connected, but he was not the exotic aristocrat that his self-styled title – Normand Vivian Dudley Van de Brecht de Vater – implied. He had been born Norman

Vivian Vater, son of a South Wales miner.

When de Vater married, his best man was Jeremy Thorpe. Sometime in 1960, Thorpe had visited the stables, and de Vater introduced him to the personable young stable hand Norman Lianche-Josiffe. Thorpe invited Norman to look him up at the House of Commons if ever he needed advice. The picture below shows Scott prepared for dressage during the year of his trial.

solicitor's office, but this job soon ended. He stole a saddle and some feed for his pony, and, on 23 April 1956, he was found guilty on two charges of theft at Bromley Juvenile Court and put on probation. Scott said it was his mother's fault for not providing him with the money.

His probation officer seems to have dealt intelligently with his young charge's problems. The pony appeared to be the boy's only real interest. Accordingly, Scott enrolled at a riding school where he worked hard, showing real flair for horsemanship. At 17 he was good enough to become a riding instructor in Cheshire.

In the autumn of 1960, back south in Oxford-

shire, Scott and his new employer, Brecht Van de Vater, parted company on bad terms. Scott's nerves were shattered, and he was introduced as an out-patient at the Ashurst Clinic in Oxford.

SECOND OVERDOSE

Twice in 1961 he took an overdose, the second time after an abortive relationship with another young man. This time he was compulsorily detained for three days at the Ashurst clinic, under Section 29 of the Mental Health Act.

Following his discharge, on 1 November 1961, he told a member of staff: 'I've had Oxfordshire, and I'm off.' His destination was London, and the House of Commons.

195

FIVE ON TRIAL

THE FINAL

The trial of Jeremy Thorpe, David Holmes, John Le Mesurier and George Deakin opened under the lofty dome of Court Number One at the Old Bailey on 8 May 1979. Thorpe, his face set and pale, joined the other three defendants in the dock, facing the judge's bench across the well of the court. They sat in high-backed chairs; that of Thorpe's was padded with red cushions because of his chronically bad back. Despite the spring weather, Thorpe wore an overcoat with a velvet collar. The judge was Sir Joseph Donaldson Cantley, 68 years old, with 15 years on the bench.

Thorpe, Holmes, Le Mesurier and Deakin were charged with conspiring together and with others between 1 October 1968 and 1 November 1977 to murder Norman Scott. In addition, Thorpe was accused of unlawfully inciting Holmes between 1

January and 31 March 1969 to murder Norman Scott.

Peter Taylor QC opened for the prosecution. His task was to prove four things: first, that there had been a homosexual affair between Thorpe and Scott; second, Thorpe's determination to keep Scott quiet after the affair; third, Thorpe's attempt to incite David Holmes to kill Scott when the threat of exposure increased; and finally, the conspiracy to kill Scott when all else had failed. Taylor opened the prosecution case with 8 November, 1961, when Thorpe had driven Scott and his Jack Russell terrier, 'Mrs Tish', from the House of Commons to his mother's house in Surrey.

THE FIRST NIGHT

'That night,' said Taylor, 'Mr Thorpe visited Josiffe's room on more than one occasion. [Scott was then still called Norman Josiffe.] The first time he brought and left with Josiffe a book entitled *Giovanni's Room*. It is a novel describing a relationship between two men. Later, Mr Thorpe returned to the bedroom, sat on the bed and talked to him.'

On the ninth day of the trial, Scott was to explain what he alleged to have happened that

Sir David Napley (above), a distinguished lawyer and former president of the Law Society, became Jeremy Thorpe's solicitor at the time of the Minehead committal proceedings in mid-1978.

night in his own words: 'He was wearing a dressing-gown and pyjamas. He just began talking to me about how I looked so ill, that things would be all right...he said I looked like a frightened rabbit. He decided, I suppose, from then on...I was his frightened rabbit and he just hugged me and called me "poor bunny"...he got into bed with me...'

DATEFILE

MAY 8 1979
Trial of Jeremy Thorpe and three other defendants opens at the Old Bailey

MAY 18 1979
Norman Scott is called by Peter Taylor QC to give evidence to establish a motive for the alleged crime

JUNE 22 1979
The six-week trial ends with acquittal of all defendants, but Thorpe's political career is finished

MAY '79-JUN '79

ACT

THE DOG-LOVER'S PARTY

In the General Election just prior to Thorpe's trial, Auberon Waugh, the writer and satirist, stood against Thorpe in North Devon for the 'Dog Lovers' Party' (at right, Waugh's poster). His adoption meeting address, published in the *Spectator*, read in part: '...I offer myself as your Member of Parliament in the General Election on behalf of the nation's dog lovers to protest about the behaviour of the Liberal Party generally and the North Devon Constituency Liberal Association in particular. Their candidate is a man about whose attitude to dogs - not to mention his fellow human beings - little can be said with any certainty at the present time...Rinka is NOT forgotten. Rinka lives. Woof, woof. Vote Waugh to give *all* dogs the right to life, liberty and the pursuit of happiness.'

A BETTER DEAL FOR YOUR DOG

VOTE WAUGH

Thorpe sought an injunction to ban the address and commit Waugh to prison for contempt of court. The Lord Chief Justice refused the injunction, though at appeal Lord Denning agreed to ban further publication. In the event, Waugh polled 79 votes.

Left: Jeremy Thorpe stares fixedly ahead as he is driven to the Old Bailey during the period of his trial. Above left: 49-year-old George Alfred Carman QC was Thorpe's leading defence counsel. He had been a contemporary of Thorpe's at Oxford University.

> *In that case, it will have to be poison. You can slip it into his drink, David, in the pub.*

Peter Bessell quoting Thorpe on his plan to get David Holmes to murder Scott

Thorpe, according to Scott, then left the room and came back with a towel and a tube of Vaseline which he put on his penis. He laid the towel on the bed, rolled Scott over and, in Scott's words, 'made love to me'.

'I just bit the pillow,' said Scott. 'I tried not to scream because I was frightened of waking Mrs Thorpe.' Afterwards, Thorpe wiped himself, got up, and patted Scott's thigh before leaving the room. 'I just lay there with my dog,' Scott explained. 'She was by the bed. I picked her up, brought her into my bed with me, and just lay crying.' The next morning Thorpe came into his bedroom and asked him how he would like his eggs for breakfast.

The affair continued, said Taylor, in Scott's Chelsea flat and in the West Country. At Christmas 1961, in a hotel in Devon, Jeremy Thorpe made love

Above: Members of the Gay Liberation Movement greet Thorpe as he arrives at court with his wife for the judge's summing up on day 27 of the trial. Right: Prosecution witness David Miller was the

Cardiff printer who recommended his friend Andrew Newton to Le Mesurier – as someone who 'would do anything for a laugh or a giggle'. He later described Newton as a 'chicken-brain.'

to Norman Scott in a green-tiled bathroom. 'I think at that stage I loved him,' said Scott, 'but I was very troubled about the sexuality. I think I loved him. He was...showing me some sort of caring.'

Taylor read out the famous 'Bunnies' letter, and told the court that its tone was consistent with Scott's account of the relationship. Scott claimed that the affair lasted through 1962, but then deteriorated. In 1963, however, while working in Ireland, Scott still went over to England to see Thorpe 'so he could screw me.'

LETTER FROM SCOTT

Taylor went on to read the letter that Scott had written to Thorpe's mother: '...through my meeting with Jeremy that day, I gave birth to this vice that lies latent in every man.' Of a later meeting with Thorpe, Scott wrote: '...that was the day I realised that Jeremy did not care for me as a friend but only as a – Oh! I hate to write that!! It upset me terribly...'

On day four of the trial, Peter Bessell related how Thorpe had showed him Scott's letter, admitting that its contents were basically correct. After describing his early role as intermediary between

Thorpe and Scott, Bessell told of the day in 1968 when, in Thorpe's office at the House of Commons, Thorpe had first suggested getting 'rid of him.' Thorpe said that the Scott problem was 'like a black cloud' over him, threatening to destroy his career. Thorpe asked Bessell if it was really impossible to get Scott a job in America, and when he said it was, Thorpe replied: 'In that case we have got to get rid of him.'

'Are you suggesting killing him off?' asked Bessell. Thorpe replied 'Yes,' and then suggested dropping the body in a river, burying it, or concealing it under the rubble of a new motorway. Bessell pointed out that his Cornwall constituency was full of old tin mines. Thorpe grabbed him by the shoulders and shook him: 'A tin mine! That's it!' Thorpe believed the body could be dropped down an empty mineshaft.

At this point, Bessell thought the discussion had become immoral. 'It's no worse than shooting a sick dog,' said Thorpe. Bessell had to leave the House of Commons for some time, and when he came back to Thorpe's office later that night, Thorpe took up the conversation as if Bessell had never left. 'I have thought of the person who could kill Scott – David Holmes.'

A few months later, Thorpe, Bessell and Holmes met in the House of Commons. Thorpe suggested that Holmes should drive down to the West Country, get Scott drunk, drive him to a lonely spot and kill him. Bessell said Holmes looked petrified, until Bessell caught his eye and winked. Thorpe also suggested poisoning Scott. This formed the evidence for the charge of incitement to murder made against Thorpe alone.

When the prosecution finished its case, things looked very black indeed for Thorpe and his fel-

INSIDE
VIEW

FIDDLING THE PARTY'S FUNDS?

CLOSE-UP — A LANDSLIDE DEFEAT

Jeremy Thorpe's trial had originally been scheduled to open on 1 May 1979, but on 4 April, Thorpe successfully applied to the Lord Chancellor to have it deferred for a week. The General Election had been called by Labour's Prime Minister, James Callaghan, for 3 May and, despite all his looming troubles and the advice of most colleagues, Thorpe decided to fight his seat at North Devon (he is seen on the left, with hat, fraternising with the locals). Twenty years after his election at Barnstaple, Thorpe's majority of nearly 7000 was wiped out, and the Tories swept in with a lead of 8473.

low accused. But as George Carman QC, Thorpe's old Oxford associate and leading counsel, developed his case for the defence, things became much brighter.

BESSELL TESTIFIES

Peter Bessell, facing the defence counsel for the first time, agreed that he was hoping to make a good deal of money from a contract with a newspaper – £50,000 if Thorpe was convicted, £25,000 if not. The clear inference was that Bessell had good reason to want to see a conviction. Carman also got Bessell to agree that he had 'disappeared' in 1974 to escape his creditors, and that the prelude to his disappearance had been an unsuccessful scheme to swindle Jack Hayward out of half a million pounds. Bessell implied that Thorpe had been heavily involved in this scheme, but Carman managed to convey a strong impression that Bessell was an habitual liar and cheat.

Carman was equally good at handling Scott. A vital point was made when he got Scott to admit that he had been boasting about a sexual relationship with Thorpe before he went to see him at the Commons for the first time. Scott admitted that he had been mentally ill at the time and suffering from delusions. What Carman was attempting to prove was that Scott might have invented the whole story of his seduction by Thorpe.

> **But inevitably because of the prominence he has achieved...his frailties, his weaknesses have been exposed remorselessly to the public gaze.**
>
> George Carman QC, leading counsel for Thorpe referring to his client

Scott's demeanour – he was twice rebuked for outbursts of temper – made a thoroughly bad impression. He came over as an hysterical neurotic who had persecuted Jeremy Thorpe, a prominent political figure, out of sheer malice.

Newton, too, came out badly. Since his Minehead appearance he had grown a straggling beard and had lost some of his jauntiness. Examined by John Mathew QC, counsel for David Holmes, Newton admitted he had lied on oath during his trial at Exeter after shooting the dog 'to save my own skin.' 'Trickery and deceit have been your trademarks throughout this matter?' asked Mathew. 'Yes,' replied Newton.

DEAKIN'S EVIDENCE

George Deakin was the only one of the accused who chose to go into the witness box. He insisted that he had merely helped to find someone to frighten a blackmailer, and had never asked who was being blackmailed. He denied any involvement in the subsequent intimidation of Scott.

The prosecution and defence took five days to summarise their cases. Thorpe's counsel emphasised that his decision not to go into the box did not prove him guilty. He had a right to remain silent.

When Mr Justice Cantley came to his summing up, he was basically in favour of the accused. He, too, stressed that the refusal of Thorpe, Holmes and Le Mesurier to go into the witness box should not be regarded as evidence of guilt. He was scathing about the credibility of the prosecution witnesses. When he spoke of Bessell, he emphasised that his evidence about Thorpe's 'ultimate solution' to the problem of Scott was uncorroborated. He obviously found it impossible to hide his distaste for Scott. He spoke of his 'hysterically warped personality' and described him as 'an accomplished liar' and 'a crook.'

When the jury retired, they were divided six for and six against acquittal. An hour later, they were two to ten for acquittal. By the following day only one man held out for a guilty verdict, and after two days that one man was convinced. On Friday 22 June, the four accused filed back into the dock. The foreman read out Not Guilty verdicts on

The prosecution's explanation of who financed the alleged plot to kill Scott was complex. Several jury members admitted they had not fully understood the financial aspects. The prosecution said that money for the 'hit-man' was siphoned off from Liberal Party funds supplied by Jack Hayward (left), a benefactor of the Liberals. Thorpe had written to Hayward after the 1974 election, explaining that he needed £50,000 for election funds, but that it would be best if he could have it in two cheques, one for £40,000 and one for £10,000. The cheque for £40,000 went into the party funds; the other for £10,000 went into an account on Jersey belonging to Nadir Dinshaw, a Pakistani businessman and friend of Thorpe.

Dinshaw sent the money on to David Holmes. In March 1975, a further £10,000 went via Dinshaw to Holmes. Dinshaw was dubious about this second request, but Thorpe assured him that the transfer would be confidential. In 1978, when Dinshaw told Thorpe he had to tell the police the truth about the transactions, Thorpe in effect warned him not to say more than necessary, with the threat that if he did, he (Dinshaw) 'will be asked to move on' – that is, asked to leave Britain.

A SERIES OF BLUNDERS

If Andrew Newton (left, at the Old Bailey) had in fact been chosen to murder Norman Scott, the choice would have been lucky for Scott, since Newton proved inept and – according to his testimony – lacked the 'killer instinct'. First, to find Scott, Newton went to Dunstable in Bedfordshire, instead of Barnstaple, Devon. Then he tried to lure Scott to the Royal Garden Hotel in Kensington, London, with offers of modelling work, but mentioned fees so high that Scott became suspicious and did not turn up. Had Scott gone, Newton intended to hit him over the head and kill him with a coal chisel hidden in a bunch of flowers.

On the stand, Newton told how he had finally contacted Scott under the name Peter Keene and had taken him for the drive which ended with the death of the dog. Newton insisted that he had pretended the gun had jammed. It was for this failed attempt that he was paid £5000.

all four, and for a moment Thorpe stared rigidly ahead. Then he smiled, tossed the three red cushions on which he had been sitting over the side of the dock, and leaned forward to embrace his wife.

THANKSGIVING SERVICE

Two Sundays after the verdict, a thanksgiving service for Thorpe and his wife, Marion, was held at the tiny 11th century church of Bratton Fleming, on the edge of Exmoor. The vicar, one of Thorpe's most faithful followers, chose as his text: 'With God nothing shall be impossible.' The lesson of the day was from Ecclesiastes:

> *He is a fraud. He is a sponger. He is a whiner. He is a parasite. But of course, he could still be telling the truth. It is a question of belief.*
>
> Sir Joseph Cantley, trial judge, on Scott during his summing up

'Let us now praise famous men...' Loud-speakers had been rigged up, linking the church with the village hall, in expectation of a large crowd. But by the time Jeremy, Marion and Jeremy's son, Rupert, arrived the church was barely half-full, and many of the congregation were members of the press.

Talk of the case continued up and down the country. For many people, the only character in the drama to emerge untarnished was Rinka the Great Dane – perhaps the most famous dog, outside the imagination of Sir Arthur Conan Doyle, in British criminal history.

Acquitted by the Old Bailey jury of conspiring to murder Norman Scott, club owner George Deakin (above) raises his arms in victory after emerging from court. His co-defendant, Jeremy Thorpe, celebrates his acquittal by appearing on the balcony of his Orme Square home in Paddington (right) after the verdict, accompanied by his wife. Family and friends later threw a champagne celebration.

THE ONASSIS CURSE

A self-made millionaire at 23, Greek

shipping and property tycoon Aristotle

Onassis moved in the highest society

circles and romanced some of the world's

most famous women. Yet all his fabulous

wealth proved no guarantee of happiness for him or his family. A succession

of tragedies – both before and after his death in 1975 – made it seem as if

there were a curse on the Onassis dynasty.

CHAPTER ONE

THE RISE TO RICHES

ON 21 SEPTEMBER 1923, A YOUNG GREEK
STEPPED ASHORE AT BUENOS AIRES,
ARGENTINA, TO SEEK HIS FORTUNE.
DETERMINATION AND GUILE
WOULD BE HIS DRIVING FORCES

TOBACCO ROAD

DATEFILE

SEPT 21 1923

Aristotle Socrates Onassis arrives in
Buenos Aires from Greece

WINTER 1932

Onassis moves properly into the
shipping business by buying six
Canadian freighters

JUNE 15 1938

World's first supertanker, the
Ariston, ordered by Onassis, is
launched in Sweden

SEPT'23-JUN'38

ristotle Onassis was 17 years old when he left Greece to make a new life for himself in Argentina. After six months in Buenos Aires and a succession of dispiritingly menial jobs, he was on the verge of working his passage back to Europe, when a conversation with some fellow Greeks landed him a post as electrician with the local telephone company. Soon, he was working as a night-time switchboard operator, and earning more money. He had no qualms about listening in to business conversations and turning his insider knowledge to good account – some $700 – on the stock exchange.

It was in the Argentine tobacco market, however, that Onassis began to make his first big money. Convinced that he could cash in on the vogue for things Oriental then sweeping Argentina, he arranged for his father, in Greece, to send a few bales of his finest Turkish leaf tobacco. Until then, most of the leaf imported into Argentina came from Brazil or Cuba and lacked the smoothness of its European counterpart.

Breaking into the Argentine market was more difficult than he had foreseen, so Onassis decided to make his own cigarettes. The two brands he created (Primeros and Osman) were aimed at rich young women. Competition was tough and he sometimes used unscrupulous methods, such as injecting chemicals into rival cigarettes which caused them to give off a foul smell when lit. He

Above: The world's first supertanker, commissioned by Onassis and called Ariston, rolled down the slipway at Göteborg, Sweden, in June 1938.
Left: Onassis retained his interest in tobacco long after he made his first fortune in the leaf. Here, he cuts up a Havana cigar for inspection while in Long Island, USA, in 1942.
Below: In 1932, and still only 26, Onassis became Deputy Greek Consul in Argentina in recognition of his political, commercial and social connections .

> *Even when you saw him in a bar or simply walking down the street you knew he was a competitor at something. To be doing a deal was his whole life, the rest was waiting.*

Costa Gratsos, long-time friend, on Onassis in 1920s Buenos Aires

Argentina had ratified neither the Geneva Convention nor The Hague Convention on narcotics trafficking and Buenos Aires had consequently become the chief distribution point for drug imports to South America. Under the cover of his continuing trade in tobacco leaf, Onassis was able to extend his opium trading into Brazil and elsewhere on the South American continent.

also labelled one of his cigarette brands with the same name as the local leading brand and sold them at cut price; he was sued when this ruse was discovered, and he wisely settled out of court for several thousand dollars.

UNDERHAND TACTICS

To meet these damages, Onassis devised an even more underhand ploy. Most of his tobacco was transshipped at Genoa in northern Italy. He arranged with the port's extensive underworld to have it sprayed with sea water while it stood on the quayside, enabling him to claim on his insurance for 'sea damage'. This, too, was detected and its ringleader jailed. Onassis remained out of reach of any extradition treaty.

In the late 1920s, as his cigarette venture began to fail, Onassis kept himself financially afloat by importing another product that his father – like many tobacco dealers in the eastern Mediterranean – traded in. Opium. The young Onassis was a drug trafficker.

Right: In a personal photograph taken in 1930, a proud Aristotle Onassis poses beside the first car he owned.

TARIFF THREAT

In 1929, his growing business was threatened by the Greek government's announcement of a 1000 per cent increase in tariffs on imports from countries with which they had no trading agreement. Fearing a similar retaliation from Argentina, Onassis hurried back to Greece with a memorandum pleading for second thoughts. After a week, he was granted an audience with the Greek minister of foreign affairs who was responsible for the drafting of the new laws. After a chilly start to the meeting, Onassis convinced the minister of the

possible repercussions, and negotiations with Argentina were soon opened.

When he returned to Buenos Aires, Onassis – aged just 26 – was appointed Deputy Greek Consul. It was a post he lost no time in turning to his own advantage, obtaining large amounts of currency at the official rates and re-selling it on the black market at a handsome profit. He also obtained an Argentine passport.

SHIFTING TO SHIPS

Onassis was now partnered in business by Costa Gratsos, the son of a Greek shipowning family, who would remain his closest confidant for the rest of his life. With Gratsos' encouragement, Onassis began to consider the advantages of trans-acting his business in his own ships. His first pur-chase was a rusting hulk lying shipwrecked on the far banks of the River Plate near Montevideo, cap-ital of neighbouring Uruguay. No sooner had he restored it to working order than it mysteriously sank – still at anchor – in Montevideo harbour. If he was trying another insurance fraud, he was not

BACKDROP

ARGENTINA BETWEEN THE WARS

Neutrality in World War I had given a huge boost to Argentina's economy. Exports of grain, wheat and minerals soared, making the country sixth in the world's wealth league.

Traditionally, Britain had been the leading investor, but the boom at the end of the war brought a new wave of immigrants from all over Europe. They came from Greece, Turkey, Germany and Spain , but by far the most came from Italy. By 1925 Italians, mostly from the south and Sicily, made up over 40 per cent of the population.

Buenos Aires, the capital, was a cosmopolitan city of two million people. Apart from having a very European flavour, it owed its new title as the 'Paris of South America' to its broad avenues, such as the Avenida Mayo (below), a metro system and splendid architecture.

In the 1920s, Buenos Aires was a bustling city with a racy nightlife. Although prostitution had been officially illegal since 1917, it was known as a centre of the white slave trade. By 1930, the city had become the principal supply point for the distribution of drugs throughout South America.

the first Greek to have tried it; a few years earlier, Lloyd's of London had expressed concern over 'the unusual number of shipwrecks in the Greek merchant navy.'

Next to catch his eye, in the depths of the Depression in 1932, were six Canadian freighters, which he bought for the knockdown price of $20,000 apiece – less than half their scrap value.

Cargo for the ships was slow to materialise, but Onassis found a way to maximise the return on what there was; he re-registered his fleet under the flag of Panama, where shipping regulations – par-ticularly those relating to the pay and conditions of the crew – were minimal.

PROFITING FROM WAR

In 1935 Hitler abrogated the London Naval Agreement limiting the size of warships and launched a massive re-armament programme, while on the other side of the world, Japan was preparing to invade China. Onassis foresaw that

Personal photographs illustrate the Onassis lifestyle in the US before and during World War II . Below left The 32-year-old Onassis in Los Angeles in 1938. Above left: Onassis' sister Artemis, in the foreground, with his mistress Ingeborg Dedichen on Long Island in 1942. Above centre: Onassis at his desk in New York, 1942. Below right: at his Long Island home with his chef in 1944. Below centre: with Ingeborg on Malibu Beach, California, in 1943.

coal, already supplying 75 per cent of the world's energy needs, would not meet the demands of escalating war preparations, and therefore shrewdly reckoned that the market share of alternative fuel – oil – would rise rapidly. Furthermore, ships to transport it would be in equal demand.

He also worked out that by increasing the size of the then standard, 9000-tonne tanker by two-thirds, he could greatly cut operating costs. He placed an order for a 15,000 tonner with a Swedish yard and secured it against a one-year contract with J. Paul Getty to carry oil from the US to Japan. Onassis followed it up with two more orders for vessels of 15,000 and 17,500 tonnes respectively. The first, the *Ariston* , was launched in June 1938.

Onassis may have thought he was well-placed to make a financial killing in the face of the gathering storm, but he was in for a disagreeable shock. With the outbreak of World War II in September 1939, the *Ariston*, berthed in Stockholm, and another tanker still under construction in Göteborg, were promptly impounded for the war's duration by the neutral Swedish government.

SAILING TO SAFETY

Forced to rely on his 'dry' cargo ships, carrying such products as tobacco, timber and grain, Onassis sold two of them to the Japanese who were paying over-the-odds for ships needed to back up their ever-widening invasion plans. He was on the point of selling two more when the US government stepped in to block the deal. However, some of his smaller ships were later taken over by the more accommodating Argentine government.

In July 1940 Onassis sailed to New York, after a voyage in which his ship had to zigzag to avoid German U-boats patrolling the Atlantic. Onassis spent the war in safety, night-clubbing with his mistress, Ingeborg Dedichen, entertaining celebrities at their Long Island home, and conducting his business from New York and Los Angeles.

INSIDE VIEW
FLIRTING WITH FASCISTS

Democracy, always a fragile flower in Argentina's chequered history, was uprooted again in 1930 by a military coup. Backed by the large German and even larger Italian communities, the new régime leaned increasingly towards the Axis powers of fascist Germany and Italy throughout the 1930s.

Onassis was more than happy to swim with this growing tide. He owed his introduction into the ruling circle to Alberto Dodero, the son of an Italian immigrant who had made a fortune from a monopoly of the ferries crossing the River Plate between Buenos Aires and Montevideo. Another intimate was Fritz Mandl, the Jewish Austrian armaments magnate. Although not directly threatened by Hitler, Mandl had taken the precaution of transferring most of his assets to South America before Hitler invaded Vienna in 1938.

Onassis' contact with these men brought him to the attention of the local FBI agents. On re-entering the US in 1942, the Bureau's director, J Edgar Hoover, personally ordered that 'his activities and movements while in the United States should be carefully scrutinized' on the grounds that he had 'expressed sentiments inimical to the United States war effort.'

BORN INTO A GREEK MERCHANT FAMILY LIVING IN SMYRNA, THE YOUNG ONASSIS LED A PRECOCIOUS AND REBELLIOUS LIFE UNTIL 1922 WHEN THE TURKS CAPTURED HIS HOME-TOWN, SET IT ALIGHT AND MASSACRED ITS CITIZENS

BAPTISM OF

With their bundled belongings, Anatolian Greeks, Armenians, Jews and Christians crowd onto boats docked in Smyrna harbour on 1 September 1922 in order to escape the advancing Turkish troops under Kemal Ataturk.

Aristotle Socrates Onassis was probably born on 20 January 1906 in the Anatolian port of Smyrna (now Izmir in modern Turkey) – 'probably' because he later claimed to have been born in 1900 in order to conceal his youth from Argentinian officials.

His father, Socrates, had moved to Smyrna from his home village deep in the Anatolian interior, attracted by the opening of the railway connecting Smyrna with the rest of Asia Minor. There he set up a thriving business in tobacco. Aristotle was barely out of his infancy when his mother, Penelope, died. His father soon married again, but from the outset Aristotle refused to acknowledge his stepmother, Helen, as a replacement – in spite of frequent encouragement from his father's strap.

At school he regularly played truant, and always ended up bottom of his class. As a result, he was expelled from school after school. In despair, Socrates turned to his friend Michael Avramides, who was supervisor of the Evangheliki School, the most prestigious in Smyrna. Its headmaster, Elie Lithoxoos, was a stern disciplinarian. Socrates persuaded Avramides to take on his son as a personal favour.

It was a favour Avramides soon regretted. 'He was a really naughty person, a disorderly child, shocking all around him...,' he recalled many years later. 'During the whole time I spent at the school I never had such a child.' Onassis later claimed that he won a place at Oxford there, but he never even graduated from the school.

CELLAR LOVE

According to Onassis, he was only 12 when he almost lost his virginity to the family's young washerwoman in the cellar. But

AN ANATOLIAN STRUGGLE

Greeks had lived on the eastern shores of the Aegean Sea for at least three millennia, but in all that time they had rarely enjoyed any sort of autonomy. Under the Ottoman Empire (from about 1300 to 1922), they had been tolerated by the Turkish majority because of the trading links they provided with the West.

In World War One, Turkey sided with Germany and under the Treaty of Sevres in 1920, the victorious allies duly exacted their revenge, awarding Smyrna and much of the Anatolian hinterland to Greece.

This humiliation rapidly led to the overthrow of the Sultan in a military coup led by Kemal Ataturk (below, centre), the general who had masterminded the successful defence of Gallipoli five years earlier. Determined to undo the Treaty's impositions, he attacked the occupying Greek forces on 22 August, 1922, and within a fortnight he drove them back the 200 miles to the coast and marched into Smyrna.

FIRE

Socrates Onassis (left), Aristotle's father, was born in Cappadocia, central Anatolia, in 1878. After establishing himself in Smyrna he married Penelope Dologlou (above), Aristotle's mother.

his stepmother caught them before anything happened and he received another belting from his father. However, it transpired that his father was more concerned about his choice of partner than his precocity: 'Never become involved with someone who will make you lose stature if the relationship becomes known,' he advised his son.

BODY BUILDER

Much of the time spent away from school was passed at the local rowing and swimming club, building up his body to the admiring glances of the girls sunning themselves on the shoreline. He also became a regular visitor to Demiri Yolu, the city's red light district. On one rare day when he was not

playing truant, he asked his surprised teacher if he could lead a prayer group to the nearby church of St. Barbara on the saint's birthday. Once clear of the school gates, however, he did a sharp about turn and led his willing fellow-pupils down to his favourite salon.

This pleasurable adolescence was brought to an abrupt end in September 1922, when the army of Turkey's new ruler, Kemal Ataturk, marched into Smyrna – since 1919 a Greek-ruled enclave – and put the non-Turk population to the sword. In five days, some 120,000 perished in an unbridled orgy of blood-letting and nine-tenths of the city was burnt to the ground. Many people were incinerated when the churches they sought refuge in were put to the torch; others who escaped gave horrific reports of seeing the heads of raped and decapitated Greek girls

Left: Burnt-out buildings line the quay in Smyrna's French quarter after Turkish soldiers had set fire to the city during a rampage in September 1922.

tied together by the hair and tossed into the harbour.

Socrates was thrown into jail, the Onassis womenfolk removed to a transit camp on the island of Lesbos, and the family house requisitioned by a Turkish general. Ingratiating himself with the general's aide-de-camp, Onassis was allowed to stay on as his assistant – and, some say, homosexual lover.

Given the freedom of the ruined city in which to run various errands, Onassis eventually traced his father, who told him to salvage what he could from the remains of the warehouse. Finding the office safe still intact, he was able to recover a considerable sum of money and smuggle himself and it on board an American destroyer at anchor in the harbour.

Disembarking at Lesbos, he located the 17 women and children of the Onassis family and after three weeks managed to transfer them – and himself –

to the safety of Athens.

After settling them into lodgings there, Onassis set off to Istanbul on a ship with the remaining money to engineer his father's release. This he managed to do, but to his surprise and dismay his father, far from expressing gratitude, at once demanded a detailed account of where the money had gone – which his son was unable to produce.

A BITTER LESSON

'You know how it is,' he later said about his father's response, 'people forget quickly. They may have been on the verge of death but the moment they're safe all recriminations and curses come pouring out.'

Alienated from his father and anxious about his future, Onassis resolved to start a new life elsewhere – in Argentina, which had a reputation as a land of opportunity.

'SLEEPING UP'

Following his father's advice that he should 'always sleep up' – that is, have sex with women of high social status – Onassis made an additional point of choosing women who could also bring him material advantages.

His first major conquest was in Buenos Aires with a visiting Italian opera star, 35-year-old Claudia Muzio (above). At that time – the early 1920s – it was still not done for women to smoke in public, and he reckoned that by persuading her to smoke his own

gold-tipped brand of cigarette in public, she would help him boost his sales.

When Onassis turned to shipping, he took up with Ingeborg Dedichen (seen below with a face-pulling Onassis), the daughter of one of Norway's leading shipowners. She provided him with an invaluable entrée into Scandinavian shipbuilding yards. She got little in return; sometimes he would beat her up so badly in their New York apartment that he dismissed the servants for a week while she recovered.

Nor did their liaison prevent him from pursuing a clutch of Hollywood starlets, through whom he was able to introduce himself to the studio and industrial magnate, Howard Hughes.

TWO

OF SHIPS AND

EMERGING FROM THE WAR A MULTI-MILLIONAIRE, ONASSIS MARRIED FOR THE FIRST TIME AT 40. WITH FURIOUS ENERGY – AND OFTEN BREATHTAKING BRAVADO – HE LAUNCHED INTO VENTURES AS DIVERSE AS WHALING AND OIL TRANSPORTATION

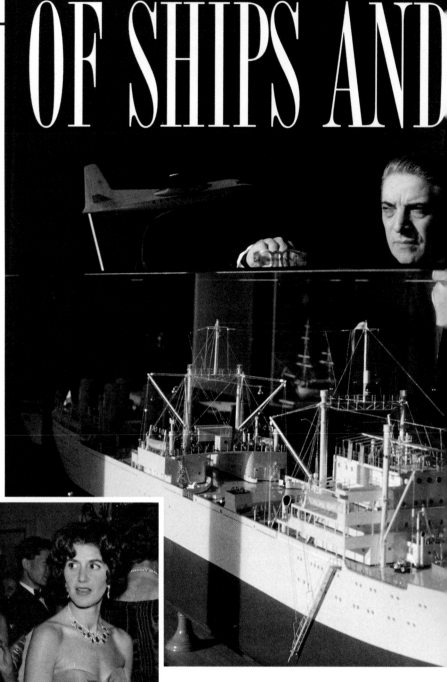

Above: Onassis' wedding reception in New York's Plaza Hotel. Tina's sister Eugenie is seated on the left beside shipping magnate Stavros Niarchos, who married her a year later. Behind Niarchos stands Tina's father, Stavros Livanos. Right: The two sisters, Tina (left) and Eugenie, remained close throughout their lives. Main picture: Onassis poses beside a model of his whaling factory ship Olympic Challenger.

DATEFILE

DECEMBER 28 1946
Aristotle Onassis marries Tina Livanos in New York City

OCTOBER 28 1950
Onassis's whaling fleet sails on its first expedition

FEBRUARY 5 1954
Onassis arrested in New York for fraud

MAY 18 1954
King Saud ratifies the oil-carrying deal with Onassis

DEC'46–MAY'54

I
f anyone benefited from World War II, it was Onassis. By 1945 his net worth was estimated to have risen to over $30 million. It was time, he decided, to acquire a status to match – in particular, a marital status. Onassis had been conducting a turbulent affair with Ingeborg Dedichen, who came from a leading Norwegian shipping family, since 1934. But in 1946, she was packed off back to Europe and replaced in his affections by a 17-year-old schoolgirl.

Athina 'Tina' Livanos was the second daughter of Stavros Livanos, the doyen of London's Greek shipowning community, who was now domiciled in New York. Born in London, Tina had been a pupil at the exclusive English boarding school, Heathfield. When Onassis first began to pay court to the Livanos mansion in 1943, it was assumed that it was Eugenie, Tina's elder sister by two years, whom he was after.

Her surprised father accordingly rebuffed his eventual request for Tina's hand, although only on the grounds that he thought it the elder sister's right to be engaged first. The impasse was resolved by the announcement of Eugenie's engagement to Onassis' contemporary and later bitter rival, Stavros Niarchos.

Onassis and Tina, 40 and 17 years old respectively, were married in New York's Greek Orthodox Cathedral on 28 December 1946. Their first child, Alexander, was born 16 months later, to be followed by a daughter, Christina, on 11 December 1950. By then the family was installed in the sumptuous Château de la Croë on the French Riviera, conveniently close to the Alpine slopes for Tina, a keen skier. It was for reasons

WHALES

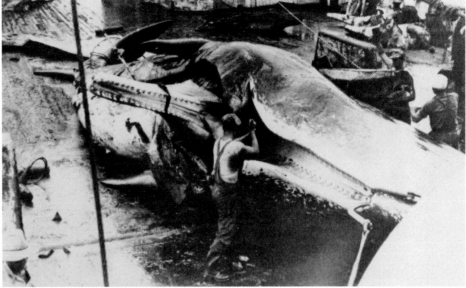

*Above: Workers on **Olympic Challenger** slice up a sperm whale to prepare the meat for processing. Onassis' whaling fleet netted him huge profits, but its illegal killing methods seriously depleted whale stocks. The fleet was eventually sold to Japan for $8.5 million.*

other than accessibility to the Alps, however, that Onassis decided to move his home and operational base back to Europe.

In 1946 the US Congress passed the Ship Sales Act in order to dispose of the enormous government-owned surplus of merchant ships left over from the war. They included a number of 16,000-tonne T-2 oil tankers. The following year, Onassis decided to purchase 20 of them, but buyers had to be American citizens. However, Onassis discovered that as long as the ships were nominally US-owned, there was nothing to prevent non-Americans from operating them. And taking the profits.

Accordingly, in September 1947, Onassis registered a new company, the United States Petroleum Carriers, in the state of Delaware. To give it a respectable front, he persuaded a group of prominent Americans to take a majority shareholding. Two other ploys completed the strategy; the ships were registered under the Liberian flag-of-convenience, removing them from US regulatory control, and chartered to an Onassis-owned Panamanian company, which would avoid liability to any US tax.

Left: Onassis and Tina in the grounds of their rented mansion, the Château de la Croë in the South of France, once home to the Duke and Duchess of Windsor.

It was not long before federal fraud investigators were on his track and, in 1953, he was indicted by a grand jury. In February 1954 Onassis was arrested, finger-printed and briefly jailed. He was eventually fined $7 million, although he was allowed to retain ownership of the ships on condition that he built more in American yards and operated them under the US flag.

GOING WHALING

Meanwhile, Onassis had perceived a gap in the market for another kind of oil – whale-oil, the basic constituent of margarine and many other everyday products – whose value was soaring with the post-war boom. Before the war, the traditional Norwegian supremacy in the industry had been challenged by the Germans. After defeat and consequent dismantling of the German fleets, including the whaling ships, thousands of German whalers and many shipbuilders were desperate for work.

Onassis commissioned the German shipyards at Kiel to 'stretch' one of his newly acquired American T-2 tankers into a factory ship and convert 17 redundant corvettes into hunter-catchers.

By October 1950, Onassis' whaling fleet was ready to sail for the Antarctic. It was crewed by Germans under the command of an ex-German Navy captain. Most of the 18 harpoon-gunners were skilled Norwegians who had collaborated with the Nazis during the war-time occupation of Norway and were unwilling to return home.

Six weeks later – and 16 days before the official opening of the blue whale season set by the International Whaling Commission (IWC) – the fleet registered its first kill, and went on killing even after the season's official close. Still Onassis was not satisfied, ordering the fleet to move north into the sperm whale fields off Peru. He even came

Above (main picture): Onassis and his family attend the launch of his oil tanker Al-Malik Saud Al-Awal in Hamburg, 1954. Inset: A painting of the tanker's launch ceremony which hung in Onassis' Monte Carlo office. Right: Arab dignitaries feast with King Ibn Saud aboard the tanker following its arrival in Jiddah, the principal seaport of Saudi Arabia.

to witness the slaughter for himself, bringing guests for whom the highlight of their visit was an invitation to try their hand at the harpoon guns.

DODGING THE BILL

This first expedition netted Onassis $4.2 million, almost covering his initial outlay on the fleet, and the next three Antarctic expeditions were as profitable. In August 1954 the fleet again arrived off Peru to hunt sperm whales, but this time the Peruvians, who had now declared a 200-mile territorial limit, were waiting. Five of the ships were seized – the factory ship and four hunter-catchers – and held pending payment of a $2.8 million penalty. It was met not by Onassis, but by Lloyd's of London; in insuring the fleet, Onassis had had the foresight to take out cover against 'war risks'.

By now, the Norwegian Whaling Association had amassed a formidable dossier of evidence against Onassis, which they presented at the 1955 annual meeting of the IWC in Moscow. It showed he had violated all whaling conventions on a massive scale. The Norwegians fined him $700,000 and impounded his whaling fleet until he paid it – only to be informed by Onassis that he had sold the fleet to Japan in the meantime. Both sides agreed a compromise, by which Onassis agreed to pay a rather smaller sum into a whale conservation fund.

SAUDI OIL MONOPOLY

While building up this whaling empire, Onassis was also examining ways to free himself from dependence on the major oil companies for charter contracts for his tankers.

Billionaire John Paul Getty provided him with an answer. In 1948 Getty was the first to break the monopoly which ARAMCO, a consortium of major American oil companies, had over the Saudi Arabian oil industry, by offering King Ibn Saud improved terms. Onassis made a similar offer for the transportation of 10 per cent of Saudi Arabia's annual oil output, a figure which he proposed to raise to 100 per cent over 10 years as ARAMCO's existing charters expired. This would make Onassis the sole shipper of Saudi oil.

When news of the proposed deal leaked out, ARAMCO was outraged. The US government also was alarmed at the prospect of so large a slice of the world's oil supply falling into such unreliable hands, and also incensed by a clause in the

INSIDE VIEW
A DAMNING DIARY

Onassis' highly profitable whaling adventure in 1954 flouted every rule drawn up by the International Whaling Commission (IWC). Evidence of his ruthless methods came from several sources on the factory ship, *Olympic Challenger*. One of the most damning was a diary kept by a crew member, Bruno Schlaghecke.

On a day well before the start of the season's official opening, he wrote: 'Killed almost only blue whales today...Woe if this leaks out.' Four days later, he went on: 'Killed only small sperm whales today. The sight of these small animals, which had not even grown teeth, makes me inwardly dumb and empty.' Nearly two months later: 'Today, October 31, production surpassed 60,000 barrels [of whale oil], an output never before recorded. More whales are continually coming in, sperm whales, blue whales, fin, humpback. This time nothing will stop them.'

On a previous expedition, another crewman recorded the shooting of a giant North Cape whale. 'As far as we knew,' he recorded, 'this species is preserved and must not be killed under any circumstances. It was...strictly forbidden by the captain to take photographs or to remove whalebones.'

> *My mistake was that I woke up too early and disturbed those who were still asleep, and as a result I got into the biggest mess of my life.*
>
> Onassis referring to his Saudi oil venture in 1954

contract forbidding Jews from having 'direct or indirect' interest in the operating company. However, with some clause changes to mollify ARAMCO, the contract was ratified by King Saud on 18 May 1954.

ARAMCO and the US government recognised that direct pressure on the Saudis could be counter-productive, given Arab reluctance to be seen bowing to the West. Instead, the squeeze was put on Onassis. He was informed that his tankers would be turned away from the ARAMCO terminal in the Gulf if they arrived to lift any Saudi oil.

Onassis responded by improving the terms of the deal and by naming his latest tanker *Al-Malik Saud Al-Awal* in honour of the King. The US government appealed for assistance to Stavros

Niarchos, whose relationship with his brother-in-law was at an all-time low. Niarchos' New York office engaged ex-FBI agent Robert Maheu to find evidence which would undermine the Onassis-Saudi deal.

Maheu bugged Onassis' New York offices, obtaining information which portrayed Onassis as a threat to US interests in the Middle East. He was also able to provide the Saudis with evidence that Onassis had bribed Saudi palace aides and ministers to the tune of $1.25 million in order to secure the contract.

Confronted with these revelations, King Saud decided to 'have done with Onassis' He did not cancel the contract outright, but reduced the terms to those of the standard market rate in the certain knowledge that Onassis would refuse them, which he did. The matter was referred to the International Court at The Hague for arbitration.

It was 1958 before the Court passed judgement – in favour of ARAMCO. Enraged, Onassis declared: 'Never before in the history of business was so much power combined to fight and destroy an individual.' By December 1955, with the ARAMCO boycott spreading and the overheads on his idle ships mounting, Onassis stared bankruptcy in the face.

SAVED BY SUEZ

As with all his other ventures, Onassis exploited developing world events to save himself from ruin. In July 1956, the Egyptian nationalist leader

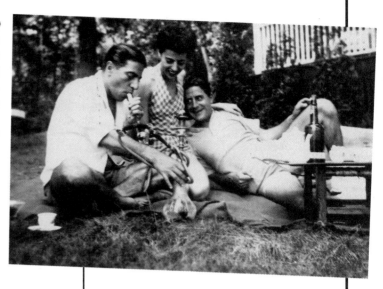

Above: Onassis shows Stavros Niarchos and his second wife Melpomene the art of smoking a hookah, at his Long Island home in 1942. Onassis and Niarchos were to become bitter enemies.

Nasser announced his intention to nationalise the Suez Canal, through which half of the world's exports of oil passed from the Gulf of Persia into the Mediterranean Sea. It was reprisal for US withdrawal of financial support (as a protest against growing Egyptian-Soviet ties) from his great project – the building of the Aswan High Dam.

Oil from the Middle East to Europe and America now had to be re-routed round southern Africa, twice the distance. As governments scrambled to ensure their supplies at any cost, Onassis was ready and waiting with his empty fleet. One journey from the Gulf to Europe reaped a profit of $2 million, and in the space of five months he made between $60 and $80 million. Onassis claimed to be 'the richest man in the world', and when Constantine Karamanlis, the new Prime Minister of Greece, sought a buyer for the national Olympic Airlines, it was naturally to Onassis that he turned.

Below: The luxury yacht Christina, which Onassis had converted from a Canadian frigate in 1953, passes through the Suez Canal on its way to Jiddah at the time of Onassis' deal to carry Saudi oil.

ONASSIS' RUTHLESS SOCIAL AMBITIONS ENABLED HIM EARLY ON TO ENTER THE HIGH SOCIETY WHOSE APPROVAL HE CRAVED. AS HIS WEALTH GREW, SO HE COURTED THE GLITTERATI OF POLITICS AND SHOW BUSINESS WITH UNBRIDLED OPULENCE

RICHES ON DISPLAY

Fireworks erupt above Onassis' yacht berthed in Monte Carlo harbour in 1953. The display was put on by the tycoon to celebrate his acquisition of the Monte Carlo casino. (Inset): In the yacht's saloon, Onassis stands beside a Madonna and Angel, supposedly by the 16th - century artist El Greco.

According to Onassis, his sights were set on the high life in 1922, when sailing to Istanbul from Athens on a mission to rescue his father from a Turkish jail. He had slipped into the First Class section and was stunned by the opulence he found. Told by a steward to get back to where he belonged, Onassis replied, 'This is where I belong.'

Onassis' mixing with high society began in late 1920s Argentina when his magnate friend Alberto Dodero introduced him to the *beau monde* of Buenos Aires. It was again through Dodero in the 1940s that Onassis entered New York society; Dodero's second wife was a former Hollywood starlet, and through them Onassis met many show busi-

A FLOATING PALACE

Monaco also provided Onassis with a haven of a different sort – a mooring place for his yacht *Christina*, which became the focal point of both his social and business life.

An ex-Canadian World War Two frigate, it was originally earmarked as an escort vessel for the Onassis whaling fleet until Onassis decided to transform it into the world's largest and most luxurious private yacht, which even ex-King Farouk of Egypt – no stranger to extravagance him-

self – would concede to be 'the last word in opulence'.

Converted in a German yard at a cost of $4 million, no expense was spared on it. The interior was decorated in marble, mosaic, lapis lazuli and antique Japanese lacquer; the dining room was dominated by four paintings, commissioned from a leading French artist, Marcel Vertes, depicting the family's out-door pastimes in the four seasons. There were also nine luxury guest suites, each named after a Greek

island. The temperature of the water in the outdoor swimming pool was controlled at a few degrees below that of the air so that guests could cool off from the heat of the day, while by night the bottom was raised to deck level to provide a dance floor.

Right: Onassis sits at the bar on the Christina. Ivory whale teeth serve as arm-rests around the counter and as foot-rests for the seats. The stools are covered with white whale foreskin. 'Madam,' Onassis once joked to Greta Garbo, 'you are now sitting on the largest penis the the world.'

STAR PARADE

ness celebrities, including movie mogul (and fellow Greek) Spyros Skouras. When Dodero bought an estate on Center Island, off the north shore of Long Island, Onassis followed suit in 1941 and rented a nearby weekend cottage, in addition to his apartment in Manhattan.

While in the USA, Onassis regularly left his mistress, Ingeborg Dedichen, in New York and flew to California, where he took a suite in the Beverly Hills Hotel. His conquests there included actresses Gloria Swanson (who once had an affair with Joe Kennedy Sr.), Paulette Goddard and Veronica Lake, and sugar heiress Geraldine Spreckles.

ARCH-RIVALRY

After marrying Tina Livanos in 1946, Onassis's social setting was largely dictated by rivalry with Stavros Niarchos. When Tina and Onassis took a four-storey house in New York's Sutton Square, Niarchos and his wife Eugenie (Tina's sister) moved into a larger house round the corner in Sutton Place. When the Onassises rented the Château de la Croë on the Cap d'Antibes, they

The company that Onassis entertained on board the *Christina* was just as important to his public image as the yacht itself. His guests ranged from Hollywood megastars to figures of politics and royalty: the West German Chancellor Konrad Adenauer,

found the Niarchoses just down the coast in the equally magnificent Château de la Garoupe. It was in order to outdo Niarchos' sleek, three-masted schooner, the *Creole*, that Onassis decided to convert a former 98m-long Canadian frigate into what was then the largest private yacht in the world, the *Christina*.

Onassis later liked to claim that he was drawn to Monaco –

Greta Garbo, Elizabeth Taylor (far left, with Onassis centre and Richard Burton, left) the Rainiers and Princess Margaret.

His greatest catch was Winston Churchill (right) who had retired at the age of 80 and looked forward to passing his last years at ease. Introduced through his friendship with Randolph, Onassis went to every length to meet the Grand Old Man's smallest whims. Lord Moran, Churchill's personal physi-

the 1.9 square kilometre principality in the middle of the French Riviera – by nostalgic memories of glimpsing it from the boat that first bore him to Buenos Aires. But it was Monaco's status as a tax haven that was the real attraction; he referred to the principality as his 'headquarters of convenience'. Its major assets – the Monte Carlo Casino and Hôtel de Paris – were owned by a

Left: The Monte Carlo casino was probably the most famous gambling house in the world. Onassis gained control of it in 1953. Below: Another Onassis property in Monte Carlo was the Monaco Yacht Club. Right: Onassis loved being with celebrities. Here he dances with Italian film star, Gina Lollobrigida, at a ball in 1967.

cian, recorded his host's devotion: 'He hardly takes his eyes off his guest: one moment he will fetch him a glass of whisky, and the next, when Winston finds it cool on deck, he will tuck him in a blanket. Once when we were waiting for dinner, he pulled his chair nearer and held a teaspoon of caviar to Winston's lips, as one feeds a baby...'

company openly quoted on the Paris Stock Exchange, enabling Onassis, at the start of 1953, to buy up a one-third interest.

This exercise did not go unnoticed by the ruling Prince Rainier, but he welcomed the prospect of new investment and teamed up with Onassis to take over control of the company. In order to attract big-spending Americans, Onassis proposed that a suitably eye-catching wife should be found for Rainier. In In 1955 Marilyn Monroe was approached, and readily agreed to a meeting, but Rainier surprised everyone with his own choice from Hollywood – the film actress Grace Kelly.

IN PURSUIT

IN HIS SEARCH FOR THE 'CONSUMMATE WOMAN' ONASSIS SET HIS SIGHTS ON OPERA'S FAMED *DIVA*, MARIA CALLAS. WHEN HE TIRED OF HER, HE WOOED AND WON THE WOMAN HE REGARDED AS THE GREATEST PRIZE OF ALL - AMERICA'S FORMER FIRST LADY

T he marriage vows Onassis made to Tina did not curtail his sexual wanderings. Being a confirmed womaniser, he was seeking his pleasures elsewhere within months of marrying. In the early 1950s, when the Onassises were living at Château de la Croë on the French Riviera, Tina met Jeanne Rhinelander, an old school friend then living in nearby Grasse. Onassis was no less pleased to meet her; when Tina paid a visit to Rhinelander at her Grasse château one day, she discovered the two of them in bed together.

Shortly afterwards, in spring 1954, the Onassises gave up the tenancy of the Château de la Croë and moved into apartments in Monte Carlo, but with the *Christina*'s arrival in the harbour, more and more of their time was spent on the yacht. 'I suppose that *Christina* is my real home,' Tina told a questioner in 1956.

DATEFILE

AUGUST 1959
Callas deserts Meneghini for Onassis

OCTOBER 4 1963
Jackie Kennedy takes an Aegean cruise with Onasis

NOV 22 1963
President Kennedy is assassinated

JUNE 5 1968
Robert Kennedy is shot dead in Los Angeles

OCTOBER 20 1968
Onassis and Jackie Kennedy marry on Skorpios

AUG'59-OCT'68

Not only did the yacht become the hub of Onassis' business empire and the set for his image-building, but it was also used by Onassis as his 'lover's lair'. Any good-looking woman who accepted an invitation aboard was considered fair game, although he eventually had to admit defeat with one regular guest – for all his persistence, Greta Garbo drew the line at sex. Even his appetite had its limits, however: finding one hopeful but unwanted guest installed in his bed, Onassis had

her air-lifted ashore by helicopter.

Unsurprisingly, Tina began to develop liaisons of her own. 'He had his friends and I started to have mine,' as she put it. In spite of his own infidelity, Tina's affairs (when discovered) roused Onassis to fury. This usually resulted in violent beatings. When the children started school in Paris, Tina began increasingly to divide her time between the Onassis apartment in the French capital and the ski-slopes. There at least she was safe,

OF PERFECTION

Poise, beauty and social status marked each of the three women who dominated Onassis' later life. They were (below, left to right): Tina Livanos, his first wife and mother of his children; opera star Maria Callas; and his second wife, Jacqeline Kennedy, seen here in the late 1950s.

because Onassis had no taste for winter sports; 'When I went skiing, it was mainly on my backside,' he once confessed.

In early June 1959, they both sailed to Venice for the summer season's annual ball given by the Countess Castelbarco. Tina was dressed in a stunning new gown and a cascade of diamonds, emeralds and rubies. But Onassis had eyes only for the guest of honour, opera *diva* Maria Callas, whom he had first met two years earlier at a ball held by the American socialite, Elsa Maxwell. Of that first meeting he explained: 'There was a natural curiosity; after all, we were the two most famous living Greeks in the world!' Now, at the 1959 Venice ball, he invited Callas and her husband, the rich building-materials manufacturer Giovanni Meneghini, to join them on a cruise of the Mediterranean, but Callas, at the height of her powers, was obliged by her many singing engagements to refuse.

Never one to take no for an answer, Onassis pursued her to London and commandeered 30 of the best seats at Covent Garden for her debut in *Medea* in mid-June 1959. Throwing a spectacular party for her afterwards at the Dorchester hotel, he renewed his invitation to a cruise, and this time she accepted. It was a fateful decision.

In July, as the *Christina* headed into the Aegean, Onassis refused to allow even the presence of Winston Churchill – his other illustrious

Below: Maria Callas (centre) relaxes at a café on the Venice Lido with Onassis and Elsa Maxwell (left), the American society hostess. Callas first met Onassis in 1957 – the year of this photo – at a ball given by Maxwell. Right: As Callas leaves a party celebrating her 1959 Covent Garden performance in Medea, Onassis (left) and her husband, Meneghini, both clasp her in a display of adoration.

guest – to inhibit his designs. Meneghini, however, sailed on in blissful ignorance, until one night a tearful Tina woke him to announce that she had just caught their respective spouses *in flagrante delicto*. When confronted, Callas confessed that she was in love with Onassis.

Meneghini tried to tell himself that it was only a temporary infatuation and he and Callas returned to Italy together, but a few days later Onassis reappeared at their home on Lake Garda to claim her. 'How much do you want for her?' Onassis demanded. 'Five million dollars? You've got it. Ten? Take it.' The cuckolded husband told Onassis to 'stick the money up his arse', but he woke the next morning to find himself alone.

FILING FOR DIVORCE

Still hoping that his wife would 'come to her senses' and return to him, Meneghini would only agree to a legal separation. Tina, however, at once took custody of the children and filed for divorce – citing not Callas, but Jeanne Rhinelander, her old school friend. Onassis begged Tina to reconsider, even invoking their friendship with the Churchills as a reason for not proceeding, but she was unmoved by his pleas.

Tina eventually settled for a 'quickie' divorce in Alabama in June 1960 to avoid the damaging publicity that a long, drawn-out divorce suit in New York would have inflicted on her family. Not long after, she broke her leg skiing in St Moritz and flew for treatment to England. One of those to visit her in hospital was the Marquess of Blandford, heir to the Duke of Marlborough and relative of Churchill. Shortly afterwards he became her second husband.

When would Onassis marry Callas? For

CLOSE-UP   THE ORIGINS OF A DIVA

Callas as she appears in Passolini's 1970 film Medea

Born Maria Anna Sofia Calogeropoulos in New York on 3 December 1923, Maria Callas was the second daughter of Greek immigrants who had recently arrived in America from Athens. The family changed their surname to Callas in 1926. Her youth was scarred by poverty and obesity (the result of compulsive overeating after a serious car accident). Her only assets were her remarkable voice and a mother determined to gain recognition for her daughter's talent.

Returning to Greece in 1937, Maria made her first major début five years later, aged 19, in *Tosca*, but because of her obesity, it was not until 1947 that she was taken on for her first major part, in the Verona production of *La Gioconda*. In the audience was millionaire building manufacturer Giovanni Meneghini. Enthralled by her performance, he gave up his industrial interests to become her business manager. In 1949, he became her husband.

He persuaded Maria to lose 40 kilos in weight, and she began to take the opera houses of the world by storm. Not only did her voice prove to have a unique range, but her tempestuous temperament gave her performances a dramatic power which audiences had never before seen in leading *divas*. 'As long as I hear them stirring and hissing like snakes out there, I know I'm on top,' she once said.

months the popular press could think of little else. The two celebrities were regularly sighted together in nightclubs. 'It is impossible for them to dance cheek-to-cheek as Miss Callas is slightly taller than Mr. Onassis,' it was reported. 'But as they danced she has lowered her head to nibble his ear and he has smiled rapturously.'

On 10 August 1960 Callas publicly announced their intention to marry – only to hear Onassis reject the idea the next day as 'a fantasy'. He was happy enough for the moment to bask in the extra publicity his relationship with Callas was bringing him. Also, his children refused to acknowledge her, blaming her for the break-up of their parents' marriage. Onassis did little to conceal his distaste for opera; his ambition was to promote Callas as a film star. When she turned down the female lead in *The Guns of Navarone* that he had arranged for her with his friend Anthony Quinn, he was furious.

As she continued to scale new operatic heights, his satisfaction turned gradually to resentment, and it became obvious that – just as Meneghini had

Below: Jacqueline Bouvier Kennedy (left) and her sister, Princess Lee Radziwill, tour the ruins of Knossos on Crete during a 1963 cruise of the Mediterranean aboard Onassis' yacht Christina. The propriety of a trip with Onassis worried many in the USA.

warned – he had no intention of marrying her. Once again his eyes began to wander, and this time they settled on a woman he believed was the pinnacle of all – Jacqueline ('Jackie') Kennedy.

STALKING HIS PREY

Onassis first met the Kennedys in the summer of 1958 when they were invited on board the *Christina* in Monte Carlo harbour to meet Winston Churchill. Kennedy, then a Senator from Massachusetts, and Churchill were soon engrossed in an exchange of views, leaving the host to show Jackie over the yacht. 'There's something provocative about that lady,' he remarked later to his long-time crony, Costa Gratsos. 'She's got a carnal soul.'

Onassis next saw Jackie in 1961 when she toured Greece with her sister, Lee Radziwill. Onassis called on her at the villa of fellow shipping tycoon Markos Nomikos. At the time, the outside world was still expecting the announcement of his marriage to Callas, but a close observer remarked that Onassis 'would forget Maria in a minute if he thought that he had a chance with Jackie'. Onassis forestalled any speculation about his intentions by feeding the press the story that Lee was replacing Callas in his affections.

Jacqueline Bouvier (above, with her husband, John F Kennedy) and her younger sister Lee were born into old New York society and had been imbued from birth with respect for money and social prestige. Jackie was 13 years old when their parents divorced; their mother was awarded custody, but it was their father, John Vernou Bouvier III, nicknamed Black Jack, a debonair Wall Street broker, who retained their loyalty. Their hankering after a father figure would be a strong influence on their choice of husbands.

John Kennedy was 10 years Jackie's senior and already a Senator when she married him in 1953. Although an inveterate womaniser like Jackie's father, John offered the compensation of being heir to the Kennedy fortune. Even this proved insufficient for Jackie's extravagant tastes, which reached new heights on her arrival in the White House as First Lady. 'Why can't I have that?' she demanded when she overheard John telling a guest that he donated his Presidential salary to charity.

In August 1963, Jackie gave birth to her third child, Patrick, who lived only a few days. Onassis suggested that an Aegean cruise aboard the *Christina* might help lift her depression. John Kennedy, by now US President and facing re-election in 1964, was less than enthusiastic about his wife associating with a man who only a few years earlier had been indicted for fraud by a federal grand jury. In addition, he was divorced and was still openly having an affair with an opera star. Kennedy made it a condition that Jackie should be accompanied by his Under-Secretary of Commerce, Franklin D. Roosevelt, Jr. and his wife. Her sister Lee also was to go with her. This drew the comment, from Attorney General Robert 'Bobby' Kennedy to his sister-in-law: 'And just tell Lee to cool it, will you?' Even he believed there was truth in the Onassis-Lee Radziwill rumour.

CRUISING IN THE MED

Onassis went to every length to ensure the success of the cruise. In addition to the usual crates of champagne, caviar and lobsters, he laid on a dance orchestra, two hairdressers and a masseuse. At first he remained discreetly out of sight, but when they reached Izmir in Turkey, Jackie insisted that he give her a personal guided tour of his birthplace. It was not long before America's front pages were filled with photos of a happy First Lady ambling around the sidestreets of Izmir or relaxing in a

Above: Aristotle Onassis leads his new wife, Jackie, from the chapel on the island of Skorpios after their wedding in October 1968. The Greek Orthodox ceremony was conducted partly in English for the benefit of his American bride and her family. Right: Onassis entertains Jackie and other guests on the Christina. Inset (right): The Christina lies moored beside the small quay on Skorpios and within easy commuting distance of the Onassis villa.

bikini alone with Onassis. In the US, questions were raised about propriety and even whether Onassis might not be using Under-Secretary Roosevelt to gain favour with the US Maritime Administration.

Jackie resolutely rejected the President's demands to cut the cruise short, but she did agree that on her return she would accompany him on an electioneering tour of Texas later in the year. She was beside Kennedy in the Presidential limousine when an assassin's bullets cut him down on 22 November.

Onassis was in Hamburg for the launch of his latest and largest tanker, *Olympic Chivalry*, when he heard the news. He immediately flew to Washington and attended the funeral as a guest of the White House – one of only a handful outside the immediate Kennedy family to do so.

A year later, Onassis was entertaining the late President's widow alone at his Avenue Foch apartment in Paris. So concerned was he to hide her presence that he ordered his servants to remain in their rooms during her stay and served dinner himself. Once back in the US, Jackie and her two children moved from Washington to New York, where Onassis retained a suite at the Hotel Pierre in Manhattan. Although Jackie had many escorts, she continued to have

Left: Rumours of a possible Onassis-Jackie Kennedy marriage circulated for weeks before it was officially confirmed by Jackie's mother, Mrs Hugh D. Auchincloss, on 17 October 1968.

a clandestine courtship with Onassis on both sides of the Atlantic. Even when Onassis and Jackie were sighted together, the very idea of such a match appeared so incongruous that little or no speculation was excited.

By May 1968 Jackie was ready to accept Onassis' proposal of marriage, on the sole condition

A MODERN ULYSSES

Onassis had long fancied himself as a modern Ulysses, the mythological prince of the island of Ithaca and seafaring hero of the Trojan Wars. Once he even considered buying Ithaca itself – until he was informed that the Ionian island's population numbered 55,000.

Forced to scale down his ambitions, he settled for Skorpios, a 162-hectare island lying three kilometres off the island of Lefkas but within sight of Ithaca, and empty except for olive groves and a tiny Greek Orthodox chapel. After marrying Jackie Kennedy, he gave her a free hand for the construction of a villa designed by her favourite New York architect – the Onassises referred to it as the 'Erechtheum', after a small temple on the Acropolis. It was barely completed before Onassis' death and today stands as a monument to Jackie's extravagance.

BACKDROP

> She's being held up as a model of propriety, constancy and so many of those boring American female virtues. She's now utterly devoid of mystery. She needs a small scandal to bring her alive.
>
> Onassis on Jackie Kennedy, 1968

that they should wait until November's presidential election, which her brother-in-law Robert Kennedy looked increasingly likely to win, was safely out of the way; 'Do you realise that this could cost me five states?' Robert had pleaded when she had first revealed her plans to him.

Onassis began to fear that she would never be mistress of her own fate as long as Robert 'has a political bone left in his body.' When the news reached him on 5 June that Robert had been assassinated in a Los Angeles hotel, Onassis made no secret of his satisfaction: 'She's free of the Kennedys, the last link just broke,' he exulted to Gratsos.

In August the surviving Kennedy brother, Edward 'Teddy', flew to Greece to negotiate the marriage contract. A deal was worked out whereby, on Onassis' death, Jackie would receive a cash settlement of $1.5m – a figure that Jackie's New York lawyers were later able to double – in return for a waiver to any further claims on his estate.

In spite of their now open liaison, the secret came as a profound shock to the world when it finally leaked out on 15 October in the *Boston Herald-Traveler*.

A SKORPIOS WEDDING

The wedding was quickly brought forward to avoid prolonged publicity, and took place just five days later on Skorpios, the Ionian island that Onassis had bought some years earlier. To maintain privacy, Onassis turned to his friends in the new military junta for the services of the Greek Navy to keep the pressmen at bay.

The ceremony took place at 5.15pm in the island's small chapel of Panayitsa ('Little Virgin'). The drizzly weather seemed to complement the strangely quiet and serious atmosphere. Jackie's children, Caroline and John Jr, seemed either dazed or distant throughout the ceremony, while Onassis' children, Alexander and Christina, looked grim. The service was conducted in Greek and English; they sipped wine from a silver chalice and were led three times round the altar. Guests pelted them with flower petals, rice and sugared almonds – rice for fertility and sugar for happiness – when they emerged from the chapel. They then boarded the *Christina* where they posed for photographers.

OF ALL HIS MANY WOMEN, INGEBORG DEDICHEN KNEW ONASSIS BEST. DESPITE MANY PROMISES OF MARRIAGE, ONASSIS EVENTUALLY REJECTED HER FOR THE 17-YEAR-OLD TINA LIVANOS. HERE SHE REMEMBERS THEIR 12 TURBULENT YEARS TOGETHER – AND THEIR PARTING.

Onassis met Dedichen aboard a transatlantic liner in 1934. The strikingly tall and blonde Norwegian whaling heiress, already in the middle

Above: Ingeborg Dedichen (centre), with Onassis and his sister, Artemis, in 1938. Opposite: Dedichen photographed in the late 1950s.

of a second divorce, was returning home to Paris from a fashionable voyage to Antarctica. She was unimpressed by Onassis' appearance.

'He was squat, with a heavy head rising straight out of his brawny shoulders; black-haired and olive-skinned, he had all the marks of a typical Levantine docker. However, these were offset by the magnetic intelligence radiating from his unforgettably expressive eyes, by a voice that was both measured and seductive, and by a dazzling smile fixed irresistibly on his fleshy lips.'

Arriving at Genoa, in Italy, he persuaded her to drive with him in his Cadillac to Venice. It was to be the start of their long affair.

ON ONASSIS THE LOVER

Mamita, 'Little Mother', was the name that Onassis invented for Dedichen. His lack of education, even of basic manners, drew out her maternal instincts, but his attraction was primarily physical.

'Thanks to Ari, I appreciated the meaning of the French expression "to have someone in the skin". His had a unique scent, texture, warmth, smoothness and sensuality of which I never tired, and which raised me to a pitch of fulfilment that exceeded even the act of sex itself.'

In the mid-1930s, from his operational base in London, Onassis continued writing to Dedichen. 'He wrote passionate letters to me almost every day expressing his undying love. He also used to telephone me daily, exulting when he could tell me of his next visit to Paris or popping up unexpectedly like a Jack-in-the-box to assure himself of my fidelity.'

ON HIS JEALOUSY

The prodigal amount of gifts Onassis lavished on Dedichen was matched by the extent of his jealousy.

'He would have been jealous of his own shadow! It was a malign fever, sparked off for the slightest reason. He loved me, seeking to keep me in his possession, but at the same time his jealousy distanced him from me. He looked on me as his thing, his object, which may have been typical of the Middle East, but it was completely at odds with my Norwegian character.'

After they moved to New York in 1940, Onassis' jealousy took an increasingly violent turn. He once beat her up and locked her in a spare room overnight.

'The next morning he hurriedly ejected the servants to prevent his friends from knowing what had happened. He deigned to let me out again towards noon. My face was like a balloon, I had a black eye, my body was covered with bruises and the tendons in my left hand were torn.'

ON ONASSIS' INFIDELITY

Onassis' insistence on Dedichen's fidelity did not compel him to behave similarly.

'In the course of our stay in America, Ari suddenly began to play cat and mouse with me. He disappeared for weeks at a time to places that had nothing to do with his business, returning only when he wanted to unbosom himself or make love. "Mamita, we're not going to get married just yet, so you can give me certain licence. I want a taste of the lifestyle that I've been too busy to enjoy to date." '

ON MARRIAGE

Despite his reluctance to marry Dedichen, Onassis nevertheless proposed to her several times. In 1945, he proposed again, just as she was undergoing an operation to cure her infertility. Bursting into her hospital room unannounced, he furiously accused her of trying to make him the object of gossip among the Greek community, and had to be

> *His [skin] had a unique scent, texture, warmth, smoothness and sensuality of which I never tired, and which raised me to a pitch of fulfilment…*

ordered out by her surgeon. Eventually, Dedichen decided to move into a separate apartment.

'One evening, exhausted by his continual torturings and at the end of my tether, I tried to commit suicide with an overdose of Nembutal. Ari telephoned and, getting no reply, he hurried round and found me unconscious. He rang a friend for help, and together they plunged me into a bath of cold water and revived me.

'When he began interesting himself in Tina Livanos, he was still reluctant to give up his bird in hand for a problematic union which her father was opposing, and he promised to marry me once more…But knowing the usual denouement, I realised that everything he told me was calculated and was finally convinced that he would never marry me.'

ON THE FINAL BETRAYAL

In 1946 Ingeborg moved back to Paris, with a promise from Onassis to set her up financially for life. Even after his marriage to Tina Livanos, he continued to visit her regularly.

'On his last visit we had a little love session, but I discovered he had an ulterior motive; he asked if he could take away all the photos of us together to have them copied, but I refused. Without doubt he wanted to suppress all the evidence of our liaison!

'My final sight of him was at the Paris Opera in 1964, when Callas was singing Norma. In the foyer I saw Ari deep in conversation with Rudolf Bing, the famous Director of the Met [New York Metropolitan Opera]. Ari saw me, but pretended not to know me. He could have made just a small gesture of recognition, but he preferred to obliterate me, wishing me forever invisible.'

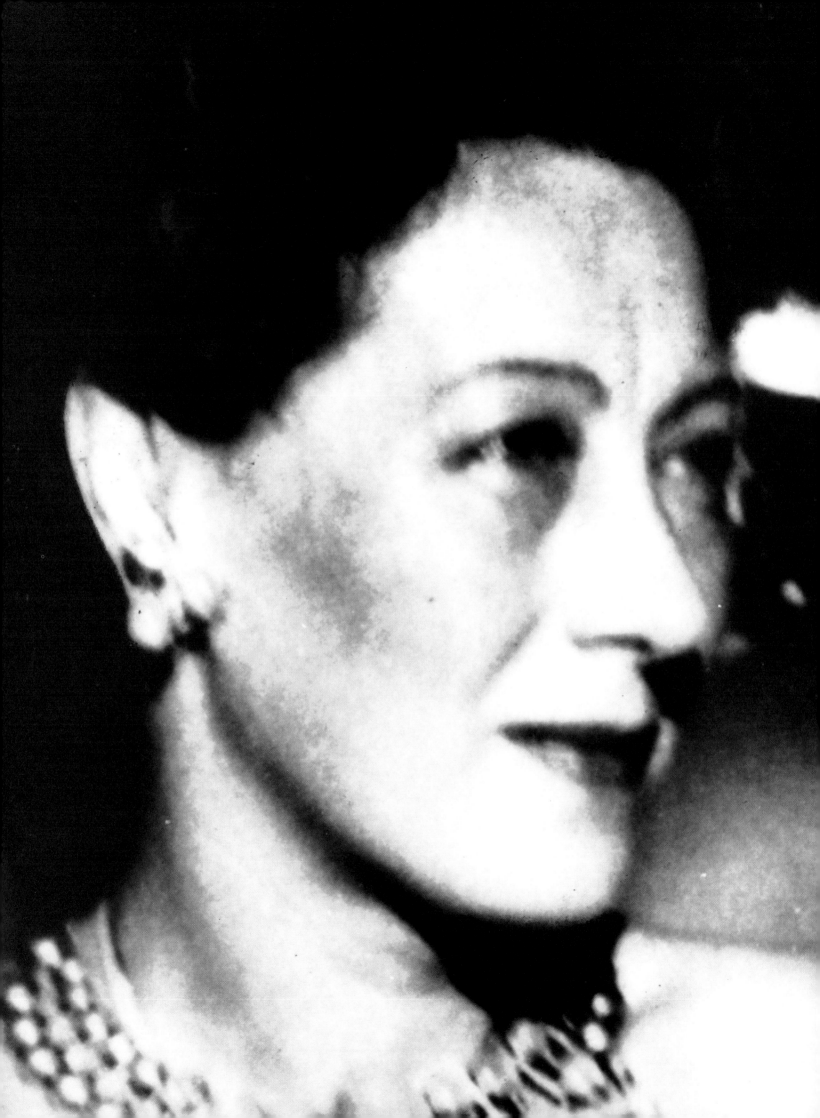

FOUR

THE TIDE TURNS

LOSING THE

FROM 1969 ONWARDS, ONASSIS BEGAN TO LOSE HIS NEAR-LEGENDARY SUCCESS IN BUSINESS AND PERSONAL MATTERS. A FAILED DEAL WITH GREECE'S RULERS AND A DISASTROUS OIL SPILL COINCIDED WITH GROWING FRUSTRATION WITH HIS MEGA-SPENDING WIFE

Onassis' marriage to Jackie Kennedy was only four days old when he flew to Athens from Skorpios to sign a multi-million dollar deal with Colonel George Papadopoulos, the head of Greece's military junta which had toppled the democratic government in April 1967. 'On that day,' said a close observer, 'Onassis was the Sun King. He had everything.'A week later he was back in Athens again for the press conference announcing the deal to the world.

Onassis had first raised the deal, code-named Project Omega, with Greece's previous (legitimate) government. Under it he planned to build an alumina refinery, an aluminium smelter and an oil refinery; the aluminium would be bartered to Russia in return for the crude oil to supply the refinery – and to be carried, naturally, by Onassis tankers. Desperate for investment with which to legitimise their régime, the colonels accepted a new condition from Onassis giving him control of

At a reception in Athens in 1968, Onassis (above left) greets a bald Stylianos Pattakos, Greece's First Deputy Prime Minister and a leader of the coup that suspended parliamentary government in 1967..The Greek junta had recently cancelled its $400 million deal (Project Omega) with Onassis. Beside Onassis is Professor Yanni Georgakis, his friend and Chairman of Olympic Airways.

DATEFILE

OCTOBER 24 1968

Onassis' meets with Greek military dictator Papadopoulos to discuss Project Omega

FEBRUARY 4 1970

Onassis' tanker *Arrow* runs aground causing massive oil spill off Nova Scotia

FEBRUARY 1970

Publication of Jackie Onassis' private letters to Roswell Gilpatric

JANUARY 3 1973

Onassis sees son Alexander for the last time

OCT '68 – JAN '73

UPPER HAND

Below right: Mikis Theodorakis, the left-wing Greek composer, arrives in London on 24 June 1970 for his first British concert, at the Royal Albert Hall. Ten weeks earlier, in April, he had been released from a Greek prolitical prison partly due to the influence of Onassis. Below left: Stavros Niarchos, Onassis' rival in the Project Omega deal with Greece's military rulers.

a state-owned refinery operated by his arch-rival Niarchos.

Onassis had banked on one of the major American aluminium companies putting up the necessary capital. Already wary of any investment in a country under such an undemocratic régime, the companies baulked altogether when Onassis further demanded that he should have a controlling share in the project. 'His must-win mentality tipped over into pure megalomania,' an Alcoa executive commented. 'He seemed to think that we'd agree to just about anything for an invitation to dine with him and Jackie...'

REFINERY WRANGLE

Onassis' request that the Greek government itself should then finance it set off a bitter internal debate within the regime, which was compounded in March 1969, when Niarchos stepped in with a rival, cheaper offer. A year later, after much acrimonious wrangling, a compromise was finally reached whereby Onassis was given the go-ahead for a very much smaller investment and Niarchos was allowed to retain control of his state-owned refinery.

Shortly afterwards, Onassis was persuaded to use his influence with Papadopoulos (to whom he had granted the rent-free use of a luxury villa) to free the left-wing composer Mikis Theodorakis. When Onassis refused to plead for the release of other prisoners, Theodorakis promptly branded him as an 'enemy of the people'. In 1971,

Right: The 1973 Arab-Israeli war caused a slump in the tanker charter market, forcing Onassis to lay off a third of his fleet of over 100 ships and cancel an order for two ultra-large crude carriers.

Above: George Papadopoulos, the Greek military dictator, initially welcomed Onassis' investment scheme since it offered much-needed respect for his regime. He was overthrown in a 1973 coup.

Onassis demanded new concessions on Omega, but the government refused. The project was eventually abandoned.

On 4 February 1970 the oldest tanker in the Onassis fleet, *Arrow,* ran aground off Nova Scotia in Canada, and broke up, spilling 11,000 gallons of crude oil on to the coastline. The Canadian government launched a $4 million cleaning-up operation to remove it. The Greek captain of the Liberian-registered ship stated that his navigational equipment had been out of order, but when attempts were made to recover costs from its nominal owners, Sunstone Marine of Panama, it was found that the ship represented the company's sole asset and that Sunstone was now effectively bankrupt. The Canadian taxpayers were thus left to pick up the bill – a total of $3 million.

Three years later, the citizens of New Hampshire, USA, not far down the coast from Nova Scotia, had their own battle with Onassis, when he applied for permission to build a refinery

> '*The boss is the only man in the world who can handle two honeymoons at the same time: one with Jackie, the other with Papadopoulos*'
>
> A favourite joke among Onassis' staff in Athens, 1968

on their coastline. With the State Governor, desperate to bring new employment to the area, on his side, Onassis regarded his application as a mere formality, but he had reckoned without the local people's legendary independence of spirit. (The state motto was 'Live free or die'.)

Already outraged by the underhand methods used by Onassis' agents to buy the required land (pretending it was to be used for an old people's home, a bird sanctuary and a beach club), the protesters were further encouraged by the recent memory of the Nova Scotia disaster. Thousands signed an anti-refinery petition. 'These ecology nuts piss me off,' Onassis commented bitterly. The result was that the New Hampshire state legislature threw out Onassis' proposal for a refinery by a 10-1 majority.

The year 1973 had begun well for the oil industry on the back of a world economic boom, encouraging Onassis to place orders for a further six supertankers. However, the outbreak of another Arab-Israeli war in October and the quadrupling of

Main picture: Athens Airport, home of Greece's national airline, Olympic Airways, stood at the centre of a battle between Onassis and the Greek government over control of the airline which had been losing money under Onassis' ownership. Left: A tired Onassis and his advisers arrive for a late-night meeting with government representatives.

CLOSE-UP

A CASE FOR DIVORCE

In 1970, amid a spate of failures in business, Onassis faced a personal embarrassment. A letter that Jackie had written to a close friend only days after her marriage to Onassis was published in America. It was addressed to Roswell Gilpatric (below, with Jackie), the man who had once escorted her on a trip to Mexico, and in it Jackie apologised for not informing him in advance of her marriage to Onassis.

"Dearest Ros,

I would have told you before I left, but then everything happened so much more quickly than I'd planned. I saw somewhere what you had said and I was very touched – dear Ros – I hope you know all you were and are and ever will be to me.

With my love,

Jackie."

To the jealous Onassis, this was a public humiliation he could not forget.

Onassis' marriage to Jackie came under increasing strain as she spent more and more time away from him at her Manhattan apartment. When he wanted to stay over, there were always reasons why she could not let him do so – the decorators were busy or friends of the children were sleeping over. Onassis was forced to lodge at his hotel suite.

Having had enough, he consulted Manhattan attorney Roy Cohn and ordered him to build an iron-clad case against Jackie for divorce. He also let his public relations team meet with the influential American columnist, Jack Anderson. He was told that the Onassis marriage had been reduced to a monthly presentation of bills and the couple were totally incompatible. Onassis wanted out.

the price of oil turned the boom into slump overnight. Onassis was forced to lay up one third of his fleet and to cancel two of the supertankers, with the loss of his $12 million deposit.

OLYMPIC IN TROUBLE

War and recession had its effects on another Onassis business operation, Olympic Airways, which the magnate had taken over from the government in 1956. Financial loss was compounded by the threat of war between Greece and Turkey over Cyprus and the collapse of the Greek junta – political instability that kept many tourists away. Onassis once described the airline as 'a hobby

enterprise' and in almost two decades under his ownership it had made an annual profit only three times; now, by December 1974, Olympic Airways was unable to generate even enough day-to-day cash to keep its planes in the air.

One of the clauses which he had negotiated with the government on taking over the airline allowed him to withdraw from the agreement at any time on six months' notice. Such was the reluctance of successive governments to see it applied that over the years he had been able to use it to wring ever more generous concessions from them. This time he threatened to withdraw once more, but Greece's new premier, Constantine Karamanlis, called his bluff and announced that he would buy Olympic back.

BORN TO SHOP

The pattern of Onassis' married life with Jackie was set during their much-interrupted honeymoon on Skorpios. As Onassis continued to fly to all points of the compass in pursuit of business, Jackie returned to New York where she could be near her children; her son John Jr. attended school in New York City, and daughter Caroline in Massachusetts. For Jackie, the attractions of New York were the boutiques and department stores of Manhattan's Madison Avenue.

In her first year of the marriage, Jackie is reckoned to have spent over a million dollars on new clothes alone. Onassis was at first happy to bask in the reflected glory of her appearance. 'There's nothing strange in the fact that my wife spends large sums of money,' he remarked. 'Think how people would react if Mrs Onassis wore the same dresses for two years.' On a less tasteful note, he openly boasted of her sexual demands: 'Five times a night! She surpasses all the other women I've ever known.'

MARRIAGE STRAINS

As Jackie's bills continued to roll in, Onassis grew less charitable, cutting her allowance by a third and moving the account to Monte Carlo where he could keep a closer eye on it. 'What does she do with all these clothes?' he complained. 'I never see her in anything but jeans!' However, it was the publication of an intimate letter which she had written during their honeymoon to a former beau that first made him reconsider the wisdom of having married her. 'My God, what a fool I've made of myself!' he told Costa Gratsos.

In retaliation, he very publicly dined with Maria Callas at Maxim's in Paris. This, in turn, provoked Jackie to fly there the next day and demand to dine at the very same table. Worse was

Jackie Kennedy Onassis arrives in London, Christmas 1969, without Onassis. She often left him to visit her sister in England , the Kennedys in Massachusetts, ski in Switzerland or shop in New York.

to come when Jackie decided to sue the American photographer Ron Galella for invasion of privacy. Onassis refused to have any part in it, saying that it would 'only give him millions of dollars of publicity at our expense.' After almost 5000 pages of testimony, Galella was ordered not to go any closer to Jackie than seven metres. She also attracted a lawyer's bill of over $300,000. For Onassis it was the last straw. He could no longer stand her spending, and the fact that she was never there when he needed her. In 1973 he began to discuss divorce proceedings with Roy Cohn, described by *Esquire* magazine as 'the toughest, meanest, vilest, and one of the most brilliant lawyers in America.'

'The old man's seeing sense at last,' Alexander said after Onassis dined with him on 3 January 1973. 'He's divorcing the Widow', using his nickname for Jackie, 'and selling the albatross', referring to the Piaggio seaplane on the *Christina*. It was the last time father and son saw each other.

POWERS OF THE FATHER

Left: A happy interlude for an estranged family. Aristotle and Tina Onassis pose with their children – Alexander, aged nine, and Christina, aged seven – during a rare family get-together in 1957.

Above: Nannies attend to Alexander and Christina's every need at Onassis' 15-room apartment in Avenue Foch, Paris.

ONASSIS LEARNED THE MEANING OF PATERNAL AUTHORITY AT AN EARLY AGE. AS A FATHER, HE WAS DETERMINED TO TEACH HIS OWN CHILDREN THE SAME LESSON

As a boy, fondly called Aristo by his family, Aristotle Onassis had long been aware of the emotional distance between himself and his father, Socrates. In his determination to provide well for his wife and children, Socrates became increasingly estranged from them as he became more and more obsessed with business.

Aristotle found a surrogate father in his Uncle Alexander, a natural rebel like himself and a leading light in the Greek separatist movement in Anatolia. Alexander inspired his nephew with ideas and concepts that would shape his whole life, telling stories of power and revenge, and teaching him about Greek notions of passion, loyalty and love. From Alexander, Aristo inherited a spirit of defiance that would remain with him throughout his life.

JUVENILE RAGE

At school, Aristo earned a reputation for being the child with the poorest average in class, and the worst temperament. After expulsion from a string of schools, he was enrolled at the Evangheliki School, a small and expensive private college.

Socrates was unconcerned by his son's academic failures, believing that the school could offer Aristo little in the way of sound business training. He told his second wife, Helen: 'Great scholars do not make good businessmen and are seldom rich. Too much education might fill his head with ideas above business.'

To Socrates' mind, Aristo's serious learning began when school finished. Every evening, he set his son to work in the office, where he encouraged him to familiarize himself with the world of business and learn everything he could about the merchant's trade.

When Aristo's step-mother protested that the boy should be working at his school lessons, Socrates replied that at school, Aristo would learn only how to be 'a clerkly bourgeois,

a servant with an education'. He preferred to instruct Aristo himself, teaching him about life's harsh realities and the necessity of placing financial gain above almost everything else.

PARENTAL NEGLECT

While Socrates Onassis paid careful attention to selected areas of his son's education, Aristotle Onassis' approach to his own children's upbringing may best be described as one of general neglect punctuated by malicious interference in their personal affairs. Throughout

Left: Christina Onassis, aged 20, and her first husband Joseph Bolker attend a function in Los Angeles in 1970.

Below left: Alexander Onassis and his first great love – Baroness Thyssen-Bornemisza, formerly the top English model Fiona Campbell-Walters.

Christina was made a substitute for parental interest and affection. At the age of six, Alexander was the owner of a petrol-driven model racing car; at 11, he was given a speed boat, which he promptly wrote off in a collision with one of the *Christina's* lifeboats.

THE WAGES OF DIVORCE

Surrounded by nannies and servants at home and attending school only intermittently, the Onassis children enjoyed no friends of their own age and both developed a painful shyness. In these circumstances, it was only to be expected that their parents' divorce would affect them particularly badly.

If they took badly to their mother's displacement by Maria Callas – in spite of Maria's well-meaning attempts to accommodate them – it was

even less likely that, as young adults, they would accept Jackie Kennedy into the family. It required all their father's powers of persuasion even to get them to attend the wedding. 'My father needed a wife, but I certainly didn't need a stepmother,' Alexander commented later. 'I don't understand his fascination for the Kennedy woman.'

Alexander sought consolation in the company of an older woman. He was only 12 when he had first been bowled over by the beauty of Baroness Thyssen, formerly the top English model Fiona Campbell-Walters. Six years later, when his mother arranged a dinner party for him, he demanded that the Baroness, then 33 and happily divorced, should also be asked. They began an affair and, rather to her surprise, she quickly became his 'mistress, mother and priest confessor'.

IMPOSSIBLE LIAISON

Onassis made no attempt to conceal his disapproval, but he was even more concerned about his daughter's liaisons. He had already arranged for Christina to marry Peter Goulandris, the 23-year-old heir to another Greek shipping empire worth $1.5 billion, when she suddenly announced her intention to marry Joseph Bolker. Known as the 'dinky millionaire', Bolker was a Californian property magnate who had two characteristics which her father had grown to hate:

he was an American and a Jew. To make matters worse, he was also 29 years older than Christina and the father of four children. When Christina, aged 20, married Bolker in a quick ceremony in Las Vegas, her father exploded with rage. 'He was mad enough to chew nails', recalled his right-hand man John W. Meyer in a later interview.

STRONG-ARM TACTICS

Immediately cutting off Christina's income, Onassis dispatched Meyer – along with two heavily-armed body guards – to talk her out of the marriage. When that failed, he had her bombarded with anonymous telephone calls alleging every possible slander against her husband. Gradually, these ploys took their toll on the marriage, and Christina realised that if she did not relent, her husband would suffer the full effects of her father's power and animosity. They filed for divorce less than a year after their ill-conceived union.

'I'm just trying to work out a life I can live with. Doesn't Daddy want me to be happy?' Christina had pleaded earlier. She had her answer: No, unless it was on his terms.

Below: An 11-year-old Alexander shows off his very own speedboat in the harbour of Itea, near Delphi. It was his second – he wrecked the first one two years earlier in a high-speed accident.

Alexander and Christina's childhood, Onassis and his first wife Tina travelled almost constantly in the interests of his business empire, scrawling their affection on postcards sent from distant places and seeing their children only occasionally.

Anything that money could buy for Alexander and

IN SEARCH OF A MOTHER'S LOVE

The death of Penelope Onassis in 1912 robbed the young Aristotle of one of the most important things in an infant's life – a mother's love. Onassis' spectacular financial successes and destructive love affairs in later years may be understood as attempts to compensate symbolically for that loss.

The awful irony of Onassis' emotional life was that, while seeking to reclaim his mother in his relationships with women, he punished

his lovers for his mother's absence, thereby alienating himself from the very people who could have given him the one thing his money could not buy.

Ingeborg Dedichen felt the full force of Onassis' pent-up rage when she shared his apartment in New York in the 1930's. In a fit of uncontrollable violence, Onassis kicked and hit her until he gave up from exhaustion. 'He left no marks on my body,' she said. 'He knew how to hit like an expert.'

CHAPTER FIVE

A CURSED DYNASTY

THE BLOWS

ONASSIS' FINAL YEARS WERE SCARRED BY PERSONAL TRAGEDY; THE DEATH OF HIS SON IN A PLANE CRASH WAS THE MOST BITTER BLOW. FOR HIS DAUGHTER, CHRISTINA, THE BURDEN OF INHERITING THE ONASSIS EMPIRE ULTIMATELY PROVED TOO MUCH

O n the night of 3 May 1970, Stavros Niarchos found his wife Eugenie unconscious in bed at their Aegean island home. She had taken an overdose of 25 sleeping tablets. By the time doctors arrived, after midnight, she was dead. Her body was also covered with multiple bruises, some of them severe enough to have caused internal bleeding.

Eugenie's husband, Stavros, explained that the bruises had occurred during his vain attempts to revive her. An autopsy found that she had died of an overdose, but doubts remained and a second examination of the body was ordered, which blamed her injuries. To clear up the inconsistency, the investigating magistrate from Piraeus, Constantine Fafoutis, set up a third inquiry; this blamed Eugenie's death partly on the tablets and partly on Stavros's violent efforts to revive her. When Fafoutis recommended that Niarchos should be charged with involuntary homicide and submitted an indictment to the High Court, the judges

DATEFILE

MAY 3/4 1970
Eugenie Niarchos dies

JANUARY 22 1973
Alexander Onassis has airplane crash. His life support system is turned off the next day

OCTOBER 10 1974
Tina Niarchos dies of drug overdose

MARCH 15 1975
Aristotle Onassis dies in Paris

NOV 19 1988
Christina dies in Buenos Aires

MAY'70-NOV'88

Christina Onassis drops a single rose into her father's grave during his funeral on 18 March 1975. Onassis died in Paris and was flown to Greece for burial on Skorpios island, beside the grave of his son Alexander. Nearly 15 years later, Christina herself was to be buried close to her father and brother.

OF FATE

Alexander Onassis, Aristotle's son, was a skilled pilot who ran Olympic Aviation, a branch of Olympic Airways, before the air crash of January 1973 which killed him at the age of 24. His death was a terrible blow to Onassis.

Above: Stavros Niarchos, the Greek shipowner, and his third wife, Eugenie, whom he married in November 1947, almost a year after her sister, Tina, married Onassis. In May 1970, the 44-year-old Eugenie died after an overdose of sleeping tablets.

ruled that Eugenie's death was suicide and, as far as the law was concerned, the case was closed.

Because of Onassis' deep distrust of his rival Niarchos, he was all for pursuing the case further, but he was talked out of it by his son Alexander for the sake of the rest of the family – especially his cousins, the Niarchos children. 'Their mother's dead, and all you can think about is getting even with their father,' he accused Onassis.

Eighteen months later ties between the two families became closer still; to the astonishment and fury of Onassis, his ex-wife Tina divorced the Marquess of Blandford and stepped into her sister's shoes as the bride of Niarchos.

DEATH IN THE AIR

As Onassis' only son and heir, Alexander occupied a very special, albeit ambivalent, place in his father's universe. When Alexander failed his exams at 16, Onassis, announcing that he was 'not going to piddle away good money on a lazy kid', took him out of school and set him to work in his Monte Carlo office.

When he gained his pilot's licence, Alexander was allowed to take charge of a small subsidiary of Olympic Airways – Olympic Aviation – which ran local flights to the Greek islands. Alexander was

soon making a better job of it than Onassis was making of the parent company, although his father refused to give him any credit for doing so.

One of Olympic Aviation's planes was an elderly Piaggio seaplane which was used to ferry guests between the *Christina* or Skorpios and mainland Greece. Alexander considered it danger-ously unsafe and at last got his father to agree to replace it. Before the replacement (a helicopter) came, however, Onassis had decided to take the *Christina* to Miami, along with the Piaggio and a trained pilot. Unfortunately, the regular pilot was out of action and an American pilot, Donald McCusker, was hired.

Although experienced with seaplanes, McCusker had never flown a Piaggio before and Alexander arranged to take him up and show him the ropes. On the afternoon of 22 January 1973, Alexander and McCusker took off immediately behind an Air France Boeing 727 at Athens air-port. Seconds later, still below 1000 feet in the air, the seaplane dipped sharply to the right, touched the ground with a wing tip and cartwheeled 1000 metres along the runway.

Although outwardly barely scratched, Alexander suffered massive brain damage and he was taken to hospital and put on a life-support sys-tem. Onassis, in New York with Jackie at the time

of the crash, flew in top neurosurgeons from London and Boston, but their verdict was the same – Alexander was brain-dead. Only the life-support system was keeping him alive. He was kept on it only long enough for his sister Christina to return from Brazil to say her farewells.

Hands tightly clasped, a grief-stricken Christina and her father leave the First Cemetery of Athens where Alexander's body was laid out in a chapel before being taken to Skorpios for burial.

As the family gathered together in the hospital, Jackie approached Alexander's friend and lover, Fiona Thyssen-Bornemisza with a question: in Onassis's discussion with Alexander about his divorce from Jackie, how big a sum had been mentioned as a settlement?

The crash investigators concluded that the cables controlling the ailerons – the movable flaps on the trailing edges of the wings – had been wrongly reconnected during the seaplane's last service. This would have caused the aircraft to turn in a direction opposite to that required by the pilot.

A further report confirmed that such a mistake was easily made, but Onassis was already convinced that it had been the work of his enemies in the junta and their allies in the CIA. He offered a million dollars reward for information, but not a single person came forward to claim it.

Onassis then began to blame McCusker, even though Alexander had been the pilot, and forbade Olympic's lawyers to concede so much as a cent in compensation for his serious injuries. However, three years after Onassis' own death, Olympic agreed a settlement of $800,000.

With Christina now his sole heir, Onassis decided that she should be groomed to take over his empire under the personal tuition of his old friend Costa Gratsos. At first, she seemed to be making fine progress and even Onassis conceded that 'it seems just possible she might some day prove herself capable of running the family.' All seemed well until a series of tragedies struck. In August 1974, Christina was rushed to hospital in London after a massive drug overdose. She recovered, but the episode had a demoralising effect on her mother, Tina, who was disillusioned

> *She simply didn't care. She did nothing with her face, her hair was a mess... it was as if she wanted to punish the world for making her so rich and so bloody unhappy*

A Paris fashion house executive on fitting sessions with Christina Onassis, in 1981 with her marriage to Niarchos as well as addicted to barbiturates. On 10 October, Tina was found dead in her room in Niarchos's Paris mansion.

Christina immediately obtained a warrant for a post mortem. Its verdict was that Tina had died from acute oedema of the lung, but Niarchos was still sufficiently provoked by Christina's interference to issue a statement implying that her own suicide attempt had contributed to her mother's death. 'My aunt, my brother, now my mother – what is happening to us?' lamented Christina at the funeral.

To Onassis' personal misfortunes was added his declining health. He had difficulty swallowing food, talking clearly and keeping his eyes open – his eyelids became so weak they had to be held up with sticking tape. His doctors told him he was suffering from a wasting disease, *myasthenia gravis*.

In late October 1974, Onassis entered a New York hospital for a series of cortisone injections. These caused his face to puff up and did nothing to improve his temper. After seeing him throw a tantrum for being kept waiting for an appointment, his heart specialist described him as having had a

'cortisone rage'. 'And when he's not on cortisone?' the nurse rejoined.

At this stage that Onassis was faced with the ruin of Olympic Airways and the Greek government's decision to take it back into public ownership. Discharging himself from hospital, he flew to Athens to take charge of negotiations. His usual tactics of threats and procrastination proved useless; on 15 January 1975 he signed the takeover agreement. His successor believed the loss of Olympic broke Onassis' will to live: 'Emotionally, and for his sense of grandeur, it was the final blow.'

Opposite page (inset): Depression and weight trouble plagued Christina for years. By July 1983, when this photo was taken, her fight to slim had become a popular topic in gossip columns; it was not helped by her addiction to cola drinks. Above left: In 1975 Christina marries her second husband , Alexander Andreadis, in a small chapel in Glyfada, near Athens. Left: Christina weds her third husband, Sergei Kauzov (centre) in Moscow's Central Palace of Marriage in August 1978. Above: Momentary happiness for Christina in 1985 as she poses with fourth and last husband, Thierry Roussel, and their daughter Athina. Main picture: Christina and Roussel stroll along the shoreline.

In early February Onassis collapsed with an attack of gallstones and was flown to Paris to have his gall bladder removed. Since he seemed to be making a gradual recovery from the operation, Jackie – who had flown in from New York to be with him – returned to America. To boost his morale, Christina brought Peter Goulandris to his bedside saying that they had decided to go ahead with the marriage that Onassis had long wanted. Shortly afterwards, Onassis suffered a relapse brought on by bronchial pneumonia. On 15 March, aged 69, he died, with Christina at his bedside.

FINAL JOURNEY

Jackie was still in New York when the end came, and her attempts at sympathy when she rejoined the family in Greece did nothing to lessen their hostility towards her. Senator Edward Kennedy accompanied her to the funeral. The body was brought from Paris to the NATO air base at Aktion in western Greece. From there the cortege drove to the fishing village of Nidri on Lefkas island, where the mourners could embark for the final journey to Skorpios. Christina was sharing the leading car with Jackie and the Senator when she suddenly left

it and got into the car behind; it was alleged that Kennedy chose that moment to raise the question of the will and what was in it for Jackie.

CHRISTINA IN CHARGE

Christina moved swiftly to take charge of the ailing empire. 'From now on, gentlemen,' she told the board of British Petroleum, 'if there is anything to discuss or to be decided, you will be dealing with me.' She also started with good luck: one of the supertankers whose construction Onassis had been unable to cancel ran aground while on its maiden voyage and she collected $50 million in insurance.

Christina was just as quick to settle her marital affairs. The pledge to marry Goulandris had been no more than a charade, and he was rapidly replaced by Alexander Andreadis, the son of a prominent Greek banker and shipyard owner. They were married barely four months after her father's death, but disintegrated even faster. Flying to Moscow to negotiate a charter contract with the Soviet shipping agency, Sovfracht, she began an affair with its tanker division's 40-year-old – and married – director, Sergei Kauzov.

After the marriage to Andreadis was dissolved in July 1977, Christina continued her affair with Kauzov, who had connections with the KGB. The relationship worried Western Intelligence, who feared the Onassis tanker fleet might fall under

Soviet influence. Gratsos was called in by the US State Department to relay the implications to her, but she swept them aside and in August 1978 married Kauzov in a Moscow registry office. The marriage lasted less than a year, and Kauzov was paid off with a parting gift of a 78,000-ton tanker.

Now lonely again, Christina devoured junk food and Coca-Cola and rapidly put on weight. Her morale improved in 1983 when she lost a lot of weight in a slimming clinic, then fell in love with 34-year-old Thierry Roussel, heir to a pharmaceutical fortune and considered one of the most eligible bachelors in France. They were married in March 1984. The following January Christina seemed to have found the fulfilment she had been seeking for so long when she gave birth to a daughter, named Athina after her mother.

Even this did not hold the marriage together, and again Christina turned to the divorce courts. The huge settlement paid to Roussel might indicate that it was Christina who had wanted to end it, but the opposite was the case: part of the sum was payment for a bank of his sperm by which she hoped to bear another child.

Unable to find happiness in Europe, she went to Buenos Aires, the city from which her father had risen from such humble beginnings. Her search for a fresh start ended tragically. On 19 November 1988 Christina was found dead in her bath. The coroner decided that she had died of 'acute pulmonary oedema' – natural causes; but because of her dependency on drugs, it was almost impossible to detect a deliberate overdose.

CLOSE-UP

THE ONASSIS WILL

Under his last will, written in January 1974, Onassis set up two companies – the first containing all his assets which Christina inherited, and the second which held the shares of the first company. The controlling interest in the second company was to go to a charitable foundation set up in the name of his dead son Alexander. This meant that Christina could not dispose of the Onassis assets. Jackie would receive an annual income of $200,000, but Onassis inserted a clause cutting her out completely if she challenged the will; however, if she challenged it successfully, she was to get no more than 12.5 per cent of the total estate, the minimum permitted by Greek law.

Predictably, Jackie did indeed challenge it, while on the other side Christina showed herself prepared to pay almost anything to excise Jackie's interest. After 18 months of intense wrangling between the rival lawyers, Jackie agreed to surrender her annuity and her 25 per cent share in the yacht *Christina* and the island of Skorpios for a sum of $37 million.

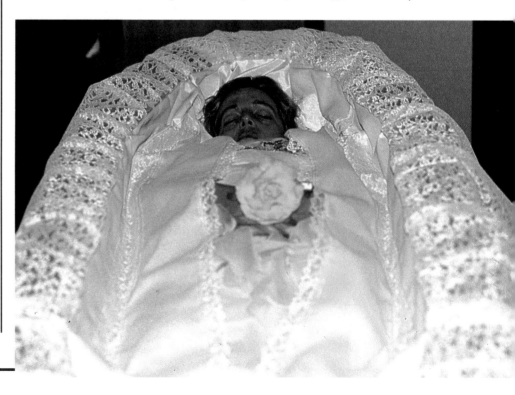

WATERGATE

Was the White House really the centre of a widespread network of political corruption? In 1973, the American public looked on with horrified fascination as Senate hearings began to probe at the truth behind the burglary of the Democrats' campaign headquarters in the Watergate building. Despite an extensive cover-up, facts emerged that showed Nixon's White House to be a hot bed of insecurity, misplaced loyalty and fear – and revealed a President spurred on by an insatiable appetite for power and public acclaim

Richard M Nixon, **a controversial but popular President since 1968 who yearned to be seen as a respected statesman.**

John Ehrlichman, **Nixon's Domestic Affairs adviser. He supervised the President's illegal intelligence unit.**

John Mitchell, **former Attorney-General who became Director of Nixon's election committee.**

Robert Haldeman, **White House Chief of Staff who played a key role in Nixon's election campaigns.**

John Dean, **an ambitious Justice Department lawyer who became counsel to President Nixon.**

ONE

A PLAN MISFIRES

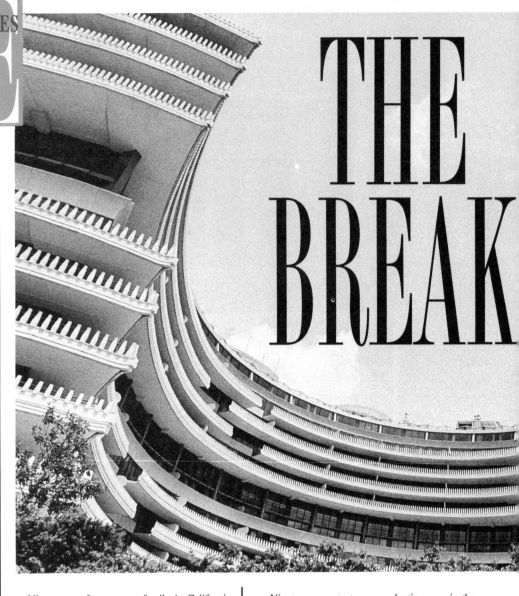

THE BREAK

WHEN FIVE MEN WERE CAUGHT IN THE OFFICES OF WASHINGTON'S PLUSH WATERGATE BUILDING, IT SEEMED LIKE A ROUTINE BURGLARY. THE BUGGING DEVICES, MONEY AND PHOTOGRAPHIC EQUIPMENT THEY CARRIED, HOWEVER, MARKED THEM DOWN AS RATHER SPECIAL BURGLARS

The greatest scandal in American history opened in the silence of the night on 17 June 1972, in the basement of the Watergate building in Washington. A burglary was discovered – a shabby, incompetent burglary which, through detective work, public inquiries and revelations in the press, led in 26 months to a crescendo of crises that forced the resignation of President Richard M Nixon.

The driving force behind what the President's re-election campaign director, John Mitchell, called 'the White House horrors', was Nixon's unsleeping paranoia. He was convinced that there was a long-standing conspiracy against him by the media, the Kennedy political clan, the elite eastern universities and the Democrats. He also suspected those rich, influential and liberal Washingtonians who lived in elegant houses in the Georgetown section of the capital and gave dinner and cocktail parties at which, he believed, they plotted against him out of personal malice.

Nixon came from a poor family in California and clawed his way to the top fighting the 'eastern liberal establishment' all the way. He despised the Kennedys – before and after the deaths of President John Kennedy and his brother Robert – more than anyone else. He hated them because they had style and wit, qualities he conspicuously lacked, because they were born rich, and because they had publicly mocked him and almost destroyed his career. The chip on his shoulder eventually destroyed him.

Nineteen seventy-two was election year in the US. Although Nixon had won presidential office with only a narrow margin in 1968, by June 1972 he was 19 points ahead of his likely Democratic rival, Senator George McGovern, in the opinion polls. Nixon's campaign was directed by the Committee for the Re-election of the President (CRP, dubbed CREEP by Nixon's more vitriolic critics), which was controlled by the White House. Its officials seemed prepared to go to any lengths to ensure victory.

DATEFILE

JUNE 17 1972
Five burglars arrested trying to bug Democratic campaign headquarters; they appear in court same day

JUNE 17-19 1972
Police trace links between burglars and President Nixon's campaign headquarters

JUNE 19 1972
The White House denies all knowledge of Watergate break-in

JUN 17-19 '72

INSIDE VIEW

COUNTDOWN TO ARREST

Main picture and inset: Washington DC's Watergate Complex, a prestigious development on the Potomac River comprising a hotel, shops, apartments and offices. Below: The security guard Frank Wills who first discovered evidence of the break-in.

N

CLOSE-UP: LIDDY'S MASTER PLAN

The original plan devised by CRP's finance counsel Gordon Liddy (above) to undermine the Democratic Party, code-named 'Operation Gemstone', had four parts. 'Operation Diamond' would deal with any protests against President Nixon during the Republican convention in Miami. Liddy wanted anti-war groups to be infiltrated with informants, while trained provocateurs would break up street demonstrations by starting fights. Another operational arm would be ready to drug and kidnap radical leaders and smuggle them across the border into Mexico until the convention was over.

'Operation Ruby' would gather intelligence during the Democratic convention, which was also to be held in Miami. Liddy planned to have spies infiltrate the offices of selected Democrats, and to moor a pleasure craft on a canal in front of the convention hotel. It would be staffed with 'the finest call girls in the country' and Democratic delegates would be lured aboard and persuaded to give up their secrets. 'They are not dumb broads,' Liddy said, 'but girls who can be trained and programmed.'

'Operation Sapphire' was designed to sabotage the Democratic convention by such tricks as turning off the air-conditioning.

The fourth project, 'Operation Crystal' involved bugging the Democrats. This was the only part of Liddy's plan that was approved.

The Democratic National Committee (DNC) – the ruling body of the Democratic Party – had its temporary headquarters in the Watergate office, apartment, hotel and shopping complex on the banks of the Potomac River in Washington. It was an odd place for Democrats: Watergate symbolised the rich, Republican classes in America. The former Attorney General, John Mitchell, who was now head of CRP, lived there. So did CRP's finance director, Maurice Stans, and President Nixon's personal secretary, Rose Mary Woods.

The DNC had taken a short lease on a sixth-floor office. At 1am on that June night, a security guard in the Watergate complex set out on his rounds. He was a 24-year-old, black drop-out from high school called Frank Wills. He found that a door into the basement parking garage had been taped. It had a spring catch, and the tape was wrapped across it horizontally to prevent it locking. A professional would have put the tape on vertically, so that nothing was visible. Wills was not alarmed. He removed the tape – thus locking

The police who made the Watergate arrest later found a recording which showed the alarm being raised at the burglars' base. It revealed that, in spite of the high stakes, the men in command of the break-in were poorly briefed.

At 1.55am on 17 June, Baldwin, the look-out in the Howard Johnson motel opposite the Watergate, saw three men move out onto the balcony of the DNC offices. He immediately radioed Howard Hunt (left) and Liddy, who were waiting in their room in the Watergate hotel:

BALDWIN: Base One to Unit One.
HUNT: What have you got?
BALDWIN: Are our people dressed in suits or dressed casually?
HUNT: What?
BALDWIN: Are our people dressed in suits or dressed casually?
HUNT: Our people are dressed in suits.
BALDWIN: Well, we've got problems. We've got some people dressed casually, and they've got guns.
The casually dressed people were police officers. They had problems all right!

> *But at some point that Saturday morning I realized that this...was a crime that could destroy us all. The cover-up, thus, was immediate and automatic; no one ever considered that there would not be a cover-up.*
>
> Jeb Magruder, deputy director, CRP, from his autobiography *An American Life*

PERSPECTIVE

THE CIA CONNECTION

The Central Intelligence Agency (CIA) and its agents played a considerable role in Watergate. The five burglars and their boss, Howard Hunt, had or were thought to have had connections with the CIA. The agency's director, Richard Helms, and deputy director, Vernon Walters, were co-opted into the cover-up by President Nixon (although they backed out of it soon afterwards), and details of various shady CIA dealings kept appearing and disappearing during the investigations.

Some have pointed to evidence that the entire Watergate episode was a CIA plot to destroy Nixon, but this angle remains unresolved.

What is clear, however, is that the CIA had plenty of its own secrets to hide, starting with the fact that it had regularly employed people as unreliable and dangerous as Howard Hunt. Its executives were deeply worried that the expanding Watergate scandal would engulf the agency. This was a reasonable concern. Ten months after Nixon resigned, some of the worst of the CIA violations - such as wiretaps and break-ins - were disclosed in the Rockefeller report.

the door – and went out for a cheeseburger at the Howard Johnson motel across the street.

At 1.45am Wills went through the garage again, and found that the door had been taped a second time. Realising that there were burglars in the building, he called the police. A three-man patrol arrived. Immediate investigation revealed other doors taped on the sixth floor.

ARREST

Alfred Baldwin, the burglars' look-out in room 419 in the Howard Johnson motel, saw three men, dressed casually and carrying guns, appear on the DNC balcony. He sent a warning by radio to the two leaders of the operation, Howard Hunt and Gordon Liddy, waiting in a room in the Watergate hotel. It was too late. The police who were moving from room to room in the DNC HQ, finally discovered five men who were trying to conceal themselves behind desks in a secretary's office. They were wearing blue rubber gloves and were carrying electronic gear, cameras and 40 rolls of film, and about $2000 in hundred-dollar bills.

Right: The five burglars caught in the Watergate building. From left to right: Eugenio Martinez, Bernard Barker, Virgilio Gonzales, James McCord and Frank Sturgis. They appeared in court at a preliminary hearing on 17 June, the same day as the break-in.

The burglars all gave aliases to the police, but two of them had keys to their rooms in the Watergate hotel. There, police found a further $3566 in cash, including $3200 in sequentially numbered hundred-dollar bills. They also found address books containing the name Howard Hunt and his telephone number at the 'W.H.' and the 'W. House.'

The burglars then abandoned their aliases. Of the five men, one was James McCord, security coordi-

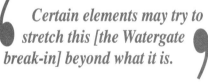

> *Certain elements may try to stretch this [the Watergate break-in] beyond what it is.*
>
> Ronald Ziegler, President Nixon's press secretary

nator for CRP; three were Cuban-Americans; and the fifth, Frank Sturgis, had been involved in the American invasion of Cuba at the Bay of Pigs in 1961. All had worked for the US foreign intelligence service, the Central Intelligence Agency (CIA). It was becoming obvious to the police that these were no ordinary burglars intent on just theft.

Later, as the long saga unfolded, it emerged that this was the second time Hunt and Liddy had

Left: Devices similar to this telephone bug were discovered in McCord's possession. McCord was an acknowledged expert in electronic surveillance.

sent their team into the DNC office. The first occasion was 29 May 1972, when McCord had put taps on two telephones, one used by the DNC chairman, Larry O'Brien, the other belonging to his deputy, Spencer Oliver. This second tap was in a private room used by secretaries and produced nothing of political significance, only graphic details of the women's sex-lives.

MISSED TARGET

The main target, however, was O'Brien, but McCord's bugging device failed. He had set it at low power to evade detection but, as a result, it was inaudible in the burglars' listening post at the Howard Johnson motel. The burglars were, therefore, sent back to the DNC to install a better phone-tap and other listening devices. They went in on 17 June, and were caught.

According to Liddy's plan, which was codenamed 'Operation Crystal' (see Close-up, page 131), the burglary was intended to install bugs in the presidential election headquarters of Senator George McGovern on Capitol Hill, situated on the other side of Washington. McGovern was a prime target as he had defeated his rivals in the primary contests and was about to be formally nominated as Democratic candidate for president in the elections due to be held in November of that year.

Liddy already had a spy in the McGovern office, but this contact was unable, or unwilling, to allow Liddy access to the building. On several nights in mid-June, Liddy prowled around the building, but there was always someone there, or a security guard outside the door, and the burglary was never attempted.

On the Saturday morning of 17 June, radio news carried a short report that burglars had been arrested at the DNC. The five burglars appeared in court, gave their names, and stated that their profession was 'anti-communist'. McCord said that he was a 'security consultant', who had worked for the government until recently. When asked by the judge what branch of government, he replied quietly, 'CIA.' With this almost off-hand admission came the first public indication that something out of the ordinary was afoot.

WHITE HOUSE DENIALS

In the next few days, the Washington Police Department established that there were connections between the burglars and both CRP and the CIA, and an indirect connection with the White House itself. They set about tracing all those suspicious hundred-dollar bills, and eventually found that they came from CRP. News of these links

> *We learned of this bugging attempt only because it was bungled. How many other attempts have there been and just who was involved?*
>
> Larry O'Brien, chairman, Democratic National Committee

soon reached the newspapers, and CRP's director, John Mitchell, issued a statement disassociating the committee from McCord.

'The person involved,' Mitchell said, 'is the proprietor of a private security agency who was employed by our committee months ago to assist with the installation of our security system. We want to emphasize that this man and the other people involved were not operating on either our behalf or with our consent.'

In answering a question about the break-in, the President's press secretary, Ronald Ziegler, said that the Watergate incident was 'a third-rate burglary attempt,' and not worth further comment.

THE EARLY 1970s WITNESSED A HOST OF ILLEGAL ACTIVITIES THAT WERE PLANNED AND DIRECTED FROM THE WHITE HOUSE. IF WATERGATE HAD NEVER BEEN FOUND OUT, THERE WAS NO SHORTAGE OF OTHER COVERT OPERATIONS THAT COULD HAVE SPELLED DISASTER FOR PRESIDENT NIXON AND HIS STAFF

PALACE OF

T he Watergate burglary turned out to be just the tip of the iceberg. Howard Hunt and Gordon Liddy had organised a series of burglaries, wire-taps and other illegal activities for their White House superiors, who were acting at the behest of Richard Nixon. Sooner or later, they were bound to get caught.

Nixon used these unofficial 'spooks' because he could not rely on the help of the Federal Bureau of Investigation (FBI) and the Central Intelligence Agency (CIA).

Nixon had decided that he was being sabotaged by FBI Director J Edgar Hoover and CIA Director Richard Helms. He allowed his staff to set up a secret agency inside the White House to direct and coordinate all counter-intelligence opera-

FBI Director, J Edgar Hoover (above), had a network of informants spying on the 'New Left'. From February 1970, he severely limited FBI cooperation with the CIA and Nixon.

tions around the country.

Hoover blocked the plan by not cooperating. He was too entrenched for Nixon to fire, so the President had to shelve the project. Instead, he ordered a 'Special Investigations Unit' to be set up. It was installed in Room 16 of the Executive Office Building, beside the White House.

WAR ON ENEMIES

Nixon also used other branches of government against his enemies. He set the Internal Revenue Service to work, harassing institutions, journalists and

politicians who displeased him, including Larry O'Brien, chairman of the Democratic National Committee. He had the FBI tap the telephones of journalists and even members of his own staff whom he suspected of leaking information.

His staff produced an 'enemies list' of people who were to be discredited. On recordings, the President's counsel, John Dean, is heard to say the objective was 'to use the available federal machinery to screw our political enemies.'

In June 1971, the *New York Times* and other newspapers published the Pentagon Papers, documents on

the origins of the Vietnam War, that had been leaked by a former senior official, Daniel Ellsberg. The President saw it as further proof of the conspiracy against him and vowed that leaks would be stopped. The Special Investigations Unit was put on the task; hence their nickname, 'the Plumbers'.

The unit did much more than plug leaks. It was an illegal intelligence organisation, intended to tap telephones, read mail and conduct 'surreptitious entries' (burglaries). Its directors were Egil Krogh and David Young, who acted under the general supervision of John Ehrlichman, one of Nixon's most senior aides.

Soon recruited by the Plumbers were Howard Hunt,

PLUGGING THE LEAKS

In June 1971, Nixon was furious at the leak of the Pentagon Papers, which detailed US escalation of the Vietnam War. He told his special counsel Chuck Colson: 'I don't give a damn how it is done, do whatever has to be done to stop these leaks and prevent further unauthorised disclosures; I don't want to be told

why it can't be done. This government cannot survive, it cannot function if anyone can run out and leak whatever documents he wants to. I want to know who is behind this and I want the most complete investigation that can be conducted. I don't want excuses. I want it done, whatever the cost.'

DIRTY TRICKS

In an office across the road from the White House (left), David Young (below) and Egil Krogh (right) directed the activities of an intelligence gathering unit known as the Plumbers, whose intention was to subvert President Nixon's political enemies.

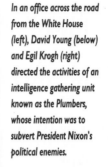

White House Chief of Staff, Bob Haldeman, instructed Jeb Magruder, Deputy Director of Nixon's re-election campaign, to take Liddy onto the staff to conduct 'intelligence-gathering operations'. Liddy prepared an elaborate scheme for spying on the Democrats, and submitted it in January 1972 to John Mitchell, who was then Attorney-General. The meeting was also attended by Magruder and John Dean, the President's counsel.

ILLEGAL PROJECT

Mitchell turned the plan down as too elaborate and too expensive, and suggested Liddy revise it. The same group gathered on 4 February to hear the revised version. Dean claims he thought he had killed the project when pointing out the illegalities. He was mistaken.

But by June 1972, Nixon was running 19 points ahead of McGovern in the opinion polls and was virtually assured of victory in the election. Perhaps the strangest irony attached to the Watergate raid was that it was quite unnecessary for Nixon's political survival.

an ex-CIA agent, and Gordon Liddy, ex-FBI. The Plumbers devised a number of outrageous schemes, some of which were never carried out.

However, the Plumbers seriously applied themselves to the task of investigating and discrediting Daniel Ellsberg. They persuaded the CIA to prepare a 'psychological profile', which they hoped to leak to the press. It was insufficiently damning, however, so they decided to raid Ellsberg's psychiatrist's office, to photograph his files.

Hunt used CIA contacts to provide him with disguises and equipment, and recruited a group of former CIA agents among the Cuban exiles in Miami. They raided the office in September 1971, but found nothing useful.

It is possible that the Plumbers conducted a number of other burglaries. At least a dozen prominent anti-war activists and their lawyers were burgled during this period, by people who were more interested in confidential documents than anything of value

GORDON LIDDY'S SHORT FUSE

Jeb Magruder (left), Deputy Director of the Committee for the Re-election of the President (CRP), did not get on with his chief lawyer and spook, Gordon Liddy. He thought he spent too much time plotting covert activities. One day, in March 1972, Magruder met Liddy in the CRP foyer and asked:

'Gordon, where are those reports you promised me?'

Liddy angrily replied: They're not ready.' 'Well, the delay is causing me problems,' said Magruder. 'If you're going to be our general counsel, you've got to do your work.'
As Magruder spoke, he casually put his hand on Liddy's shoulder. 'Get your hand off me,' Liddy shouted. 'Get your hand off me or I'll kill you!'

THE COVER

THE WATERGATE ARRESTS SPREAD PANIC INSIDE THE WHITE HOUSE. PRESIDENT NIXON'S MOST SENIOR AIDES ABANDONED THEIR PUBLIC DUTIES TO HATCH A FURTIVE CONSPIRACY TO DECEIVE THE COURTS AND THE PUBLIC

Immediately after the burglars were arrested, Hunt and Liddy fled from their room in the Watergate hotel. Driving away, they were alarmed to see swarms of police converging on the building. Hunt then fetched a truck and returned to the Howard Johnson motel, where his look-out, Alfred Baldwin, was still watching developments. The two men loaded all their electronic gear into the truck and Hunt drove the equipment to McCord's house in the suburbs, handing it over to his wife. He then set about finding lawyers for the Cubans.

HOLDING THE FORT

When the news broke that burglars had been arrested inside the temporary headquarters of the Democratic Party, President Nixon was in the Bahamas, staying with a friend on a private island. His Chief of Staff, Bob Haldeman, was in Key Biscayne, an island off Miami, Florida. John Mitchell, director of the Committee for the Re-election of the President (CRP), and other leaders of CRP were in Los Angeles for a fund-raising

Two Washington Post *junior reporters, Carl Bernstein (left) and Bob Woodward, were assigned to the Watergate burglary story. They were to make history and build their own careers in exposing the White House connection. Together with their mysterious contact, 'Deep Throat', they have entered newspaper folklore.*

DATEFILE

JUNE 18 1972

White House aides destroy files linking Watergate burglary to senior officials

JUNE 23 1972

President Nixon agrees to a plan to block FBI investigation of 'dirty money'

JULY 1 1972

John Mitchell resigns as director of Nixon's re-election committee

JUNE-JULY '72

event, and John Dean, counsel to the President, was in the Philippines. The President's Domestic Policy Adviser, John Ehrlichman, was holding the fort in Washington.

Liddy went to the CRP headquarters on Saturday morning, 17 June, and started destroying all documents linked to the Watergate burglary and even some of the incriminating $100 bills. At 11.30am he telephoned CRP's Deputy Director,

Jeb Magruder, the man who had authorised the break-in, in Los Angeles. It was breakfast time on the West Coast and Magruder was in the hotel dining room with other CRP officials, eating kippers. A waiter brought a telephone to his table.

Liddy told him that he had to find a secure phone. Magruder asked why. 'Our security chief was arrested in the Democratic headquarters in the Watergate last night,' Liddy told him. Magruder

UP

Nixon's Chief of Staff, Bob Haldeman (left) had his files purged of anything linking the White House to the burglary. The President's legal counsel, John Dean (above), took incriminating files from Hunt's safe, but ignored advice to destroy them.

General, Richard Kleindienst, who had succeeded Mitchell only a few months earlier. Liddy found him at a golf club.

'Mitchell has sent me out here to talk to you,' Liddy explained in the confidentiality of a locker-room, 'and he wants those five people arrested last night out of jail.' Kleindienst was outraged at the crass stupidity of the approach. He called Henry Petersen, the prosecutor handling the case, and told him to treat the five suspects exactly as he would anyone else. However, he did not tell Petersen about Liddy.

In Washington, police had discovered that the Howard Hunt mentioned in two of the burglars' address books worked at the White House. The President's special counsel, Charles Colson, assured them that Hunt had ended connections with him in March. Magruder and Dean flew back to Washington. The files of 'Operation Gemstone' contained the transcripts of conversations picked up by the one successful wiretap installed in the DNC office on 29 May. Magruder burned the files in his fireplace at home.

CLEANING THE FILES

At the same time, Nixon's Chief of Staff, Haldeman, told an assistant to ensure that 'the files are clean.' The aide dutifully shredded every incriminating piece of paper. Ehrlichman and Dean agreed that Hunt should vanish. He quickly left for

Los Angeles, and Dean had the safe in Hunt's office opened. It contained documents referring to earlier operations carried out by a shady White House unit called the 'Plumbers', as well as bugging equipment, a gun, two notebooks and a pop-up address book. 'Why don't you deep six it?'

THE HUSTON PLAN

The Watergate affair endangered one of President Nixon's most secretive and illegal operations. In 1970, he had approved a set of covert measures against 'domestic security threats' known as the 'Huston Plan', named after the former White House aide, Thomas Huston, who drafted it. The plan led to the creation of the 'Plumbers Unit', so-called because their prime task was to investigate security leaks at the White House.

The plan also called for increased wire-tapping of telephones, the opening of private mail, the monitoring of international telephone calls made from America, and broader surveillance of college campuses. Huston acknowledged to Nixon that parts of the plan were 'clearly illegal.'

The Nixon White House invoked national security to justify the secret plan, which was largely designed to spy on Nixon's critics in politics, academic life and the press.

replied: 'What? You mean McCord?' He dashed to a pay phone in a private corner of the hotel, called Liddy back, and learned the worst.

Magruder was appalled. After breakfast he said to a colleague, 'Oh God, why didn't I fire that idiot Liddy when I had the chance?' He then reported to his boss, John Mitchell.

The first thing was to get the burglars out of jail. Liddy was instructed to see the Attorney

'Certain crucial events took place
on park benches in meetings
as covert as the microfilm
exchanges in spy movies.'

John Dean in his autobiography
Blind Ambition

Ehrlichman allegedly told Dean, who looked perplexed. 'Well,' explained Ehrlichman, 'when you cross over the river on your way home, just toss the briefcase in the river.'

Dean declined, and later handed the files to Patrick Gray, acting head of the Federal Bureau of Investigation (FBI), which deals with security inside the USA. Gray participated in the Watergate cover-up without ever admitting to himself that he was, in fact, obstructing justice. Dean told him that the files had nothing to do with Watergate, and concerned national security. Gray kept them at home for six months, then burned them, with holiday wrapping paper, a few days after Christmas. Dean kept the notebooks and address book.

The CIA also lent a hand. McCord had been in the agency for over 20 years, before setting up his own security firm, and joining CRP. On the morning after the arrests, a man from headquarters was sent to McCord's house to ensure that incriminating evidence was destroyed. McCord later disposed of the bugging equipment which Hunt had taken there after the burglary.

Jeb Magruder, Deputy Director of CRP (right), burned files in his own fireplace. Top White House aide, John Ehrlichman (below), allegedly told John Dean to 'deep six' the contents of Hunt's safe.

PERSPECTIVE

'DEEP THROAT'

Woodward and Bernstein developed most of their stories on Watergate by asking questions of hundreds of people, relentlessly, day after day. They went exhaustively through lists of people working at CRP and interrogated all of them. Most refused to speak, but the two reporters gradually found people whose conscience was greater than their fear for their jobs.

Woodward also had a secret source, nicknamed 'Deep Throat' after a pornographic movie of that name. He was a government official (and much ink has been spilled trying to establish his identity), who was well informed about Watergate. He seldom gave Woodward specific information, but urged him to follow the money trail, and frequently guided him by confirming or quashing stories which the *Washington Post* had prepared for publication.

If Woodward wanted an urgent interview, he moved a potted plant with a red flag in it on his balcony; if the other wanted a talk, Deep Throat would leave a scribbled message in Woodward's morning newspaper (how he managed this was never disclosed). The two men always met in an underground garage at about 2am. Deep Throat's main contribution was to confirm how serious the Watergate affair was.

The link between McCord and the CIA was all the press had to go on that first day. Reporters did not discover his employment by CRP until two days later. The *Washington Post* had assigned two junior reporters, Bob Woodward and Carl Bernstein, to cover the break-in and they grasped the biggest break of their careers with tenacity. Soon, the *Washington Post* was delving deeply into the backgrounds of everyone linked to the Watergate burglary.

The White House knew that the five burglars needed to be persuaded to be discreet. Hunt kept the Cubans quiet. A former CIA agent, he had been one of the organisers of the abortive invasion of Cuba in 1961, in which the Cuban burglars were involved. Mitchell and Magruder agreed to pay their legal bills and their families' expenses. Nixon's private lawyer, Herb Kalmbach, was given large sums from CRP's secret slush fund and passed them on to the five. Later, payments also went to Hunt and Liddy, and soon escalated into hundreds of thousands of dollars. Always they were made in cash, in $100 bills, carried around the country by Kalmbach and other 'bag men' in briefcases and brown envelopes.

Charles Colson, special Counsel to the President (above), told the police that Hunt's connection with the White House had ended months before the Watergate break-in. Herb Kalmbach, Nixon's private lawyer (right), distributed CRP slush funds to the burglars to pay for their legal expenses.

THROWN TO THE WOLVES

At first the damage-control team in the White House hoped that Hunt and Liddy could be shielded from the police investigation. It was a vain and naive hope. Both men had left their tracks all over the case. Then the White House decided that Hunt and Liddy would be thrown to the wolves. If the trail was followed any higher, first to Magruder, then Mitchell, it would soon implicate the President himself.

The most incriminating evidence was the trail of the money. Liddy had been authorised to draw $250,000 from CRP by Mitchell and Magruder. Hugh Sloan, the CRP treasurer, had paid Liddy $199,000. When Liddy's involvement with Watergate emerged, Sloan realised that his own superiors must have authorised the break-in. Sloan resigned. Then, on 30 June 1972, came another hint that the Watergate break-in involved powerful public figures. John Mitchell suddenly resigned as the director of CRP, only four months before the presidential elections, giving as his reason the fact that his wife had just left him.

The White House cover-up team was terrified that the FBI would trace the $100 bills to CRP, and also discover that the money consisted of illegal campaign contributions. The law forbade corporations to contribute to political campaigns and a new law, effective only since 7 April 1972, required all contributions to be declared publicly. Previously, campaign contributions had been closely guarded secrets. CRP had taken in hundreds of thousands of dollars in illegal contributions since the new law came into effect. Some had been 'laundered' in Mexico, so that they could never be traced back from CRP to the contributors, and part of that money had financed the Watergate burglary. If the FBI looked closely, it would find not one but three crimes – the burglary, the cover-up and money laundering.

INSIDE VIEW
DOMESTIC SPYING

The Nixon Administration not only spied on its enemies, but maintained surveillance on itself. Dr Henry Kissinger, the President's National Security Adviser, had wire-taps put on the telephones of several senior assistants; William Safire, one of Nixon's top speechwriters; and some of Kissinger's friends and contacts in the press.

Meanwhile, the joint Chiefs of Staff, the military commanders in the Pentagon, were spying on Kissinger. A navy warrant officer, Yeoman Charles Radford, seconded to the National Security Council, was found to be copying secret NSC documents and sending them to his superiors at the Pentagon.

The affair was uncovered when a journalist, Jack Anderson (right), published a secret memorandum on American policy towards the war between India and Pakistan in 1971. Nixon wanted the USA to tilt in Pakistan's favour. The investigators who tapped Radford's phone never proved he was the source of the leak, but they did prove that Radford was spying for the joint Chiefs. Radford was banished to a navy station in Oregon.

NIXON'S

RICHARD NIXON'S PRESIDENCY REPRESENTED A REACTION AGAINST A PERIOD OF SUSTAINED SOCIAL CHANGE. HIS ADMINISTRATION WAS A JOYLESS CROWD IN A CITY WHERE POLITICS WAS – AND REMAINS – THE MAIN DIVERSION

The seat of power: an aerial view of the Capitol (right) and the memorial to one of America's greatest presidents, Abraham Lincoln (above).

Richard Nixon became president in the midst of a social upheaval that at times threatened political revolution. The civil rights movement had begun to redress the country's political and social discrimination against blacks, without ending their poverty. There were serious ghetto riots in Newark, Washington, Detroit, Los Angeles and many other cities.

The 'baby boom' generation reached the universities and joined in the world-wide student revolt of 1968. The feminist movement became a political force for the first time. Above all, the protests against the Vietnam War dominated the country's politics and society from the mid-1960s until the United States escaped from the morass in 1973.

It was a frantic period, not at all like the self-satisfied 1950s or 1980s. In the 1960s,

Americans had to face the fact that theirs was a violent society. There was a series of assassinations: President Kennedy and his brother Robert; the black leaders Martin Luther King, Medgar Evers and Malcolm X; and the prominent fascist, George Lincoln Rockwell.

VIOLENT SOCIETY

A riot at the Democratic Party convention in Chicago marred the climax of the 1968 election campaign: tensions were so acute that President Johnson himself was unable to attend.

The 1960s generation is inclined to believe that it liberated sex, abruptly breaking clear of Victorian inhibitions, and there was certainly more promiscuity than in earlier decades, helped by the introduction of the birth-control pill. The Supreme Court decision to permit abortion, in

Peace marches in Washington in 1967 (left) were already setting the tone for Nixon's future presidency.

1973, was a major landmark. Furthermore, the same period saw the liberalisation of pornography, and the 1960s generation was also the first to use drugs in quantity.

Every revolution provokes its counter-revolution, and conservatives who deplored pornography and 'sex, drugs and rock and roll', voted for Richard Nixon. The anti-war movement which drove Lyndon Johnson out of the White House and ended American involvement in the Vietnam War was a leftist, Democratic phenomenon. One of its effects

WASHINGTON

The Watergate complex (below) in Washington will always be linked with the Nixon presidency and his downfall.

has been that the Republicans have won four of the past five presidential elections.

DULL WASHINGTON

When Nixon returned to Washington in triumph, in January 1969, he found that it had not changed very much since he had left in defeat, eight years earlier. Washington was a dull town, compared with New York or Los Angeles (and still is). There has never been much 'high society' there, except for the brief time John and Jackie Kennedy lived in the White House. In the Nixon days, there were still a few great hostesses, including Margaret Merriweather Post, the cereal heiress, and Alice Longworth, the aged daughter of President Theodore Roosevelt.

There were a few survivors of the heroic era of the 1940s, like Averell Harriman and

David Bruce, both multi-millionaire Democratic diplomats, who held court in Georgetown, or the columnist Walter Lippmann. But that was all.

There were no famous nightclubs, or discos, where the rich, famous and glamorous could see and be seen. There were only restaurants, where members of Congress, members of the White House staff, and the ubiquitous lobbyists had lunch. Cultural life was mediocre and episodic; Washington's favourite indoor sport was political gossip. It must be said that very little has changed since then.

There were, and still are, cocktail parties and dinner parties in Georgetown, but Nixon detested such events and the people who attended them, so White House staff shunned them. There was a strong streak of puritanism in the Nixon camp (quite unlike the

Reagan crowd of the 1980s). The only senior administration figure who ignored the President's disapproval was Henry Kissinger, who delighted in his transformation from dull Harvard professor to media star. He was much sought-after on the cocktail circuit.

Washington goes to bed early because it rises early, particularly politicians and their

staffs, who are at their desks at 7.00 am. The concept of the 18-hour working day is cultivated by politicians and their staffs, hoping to prove their devotion to the public interest and to their superiors. Its effect tends to be pernicious (people who overwork make mistakes), ruining the city's social life.

SYMBOLIC PLACE

Washington is not a very cultural city and barely sustains its orchestra and seasonal opera. The Kennedy Centre was as much a political statement as a temple of the arts.

The Watergate buildings were already a Republican symbol of another sort. It was one of their strongholds, a plutocratic complex of shops, offices and apartments on the Potomac River situated next to the Kennedy Centre for the Performing Arts. It was a symbolic juxtaposition – culture and wealth, both tidily separate from the rest of the city.

A major demonstration on Capitol Hill in 1971 (left) reflected the growing popular opposition to the war in Vietnam.

A CONSPIRACY

IN NOVEMBER 1972, PRESIDENT NIXON WAS

RE-ELECTED IN A LANDSLIDE OVER HIS LIBERAL,

DEMOCRATIC OPPONENT. ALTHOUGH HE ASKED

AMERICANS TO PUT WATERGATE BEHIND THEM,

THE COVER-UP WAS VERY MUCH ALIVE – AND

THREATENING TO FALL APART

Trouble resumed after President Nixon's election victory in November 1972. Hunt called Colson and demanded more hush money. Colson recorded the conversation. By then, everyone involved in the cover-up was recording each other.

'Commitments that were made to all of us at the outset have not been kept,' Hunt told Colson. '...There's a great deal of financial expense that has not been covered and what we've been getting has been coming in minor dribs and drabs...we're protecting the guys who were really responsible.'

HALDEMAN OPENS THE SAFE

Hunt set a deadline, 25 November, for a settlement. This was blackmail. Hunt had already received over $200,000. Now he extorted further huge sums, clearly hush money. The money was drawn from the $350,000 kept in Haldeman's safe, funds left over from the 1968 presidential campaign. Moving such sums in cash involved lawyers, fund-raisers and 'bagmen' (collectors or

DATEFILE

NOVEMBER 7 1972

President Nixon is re-elected for his second term by a huge majority

FEBRUARY 7 1973

The Senate votes to establish a Select Committee on the President's campaign activities

MARCH 23 1973

Watergate burglars sentenced to long terms of imprisonment

NOV '72-MAR '73

246

INTACT

distributors of money). Packets of money would be left in phone booths or left-luggage lockers.

Hunt passed part of the funds on to the burglars' lawyers, using his wife as a courier. She was killed in a plane crash on 8 December 1972 and over $10,000 in cash was found in her handbag. Distraught, Hunt demanded that Colson promise that he would be got out of jail if he pleaded guilty at the trial.

'There is a limit to the endurance of any man trapped in a hostile situation,' he wrote in a letter to Colson on 31 December. Almost at the same time, McCord sent a message to Dean: 'If Helms [Director of the CIA] goes and the Watergate operation is laid at the CIA's feet, where it does not belong, every tree in the forest will fall.'

LOOKING AFTER HUNT

Colson and Ehrlichman both approached the President, the only man who could offer a pardon. They obtained a secret assurance: if Hunt and the others kept quiet, they would be pardoned by the following Christmas of 1973. Hunt was satisfied with the arrangement, agreed to plead guilty, and persuaded four of the five burglars to follow his example. Liddy, obsessed with his self-image as the strong, silent leader, refused to agree to plead guilty, but he was also refusing to answer any

Left: The President and Mrs Nixon on the pre-election glory trail in October 1972.
Right: Judge John Sirica, who handed out exemplary sentences to Hunt and Liddy and the five Watergate burglars at the Washington District Federal Court (below). However, Hunt in fact served less than three years and the others a lot less.

questions by the authorities. McCord was left as the weak link, unmoved by hush money or Hunt's promises of clemency.

The trial of the 'Watergate Seven' (the five burglars, plus Liddy and Hunt) opened in Washington's District Court House on 8 January 1973. All defendants except Liddy and McCord pleaded guilty and all were convicted. Judge Sirica expressed strong doubts that the prosecutors had reached the bottom of the case. Sentencing was set for 23 March.

SKILFUL SIDE-STEPPING

An attempt to investigate Watergate before the election, by the House of Representatives Banking Committee, was foiled by skilful Republican manoeuvreing. The Democratic majority in the Senate, however, was determined to hold an inquiry and, despite Nixon's manipulative tactics,

UNITED STATES COURT HOUSE

Right: The magisterial Senior Senator from North Carolina, Sam Ervin, the leading legal brain in both Houses of Congress, was named as Chairman of the Senate Select Committee on Presidential Campaign Activities – more popularly known as the Watergate, or Ervin, Committee.

they secured the necessary resolution in the Senate on 7 February 1973. Sam Ervin, the Senior Senator for North Carolina and the Senate's leading constitutional expert, was nominated to be chairman of a Senate Select Committee on Presidential Campaign Activities (often referred to as the Watergate Committee or Ervin Committee).

The cover-up was still holding firm, but Dean was acutely aware of the dangers. It was a large conspiracy, one that might unravel if any one conspirator cracked. Mitchell, Magruder, and many lesser players, had already perjured themselves to a grand jury on the question of their involvement in the burglary and the money trail, particularly on the issue of why Liddy was given $250,000 from CRP funds. Many of the conspirators would have to testify in public, under oath, to the Ervin Committee.

DEAN EXPOSED

The dangers became starkly clear in March 1973 when the Senate Judiciary Committee began hearings on Pat Gray's nomination as Director of the FBI. Gray told the Committee that he had

GRAND JURIES AND PROSECUTORS

The American system of justice differs in important respects from British practice. Certain crimes, such as the set of offences known as Watergate, are investigated by the Federal Bureau of Investigation (FBI) rather than a local police force. The FBI, which is answerable to the Attorney-General, passes evidence to federal prosecutors, who may convene a grand jury. This is a stage of the legal process which English legislators chose to abolish about 150 years ago.

Suspects and witnesses are brought before the grand jury, which consists of ordinary citizens chosen in the same way as a trial jury. After hearing all the evidence, the grand jury votes on whether or not to indict the suspect on particular offences. If indicted, he or she is then brought to trial.

turned over details of the FBI investigation to Dean and even allowed him to attend FBI interviews with Watergate figures. The hearings suddenly brought Dean – much to his consternation – out of the White House shadows.

Pat Gray claimed that Dean had probably lied about Watergate. The Senate Committee wanted to summon Dean and other White House officials to testify. Both Dean and the President invoked 'executive privilege', under which the President may refuse to accede to Congressional demands. Congress objected vigorously.

Gray continued to make heavy weather of his nomination hearings, and John Ehrlichman observed to Dean, 'I think we ought to let him hang there. Let him twist slowly, slowly in the wind.' Then Gray admitted burning material taken from Hunt's safe. With that highly incriminating admission, his hopes of confirmation as Director

> *People are going to start perjuring themselves very quickly...to protect other people in the line.*
>
> John Dean to President Nixon

of the FBI were also in embers.

As the day of sentencing the Watergate burglars approached, Hunt resumed his demands for hush money. This time he needed $132,000. To Dean, this was the last straw. He refused to have anything further to do with hush money payments, and decided to confront the President with the depth of the crisis.

On 20 March 1973, three days before the seven defendants were to be sentenced, McCord sent a letter to Sirica that proved crucial to the unravelling of the conspiracy. 'In the interest of restoring faith in the criminal justice system,' he wrote, 'I will state the following:

'There was political pressure applied to the defendants to plead guilty and remain silent. Perjury occurred during the trial...Others involved in the Watergate operation were not identified during the trial...The Cubans may have been

BACKDROP

misled by others into believing it was a CIA operation. I know for a fact that it was not.'

Sirica read out the letter in court before handing out sentences on 23 March. He sentenced Liddy to between six years eight months and 20 years in jail, and fined him $40,000. Liddy had been utterly uncooperative, and Judge Sirica intended his sentence to be a warning to the others. Maximum provisional sentences of 35 years were given to Hunt and 40 years each for the four Miami burglars. He reserved McCord's sentence while he studied his letter. Final sentences were all greatly reduced. In the end, no burglar served more than 14 months in jail, but Hunt served just over two years seven months.

Two days before, on 21 March 1973, Dean had told Nixon: 'We have a cancer within – close to the Presidency – that's growing. It's growing daily.'

NIXON TALKS MONEY

Nixon was disturbed by Hunt's latest demands for money. Dean said the total bill might come to a million dollars. Nixon commented, 'We could get that.' Later, he added, 'What I mean is, you could get a million dollars. And you could get it in cash. I know where it could be gotten.'

Nixon rejected Dean's suggestion that he cut his losses, and accept that a number of his associates would go to jail. Instead, he returned repeatedly to the hush money: 'Don't you, just looking at the

immediate problem, don't you have to handle Hunt's financial situation damn soon? You've got to keep the cap on the bottle that much in order to have any options...At the moment, don't you agree that you'd better get the Hunt thing?'

THE FINAL ACT

Dean was back in the cover-up. He passed the message on to the current bagman, a financier called Fred LaRue, who made a final payment of $75,000 to Hunt's lawyer. Once again, the money was in $100 bills and came from the remainder of the $350,000 in Haldeman's safe. The total hush money paid came to $429,500. It was the last act of a cover-up that had begun nine months before, on the morning after the burglary.

Above: Mississippi financier and unpaid CRP officer, Fred LaRue, who made a final payment of $75,000 to Hunt's lawyer, on Dean's say-so. The money was left-over 1968 campaign funds.

Below: When the 'Watergate Seven' were sentenced on 23 March 1973, Judge Sirica read out in court a letter from McCord stating that political pressure had been applied to persuade the defendants to plead guilty and otherwise remain silent. McCord's letter was a crucial blow to the cover-up conspiracy.

PERSPECTIVE

THE WHITE HOUSE

The term 'White House' means the Executive Office of the presidency, a large bureaucracy that occupies the White House itself, the Executive Office Building next door, and various other buildings. The White House is, therefore, like a royal court. The most powerful men are those who work closest to the president. In Nixon's first term of office (1968-72), foreign policy was conducted by his National Security Adviser, Henry Kissinger, not by his Secretary of State. When Kissinger became Secretary of State himself in October 1973, he retained his national

security post, and his corner office in the White House.

Nixon's Chief of Staff was H R ('Bob') Haldeman. The head of Domestic Affairs was John Ehrlichman. These two, and Kissinger, between them, ran the United States government for Richard Nixon. Haldeman sent his own aides to run the Committee for the Re-election of the President (CRP), and supervised them closely. Ehrlichman and another aide, Charles Colson, who was known as Nixon's chief hatchet man, supervised the 'Plumbers' and their illegal activities.

Watergate spy tells 'pressure' to plead guilty

Vote perils tax relief --Walker

By Henry Hanson
Of Our Springfield Bureau

SPRINGFIELD, Ill. —Gov. Dan Walker Friday charged that tax relief has been jeopardized because the House override his veto of a CTA subsidy bill.

"We tried to save $3 million of state funds for tax relief and we lost," Walker told a press conference here.

To preserve the chances of tax relief, Walker said he

Walker names Fogel to new advisory post. Page 3.

How they voted on CTA veto. Page 9.

Mi- that his the ela- high

would have to trim $3 million from his budget.

The House voted 113 to 49 Thursday to override Walker's

Former Beatle John Lennon, who was ordered to leave the United States within 60 days, with his wife Yoko Ono in New York recently. His wife will be allowed to stay. (AP)

Lennon must get out of U.S.

Charges perjury and cover-up

By Robert Signer
Of Our Washington Bureau

WASHINGTON — A federal judge imposed severe sentences on the Watergate defendants Friday amid sensational new charges by one of the defendants that witnesses lied and shielded others involved in the political espionage during the trial.

The defendant, James W. McCord Jr., said "political pressure" was applied on the

James W. McCord Jr.

Full text of McCord's letter. Page 16.

seven accused men "to plead guilty and remain silent." McCord, saying his family feared for his life if he disclosed all he knew about the case, asked to meet privately with U.S. District Court Judge

2d murder at hotel for retirees

By Edmund J. Rooney

An 82-year-old woman was

AS ONE OF PRESIDENT NIXON'S TOP AIDES, JOHN EHRLICHMAN HAD A UNIQUE VIEW OF THE WATERGATE AFFAIR. HERE HE CHALLENGES MANY OF THE ACCEPTED TRUTHS AND ARGUES FOR A MORE SERIOUS APPRAISAL OF THE PERIOD

I was on Richard Nixon's White House staff from late 1968 to April 1973. During most of that time I was Nixon's assistant for Domestic Affairs, handling problems of the economy, transportation, civil rights, labor, the environment and natural resources, and hundreds of other national policy questions.

The disparate incidents lumped together as 'Watergate' commanded a tiny fraction of my time and attention, yet I will forever be tagged with them. Journalists and historians have tried in vain to explain why the Watergate break-in occurred at Democrat headquarters. I sat through hundreds of hours of judicial proceedings, but that central question was never answered.

ON THE BURGLARY

The prosecutor's explanation – that the purpose was to plant listening devices in Chairman Larry O'Brien's office – never made sense to me. To hear what? That moribund headquarters was not the nerve-center of the Democrats' presidential campaign. In fact, Mr O'Brien had moved his office to Florida.

Why a burglary? At that time, Richard Nixon was far ahead in the polls and gaining ground every day. The burglars were (except for Liddy) an all-CIA crew; no one has ever established who gave them orders, nor what those orders were.

The cover-ups are less mysterious. In 1974, I was convicted of failing to call the cops when Howard Hunt and Gordon Liddy broke into a psychiatrist's office in Beverly Hills, in 1971, to see Daniel Ellsberg's reports. Ellsberg, a former government man, purloined highly classified documents about the Vietnam War and turned them over to several newspapers.

Henry Kissinger and the President feared Ellsberg might release other secrets, so the FBI was asked to investigate him. The President was dissatisfied with the pace of the FBI's efforts and sent Hunt and Liddy to California to get results. Neither Nixon nor I knew they would break into the psychiatrist's office. When I heard what they had done, I told them to abort their failed adventure. But calling the cops would have compromised the President's investigation of Ellsberg.

The Watergate break-in happened in June 1972. Nixon decided to postpone dealing with its cover-up (and that of the Beverly Hills break-in) until after the November presidential election. He assumed John Mitchell [CRP campaign director] or Charles Colson [Nixon's special counsel], or both, were involved in Watergate and sought to avoid the political embarrassment it would have caused. That aside, Richard Nixon was a conspiracy

> **Richard Nixon was a conspiracy junkie...Something like the Watergate case attracted him irresistibly. He couldn't leave it alone.**

junkie. He loved to be involved in plots and counterplots. Something like the Watergate case attracted him irresistibly. He couldn't leave it alone.

ON NIXON'S DOWNFALL

Once he had won his November 1972 re-election, Nixon could have put Watergate behind him. Had he made a clean breast of the whole thing as he then knew it, I think the American people would have been happy to forgive and forget. Several people on his staff (including me) urged him to do just that.

But from February to April 1973, he would not come clean. He says now that he believed he was protecting his friends. I think he was simply incapable of admitting his mistakes and delivering himself to his foes.

During that time, the general manager of the cover-up, the President's counsel, John Dean, began to realize that his complex of falsehoods and crimes was unravelling. He systematically blamed others for his own actions. For example, Dean told Liddy to give Howard Hunt orders to 'leave the country.' Later, Dean claimed I had told him to instruct Hunt to flee in the course of a meeting in my office. That is a falsehood, and the other two people at the meeting also say that is false, but Dean's lie persists.

Dean destroyed key documents from Howard Hunt's safe, then he charged that I suggested that he 'deep-six' the safe's contents in the Potomac River. I did not, but his charge lives on. I believe they were papers that incriminated Dean.

Oddly, John Dean has been canonized by journalists for his memory and truthfulness. He has testified under oath about Watergate at least four times and has written a book about it. When these versions are compared with the White House tapes, they are seen to be widely and materially different, but no journalist of the time made such an analysis.

Did I say Pat Gray [Acting Director, FBI] should be left to 'twist slowly in the wind' before a Senate Committee? No. Apparently every 'newsie' in Washington thinks I did, but I didn't. Their readers must think I was callous and hard-hearted. In fact, I was describing what Richard Nixon had done by abandoning Gray's nomination to be FBI director, without formally withdrawing it from the Judiciary Committee.

As Nixon was about to resign, did I 'frantically implore' him to pardon Bob Haldeman and me? No. Not directly or indirectly. I had instructed my attorney that I would not accept a pardon if it were offered. Haldeman and others sought a pardon, but I did not.

ON THE MEDIA'S POWER

Part of the difficulty in erasing such falsehoods is that they were made during the Senate hearings, which were televised over four networks day after day for many weeks. The show attracted a very large audience and saturated the public mind. The result is that the 'facts' charged persist, even though they are untrue.

The landscape of Watergate is littered with errors of fact like that. I have long ago ceased any effort to correct them; I appreciate this opportunity to mention a few. I also look forward to the time when the slapdash newspaper files are forgotten and some solid history of the time becomes available.

Ehrlichman (today, right) feels that the media should reappraise their portrayal of him during the scandal (left).

FOUR

WHITE HOUSE MASSACRE

BATTLE WITH

AS IT BECAME CLEAR THAT A COMPLETE COVER-UP WOULD NOT WORK, SCAPEGOATS HAD TO BE SACRIFICED TO PROTECT THE WHITE HOUSE. HOWEVER, THOSE NOMINATED TO TAKE THE BLAME BEGAN TO LOOK TO THEIR OWN INTERESTS

D ean, Haldeman and Ehrlichman, and President Nixon himself, were all ready to throw Magruder to the wolves. The first three were also prepared to abandon John Mitchell. In Haldeman's term, it was time 'to draw the wagons around the White House.' Nixon still felt some loyalty to his former law-partner, and was afraid that abandoning Mitchell would simply precipitate further trouble. On 22 March 1973, the President told the former Attorney-General: '...I want you all to stonewall it, let them plead the Fifth Amendment, cover-up or anything else if it'll save it – save the plan.'

WHITE HOUSE SCAPEGOAT

Another scapegoat was needed, and the conspirators elected John Dean. He was instructed to prepare a report which would exonerate the President and senior White House staff. John Ehrlichman called it a 'modified, limited hang-

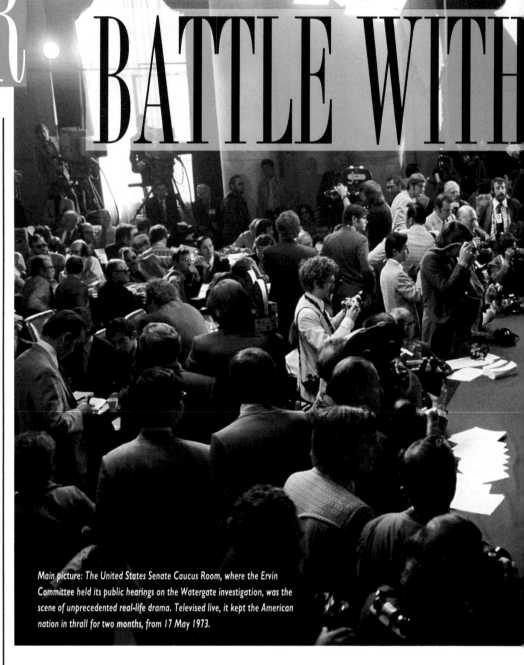

Main picture: The United States Senate Caucus Room, where the Ervin Committee held its public hearings on the Watergate investigation, was the scene of unprecedented real-life drama. Televised live, it kept the American nation in thrall for two months, from 17 May 1973.

out.' In other words, Dean would appear to be wholly candid and, it was hoped, incriminate himself. He was dispatched to the President's official country residence, Camp David, in the Maryland hills north of Washington, on 22 March, to prepare the report. While there, Dean faced his situation. After several days of worry, he called a lawyer. On 3 April, federal prosecutors were told that Dean was ready to talk.

Dean broke the news to Haldeman, who remarked, 'Just remember that once the toothpaste is out of the tube, it's going to be very tough to get it back in.' Dean was not the only rat abandoning ship. Colson and others had hired lawyers, and Magruder was steeling himself to confess.

The public was unaware of all this, but the press was pursuing the case relentlessly. In the

middle of April, Nixon and his remaining loyalists, Haldeman and Ehrlichman, learnt that Magruder, like McCord, was talking to the prosecutors, and realised that the cover-up was close to disintegrating. Mitchell refused to go quietly. He told Ehrlichman that the Watergate affair

> I neither authorised nor encouraged subordinates to engage in illegal or improper campaign activities. That was, and is, the simple truth.
>
> President Nixon, 15 August 1973

CONGRESS

Above: President Nixon eventually had to ditch even his most trusted White House aides, Haldeman and Ehrlichman. Left: Jeb Magruder, Deputy Director of Nixon's re-election committee, was the White House's first choice as scapegoat.

originated in the White House, and that he had been sucked into it. Then Dean gave Ehrlichman a list of the people who would probably go to jail. It included Magruder, Mitchell, Dean, Colson, Haldeman and Ehrlichman.

The last three conspirators – Nixon, Haldeman and Ehrlichman – squirmed about, desperately seeking an escape. Nixon issued a strong statement on 17 April, denouncing wrong-doing. It was not enough. The prosecutors were about to summon Haldeman and Ehrlichman to the grand jury.

LAST ACT OF BETRAYAL

It was now clear to Nixon that he would have to abandon his last two loyalists to save himself. On 29 April, Haldeman and Ehrlichman, and the Attorney-General, Richard Kleindienst, resigned. Dean was sacked. Nixon made the announcement the following day and the Watergate whirlwind engulfed Washington.

The Ervin Committee public hearings began on 17 May 1973. They were held in a grand hall in the Senate office building, known as the Caucus Room, and televised live. For the next two months the whole nation watched, riveted and amazed.

The proceedings were dominated by Senator Ervin himself, a patriarchal figure with a deep southern drawl and expressive eyebrows, who liked to present himself as a small-town lawyer who happened also to be a senator. He was, in fact, a graduate of Harvard Law School and had one of the sharpest brains in the Senate.

There were four Democrats and three Republicans on the Senate Committee. Apart from Ervin, the other Democrats were: Herman Talmadge of Georgia (the only one who was Ervin's intellectual match, and who had an even more pronounced drawl); Daniel Inouye of Hawaii, a Japanese-American, who had lost an arm in the war; and Joseph Montoya, a lightweight from New Mexico.

The senior Republican was Howard Baker of Tennessee, who did his best to protect Nixon while preserving his own reputation. Early in the

Kleindienst, 3 top Nixon aides quit!

...hman, Dean out

Chicago Tribune
THE WORLD'S GREATEST NEWSPAPER
Tuesday, June 26, 1973

*** Final

Nixon had role in coverup, hush money payoffs: Dean

Parochaid ruled illegal by high court

President's 2 key aides also linked

Dean's charges

Above: The headlines spell out the beginning of the end for Richard Nixon. Once his two steadfast co-conspirators and the Attorney-General had been forced to resign, there was nothing to stop the damning revelations from pouring out.

hearings, he started asking witnesses 'What did the President know, and when did he know it?' He hoped to elicit testimony exonerating Nixon. It did not work out like that.

The other Republicans were: Lowell Weicker of Connecticut, an eccentric and independent senator whom Nixon soon added to his list of enemies; and Edward Gurney of Florida, who remained loyal to Nixon until the bitter end.

The hearings began with the minor characters in the plot, but reached the nub of the matter on 14 June, when Jeb Magruder testified. Magruder spelt out the details of the burglary and the cover-up, and laid the blame firmly on John Mitchell and Bob Haldeman. Then the star witness, John Dean, former counsel to the President and operations officer for the cover-up, took the stand on 25 June and the proceedings caught fire.

> *While the President was involved, he did not realise or appreciate at any time the implications of his involvement.*
>
> John Dean to Senate Select Committee, 25 June 1973

Dean wore heavy, horn-rimmed spectacles and peered owlishly up at the seven senators from time to time as he read his 245-page opening statement, and then endured five days of interrogation. His tone was mild, his demeanour respectful, even obsequious, and his testimony was devastating.

SMEAR CAMPAIGN

The White House had mounted an immense public relations effort to discredit Dean in advance. All that was blown away in the Caucus Room. Dean's testimony was a high-point of the entire Watergate affair. Government came to a halt as civil servants, members of Congress and their staffs, plus millions of people across the country, ignored their work to watch the unfolding drama on television.

Dean described in great detail the dozens of conversations he had with President Nixon, plotting the cover-up – Nixon's gloating over the success of the cover-up in September 1972; the occasion when the President admitted discussing a pardon for McCord; the 'cancer within the presidency' conversation in March, when the

Chief burglar, James McCord, explains the bugging system to the Senate hearing. Nixon promised him a pardon, according to John Dean.

Main picture: John Dean was the investigation's star witness. Millions of people were riveted to their television screens as he implicated the President himself. Meanwhile, Haldeman (right) gave nothing away.

President speculated that he could get a million dollars for hush money.

Dean explained the origins of the Watergate burglary, Nixon's list of enemies, the Huston Plan, and the Ellsberg break-in. Baker's question, 'What did the President know and when did he know it?' was answered, and politicians began seriously to talk about impeachment.

The other witnesses did little to retrieve the President's reputation. Mitchell was wholly uncooperative. He claimed to remember nothing, but commented: 'I still believe that the most important thing to this country was the re-election of Richard Nixon. And I was not about to countenance anything that would stand in the way of that re-election.'

FIGHTING BACK

Haldeman gave nothing away. He insisted again and again that the President had known nothing about Watergate, before or after. Ehrlichman, who had often played the good guy in his partnership with Haldeman, fought the committee savagely. At one point, defending the investigations into the private lives of Nixon's 'enemies', he seemed on the brink of revealing some of Congress's dirty secrets, notably members' alcoholism and philandering. Ehrlichman and Haldeman were both teetotal Christian Scientists and insisted on strict sobriety in their staffs.

Political Washington held its breath: two members of the Committee as well as

numerous other influential members of Congress were heavy drinkers. Members of the Committee conspicuously refrained from asking Ehrlichman to name names, and passed to other matters.

In the aftermath of the forced resignations of Haldeman, Ehrlichman and Kleindienst, a new Attorney-General was appointed. He was Elliot Richardson, who had held several senior posts in the Nixon administration, and had just been appointed Secretary of Defence when he replaced Kleindienst. One of Richardson's first moves was the appointment of a special prosecutor –

FINAL

DAILY ⓐ NEWS
NEW YORK'S PICTURE NEWSPAPER ⓐ

Vol. 55. No. 14   New York, N.Y. 10017. Wednesday, July 11, 1973*   15¢

MITCHELL: I WAS IN ON COVERUP

But Didn't Tell Nixon About It; Calls Magruder 'Damnable' Liar

Denies He OKd Break-In

CRP Director and former Attorney-General, John Mitchell, held the loyalty of his old friend, Richard Nixon, until the investigations became too close to the President for comfort. He told the hearing he still believed the most important consideration was the re-electing of the President.

Professor Archibald Cox – to investigate Watergate. Cox was a Democrat from Harvard University, and had been Solicitor General in the Kennedy administration of the early 1960s. From the start Nixon feared and hated him.

SENSATIONAL DISCLOSURE

On 16 July 1973, the Ervin Committee produced a sensational disclosure. A former senior assistant to the President, Alexander Butterfield, testified that there was a taping system in the President's two offices – one in the Executive Office Building (next to the White House), and in the formal Oval Office in the White House – as well as in the cabinet room, and on many White House telephones. It meant that President Nixon could prove his innocence and prove that Dean was lying or, if the President was guilty, the tapes would show it. The Ervin Committee issued a subpoena for five tapes, and Cox subpoenaed nine.

Nixon refused to deliver the tapes to either the Ervin Committee or to Cox. He argued that 'if the special prosecutor should be successful in the attempt to compel disclosure of recordings of Presidential conversations, the damage to the institution of the Presidency will be severe and irreparable.'

NO CONSTITUTIONAL PROTECTION

The Committee and Cox both went to court. It soon emerged that the courts, in the person of Judge Sirica, who had sentenced the Watergate

burglars, were disinclined to intervene between the President and Congress, and rejected the Committee's subpoenas.

The special prosecutor's case was different, however. Cox needed the tapes for a criminal investigation, and the courts agreed that nothing in the Constitution protected the presidency in such circumstances.

COUNTER-ATTACK

Nixon counter-attacked with a series of speeches on Watergate throughout April, and in May and again in mid-August. 'The time has come to turn Watergate over to the courts, and for the rest of us to get on with the urgent business of our nation,' the President said.

After one speech, his press spokesman, Ron Ziegler, stated,

PERSPECTIVE

THE VICES OF A VICE-PRESIDENT

Early in August 1973, President Nixon learned that federal prosecutors in Baltimore were preparing to indict the Vice-President, Spiro Agnew, (right) on charges of accepting bribes. Agnew had risen rapidly from municipal office in the Baltimore suburbs, to Governor of Maryland, to Vice-President. It transpired that he had accepted bribes from Maryland businessmen who wanted state contracts. Some of those payments were made after Agnew became Vice-President, and were delivered in brown envelopes to him personally at the White House.

The scandal became public later in August 1973 and

Agnew resigned on 12 October. He received a suspended prison sentence and a fine. The episode was a further blow to the President; he had the poor judgement to select a crook as a man who might succeed him as president

NIXON AND THE TAPES

An abiding mystery of Watergate is why Nixon did not destroy the notorious White House tapes. One answer is that he made a calamitous misjudgment. His chief of staff, Haldeman, listened to several recordings, and reported that the tapes were, on balance, favourable to the President. Nixon had originally installed the tapes in the belief that they would be his personal property after he left office, and very valuable. He was convinced that he would never be forced to surrender control over them.

By the time the President discovered that the tapes were desperately incriminating, and that refusing to surrender them would bring his impeachment, it was too late to destroy them. After a subpoena had been issued, anyone who tampered with them, let alone destroyed them, would be guilty of obstruction of justice, and would go to jail. The secret servicemen who guarded the tapes would protect the President's life with their own, if necessary, but they would not go to jail for him.

'The President refers to the fact that there is new material; therefore, this is the operative statement. The others are inoperative.' This meant, effectively, that Nixon had been lying.

DESPERATE MEASURES

The President's standing in the polls continued to sink, and public debate concentrated on the tapes. On 29 August, Judge Sirica ruled that Nixon must deliver the tapes to Cox, the special prosecutor. The Appeals Court upheld his rulings.

Nixon resorted to yet another desperate measure. He would prepare a summary of the contents of the nine tapes sought by Cox, and have a respected, elderly Democratic senator, John Stennis of Mississippi, read transcripts of the tapes to make sure the summaries were accurate. Also, Cox would be fired.

On 14 October, the Attorney-General, Elliot Richardson, was ordered by Nixon's new Chief-of-Staff, General Alexander Haig, to fire Cox. Richardson refused. Haig then proposed the Stennis gambit. Would Richardson and Cox accept

Right: The first anniversary of the Watergate break-in – 17 June 1973 – was commemorated by an anti-Nixon march outside the White House. The placards proclaimed the sentiment: Nixon Must Go.

the summaries of the tapes, authenticated by Senator John Stennis? Cox replied that he might, but laid down a series of strict conditions, as did Senators Stennis, Ervin and Baker. But time was against the compromise. The White House needed an immediate reply, because the deadline for appealing to the Supreme Court was close. Cox and Richardson refused to be rushed.

On the evening of Friday, 19 October 1973, the White House announced that the President had ordered Cox to stop subpoenaing White House papers, and gave details of the Stennis plan. The next day, Cox told a press conference why he could not accept these instructions, but that he would not resign.

MASS RESIGNATIONS

Nixon promptly ordered Richardson to fire Cox. Richardson and his deputy, William Ruckelshaus, had agreed that they would resign rather than obey the President's order. The Solicitor-General, Robert Bork, the number three man in the Justice Department, agreed to fire Cox.

Richardson resigned in person at the White House late on the Saturday afternoon. Ruckelshaus resigned over the telephone, to Haig. Bork then fired Cox.

> *A few men gambled that Americans wanted the quiet of efficiency rather than the turbulence of truth*
>
> Senator Lowell Weicker, 17 May 1973

These dramatic and ruthless manoeuvreings, which became known as the Saturday Night Massacre, burst upon the public totally unexpectedly. There was a wild surge of public outrage. Washington was inundated with telegrams and letters denouncing the President. He was accused of overthrowing the Constitution, organising a *coup d'état*, all to protect his guilty secret. The Saturday Night Massacre confirmed the President's guilt over Watergate in public opinion. More importantly, dozens of members of Congress introduced resolutions calling for the President's impeachment.

HERO OR TRAITOR?

RICHARD NIXON, 37TH PRESIDENT OF THE UNITED STATES, WAS OF HUMBLE, SMALL-TOWN ORIGINS. THE CHILDHOOD INSECURITIES WHICH HE RETAINED THROUGHOUT HIS CAREER MADE HIM FRETFUL, SUSPICIOUS, AND TOO EAGER TO DEAL WITH SUPPOSED 'ENEMIES'

R ichard Milhous Nixon was born in January 1913, in Yorba Linda, a farming district about 50 km east of Los Angeles. His father was a dour, strict Methodist from Ohio, who moved to California in search of work. Nixon's mother, Hannah, was a Quaker, and she tried to bring up her children with her faith's pacifist doctrines .

Richard was a second son; his older brother, Harold, died of tuberculosis. Hannah Nixon took Harold and two other tubercular children to Arizona in a vain attempt to save them.

Above: Nixon as a member of Whittier College football team. He has put his love of sports down to 'a highly competitive instinct'. Below left: Young attorney Nixon poses by the door of his law firm, Bewley, Knoop & Nixon.

She was away for three years while Richard was a child, and the insecurities and unhappiness of that time left a permanent mark. Nixon mentioned this in his farewell speech.

He was the son of a bullying failure married to a saint (Nixon's own term). There was no love in his childhood and he grew up insecure and aggressive. At school and university he was always seeking approval from his peers while secretly despising them. He became distrustful, self-reliant, suspicious and vindictive.

He was a good debater at school and, later, at Whittier College in California. From Whittier, he won a scholarship to the Duke University Law School in North Carolina.

At the beginning of World War II, he spent a brief spell as a legal bureaucrat rationing tyres, which left him with a mistrust of bureaucracy. Despite his mother's pacifism, he joined the navy during the War and saw active service in the Pacific.

WITCH-HUNTER

Nixon was elected to Congress in 1946, defeating a liberal Democrat by claiming that his opponent was in the pay of Communist-dominated unions.

During a short and spectacular career in the House of Representatives, he was on the notorious House Un-American Activities Committee and led the witch hunt against alleged Communists. Most memorably, he prosecuted a former senior diplomat, Alger Hiss, who was finally convicted of perjury. The notoriety from the Hiss case allowed him to run for the Senate in California in 1950. He defeated a prominent liberal Democrat, Helen Douglas, relentlessly smearing her as a crypto-Communist.

In 1952, Dwight Eisenhower chose him as Vice-Presidential candidate. Nixon was almost dropped from the ticket when it was discovered that some rich friends had set up a secret fund for him.

'FOLK HERO'

He defended himself in a half-hour television broadcast in which he described his humble

Left: Nixon has won praise for promoting relations with China and the USSR. Here, as Vice-President, he asserts himself at a July 1959 Moscow meeting with Soviet First Secretary Nikita Khrushchev. Below: Nixon in 1973, the year it all began to fall apart for the ambitious Republican from Yorba Linda.

background and honesty: the only gift he had ever accepted, he said, was a dog, 'Checkers', given to his daughters. 'And whatever they say, we are going to keep her'. The speech instantly entered American mythology and, in the process, Nixon won the abiding loyalty of a large class of Americans who saw his success as a model for themselves.

Vice-President Nixon was the Republican's natural choice to oppose John Kennedy in the 1960 presidential election. Kennedy won by the narrowest of margins, amidst allegations of ballot rigging in his favour.

Nixon ran for Governor of California in 1962, and lost. But he was still able to emerge in 1968 as the presidential candidate who best represented the

centre ground of the party. He won the closest election in recent American history, defeating the Democrat's Hubert Humphrey.

NIXON IN PERSPECTIVE

The narrowness of Nixon's defeat in 1960, and of his victory in 1968, reinforced his tendency to 'fight dirty' and also

his insecurity. He craved an overwhelming electoral mandate, and determined that he would do anything to win such a victory in 1972.

Nixon had preserved his early insecurities intact as he scaled the heights of the political system. He retained the instinct to fight back when opposed and to go for the kill immediately.

Whatever his personal faults, Nixon was one of the ablest of recent American presidents. His foreign policy was consistent and far-sighted. He believed in an accommodation with the Soviet Union, and set about negotiating it. The first Strategic Arms Limitation Talks (SALT I) was his work. There have been few moments more dramatic than Nixon's reconciliation meeting with China's Chairman Mao Tse-tung in 1972.

TAXES AND HOUSES

In 1973, a disgruntled Inland Revenue Service employee sent a copy of Nixon's tax returns to the newspapers: the President had paid $792.81 in tax for 1970, $873.03 in 1971, and $4298 in 1972. Nixon had claimed immense deductions, and an indulgent IRS had accepted all of them.

The President had deducted the value of his 'presidential papers' presented to the National Archives. His predecessors, and many other political figures, had done the same thing. However, the law had been changed, and after

July 1969, the value of such gifts could no longer be deducted.

Nixon's staff mismanaged the affair, and the official deed of gift was not signed until after the cut-off point. Nixon still claimed his deductions, $576,000 spread over several years.

Meanwhile, some rich friends had helped him buy two exceedingly expensive houses on the ocean, at San Clemente, just south of Los Angeles, and at Key Biscayne, near Miami. It turned out that arrangements included very substantial gifts that Nixon

should have declared as income. Nixon also charged the government for many luxurious improvements to the houses.

In all, the IRS now calculated that he owed $434,787.13 in back taxes for the years 1969-72, plus interest, bringing the total to nearly half a million dollars. Nixon promised to pay it all, including nearly $150,000 on his 1969 taxes, even though the statute of limitations had run out and he was not legally bound to pay. He then resigned the presidency and forgot the promise.

FIVE RESIGNATION

FATAL

NIXON REFUSED TO ACCEPT THAT THE WHOLE COUNTRY SAW HIM AS A LIAR AND CONSPIRATOR. WHEN THE ULTIMATE DISGRACE BEFELL HIM, HE TRIED TO SALVAGE A LAST SEMBLANCE OF PERSONAL DIGNITY

S o violent was the reaction to the Saturday Night Massacre of 20 October 1973 that Nixon abandoned his opposition to Cox's demands. His new lawyer, James St Clair, announced that the President would release the nine tapes and related materials. 'This President does not defy the law,' St Clair said. The following night, the Soviet Union threatened to intervene in the Middle East War, and Henry Kissinger decided that American forces should be put on alert as a deterrent. Nixon was too distraught to take the decision.

On 1 November 1973, the President nominated a new Attorney General, Senator William Saxbe, and a new Special Prosecutor, Leon Jaworski, a distinguished conservative Democratic lawyer from Texas. However, another of the President's lawyers, Fred Buzhardt, revealed that two of the subpoenaed tapes did not exist.

One of the missing tapes was of a telephone conversation between Nixon and Mitchell on 20 June 1972, their first after the Watergate burglary. The other was a meeting between the President

DATEFILE

JULY 24 1974

Supreme Court orders Nixon to hand over vital Watergate tapes

JULY 27-30 1974

House of Representatives passes three articles of impeachment

AUGUST 9 1974

President Nixon officially resigns

JULY – AUGUST '74

and Dean on 15 April 1973, at which, according to Dean, Nixon had admitted that he had discussed a pardon for the Watergate burglars. Most suspected that Nixon had destroyed the two tapes.

GAP IN THE TAPES

There was worse to come. On 15 November 1973, Nixon assured a group of senators that there were no more surprises about the tapes. A week later, Buzhardt informed Judge Sirica that there was an inexplicable eighteen and a half-minute gap on the tape of a conversation between Nixon and

Haldeman on 20 June 1972, the result of an accident. No one believed it.

Acoustic experts established that the missing portion had been deliberately erased by at least five, and possibly as many as nine, 'separate and contiguous' erasures. Someone had ineptly swept the tape with the record button.

Nixon once again retreated and sent a further batch of 14 tapes to Sirica. These included the tape of the 21 March 1973 meeting in which Dean spoke of a 'cancer' within or near the presidency, and Nixon had ordered him to make further payments to the burglars.

EVIDENCE

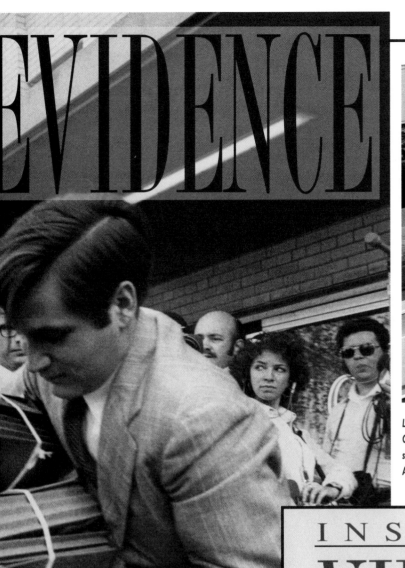

Left: Edited transcripts of 46 subpoenaed White House tapes being delivered to the House Judiciary Committee on 30 April 1974. From an earlier despatch of transcripts, it became evident that there was a sizeable gap in a June 1972 conversation between Nixon and Haldeman.

Above: The President's secretary, Rose Woods, explaining how she 'accidentally caused the erasure'.

Throughout the autumn of 1973, Nixon conducted a public relations campaign, labelled 'Operation Candor'. He travelled the country making speeches. 'I am not a crook,' he told a group of newspaper proprietors in Disney World, Florida. Nixon also released details of his finances and taxes. Nothing worked. Operation Candor was abandoned.

Sirica examined the surviving tapes, and passed them over to Jaworski, the Special Prosecutor, in December 1973. On 6 February 1974, the House of Representatives voted by 410-4 to give its Judiciary Committee the powers it

INSIDE

VIEW

THE 'SMOKING GUN' TAPES

The picture (right) shows a Capitol policeman guarding the equipment on which tapes were played to the impeachment inquiry. Extracts from tapes of three meetings between Nixon and his Chief of Staff, Bob Haldeman, on 23 June 1972, a week after the Watergate burglary, proved that Nixon had approved a plan to block the FBI investigation at the outset.

H. Now on the investigation, you know, the Democratic break-in thing, we're back in the problem area because the FBI is not under control...they've been able to trace the money – not through the money itself but through the bank sources – the banker. And, and it goes in some directions we don't want it to go...

P. ...Of course, this Hunt, that will uncover a lot of things. You open that scab, there's a hell of a lot of things, and we feel that it would be very detrimental to have this thing go any further...Is it Liddy? ...He must be a little nuts.

H. He is...

P. When you get in [unintelligible] people, say 'Look, the problem is that this will open the whole, the whole Bay of Pigs thing, and the President just feels, ah, without going into the details – don't, don't lie to them to the extent to say no involvement, just say this is a comedy of errors...They should just call the FBI in and [unintelligible] don't go any further into this case period!'

needed to investigate the President and prepare a case for impeaching him.

On 1 March 1974, Mitchell, Haldeman, Ehrlichman, Colson and three others were indicted for the Watergate break-in and cover-up. The grand jury also named Nixon as an 'unindicted co-conspirator'. Jaworski kept that decision secret.

On 11 April 1974, the House Judiciary Committee formally asked the White House for 42 tapes, setting a deadline for 25 April (it was then extended for another five days). On 16 April, Jaworski asked Sirica to subpoena the White House for a further 64 tapes. This Sirica did two days later.

The President's last counter-offensive was

> *There are frightening implications for the future of our country if we do not impeach the President.*
>
> Representative Caldwell Butler,
> 25 July 1974

launched on 29 April 1974, exactly a year after Haldeman and Ehrlichman resigned. The President announced on television that he was releasing transcripts of most of the subpoenaed tapes. The President said, 'As far as what the President personally knew and did with regard to Watergate and the cover-up is concerned, these materials, together with those already made available, will tell it all.' The next day, the White House put out 1254 pages of transcript, covering 46 tapes in all.

AUDIBLE AND RELEVANT

It was another disaster. The press selected excerpts to illustrate the most damning aspects of Nixon's involvement in the cover-up. Dean was vindicated. The House Judiciary Committee, which had the originals of 19 tapes, released its own transcript that showed the White House had been very selective. Many passages described as inaudible or 'irrelevant to Watergate' turned out to be very audible and highly relevant. Nixon's language was foul. The phrase 'expletive deleted' entered the language.

The Committee issued a new subpoena for more tapes, including one of a meeting between Nixon and Haldeman on 23 June 1972. After checking the tape himself, Nixon then flatly refused to hand it over.

The Watergate crisis reached a new peak on 24 July 1974 when the Supreme Court, the country's highest judicial body, ruled on the legal contest for the tapes. Chief Justice Warren Burger conceded that executive privilege, which Nixon invoked,

With impeachment proceedings under way, Nixon was told by senior Republicans that he had little support in the Senate. Amidst demonstrations and counter-demonstrations (main picture), the President 'resigned' on the following evening – 8 August 1974 – with a emotional televised address to the nation (right).

handling of Watergate, the basic fact remains that when all the facts were brought to my attention, I insisted on a full investigation and prosecution of those guilty.' It was a lie.

The President's son-in-law, Edward Cox, told a Republican senator that Nixon had taken to wandering the corridors of the White House, making speeches to pictures of dead presidents. Perhaps he was suicidal. Haig made sure there were no pills available and later, the Secretary of Defence, James Schlesinger, issued a directive to the armed forces that any orders from the White House should be ignored unless issued by Schlesinger himself. He was afraid Nixon might attempt a military coup.

LITTLE SENATE SUPPORT

On the afternoon of Wednesday, 7 August 1974, Senator Barry Goldwater, who was revered as the Grand Old Man of American conservatism, and other senior Republicans, went to the White House. Goldwater told Nixon that he could count on no more than 16 or 18 votes in the Senate, and that he would vote against the President himself. Nixon needed 34 votes to avoid impeachment.

Haldeman and Ehrlichman sent frantic messages to Nixon, imploring him to pardon

---

'cannot prevail over the fundamental demands of due process of law in the fair administration of criminal justice.' Courts had a right to the evidence they needed in criminal cases. The Supreme Court ordered Nixon to hand over the 64 tapes which the Special Prosecutor had demanded. The ruling was unanimous.

It was a devastating, fatal defeat for the President. Nixon had hoped there would be 'some air in the decision,' some ambiguity allowing him to procrastinate further. If he refused to obey the Supreme Court, he would be impeached.

Fearing the worst, he had instructed his lawyer Fred Buzhardt to listen to the 'smoking gun' tape of 23 June 1972. It was the first time Nixon had allowed anyone to do so. The tape proved that Nixon was in the cover-up from the beginning.

On the evening of 24 July 1974, after eight hours of hesitation, Nixon announced that he would comply with the Supreme Court ruling. Half an hour later, the House Judiciary Committee began its debate on impeachment.

There were 21 Democrats and 17 Republicans on the Committee. Each was allowed to speak for 15 minutes. The whole nation watched television as Congressmen – some liberal, some died-in-the-wool conservatives – unfolded their thoughts on the Watergate crisis.

On 27 July, the Committee voted on Article I. It charged Nixon with obstructing justice and thus failing 'to take care that the laws be faithfully executed.' The words come from the oath taken by presidents on their inauguration. The article was approved by 27 votes to 11. The Committee later approved two other articles of impeachment.

By now, Nixon's closest advisers had listened to the 23 June tape, and unanimously advised him to resign. On 5 August 1974, the fatal transcripts were released.

In his last attempt to save himself, Nixon issued a statement on the same day saying, '...Whatever mistakes I made in the

---

IMPEACHING A PRESIDENT

The guiding principle of the United States Constitution is the separation of powers. Congress passes laws, the courts clarify and explain them, and the President enforces them. The President is elected for a fixed, four-year term, and can only be removed from office by impeachment. The process is laid down by the Constitution and, before 1974, had been invoked only once, against President Andrew Johnson (right) in 1868, for removing the Secretary of War without the Senate's approval. Johnson was acquitted by a one-vote majority in the Senate.

First, the House of Representatives must rule that the President has a case to answer. Then he is tried before the Senate, and can be convicted

on a two-thirds majority. The Constitution provides a sweeping definition of the offences for which a President may be impeached. He must be found guilty of 'Treason, Bribery, or other High Crimes and Misdemeanors.'

Nixon made his final farewells as President on the morning of August 9 – he officially resigned at noon. Before entering the presidential helicopter that was to take him home, he turned for one last populist gesture (above).

a strong enough political base in the Congress to justify continuing the effort,' he explained. He would prefer to fight to the end but, in the national interest, he would resign.

'I regret deeply any injuries that may have been done in the course of the events that led to this decision, Nixon said. 'I would say only that if some of my judgments were wrong – and some were wrong – they were made in what I believed at the time to be the best interest of the nation.' It was the closest Nixon got to an apology.

LAST CEREMONY

There was one last ceremony. The following morning, Friday, 9 August 1974, Nixon said his last farewell to his colleagues in the East Room of the White House. It was televised live. In a rambling, maudlin speech that sometimes sank into self-pity, Nixon gave final advice to his countrymen: 'Those who hate you don't win unless you hate them, and then you destroy yourself.' It was his own epitaph.

The President walked out to the back lawn and mounted the presidential helicopter for the last time, to begin the humiliating flight home to California. He turned, on the top of the steps, to wave at the crowd staring at him, and for a last time raised his arms in the air in the V-for-Victory sign – this time at the moment of his defeat.

them before leaving office. His lawyers scotched any such idea.

The President took his family on a last trip down the Potomac, on the presidential yacht, on the evening of 7 August. At about midnight, Kissinger visited him and Nixon broke down, weeping and beating his head on the carpet. Haig passed the word to Vice-President Ford that he should prepare to take power.

On the afternoon of Thursday, 8 August, the White House announced that the President would address the nation on television that evening. He summoned Congressional leaders, the Cabinet, and his personal staff, to a series of meetings to tell them of his decision. Many of his staff wept. Finally, at 9pm, he faced the camera in the Oval Office for the last time. 'I no longer have

CLOSE-UP THE PARDON

Nixon's resignation took the form of a one-sentence letter to the Secretary of State, Henry Kissinger. It took effect at noon, Washington time, on 9 August 1974. Gerald Ford (above) was sworn in that afternoon.

The most important issue remaining was what to do with ex-President Nixon? He was clearly guilty of directing the Watergate cover-up, a crime for which his closest advisers were about to be put on trial. Nixon belonged in the dock, with Haldeman, Ehrlichman and Mitchell. Indeed, he was more guilty than they.

President Ford resolved the dilemma on 8 September by issuing a comprehensive pardon for Nixon for any crimes 'which he has committed or may have committed' during his presidency. Ford was much criticised for pardoning his predecessor, but his leniency spared Americans the embarrassment of seeing a man they had elected president put on trial.

Chicago Tribune ···Final

Pardon for Nixon

Ex-President has suffered enough: Ford

THE GREAT TRAIN ROBBERY

On 8 August, 1963, a Royal Mail train was robbed of over £2,500,000. The crime was unique, not only in its remarkable execution but also in the severity of the life sentences meted out – in most cases from 20 to 30 years. It seemed, to the train robbers at least, that they had been made the victims of heavy-handed retribution; if the authorities could not have the stolen money back, they would be certain to have their pound of flesh.

Wanted poster issued by police, August 1963.

METROPOLITAN POLICE

On the 8th August, 1963, the Glasgow to Euston mail train was robbed of about two and a half million pounds.

Substantial rewards will be paid to persons giving such information as will lead to the apprehension and conviction of the persons responsible.

The assistance of the public is sought to trace the whereabouts of the after described persons:

RONALD EDWARDS alias RONALD CHRISTOPHER EDWARDS, also known as "BUSTER," aged 32, florist club owner, 5ft. 6in., stocky build, complexion fresh, hair dark brown, eyes brown, London accent, scar left of nose and right forearm.

JUNE ROSE EDWARDS, alias ROTHERY, aged 30, 5ft. 3in., hair black. May be accompanied by daughter NICOLETTE, aged about 3 years.

BARBARA MARIA DALY, née ALLAN, aged 22, 5ft. 1in., hair brown. May be pregnant and accompanied by daughter LORRAINE PATRICIA, aged 1 year.

JOHN THOMAS DALY, aged 31, born at New Ross, Eire, antique dealer, 5ft. 11in., complexion fresh, hair dark brown (wavy), eyes blue, scar right of forehead.

BRUCE RICHARD REYNOLDS, alias RAYMOND ETTERIDGE and GEORGE RACHEL, aged 31, born London, motor and antique dealer, 6ft. 2in., complexion fresh, hair light brown, eyes grey (may be wearing horn-rimmed or rimless spectacles), slight cleft in chin, scar left eyelid, cheek and right forearm.

FRANCES REYNOLDS, aged about 24, 5ft. 4in., slim build, hair brown.

ROY JOHN JAMES, aged 27, born London, silversmith, 5ft. 6in., medium to slim build, complexion fresh, hair light brown, eyes hazel. Is a racing car driver.

JAMES EDWARD WHITE, alias JAMES BRYAN and JAMES EDWARD WHITEFOOT, inset many aliases, aged 43, born Paddington, London, cafe proprietor, 5ft. 10in., slim build, complexion sallow, hair and eyes brown, may wear moustache, Royal Artillery crest tattooed right forearm.

SHEREE WHITE, aged 30 to 35, 5ft. 6in., complexion light coffee-coloured, hair dark brown. May have 6 months old baby and be accompanied by white miniature poodle dog called "GIGI."

Persons having information are asked to telephone WHItehall 1212 or the nearest Police Station.

CRIME OF THE

AT 3.27AM ON THURSDAY, 8 AUGUST 1963, £2,631,684 WAS STOLEN FROM A HI-JACKED MAIL TRAIN, NEAR THE VILLAGE OF CHEDDINGTON. WITH ITS SPEED, MILITARY PRECISION AND SINGLE-MINDED BRUTALITY, THE CRIME WAS TO FIRE THE IMAGINATION OF PEOPLE THROUGHOUT THE WORLD

The light was already fading when the Royal Mail train drew away from Glasgow Central station shortly before 7pm on Wednesday, 7 August 1963. It was carrying over £2 million in bank notes. Inside, 72 postal sorters had bolted the coaches and begun sorting the 100 mailbags loaded on at Glasgow. Packed inside the bags were thousands of packets of £5 and £1 notes, dispatched by banks in Scotland to their London head offices, as well as ordinary packages and post.

The train twisted away from Glasgow, making its way south. It gradually gathered speed and crossed the border into England, picking up more mailbags and coaches. Slowly, the bags of bank notes were separated and sent to the second coach from the front of the train, known as the 'High Value Package' (HVP) coach, where they were stacked in locked cupboards.

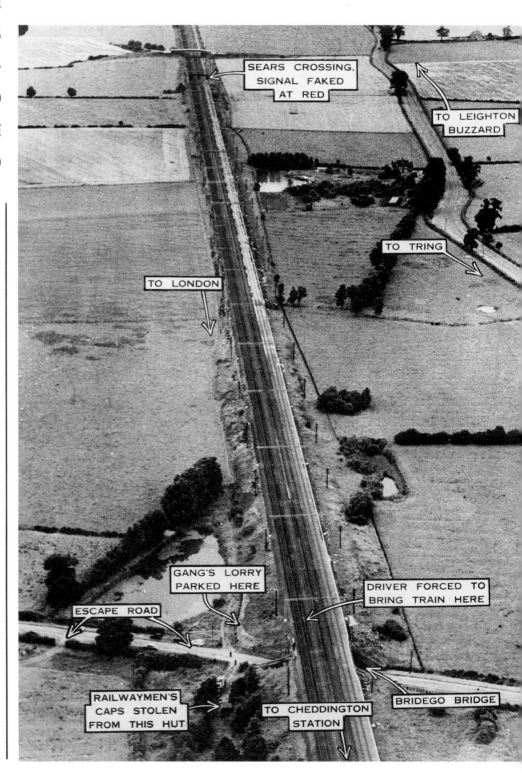

SEARS CROSSING, SIGNAL FAKED AT RED

TO LEIGHTON BUZZARD

TO TRING

TO LONDON

GANG'S LORRY PARKED HERE

DRIVER FORCED TO BRING TRAIN HERE

ESCAPE ROAD

RAILWAYMEN'S CAPS STOLEN FROM THIS HUT

TO CHEDDINGTON STATION

BRIDEGO BRIDGE

DATEFILE

AUGUST 7 1963
7pm – Royal Mail train leaves Glasgow for London.

AUGUST 8 1963
1.30am – The robbers arrive at Bridego Bridge.

AUGUST 8 1963
3.03am – The Royal Mail train is halted by a red signal at Sears Crossing.

AUGUST 8 1963
3.27am – The robbers get away with £2,631,634.

AUG 7 - AUG 8

CENTURY

Far left: Aerial view of the stretch of track where the Royal Mail train was halted and robbed.
Below left: The train left Glasgow Station with old mail coaches. New anti-bandit models were out of action on the night of 7 August.
Left: Driver Mills, who suffered head wounds in the robbery.

Both Mills and Whitby were slightly puzzled by the sight of a green light in the far distance. Whitby got down onto the path to look for one of the telephones which were installed at the foot of every signal box. It was customary, whenever a Home Signal showed red, for the crew to telephone the nearest signalman – in this case at Cheddington Station – to check that there was no signal failure.

AMBUSH

Whitby located a telephone on the side of the tracks closest to the B488 road. On the other side of the signal gantry, five masked men in blue boiler suits, gripping pick-axes and coshes, silently crouched down. As Whitby picked up the telephone, two more hooded figures emerged noiselessly from the thickets on his side of the tracks and moved to the coupling between the HVP coach and the third van.

Above: Fireman David Whitby stepped down from the Royal Mail train to investigate the red signal. He tried to telephone from Sears Crossing. He found the lines cut and himself a prisoner.

The telephone line was dead. Whitby saw that the wires were cut. Surprised, but not suspicious, he shouted to Mills and began walking back along the path. As he did so, he noticed the figure of a man standing behind the HVP coach. Whitby thought it must be one of the postal workers.

Close to midnight, the train picked up more mailbags at Crewe, where a new driver, 57-year-old veteran Jack Mills, and his fireman, David Whitby, took over. The train left Crewe on schedule at 12.30am.

MOVING INTO POSITION

At the same time, over 100 miles to the south, two Land Rover jeeps and a three-ton army lorry drove slowly down a track from an isolated farmhouse near Oakley, Buckinghamshire. The convoy turned left onto the unlit B4011 route and headed east.

There were 16 men in the vehicles. The majority wore army uniforms, but this was not an unusual sight as there was a military base nearby at Bicester. The convoy kept to quiet lanes, winding through the sleeping villages of Wingrave, Whitchurch and Chilton.

By 1.30am, the convoy had ended its 27-mile journey and parked by a railway bridge on a deserted lane north of the village of Cheddington. The men put blue boiler suits over their uniforms and collected pick-axes and a crowbar from a nearby workman's hut.

On the mail train, the sorters were working flat out. At 3am when they passed through Leighton Buzzard, there were 128 bags of bank notes locked inside the HVP coach. In the cab, Mills and Whitby finished their last mug of tea. They were only 40 miles from Euston.

The train passed Linslade. Mills saw that a small signal up ahead, known as a 'Distant Signal', was showing amber – a simple warning to a driver that the next signal, 'the Home Signal', would show red, the halt sign.

MYSTERIOUS SIGNAL

Mills slowly braked the 2000-horsepower diesel and peered down the track. The Home Signal was 1300 yards further on at Sears Crossing bridge. There, on the signal gantry, the red light was lit up. The train pulled to a halt in the silent, deserted countryside, its diesel throbbing and headlamps shining down the track. The time was 3.03am.

Above: Roger Cordrey altered the signal at the Sears Crossing gantry to show red. John Daly altered the preceding Dwarf signal to amber, in accordance with British Railways procedures warning a train that a red signal is imminent.
Below: The severed telephone lines at Sears Crossing where David Whitby tried to telephone the signal box to question the red signal.

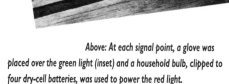

Above: At each signal point, a glove was placed over the green light (inset) and a household bulb, clipped to four dry-cell batteries, was used to power the red light.

'What's up, mate?' he called. There was no answer. The figure silently beckoned the fireman over. Whitby crossed the tracks and, in an instant, was grabbed and flung down onto the embankment, where two masked men wearing gloves pinned down his legs and neck. One held a cosh above the fireman's face.

'If you make a noise, son, you're dead,' he breathed.

'All right, mate,' said Whitby, adding, in fear: 'I'm on your side.' The man who had jumped Whitby now ran towards the engine, breaking silence to summon the squad hiding at the gantry.

Mills, sensing commotion, had looked out of the cab only to be confronted by the masked

Keep your mouths shut... there are some right bastards here.

Robber to Mills and Whitby

attacker, who raised a cosh and tried to storm the 10-foot-high ladder to the cab. Mills blocked his ascent by kicking the attacker's hands every time he got a grip on the rung.

Suddenly the darkness was full of hooded men in boiler suits, eyes glaring through balaclava eye slits or stockinged masks as they leapt onto the cab, brandishing clubs. One pushed the first attacker up the steps as two more burst through the door.

Mills was gripped, pinioned from behind and clubbed viciously on the top of his skull. He collapsed onto his seat, blood seeping down his face. One of the raiders picked up a rag and wiped some of the blood away. More hooded men in boiler-suits emerged from the darkness, racing towards the engine. At the rear of the HVP coach, two men quickly decoupled the diesel and front two coaches from the rest of the train and unscrewed the vacuum pipe.

There was no sign of alarm from inside the HVP coach. Brief delays were common and the five HVP sorters were still hard at work. The

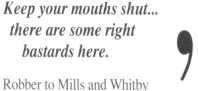

Above: The Royal Mail's relief driver shows police how the robbers uncoupled the train. The robbers' getaway driver, Roy James learned how to do this from a book and then by practising in railway sheds, furtively at night. The knowledge was shared with Jimmy White who acted as back-up.

parcels coach, immediately behind the engine, was locked and unoccupied and there was no passageway linking the locomotive to the HPV coach.

Moving swiftly and quietly, the raiders bundled Whitby into the cab, pulled the bleeding Mills out of his seat and roughly handcuffed the two men together. The two were then hauled towards the narrow passageway alongside the fan room in the centre of the engine.

At the same time, an elderly man was escorted out of the darkness and led up into the cab. The glimpse of the wounded, trussed-up driver visibly unnerved him. Trembling, he sat down and operated the driver's controls. The engine rumbled but did not move. Inside the packed cab, the mood was electric. 'Move it,' snapped a tall, powerful man in a balaclava, lifting a truncheon.

SINISTER THREATS

The old man, by now extremely agitated, pleaded that the brakes were blocked. The attacker would not listen. He grabbed the old man by the shoulders, and dragged him away from the controls. 'Get the other driver,' he snapped. Pale and shaken, Mills was untied and shoved back into the cab. 'Move this train or you'll get some stick,' said the man who appeared to be in charge. Mills revved

the engine, but the brakes were still locked. 'Move this train,' the man repeated venomously.

Mills protested that the vacuum pipes operating the brakes were not working – they had been unscrewed when the train was decoupled – but then the engine heaved forward and another man in a balaclava stepped up to Mills. 'Don't worry, mate,' he said, 'no one's going to hurt you now.'

There was a tearing sound as the steam pipe and concertina covering linking the HVP and third coaches were torn apart. Inside the HVP coach, the senior Post Office sorter, Frank Dewhurst, realising the train had broken up, pulled the communication cord and waited. Ten coaches, with 67 postal sorters working inside, were left standing in the darkness.

DISAPPEARING COACHES

In the rear of the last coach, the 61-year-old guard, Thomas Miller, saw from his brake-vacuum gauge that something was wrong. Climbing down from the train, he walked along the side of the track and was astonished to see that the locomotive and first two coaches had disappeared. He ran to the gantry telephone but, seeing that the wires had been cut, he turned round and began to walk north towards Leighton Buzzard – away from the action in the locomotive and HPV coach – in order to place warning detonators on the track to alert any approaching trains.

The raider leading the assault was leaning out of the cab as Mills slowly guided the engine forward half a mile ahead to a point marked by a

VIEW

CASING THE COACH

The train robbers got away with £2,631,684 – worth 10 times as much in 1990 – in the first ambush of a Royal Mail train in 125 years of the service. The plot certainly depended on inside information, and possibly even sabotage. The serial numbers of only about £15,000-worth of notes were recorded and the bulk of the huge theft was untraceable.

Three new anti-bandit coaches were out of action – two with hot axles, one with a damaged wheel – on the night of 7 August. Older rolling stock was used, protected only by interior bolts and padlocks on the cupboards in the High Value Package coach.

Security experts concluded that the anti-bandit coaches would have taken up to 20 minutes longer to break into with the axes and blunt instruments used by the robbers. There is no proof that they carried dynamite or firearms; they were probably informed that the older coaches (below) were in use. At Glasgow, the mailbags were loaded in view of anyone holding a platform ticket and the trains carried no police officers or armed guards. A rail guard travelled in the rear coach, but the HVP coach was always located

Left: The ransacked interior of the High Value Package van. The GPO sorters were shepherded into a corner and told they would be shot if they 'tried anything'.

Below: The communicating door at the rear of the High Value Packet van through which the robbers forced their entry.

white sheet laid down by the track in front of Bridego Bridge.

'Okay, stop,' he said. The train halted. 'On again,' came the order.

'Well, make up your minds,' Mills snapped. This time the front of the locomotive was exactly at the marker. The tension inside the cab eased slightly. Two men – one tall and slim, the other plump – could be seen standing calmly on the bridge.

'Well done, chaps,' the tall one said crisply, 'Well done.' Mills and Whitby were bundled back to the embankment and told to lie face down. Their minder let them smoke, and accepted Whitby's offer of a cigarette.

'For God's sake, keep your mouths shut,' the minder said. 'There are some right bastards here.'

As he spoke, the quiet was shattered by the crash of splintering glass and wood. One of the hooded raiders was hacking his way into the back of the HVP coach with an axe, another attacked the window with a crowbar, two more forced the

windows with coshes. Dewhurs, the senior sorter, tried to barricade the doors but heard a voice shout, 'They're bolting the doors, get the guns!'

SMASH AND GRAB

Moments later, one masked man burst into the coach, then another, then more and more raced in, as the five sorters were chased to one end of the coach, coshed on the shoulders and ordered to lie face down.

One robber grabbed the axe and smashed the padlock on the cupboards with a single blow. Another, the man who had menaced the driver in his cab, snatched a mailbag, slit it with a sheath-knife, then cut open one of the packages. 'This is it,' he breathed.

Silently, without orders, the robbers formed a chain stretching from the wrecked HVP coach through the darkness on the bridge

PERSPECTIVE

HIGHWAY ROBBERY

The Royal Mail attack evoked comparisons with the 18th-century 'highwayman' Dick Turpin, the most glamorised villain in English folklore. Born at Hempstead in Essex, Turpin robbed scores of travellers at gunpoint on lonely country roads, often in Epping Forest. He committed two murders and was executed in 1738. In legend, he is usually portrayed with a black horse, eye masks, cocked hat and the cry of 'Stand and Deliver !'

In the US, the robbery was compared to the 19th-century 'Wild West' robbers, such as Jesse James, as well as to more recent efforts of organised crime. The *New York Times* commented, tongue-in-cheek: 'How pallid our own crime syndicates are made to look, how wanting in imagination ...The know-how is distinctly British. Or were some enterprising members of the American underworld there in a patriotic effort to help even out our balance of international payments?'

Right: Part of the Royal Mail train was taken to Euston Station in London after the robbery. The engine and two High Value Package coaches were left at Bridego Bridge to be examined by police for fingerprints. None was found.

and down the embankment to a stone wall by the lane, where the 3-ton lorry was parked on a grass border, close to a pond. Dozens of heavy bags passed swiftly down the line. It was strenuous work, and even the strongest of the robbers became exhausted with the sheer number of bags.

GETAWAY

'That's enough,' the tall man at the bridge ordered suddenly. There were seven mailbags full of bank notes still left inside the HVP coach; it would have only taken a few more minutes to clear the van completely, but no one argued with the command. Mills and Whitby, handcuffed to each other, were hauled into the HVP coach and left lying face down with the sorters. 'Don't move for half an hour or we'll be back,' someone told them. 'We've got a look-out. If you move, you'll be killed.'

The gang raced off, piling into the lorry and Land Rovers. One mailbag was left on the embankment, but no one went back for it. The dismembered train stood by the bridge, while the rest of its coaches waited half a mile away. The convoy drove away back west towards the farm near Oakley. The man in charge at the bridge was sitting in the front Land Rover, listening for police bulletins on a VHF radio. It was getting light but there was little traffic on the roads.

The time was 3.27am. In 24 minutes, the gang had pulled off the biggest train robbery the world had ever seen.

Left: Bridego Bridge, near Cheddington, where the robbers forced driver Mills to take the broken mail train. On the road beneath the bridge, only 15 feet from the track, the getaway vehicles waited.

THE ROYAL MAIL

Mail trains have been running in Britain since 1838, when the first 'Travelling Post Office,' a converted horse-box (below), was drawn between Birmingham and Liverpool. This led to an Act of Parliament authorising the transport of post by rail, although mail had been sent privately on the Liverpool & Manchester Railway as early as 1830. The *Irish Mail*, the oldest named train in the world, began services in 1848.

By 1963, Royal Mail trains ran on 40 networks around Britain. The Glasgow-London train, known as the 'Up Special', left the Scottish capital at the same time every midweek evening.

The largest load of bank notes was always a day or two after August Bank Holiday. Scottish traders paid in their takings, leaving the banks with more notes than they needed. The surplus was sent to London in 'high value' packets of up to £5000 each.

TRAVELLING POST-OFFICE, ON THE LONDON AND BIRMINGHAM RAILWAY.

COMPANY OF

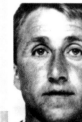

The bandits who robbed the Royal Mail train of more than £2,500,000 were a merger of two successful gangs operating in southern England. Although the larger outfit, led by Bruce Reynolds, did not need more manpower, it did require the expertise of the smaller unit in halting and robbing trains.

REYNOLDS' GANG

Reynolds' outfit, based mainly in south-west London, included Gordon Goody and Buster Edwards. It had carried out the London Airport 'City Gents' raid in 1962 (see Backdrop, p298) and had a flair for surprise and split-second timing.

Among the other members of Reynolds' crew was Charlie Wilson, 31, violently single-minded when fired up for crime, yet charming and warm-hearted when relaxed. It was also Wilson who tried to comfort driver Mills, saying no further harm would come to him. It was Wilson also who was first into the HVP coach.

Jimmy White, 44, a former paratrooper, owned a café in south London and was a master lock-breaker. Usually a solitary thief, he was to act as quartermaster. On the night of the robbery, he wore his old uniform sporting the maxim 'Who Dares, Wins' – famous as the motto of the Special Air Service Regiment.

Roy James, 28, was a silversmith by trade but also a racing driver of rare quality. Short and boyish-looking, James had won a succession of leading events against top-class drivers and was the getaway driver for Reynolds' high-speed set pieces.

Jim Hussey, 31, was a painter from south-east London who provided simple force, but was self-possessed and remained calm under pressure. Like most of the train robbers, he was considered amiable company.

John Daly, 32, Reynolds' Irish brother-in-law, was an antiques dealer with a sense of roguery. Believing Daly would bring luck to the team, Reynolds gave him an all-purpose role.

A TOUCH OF CLASS

Bruce Reynolds, the leader of the south-west London gang, was a tall, suave 32-year-old with a taste for stylish living. The son of a trade unionist, he looked down on pubs, preferring to be seen in dark glasses, parking his sports car outside elegant hotels. An imaginative planner, Reynolds seemed mild-natured and had many law-abiding friends.

Reynolds boasted of having been the youngest major in the British army, but in fact had deserted as a private. He had served jail sentences for theft since his late teens but, by 1963, he had become the leader of a band of robbers who were disciplined but also capable of brutality if they saw the need for it.

It was Reynolds who, on 8 August, stood by Bridego Bridge congratulating his troops, and it was his unchallenged word which ended the operation.

Ronnie Biggs, 34, was a small-time thief working as a carpenter in Redhill, Surrey, and married to a respectable young wife. Reynolds liked the amiable Biggs well enough but held his criminal skills in near-contempt. Biggs demanded a role in the robbery as his reward for introducing Reynolds to the retired railway driver, but he was disliked by all the other robbers.

WISBEY'S GANG

The second, smaller gang had less audacity and polish, but they were specialists in wages

THIEVES

Members of Reynolds' gang, pictured from left to right: Ronald 'Buster' Edwards, James Hussey, Charles Wilson, James White, Roy James and Ronnie Biggs. Below: Bruce Reynolds, left, pictured in the sort of smart nightclub he liked to frequent, with his wife Frances and Barbara Daly, the wife of fellow gang member John Daly, far right of picture. The photograph was issued by police on 30 August 1963.

THE MASTERMIND

The legend that a criminal mastermind planned the Great Train Robbery took root immediately after the raid, adding to the mystique of what was, in reality, a brutal assault. This shadowy figure is said to have devised the overall strategy, head-hunted the men to carry it off, and received an enormous share of the stolen millions.

A retired Scotland Yard detective, John Gosling, in his book *The Great Train Robbery* (1964, with Dennis Craig), wrote that the mastermind was a distinguished Scottish former soldier known to the robbers as 'Johnny Rainbow'. Some of the robbers themselves were to allege in Piers Paul Read's *The Train Robbers* (1978) that an 'Ulsterman' was the brains behind the robbery.

Generally, criminal plans do the rounds before they are taken up, and one theory is that Bruce Reynolds heard of the undefended 'High Value Package' coach in prison. Detective Superintendent Malcolm Fewtrell, who led the Buckinghamshire inquiry, believed, however, that Reynolds, Goody, Edwards and Welch were intelligent enough to have plotted the robbery without a mastermind.

Members of the Wisbey gang from south-east London, from left to right: Robert Welch, Roger Cordrey and Thomas Wisbey. Their use to Reynolds was their experience of wage snatches from trains.

THE LONER

snatches from trains travelling along the London-Brighton routes in Sussex.

Thomas Wisbey, 34, was the gang leader who ran a London betting shop, wore sporty jackets and had wavy, slicked-down hair. He had done a stint in the Royal Army Service Corps some years previously without a blemish to his record.

Roger Cordrey, 41, shifty and cautious, had the vital know-how of manipulating rail signals, without which the mail-train robbery would not have been at all possible. Unhappily married with four children, and a florist by trade, Cordrey had become a heavy gambler who looked older than his age. His marriage problems had been a major distraction to him on the night of 8 August.

Robert Welch was an intense, highly-strung 35-year-old, very tall, and with a powerful, lean physique. An all-rounder on Wisbey's team, he remained suspicious of Reynolds' crew.

Of the three other robbers at the train robbery, two were from Reynolds' 'firm' and one from the south-eastern outfit. However, they have never been publicly identified.

Gordon Goody (right), a thin, inscrutable man of 34, was the most quietly menacing of the robbers. Like Reynolds, he needed a challenge – one that would win applause as well as profit. A hairdresser, Goody took immense pride in his clothes, buying shirts and suits in Jermyn Street, London's high-class tailoring centre. Very much a loner, he shied away from loud places where coarser villains collected. He lived at his Irish mother's home in Putney, south London.

Where Reynolds led by bonhomie, Goody's authority grew out of the inner danger he projected, and his meticulous planning. He had been jailed twice, and on one occasion had been birched.

Goody was attracted to crimes of luxury, often for gold or jewellery. He had shown his controlled savagery during the London Airport robbery in 1962. It was Goody who led the assault team on the Royal Mail and who took charge at the perilous moment when the diesel refused to move.

THE GROUNDWORK FOR THE ROBBERY WAS METICULOUSLY LAID. THE GANG RESEARCHED AND REHEARSED SO THAT NOTHING WAS LEFT TO CHANCE. ALL THAT REMAINED WAS TO EXECUTE THE ROBBERY WITH THE SAME PRECISION AND EFFICIENCY

THE PROFESSIONALS

The first murmur of a 'big job' began buzzing through the underworld grapevine in the spring of 1963. Whispers reached the ears of Scotland Yard detectives in London, but the trail soon ran dry. The plotters had been careful men. Quiet approaches had been made to modestly-paid employees of the General Post Office and British Railways with a touch of menace and the promise of a 'drink' (pay-off) later. The robbers soon obtained the confidential documents which confirmed what they had heard: the Royal Mail carried enormous sums of unguarded, untraceable banknotes.

Above: Locomotive of the type which pulled the Royal Mail train on the night of the robbery. Reynolds spent hours in railway stations assessing the manoeuvres required to gain entry to the driver's cab.

The two gangs who merged to become the train robbers found this stage simple. They were all men capable of imparting warmth, trust and a rascally grin but could just as easily switch to viciousness.

MAPPING OUT THE GROUND

The next stage was to choose a location for the assault. Bob Wisbey and Ronald 'Buster' Edwards toured the rail route through the Hertfordshire towns of Tring and Hemel Hempstead. Using Ordnance Survey maps, they studied routes, farms, road access, signals, embankments, and police and rail stations as far north as Rugby.

Finally they chose a stretch north of Cheddington where both the Grand Union Canal and the main B4088 road veered away from the railway tracks. The tracks passed over Bridego Bridge, marked Bridge 127 and built of faded mauve bricks which rose less than 11 feet above a quiet lane. The tracks themselves, bordered by low metal railings, were only 15 feet above the road.

The nearest homestead, Rowden Farm, was

DATEFILE

MARCH-JUNE 1963

Two London gangs combine forces to rob a Mail train and plan the details as if for a military operation

AUGUST 7 1963

Train robbers assemble at Leatherslade Farm for the raid

AUGUST 8 1963

Robbers leave farm in convoy of army vehicles soon after midnight

MAR-AUG '63

BACKDROP

THE 'CITY GENTS' RAID

Shortly before 10am on 27 November 1962, two security guards were moving £62,500 in banknotes from Comet House, a London Airport office block, to a nearby bank. They halted their trolley in a corridor and called a lift. A man in a check cap, two gentlemen in bowler hats, pinstripe trousers and umbrellas lounged nearby

The lift doors opened and five hooded men stepped out. With the 'city gents,' they snatched the money, viciously coshed the guards and a clerk and sped through the front door into two waiting Jaguars. The entire raid was over in two minutes.

Only one man, a driver named Mickey Ball, was convicted for the raid. Charlie Wilson was acquitted and Gordon Goody — the man in the cap — managed to obtain a retrial at which he was acquitted. The raid was planned by Bruce Reynolds and set the scene for the commando-style assault, tinged with the same violence and black humour, on the Royal Mail train.

Left: Brian Field, the managing clerk at James and Wheater, solicitors, who was given the task of finding suitable premises at a safe distance from the scene of the crime where the gang could lie low.
Right: John Wheater, former army officer and partner in the firm who had obtained an acquittal for Goody on a previous robbery charge.

Night after night, Bruce Reynolds stood on the little lane under Bridego Bridge, checking the time at which the Royal Mail passed. Almost always, it was punctual at 3.03a.m. Often he shot cine-film of the bridge, Sears Crossing and the mail train passing through. The film was shown over and over again to other members of the gang in London. Reynolds wanted them familiar with the bridge and crossing without them running the risk of being seen loitering at night. In addition to these private viewings, there were nights when the robbers dressed up as railwaymen in dark blue boiler suits in order to study the area without arousing suspicion.

PASSING THE WORD

Meetings between the plotters were rare, however. Reynolds and the secretive Gordon Goody, the two most reflective of the robbers, both loved fishing. Buster Edwards, who knew nothing of the sport, sometimes loaded up with tackle so that brief words could pass in privacy. At other times,

less than a mile away but its windows were neither visible from the Home Signal at the gantry, nor from the dwarf signal up the tracks at Sears Crossing. Lord Rosebery's estate at Mentmore, about a mile south-west of Bridego Bridge, was shielded by tall trees.

Roger Cordrey, the gang's signals expert, was taken there the next day. 'No problem,' he remarked, 'No problem.'

messages were whispered at 'chance' meetings at dog-race meetings, racetracks or in shops. There is no proof that the complete robbery team met before it assembled in the days just before the assault.

As the day approached, security among the plotters became strict. Telephoned messages such as 'Johnny wants a sack of potatoes by Saturday' became common. Wives and girlfriends passed these instructions on without even a smirk. All

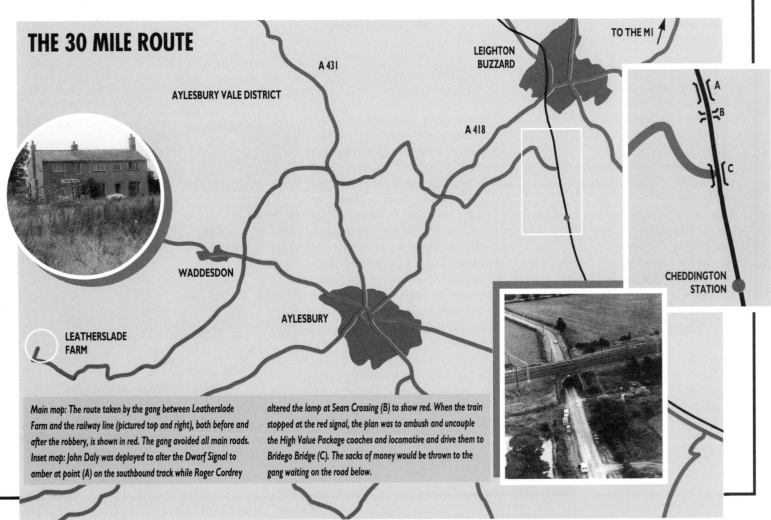

THE 30 MILE ROUTE

Main map: The route taken by the gang between Leatherslade Farm and the railway line (pictured top and right), both before and after the robbery, is shown in red. The gang avoided all main roads.
Inset map: John Daly was deployed to alter the Dwarf Signal to amber at point (A) on the southbound track while Roger Cordrey altered the lamp at Sears Crossing (B) to show red. When the train stopped at the red signal, the plan was to ambush and uncouple the High Value Package coaches and locomotive and drive them to Bridego Bridge (C). The sacks of money would be thrown to the gang waiting on the road below.

Above: The interior of a sorting coach where the money would be bagged up before transfer to the High Value Package van. Reynolds would have estimated the time when this transfer would take place when making his choice of location at which to stop the train.
Left: Reynolds studied the movement of mailbags on and off trains.

knew how their men lived and asked no questions.

At Euston Station in north London, Reynolds and Edwards loitered time after time, memorising the serial numbers of HVP coaches. Then gang members searched rail sidings at night, eventually finding an entire set of Royal Mail coaches at Stonebridge Park, which they studied closely for their weak points and interior lay-out. Roy James and Jimmy White studied handbooks to learn how to decouple coaches, and stealthily entered railway yards at night to practise.

There were flare-ups between the two camps of the robbery team. Reynolds' high-class pretensions, and Goody's habits of playing his cards close to his chest and showing off, irritated some members of the south-eastern gang, which made no claim to social or artistic graces.

FINDING A BOLT-HOLE

In June, a man called Brian Field was enlisted. Field was the managing clerk at James and Wheater, a London firm of solicitors run by a former army officer, John Wheater. The firm had defended Gordon Goody in two previous trials after which he was acquitted of involvement in a highly-publicised wages robbery at London Airport the previous winter (the 'City Gents' raid).

Field searched for isolated buildings for sale within reach of Bridego Bridge. Eventually, he noticed a modest, rather scruffy property called Leatherslade Farm up for sale at £5500. On 27 June, he visited the farm with a man called Lennie

> ‘ *What will you do with the farm?..... Can you imagine this place with a swimming pool?* ’

Exchange between Mrs Rixon and Lennie Field at Leatherslade Farm

Field – no relation – the brother of a client of James and Wheater who had recently come out of jail. Lennie Field was told that a criminal enterprise was in the making, but nothing was said about a train robbery. He was offered some of the takings on condition that he agreed to sign the lease on the farm.

The owner of Leatherslade Farm, Mrs Rixon, showed the two Fields around on 27 June. There was a 600-yard private track, some outbuildings and a few acres of land. Mrs Rixon found it curious that her visitors seemed interested only in the outbuildings. Field spoke approvingly

Right: The robbers found the isolated property they were looking for at Leatherslade Farm. Inset: Lennie Field was promised a share of the proceeds of a robbery if he would sign the lease on the farm. He was not told the robbery would involve a train.

and said his clients would be making an offer. ‘What will you do with the farm ?’ she asked as they made their departure.

‘Can you imagine this place with nice gardens all round and a swimming pool ?’ Field called back.

‘Oh yes,’ Mrs Rixon said.

‘Well if your husband lets us have the contract, you can start digging a hole,’ Field said. It was the kind of facetious joke that the villagers remembered later.

Contracts were signed on 22 July, and a deposit of £550, enough to secure possession, was paid by cheque the following day. Completion of the deal, and the rest of the payment, was to follow a few weeks later. James Wheater, Brian Field's boss, wrote to the Rixons' solicitor, stating that his clients expected to be in funds by 13 August. In fact, the clients expected to be very much in funds almost a week earlier. The Mail Train robbery was fixed for the early hours of Wednesday, 7 August.

STEALING THE 'WHEELS'

Reynolds and Jimmy White stole a light blue Land Rover in London and Gordon Goody painted it a military khaki colour. Another Land Rover and a 3-ton army lorry were purchased. Huge amounts of supplies were taken to the farm, including dozens of loaves of bread and 15 sets of cutlery.

Goody was chosen to lead the assault team to take the train, as he had knowledge of the engine's controls. With Reynolds, he had crept onto diesel locomotives at night to study the controls,

although, in the end, they hired a driver who, though he retired before diesels were introduced, nonetheless assured them he could move one.

The assault team consisted of the toughest members: Wilson, Edwards, Hussey, Wisbey, Welch and another, unidentified member of the south-eastern rail gang.

GETTING THE GO-AHEAD

On the evening of the Tuesday 6 August, Reynolds learned from an informant in Glasgow that the Royal Mail had left with only a light load. The gang, already highly tense, had to be quietly told that the raid was postponed for 24 hours.

Soon after 7pm the following evening, Wednesday 7 August, Reynolds finally got the word he wanted. The mail train was carrying a huge load of mailbags carrying the marking of High Value Packets.

The robbers assembled inside the farm. Precautions for the assault and escape had been fastidious. Reynolds and Cordrey each purchased Hitachi VHF radios to listen to police bulletins. Zeiss binoculars and walkie-talkies were also obtained and the irrepressible Roy James bought the handcuffs, telling a shop assistant that they were for amateur dramatics.

It was beginning to get dark at 7.30pm when the last man, Gordon Goody, arrived with a bag holding his balaclava, Spanish police truncheon and silk gloves. There were angry glances over his late arrival but the cautious, solitary Goody had never intended to arrive in broad daylight.

Five hours later, at half past midnight, the convoy slipped down the farm's tree-lined track. Reynolds sat in the front Land-Rover, wearing a major's uniform, as the vehicles headed for Bridego Bridge.

THE WOMEN WHO WAITED

The train robbers were a mixture of married and single men who needed loyalty and discretion from the women in their lives. Bruce Reynolds and his teenage wife, Frances, had a young son Nicky, and enjoyed life in the south of France. Goody, at 34, still lived at his Irish mother's house in Putney, south London, though he was planning to marry his girlfriend Patricia Cooper.

June Edwards, Buster's youthful sweetheart and wife, lost her first child at six weeks with a heart defect but had given birth to a daughter in 1960. Charlie Wilson was a fond husband with three daughters on whom he doted. Jimmy White, Bob Wisbey and Bob Welch were married, and Welch had a child by a mistress. Roger Cordrey's marriage was breaking up. Some stories say he hoped that new-found wealth might charm his wife back. Roy James, a boyishly handsome figure, liked female company, as did Jim Hussey. The women all knew their men's chosen careers but would not have dared to ask, or wanted to know, what they were planning on any particular occasion.

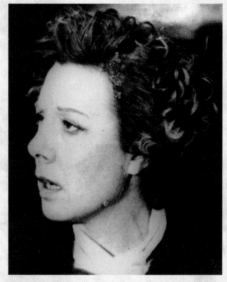

Wives and girlfriends of the robbers, clockwise from top left: Patricia Wilson, Patricia Welch, Patricia Cooper, Rene Wisbey and Cherry White.

THE GREAT TRAIN ROBBERY WAS CARRIED OUT AT A TIME WHEN THE METHODS AND REWARDS OF LARGE-SCALE PROFESSIONAL CRIME IN BRITAIN WERE RAPIDLY CHANGING. LONDON'S UNDERWORLD HAD BECOME MORE SOPHISTICATED, WITH A TASTE FOR THE HIGH-LIFE.

CHANGING FACE OI

Much of London's underworld in the early 1960s consisted of 'empires'. London's East End was controlled by the extortion and protection rackets of the notorious Kray twins, who resorted to murder when their authority was challenged. Southeast London was the fiefdom of the Richardson gang which tortured its enemies in a Rotherhithe warehouse.

The Soho world of prostitution and gambling had long been run mainly by immigrant racketeers, such as the Messina gang

Main picture: London's Soho in the 1960s blazed with signs advertising the seedy dives alongside the respectable establishments. It was a world where gangsters and celebrities often rubbed shoulders. Left: The Kray twins, Reggie, left, and Ronnie, pose with singer Judy Garland in a Soho nightclub.

of the early 1950s and a succession of shady characters with names such as 'Italian Alec' and 'Tony the Greek.'

Armed robbers were a different breed, however. They had no interest in seizing control of a criminal 'manor,' or in delegating authority to a long line of subordinates. The sheer inactivity would have bored them. They liked to work alone or with a few trusted associates, and would operate away from their immediate home locality.

In the late 1950s, wages robberies were increasingly common. Small, close-knit gangs preferred to 'snatch' large sums of cash during transportation rather than spend long hours picking safes inside a building where they could be trapped by nightwatchmen or police.

BATTLE OF WITS

Where territorial mobsters like the Krays avoided arrest by insulating themselves from direct evidence, robbers were specialists who expected to be questioned when crimes fitted their known style, and they skillfully prepared alibis beforehand.

Arrest, if it followed, was only one more stage of the battle of wits. Majority verdicts were not yet introduced and only one juror needed to be bought off to secure an acquittal.

At the time of the train robbery, the rich towns of the home counties north of London, including those of south Buckinghamshire, were frequent targets of London robbers who would commit afternoon break-ins, then race back to London on the newly built M1 motorway.

Although the train robbers had long since graduated beyond household break-ins,

CRIME

SOCIAL SCENE

Left: Charlie and Eddie Richardson outside their south-London scrapyard where they tortured their underworld enemies. Newspaper accounts of their trial made gruesome reading.

their larger crimes developed from this smash-and-grab style. Despite this, they shared with mobs like the Kray 'firm' a keen desire for respectability.

CRAVING FOR RESPECTABILITY

Like the Krays, Reynolds loved to cultivate law-abiding friends who suspected that he was a bit 'dodgy,' to use his own favourite word. The Krays ran West End night clubs at which show business celebrities felt a *frisson* of excitement at meeting gangsters in dinner jackets.

While on the run after the

train robbery, Reynolds changed his family's name and sent his children to private schools just as, today, the corrupt and ruthless 'barons' of the South American cocaine trade send their sons and daughters to the finest overseas universities.

Gordon Goody and Charlie Wilson had their own cravings for respectability. Goody, like most of the train robbers, had grown up in wartime London and led a gang of marauding youths through bombed streets. He had also once worked as a ship's steward, observing the discreet manners of rich, powerful people, and clearly envied them. But at his mother's house in south London, where Goody lived before his arrest in 1963, his room was so small that it contained little more than a bed.

The London underworld, like any closed community, had its snobbery, pecking order and hierarchies. The train robbers, like all professionals, wanted to establish their class and credentials and build wealth for their families. 'Most criminals are Tories,' a friend of one of the robbers commented. 'After all, they are capitalists.'

At home, men like the robbers were old-fashioned chauvinists, but capable of a certain gallantry provided their women asked no questions and obeyed. Reynolds, Edwards and Wilson took pride in their homes and were protective of their families.

ATTACK

For Reynolds, women had virtually no rights at all. If a girlfriend chatted too much to another man, Reynolds would cast her out of his life and possibly attack the other man.

Although the wives of successful villains wanted their men kept out of prison, there are signs that they enjoyed the mys-

tique of being married to rogues. The only one of the robbers whose marriage was breaking up was Roger Cordrey, the least prepossessing of the 'gang, and a man brought in for technical skill and not as a swashbuckler.

The other members of the gang also were neither seedy villains, nor con-men selling dud cars. Many had strong moral opinions on various subjects.

BREAKING THE RULES

The underworld of the early 1960s was a confident, brash community linking the crudest violence with streamlined new approaches to crime.

The train robbery involved cine photography, electrical expertise, walkie-talkie radios and coshes. It made a mockery of old-fashioned security systems and triggered fresh debate about the origins of criminality and the appropriate methods of dealing with it. It also undermined the belief that gangs could never trust each other. In almost every sense, the Great Train Robbery broke the rules.

nk raids in the 1960s progressed from the ordinary run of ash-and-grab. At Barclays Bank in Hemel Hempstead, the bbers used a Jaguar to force entry and get away with £8000.

MARY MANSON – THE ROBBERS' FRIEND

The male chauvinism of the London gangs was also practised by the train robbers. Women were seen as wives, mothers, even playthings, but not as confidantes or friends. The one exception was Mary Kaziah Manson (right). Mary knew most of the robbers and was particularly attached to John Daly who had shown great kindness to her during her brother's fatal illness. She was also close to Bruce Reynolds.

After the arrests, Mrs Manson looked after Reynolds' son Nicky until his mother reclaimed him,

and gave continual support and encouragement to the robbers' wives, particularly Barbara Daly, who was suffering shock, and to the Daly children. Mrs Manson and Reynolds were found to have purchased a car for cash at a garage in Chiswick, west London, on Friday, 9 August, one day after the train robbery. A charge against her was dropped at a magistrates' court. Shrewd and generous, Mrs Manson remained probably the only person who acted as friend and counsel to all the robbers and their families.

THREE
THE HUNT

PANIC AT

WHEN POLICE DISCOVERED THE HIDEOUT AT LEATHERSLADE FARM, IT SEEMED THAT SOMETHING HAD OCCURRED TO UNSETTLE THE ROBBERS. MISTAKES HAD BEEN MADE AND VITAL CLUES WHICH HAD BEEN LEFT BEHIND HELPED PUT POLICE ON THEIR TRAIL

O n the morning of 8 August 1963, the theft of £2,631,684 in bank notes, a crime of unrivalled audacity, unfolded to the astonishment of first British, then worldwide audiences. The robbers had left without leaving one single tangible clue to their identities at Sears Crossing or Bridego Bridge.

The hunt for the robbers was led by Detective Superintendent Malcolm Fewtrell, head of the Buckinghamshire CID, who promptly asked Scotland Yard for support.

THE 'SWEENEY'

The Yard attached two detectives to the rural investigation and told the Flying Squad – known colloquially as Sweeney Todd– to form a robbery unit to scour London. The Flying Squad team was led by Detective Chief Superintendent Tommy Butler, known to his colleagues as the 'Grey Fox'.

Further north, more than 100 officers searched haystacks, deserted buildings and ditches. Scores of 'suspicious' activities were reported by the public,

---

DATEFILE

AUGUST 12 1963
Police announce: 'Robbers may be within 30-mile radius.'

AUGUST 13 1963
Police discover Leathershade Farm

AUGUST 13 1963
First robber - Roger Cordrey - arrested in Bournemouth

AUG-OCT 1963
Eleven more robbers taken into custody

AUG-OCT '63

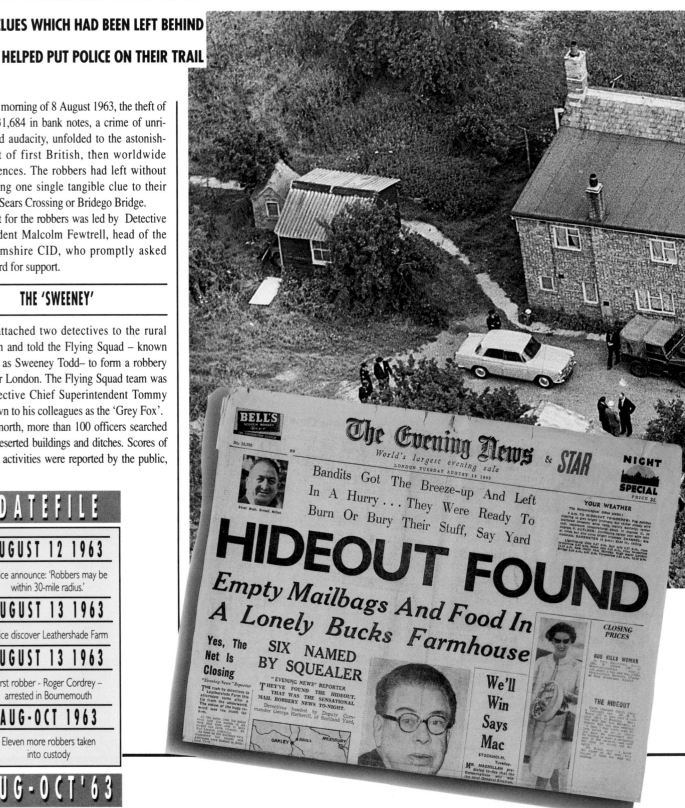

The Evening News & Star, London, Tuesday August 13 1963

Bandits Got The Breeze-up And Left In A Hurry . . . They Were Ready To Burn Or Bury Their Stuff, Say Yard

HIDEOUT FOUND
Empty Mailbags And Food In A Lonely Bucks Farmhouse

Yes, The Net Is Closing

SIX NAMED BY SQUEALER

We'll Win Says Mac

LEATHERSLADE

mostly local people who were at first curious and then suspicious of the comings and goings at Leatherslade Farm. The main suspects were identified at Scotland Yard by the style of their known crimes. Police, however, were hampered by the silence of their network of informants, despite large rewards offered by both the GPO and the Midland Bank, whose load on the train had not been insured. The robbers had either showed maximum discretion or aroused an unusual degree of fear.

> *You'll never believe this, they've stolen a train!*
>
> Police radio message, dawn, 8 August.

The fireman, David Whitby, had caught a glimpse of an army lorry parked down the embankment by Bridego Bridge. Police quickly announced that army vehicles had been used for the getaway, a statement the robbers would have heard on the midday radio bulletins.

Fewtrell and his colleague, Detective Sergeant

Main picture: Aerial view of Leatherslade Farm on 13 August – the day it was discovered by police. One of the Land Rovers used in the robbery is parked outside. Below left: The 13 August edition of the London Evening News. Above: Stores of food found at the farm indicated the robbers' initial intention to lie low for several days.

INSIDE VIEW

EYE-WITNESSES

The train robbers thought they could use Leatherslade Farm without attracting any local curiosity, but John Maris, who alerted the police after the robbery, lived on the nearby B4011 road and had seen vehicles at the farm from 29 July onwards. Another neighbour, Mr Wyatt, who visited the farm for permission to continue renting a field, noticed sleeping bags lying around and a lorry in the front drive. A man named Cunnington saw suitcases being taken to the farm in a Land-Rover on the same day.

Mrs Nappin (right), who lived near the entrance to the farm, saw the convoy leaving on the night of 8 August. The robbers did not arouse suspicion prior to the robbery, although there had been a certain amount of chatter about the men who avoided the local shops.

PERSPECTIVE

A POLICEMAN LOOKS BACK

Detective Superintendent Malcolm Fewtrell, head of Buckinghamshire CID at the time of the robbery, reflects on a crime that, over 25 years later, remains unrivaled.

'The train robbers were ruthless, professional and dedicated criminals. It was the most ambitious crime of its kind we have had in Britain. These people were determined to achieve what they set out to do. Fortunately, **only one man (driver Mills) did** resist them, and he paid heavily for his courage. The calibre of the robbers was that they would stop at nothing.

'I don't think they would have considered the possibility of being caught. Some had been caught before and had been acquitted before. They were self-possessed. They knew it was a big one and I assume they were proud of what they had done, but they never expressed it in so many words.'

The possibility of turning informer to escape a long sentence would never have been considered by any of the robbers, in Fewtrell's opinion:

'If an informer is discovered by these sort of people, he pays for it in violence. It's the law of the jungle. These people were so ruthless that if they suspected there was an informant, they'd deal with it. Most would have put the frighteners on anybody. The robbery was the work of a very experienced gang of criminals.'

In custody at Aylesbury before the trial, the robbers gave the police no difficulty, and even shared moments of humour. Gordon Goody once sent Fewtrell a magazine photograph of a mountain-climbing sherpa wearing a face-mask with the message: "The real train robber." Fewtrell asked Goody to sign it as a memento, but Goody erupted at the thought of 'signing anything for a copper' and refused point-blank.

'We had a good relationship,' Fewtrell went on to observe, 'We got on well with all of them. They were on one side and I was on the other – and they realised it. If you are a professional, you have to expect the setbacks. They would have spent the money and then started on another robbery. But I have got to condemn the audacity of the robbery. You can wonder that they had the sheer nerve to think they could get away with it. But if they hadn't made such a mess at Leatherslade Farm, they would have got away with it.

'Clearly they were capable of working the plan out for themselves. The major mistake they made was that they intended **to stay at Leatherslade Farm as long as it suited them.** They could have completed the purchase. They could quietly have destroyed the evidence and got out at their leisure.

'Why should any investigating officer start looking 30 miles in that direction? They hoped the immediate reaction would be that they were off down the M1.'

When Det. Supt. Fewtrell reached the scene of the raid, no one knew how much money had been stolen. The raid had been so swift, most victims were left more bewildered than injured.

'The first thing I saw was the 10 rear coaches and 70-odd postal workers. All they knew was that they had lost their train. When I asked what had gone, one of them replied, "Most of the mailbags ... it could be a million pounds." I remember repeating this to my wife who told me to stop exaggerating.

'I was surprised by all the publicity it caused all over the world but even more surprised when it went on year after year.'

At the age of 81, Fewtrell has delivered countless lectures on the Great Train Robbery and given interviews to journalists from Italy, Sweden and numerous other countries where the raid at Bridego Bridge is well remembered. Despite his surprise at the publicity, the robbery was the high spot of his 33-year career. He retired from the police in 1964, the day before the sentences were passed on the first batch of train robbers.

Today, Malcolm Fewtrell firmly believes that the judge was justified in passing such long sentences for the robbery.

'He was right to deter. There has never been a crime like that since. No other gang has tried this. They haven't stopped committing crime, but they don't stop trains.'

herdsman John Maris, who used a field adjoining Leatherslade Farm, had become curious about the quietness there. He peered into the shed at the back, saw the vehicles and alerted police.

The ashes of a bonfire outside Leatherslade Farm were quite cold when the police arrived at 10.50am on Tuesday, 13 August, five days after the raid. Traces of half-burned masks lay in the bonfire. Nearby, empty mailbags lay in a hastily dug open pit near a bed of flowers. A spade had been left sticking up in the clay.

One Land Rover was parked outside the front door. The other was with the yellow army lorry in the shed, covered by a tarpaulin. The white-framed windows were blacked out by rough blankets of different colours.

BROKEN BEER BOTTLES

The farm was obviously deserted. PC Wooley and Sergeant Blackman, both of Waddesdon police, prised open a window and climbed inside. They found the debris of a brief encampment. The kitchen was piled high with tins of food, beer bottles, bread, eggs and fruit, enough to feed a dozen men for a week or more. Plates of half-eaten meals lay on the table. The floor was littered with broken beer bottles.

The living room and bedrooms were full of sleeping bags, mattresses, blankets and old clothes. A game of Monopoly was left in the living room and the house was strewn with empty cigarette packets and ashtrays full of stubs. In an alcove under the stairs, the officers found a bag of potatoes and more fruit.

PC Wooley pulled the potatoes and fruit away to uncover a trapdoor. He climbed down to a cellar where he discovered a pile of mailbags and paper wrappers which were printed with the names

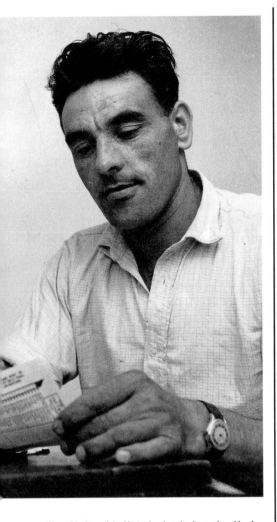

Above: Herdsman John Maris who alerted police to the robbers' hideout at Leatherslade Farm. He received £10,000 reward. Left and below left: A cartoon of Detective Superintendent Fewtrell published in the Daily Mirror, and himself, in January 1964.

McArthur, however, were struck by the threat to Mills, Whitby and the sorters not to 'move for half-an-hour.' The idea of a look-out had been a bluff, but the 30-minute period seemed significant.

THIRTY-MILE RADIUS

As the local search continued, the Buckinghamshire police announced on Monday, 12 August, that the robbers might have used a deserted building within a half-hour drive of Bridego Bridge. The radio announcements calculated that this meant within a 30-mile radius.

The robbers' trademark of precision had worked against their interests. Leatherslade was just inside the 30-mile radius. On the same day that the announcement was made,

Above: Mrs Emily Clark from Bournemouth gave police information – about two men wanting to rent her garage – which led to the arrest of Roger Cordrey. She received £14,000 reward. Below: The robbers' getaway vehicles, found abandoned at Leatherslade Farm. The number plates on the Land Rovers were false and identical to cause confusion to police during the escape.

of banks. The robbers' hideout had been found. 'The whole place is one big clue,' Detective Superintendent Malcolm Fewtrell commented on arriving with two Scotland Yard officers, Detective Superintendent Gerald McArthur and Detective Sergeant Jack Pritchard.

PANIC DEPARTURE

The mess at Leatherslade Farm, however, was not in keeping with the expert planning of the robbery. The mailbags in the unfinished pit, the plates half-full of food, and the discarded clothing indicated hurried departures. Yet such lack of preparation would be inconceivable in even amateur villains. Fewtrell knew the train robbers must have had a meticulous escape plan, cunning alibis, connec-

Left: Detective Chief Superintendent Tommy Butler of Scotland Yard, who gave up his first year of retirement to continue the search for the robbers still at large. His persistence led him to Canada, where he arrested Charles Wilson on 25 January 1968. Below: Redland Wood, Dorking, where two holdalls containing almost £101,000 were found on 16 August 1963.

tions and the money to buy loyalty and discretion. Something had gone badly wrong. The farm had no telephone and the Monopoly board suggested long periods of monotony. If the robbers had expected to be safe at the farm, what had suddenly caused them to leave such a shambles behind?

In London, Scotland Yard had already noticed similarities between the Mail Train robbery and the London Airport 'city gents' hold-up the year before: careful planning, perfect timing, brutal efficiency and speed of escape from the scene – all with a hint of impudent black humour. These suspicions turned to certainty within hours of forensic experts arriving at Leatherslade Farm. Many of the robbers had, literally, left their marks. Yet, equally interesting, was the discovery that considerable effort had been made to wipe the place clean.

It was clear that whatever had happened had left the robbers edgy and off-balance. A secret compartment was found in the army lorry. Police calculated that it could have contained only about £100,000, which meant that the lorry could not have been used to move all the money immediately after the raid.

The two Land Rovers had the same number-plate, BMG 757A, a ploy geared to the escape plan. Yet the vehicles had also been abandoned. Indeed, the atmosphere at the farm reeked of panic. The detectives felt sure the fugitives would still be rattled.

Above: The mews house, left of picture, where Roy James was arrested on the night of 10 December 1963. He was later charged for his part in the Great Train Robbery. The police raid followed a tip-off given to them that morning.

FIRST CAPTURE

Roger Cordrey, the robber with the most unsettled private life, was the first to be careless, and in bizarre circumstances for such a cautious man. On the day the discovery of the farm was announced, Tuesday, 13 August, a landlady in Bournemouth – a policeman's widow – sensed something was wrong when Cordrey's accomplice Bill Boal handed over three months' rent for a garage from a thick wad of notes – an unusual practice in 1963.

The police arrested Boal and Cordrey when they returned to the garage. In various suitcases at the garage and in Cordrey's room above a florist's shop in the town, police found almost £141,000.

The fingerprints of eight robbers – Reynolds, Welch, Wisbey, Hussey, Biggs, James, Daly and Wilson – were found at the farm, some on a vehicle, others on movable objects or the building itself. Wilson was picked up on 22 August, Biggs, Hussey and Wisbey by the middle of September and Welch by the end of October. All had been confident not only of their alibis but that incrimi-

nating prints had not been left at the farm. When asked if he objected to prints being taken, Hussey replied, 'No, I have no worries.'

THE LAST ROUND-UP

Goody had expected to be questioned. His alibi initially held firm and there were no fingerprints of his found at the farm, where he had never once taken off his gloves. But he was re-arrested in Leicester and charged on 3 October after forensic reports linked him to paint at Leatherslade Farm.

Leonard Field, the nominal purchaser of the farm, was arrested early in September, followed by Brian Field after the discovery, in Dorking Woods, Surrey, of an abandoned briefcase containing £100,900 in notes from the robbery. John Wheater, the solicitor manipulated by Brian Field, was implicated through the farm purchase and arrested in October.

While making inquiries around Dorking, police found a further £30,440 in a deserted caravan, which was covered in Jimmy White's fingerprints. John Daly, arrested in his pyjamas and dressing gown, was the next to be tracked down and Roy James' elusiveness ended in a rooftop chase in London, on 10 December. He had a hold-all containing £12,041. But Reynolds, Edwards and White were still missing, and so was about £2 million.

CLOSE-UP

THE ESCAPE

One baffling aspect of such a unique and brilliantly executed crime was the bungled escape from Leatherslade Farm. This has prompted theories of a 'Judas' who never arrived to remove all incriminating evidence. Senior detectives, however, knew that the robbers would expect them to suspect that a London gang would have fled immediately down the M1 motorway to the east of Bridego Bridge.

The police decided that the gang may have believed that a farm, 30 miles west of the robbery and well away from main roads, would never be suspected. It seemed likely that the robbers had planned to stay some weeks, complete the purchase and install a plausible owner who would destroy the evidence in his own time. The careless warning to the rail crew and sorters not to move for half-an-hour destroyed the plan, and the radio announcement of a local search panicked the robbers.

Despite their haste, the clean-up was thorough, but not good enough to remove every trace of fingerprints, such as one on the underside of the hand rail in the bath.

FACE TO FACE WITH *Buster Edwards*

RONALD 'BUSTER' EDWARDS, WENT ON THE RUN AFTER THE TRAIN ROBBERY; HE SURRENDERED IN SEPTEMBER 1966 AND SERVED NINE YEARS IN PRISON. HE TALKS TO *SCANDAL* ABOUT THE CRIME THAT HAS BROUGHT HIM LIFE-LONG NOTORIETY.

Buster Edwards recalls the professionalism of his own team, emphasising that getting the correct information beforehand is the key to any successful robbery.

'We were a professional team and had already done some very big robberies. I knew a couple of 'firms' that could also have pulled off the train robbery, but we were the ones that got the information.'

ON PUBLICITY

Edwards believes that none of the gang had ever thought that the robbery would receive such publicity on a national as well as worldwide scale, let alone achieve legendary status.

> **❚❚ I am very proud of what I did, and have no regrets. ❚❚**

'I don't think we realised there would be publicity like there has been. But we would not have been deterred. Our doubts were that it was out of London. The trouble was getting back to London, or you stand out like a sore thumb.'

ON THE MONEY

He concedes that some robbers had been overwhelmed by their then massive £148,000 shares of the £2.6 million haul.

'There was tension at the farm. The amount of money frightened people. Two people said, "No, I want £50,000 for my whack." It was a frightening amount of paper. The police were looking everywhere and, in the end, we changed our [escape] plan. By the Friday [9 August, 1963], it seemed the best thing we could do was leave.'.

ON THE SENTENCES

Edwards maintains that the train robbery was professionally carried out and that the injuries to the driver, Jack Mills, were in fact much milder than the public were led to believe, being later exaggerated both at the trial and by the press

'I am very proud of what I did and have got no regrets. In every person there's a thief who would love to do it if he had the arsehole. But I am sorry for Mills – he was used.

'The sentences were a disgrace. They were nothing to do with the injuries Mills got. It had got to the point where they were going to throw the book. Even 20 years was an enormous sentence.'

'Going to prison is only a question of averages. When I was very young, I was upset that I wasn't a part of the people who had done time in prison. I thought I was missing something. Prison was glamorised. They only tell you the good things. It was only when I got inside I found out.'

ON GUNS

Edwards would not be drawn on whether members of the gang were armed on the night of the robbery. But he points out the irony of how the stiff sentences designed to deter violent crime might have had some bearing on the increase in armed robbery in the years that followed.

'Since the train robbery, there have been brilliant but terrible crimes. Because of the 30-year sentences, everyone carries guns. If the train robbery was 10 years later, guns would have been taken.'

ON THE TEAM

Edwards dismisses the idea of a mastermind. They were all in it together and applied themselves to their work as a team.

'There are no top people, everyone had their jobs. Goody was a good thief – we all were – and Roy James was a marvellous driver.'

But Edwards was less than flattering about Biggs' role, recalling one incident with evident amusement.

'Ronnie Biggs was a gas-meter man. Charlie Wilson was digging a hole at the farm, and Biggs thought it was to bury him in.'

> **❚❚ Manual robbery is dying. The thing now is fraud. ❚❚**

ON PLANS GOING WRONG

Despite all the careful planning that had preceded the robbery, there were unexpected 'glitches' – moments when things didn't go completely as expected.

'Some things did not work to plan. Cordrey told us the fireman [Whitby] would get down on the right hand side, where there were people waiting by the signal. But he got down on the left hand side.

'The driver we brought didn't know anything about diesels. If we could not have driven the diesel forward, we would not have got inside the coaches. There were 70 people or so in there. That was too many. One of us would have shouted "Swallow" [leave].

ON CRIME TODAY

Edwards reflects on the changing face of crime, with some envy of modern professionals, but also some pride in his own perfectionism.

'When I look back, I'm very envious of the young professionals. I used to want everything to be right, 99 per cent in my favour. I loved looking at bits of work. I used to take my daughter to watch money being taken out of a bank.

'Manual robbery is dying. The thing now is fraud. We were called thieves. In the City [London's financial district], they're called unlucky – you shouldn't get caught.

'I love reading about robberies in the paper but it is rare to have a big robbery these days. I'm afraid the young chaps aren't into robbery. They're into drugs.'

Buster Edwards has run a flower stall at Waterloo Station since he was released from prison in 1975. Flower selling was also his trade before the Great Train Robbery.

TRIAL AND

THE TRIAL OF THE GREAT TRAIN ROBBERS BEGAN AT AYLESBURY ON 20 JANUARY 1964 AND LASTED 51 DAYS. HIGH-POINTS SUCH AS SENDING BIGGS FOR RE-TRIAL AND GOODY'S EVIDENCE WERE ECLIPSED BY THE SEVERITY OF THE SENTENCES

Crowds packed the streets of Aylesbury on Monday, 20 January 1964, when the train robbers were transported in black police vans to the hastily converted Rural District Council Offices. The local Assize Court was too small for the trial, which required an attendance of more than three dozen barristers in addition to a huge number of British and foreign journalists.

By 10.27am, Mr Justice Edmund Davies – once a fiery Welsh barrister, now a self-possessed

Left: Barristers take their tea-break outside the make-shift court at Aylesbury. In the foreground by the car is Arthur James QC who led for the prosecution. Below: Judge Edmund Davies.

High Court judge – and the 12-man jury were all in place. The defendants stood in the dock to answer charges 'against the Peace of our Sovereign Lady the Queen, her Crown and Dignity.'

It took 30 minutes to read the indictments. Cordrey, the signals expert, admitted conspiracy to rob and receiving stolen money. His plea of not guilty to robbery – in effect, of not having changed the railway signals – was accepted and he was taken away to be sentenced later. The remaining defendants denied a barrage of conspiracy and robbery charges. John Wheater, the most miserable, lonely figure in the dock, faced relatively minor charges, which he nonetheless denied.

LOW-KEY

The trial itself was low-key in comparison with the crime involved. There were no fierce clashes between counsel and witness, no vitriolic accusations from defendants – few of whom gave evidence – and no unexpected witnesses nor mysterious masterminds.

The press benches soon thinned out. Arthur James QC needed 10 hours to outline the prosecution case, during which two remarkable facts

---

DATEFILE

JANUARY 20 1964
The trial of the robbers begins at Aylesbury

FEBRUARY 3 1964
Biggs sent for re-trial; Daly freed through lack of evidence

MARCH 26 1964
The jury delivers the verdicts

APRIL 15 1964
Judge Davies passes sentence

JAN-APR '64

PUNISHMENT

emerged. In the first place, not one forensic clue had been found at either Sears Crossing or Bridego Bridge, while the fingerprints of seven men had been identified at Leatherslade farm. Secondly, according to the prosecution, there were also paint scraps to link Goody and Boal to the farm.

In the early days of the trial, the shaken-looking driver Jack Mills began to give his evidence. He was unable to identify any of the defendants. Evidence from the farm created banal images in marked contrast to the ruthless reality of the raid on the train. Scotland Yard's fingerprint expert, Detective Superintendent Maurice Ray, spoke of Welch's prints on a beer can, Biggs' on a bottle of tomato ketchup and Monopoly board, and James' on a plate.

STICKING TOGETHER

Cordrey, awaiting sentence at Aylesbury Prison, wanted to testify that Boal was innocent, but was dissuaded when told he would then be asked if the others were innocent also. A remarkable feature of the train robbers was their absolute refusal to turn Queen's Evidence and give evidence against each other. Pride, it seemed, bound them together.

The 13th day of the trial saw the presentation of the only complex piece of evidence. Dr Ian Holden, a consultant on the Scotland Yard laboratory team, said that tiny scraps of paint found on a pair of suede shoes belonging to Goody matched the paint on one of the Land Rovers.

'If I had to go out and find another pair of shoes with both those paints on, even if my life depended on it, I do not think I would even bother to try,' Dr

Main picture: The robbers look out from a police prison van as they are driven away from Aylesbury after the first day of the trial.
Top left: The London Evening News announces the total number of years in jail handed down to the robbers.
Inset: Driver Mills suffered severe head wounds during the attack. He was still shaken, five months later, when he gave evidence at the trial.

INSIDE VIEW

WERE GUNS USED?

The robbers' cry of 'They're bolting the doors – get the guns!' during the assault on the HVP coach was recounted to the Aylesbury jury. There was no evidence of firearms being seen or heard at the hold-up but, in summing-up, Mr Justice Edmund-Davies asked whether the cry really was bravado. The defendants could not dispute this since they denied being at the robbery. Privately, however, they were bitter because, they claimed later, a firm decision had been made not to take guns. The relatively limited violence used in the train robbery helped to win acclaim for the robbers from people who might have responded differently had they known something of their earlier crimes.

However, Detective Chief Superintendent Jack Slipper (left), who hunted the robbers in London with the Flying Squad, stated in his memoirs *Slipper of the Yard* (1981) that, if the robbers had been cornered at Leatherslade Farm, the myth of 'gentlemen' bandits would have been shattered. 'They were armed, and they had £2.6 million inside the farm,' he wrote. 'I don't doubt there would have been a blood-bath.'

Above left: Sebag Shaw QC, defence counsel for Gordon Goody, arrives at the court. He challenged every juror put forward for the trial, alleging bribes had been offered to five of them. Judge Davies rejected the challenge as 'pure speculation'.

Above: The London Evening News headlines announce the verdicts of the jury, seen in their coach (above) returning to court.

Holden said. He also described how he had discovered flakes in Boal's pocket matching a can of yellow paint at the farm.

On the 14th day, Biggs was sent for retrial, after a police officer inadvertently let slip to the jury that Biggs had a prison record. Three days later, John Daly, brother-in-law of the absent Reynolds, left the dock a free man. The only evidence against him was a fingerprint found on a movable object (the Monopoly board) at the farm. The judge directed the jury to acquit Daly, with the words 'suspicion alone is not enough.'

Only when Goody began to give evidence, on Thursday, 20 February, did any suggestion emerge of the driving needed to pull off the robbery. His counsel, Sebag Shaw, QC, dismissed the paint evidence as a story of 'Goody Two Shoes'. 'Are you meticulous about your dress?' he asked Goody. Everyone could see that Goody was dressed more smartly than most of the barristers.

THE CHARISMATIC GOODY

'I like to think so,' Goody replied. His alibi involved the smuggling of watches from Ireland and staying with his girlfriend Patricia Wilson, who gamely supported it in her evidence. He also spoke about his acquittal at the end of the London Airport robbery trial and why he had gone into hiding after the raid. 'Every time a robbery is committed locally they pay me a visit,' he explained.

At last the public galleries were looking at that untamed quality people expected of the train robbers. Goody apart, the robbers settled for drab, mundane alibis. Wisbey acknowledged making an 'innocent' trip to the farm after the robbery, but only to deliver vegetables. Welch supported the story and Hussey spoke of delivering some apples.

CLOSE-UP THE MONEY

Only £336,534 – less than 12 per cent of the total stolen money – was ever recovered from the Great Train Robbery. It has been suggested that the bulk of the missing £2,295,150 was secretly moved abroad in boats and left to nestle in continental banks. This seems improbable, however, as each robber is now thought to have received £150,000, with the remainder divided among the many helpers and informants.

Piers Paul Read, who interviewed a number of the gang for his book, The Train Robbers (1978), calculated that each member spent several thousand in expenses immediately after the robbery, and up to £30,000 each in legal fees (none got legal aid, and all hired the finest counsel). There were also families to provide for during the long years of imprisonment. The rest was spent either on life on the run, frittered away or simply stolen by once-trusted friends. Read calculated that Edwards spent nearly £70,000 in Mexico alone. A few, however, did emerge from prison to find part of their share invested in property.

The picture shows what the amount of stolen money would look like in comparison with an average-sized man.

The judge's summing-up took six days and a quarter of a million words. The jury took over two days to reach all their verdicts. Police and crowds were packed outside the building on Thursday, 26 March. At 10.30 am, the judge ordered the courtroom to be sealed.

The verdicts were complex. In essence, Goody and his associates, the luckless Boal included, were found to be the 'Great Train Robbers'. Brian Field and Leonard Field were not charged with robbery

> ‘ *Let us clear out of the way any romantic notions....this is nothing less than a sordid crime of violence inspired by vast greed... leniency would be evil.* ’
>
> Mr Justice Edmund Davies

but with conspiracy, and Wheater with obstructing the course of justice. The robbers betrayed neither surprise nor fear when the verdicts were announced, appearing as well drilled as on the night they stole £2.6 million. On 8 April, Biggs was also judged to be one of the train robbers.

The court re-assembled on 15 April to hear the sentences. The prisoners were brought up one by one. Mr Justice Edmund Jones spoke of a 'crime which by its impudence and enormity is the first of its kind in this country. I propose to do all within my power to ensure it will also be the last of its kind.' He dwelt on the 'terrifying effect' of an assault by masked, armed men and pointed out that the robbers may have carried guns.

STUNNED SILENCE

‘As the higher the price the greater the temptation. Potential criminals, who may be dazzled by the enormity of the price, must be taught that the punishment they risk will be proportionately greater,’ he said. Cordrey, who had pleaded guilty, was sentenced to 20 years' imprisonment. Then, in a stunned silence, sentences of 30 years were passed on Goody, Wilson, James, Hussey, Wisbey, Welch and Biggs. Boal received 24 years and the two Fields each got 25 years. John Wheater was jailed for only three years.

As the court broke up, it became apparent that the severity of the sentences had not only shocked the robbers, but horrified even the public and the barristers alike.

BACKDROP

Below: Ronald Biggs seen leaving court on 15 April 1963. He had heard the jury find him guilty on two counts: for conspiring to stop a train with intent to rob it and of taking part in armed robbery.

THE FUGITIVE

I t's my sad duty to inform you, Biggs, that your earliest date of release is 1984.' With this comment from the governor of Lincoln Prison, train robber Biggs began his 30-year sentence.

Biggs, close on 35, did not look like one who would escape, cross the world, evade constant pursuit and finally earn the informal title of 'the world's most wanted man'. As a fugitive, however, Biggs showed a resourcefulness he had seldom displayed as a petty thief back in England.

Not long after his transfer to London's Wandsworth Prison, Biggs proved the Lincoln governor wrong; he secured his own 'release' on 8 July 1965 when, at 3pm, he and three other prisoners went over the wall on a rope-ladder.

For weeks Biggs lay low, protected by friends, making only occasional telephone calls to his wife Charmian. Eventually, he was smuggled by boat from Tilbury to Antwerp by an underworld escape outfit known as 'The Organization'. Biggs was well able to afford their heavy charges .

In Paris, he underwent two operations for plastic surgery, which left him in screaming pain. The surgeons had cut behind each ear and pulled the skin tight across each face. Only drugs helped to ease the agony.

Biggs was given a new passport under the name of Terence Furminger, an assistant fish salesman from north London. On New Year's Eve 1965, wearing a moustache and black-rimmed glasses and carrying £4,000 in cash, 'Furminger', flew into Sydney, Australia, en route to Adelaide.

Above: The 56-year-old Ronnie Biggs celebrates 20 years on the run, in 1985.

Left: Australian police find Biggs' clothing in a Melbourne hotel when he was on the run in 1969.

'The weather is glorious, the opportunities are marvellous and the natives are friendly,' Biggs wrote to Charmian. As 'Mrs Furminger', she joined him with their sons, Nicky and Chris, in June 1966.

The 28-year-old Charmian enjoyed the easy-going neighbourliness in Australia as much as her husband did. From time to time, instalments of Biggs' loot arrived pressed inside magazines. Vowing never to return to crime, Biggs soon adopted the name of Terry King and became a respected carpenter.

MOMENTS OF PERIL

There were the occasional scares, such as when a friend noticed that Biggs had identical scars behind each ear. But there was no danger until after

CHARMIAN BIGGS — THE WIFE WHO LOVED AND LOST

'I married you for the rainy days as well as the fine ones,' Charmian Biggs told her husband before his prison escape in 1965. Four years later, when Biggs had fled their home in Australia, she was taken into custody to endure many hours of questioning.

Later, her lawyer negotiated the sale of her story to the press and television for about £30,000 and, although much of this went in taxes, a small amount got through to Biggs.

Charmian was finally allowed to take up permanent residence in Australia; opinion among her neighbours was divided. Some signed a petition on her behalf; others let down her tyres and threw milk bottles at the house.

It was nearly five years before Charmian saw Biggs again, in 1974. By then, however, his affection was for Raimunda (right), the Brazilian girl whose baby boy prevented Biggs' extradition. Charmian returned to Australia, completed her arts degree at Melbourne University, and divorced her husband.

Charmian gave birth to their fourth child, Farley, in the spring of 1967.

'Things moving in unpleasant direction... Suggest change of scenery and name, wrote 'The Organization' from London. Also, the arrests of Charlie Wilson and Bruce Reynolds in 1968 led to the reappearance of Biggs' photograph in the Australian press.

From then until late 1969, the Biggs lived a hunted, nomadic life. There were times when he wanted to take people into his confidence, but Charmian warned him not to trust anyone.

By the autumn of 1969, knowing the Australian police were on his trail, Biggs was all set on giving himself up for the children's sake, but Charmian saw it differently: 'They want to look up to you,' she told him. 'So long as you are free they can do that.'

One October evening, Charmian found their home in Adelaide surrounded by armed Australian police. Biggs was nowhere to be found, however,

having already slipped away that morning. Aided by an English friend who took grave risks for him, Biggs was taken by boat across the world, reaching Panama in February 1970, then Venezuela and finally on to Rio de Janeiro, Brazil, the following month.

Left: Charmian Biggs in 1964. She remained in Britain after Biggs' escape until it was safe for her to follow him to Australia. Their children, seen below with a Melbourne policewoman, were reunited with Biggs in 1966.

Biggs was highly attractive to women and sought their company to help him through months of fear. A year later, however, feeling desperately homesick, he made plans to return to Australia. Charmian told him to wait, and Biggs took on odd jobs for a while.

In January 1971, Biggs found out his son Nicky had died in a car crash. Sensing he would be in despair, Charmian sent a message via a London journalist: 'If I lose you, my life will become totally worthless. I'd have nothing to live for. Whatever you do, Ron, don't come back.'

LONGING FOR ENGLAND

Slowly, Biggs began to find distractions in Rio. He had always enjoyed jazz and sensual music and he added to these a taste for marijuana. But his longing for English habits — the tea, heavy meals and beer — constantly tempted him to surrender.

He had left everything behind him in Australia — not just the chasing packs of police and world's press, but also a shattered family. Inwardly, he yearned for some form of redemption, provided there would be early parole.

Without Charmian to restrain him, Biggs put out feelers among the English community in Brazil, a move that led to the fiasco of his arrest in 1974 and the failed attempt to extradite him. The train robber from south London stayed in Brazil, talking about England whenever he had the chance, still maintaining he had suffered enough to deserve a pardon.

THE LONG SENTENCES HANDED DOWN TO THE TRAIN ROBBERS DREW PROTESTS FROM ALL QUARTERS OF SOCIETY. SOME OF THE GANG APPEALED, OTHERS ESCAPED, WHILE THOSE ON THE RUN FLED THE COUNTRY. GRADUALLY, HOWEVER, ALL BUT ONE WERE RUN TO GROUND

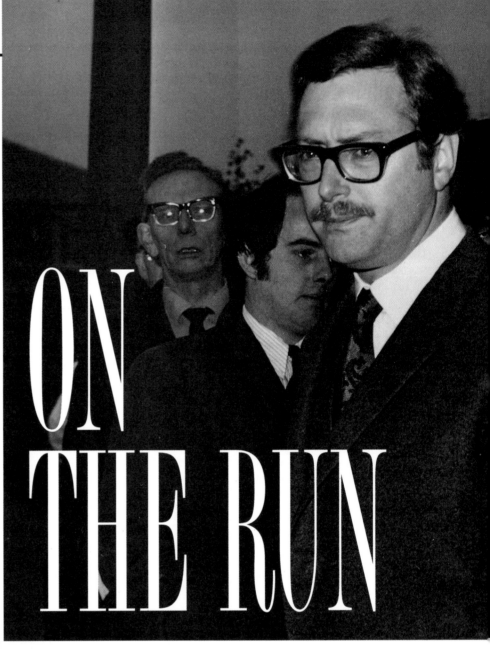

ON THE RUN

DATEFILE

AUG-SEPT 1964

Reynolds flees the country; Wilson and Biggs escape from Prison

APRIL 21 1966

Jimmy White caught

SEPTEMBER 1966

Buster Edwards returns from Mexico and surrenders in London

JAN-NOV 1968

Wilson caught in Canada and Reynolds arrested in Torquay

AUG '64 - NOV '68

The appeals were heard in the summer of 1964, but the long sentences remained unaltered. Mr Justice Atkinson described the robbery as 'an act of warfare against the community.' The convictions for conspiracy against Brian Field and Lennie Field were quashed, however, although their sentences of five years for obstructing justice held. Boal's conviction for robbery, and Cordrey's for conspiracy, were also quashed and their sentences were adjusted to 14 years for receiving.

The long terms of imprisonment became the subject of a fierce public debate over the justice of their sentences. Newspapers across the political spectrum expressed concern that prisoners convicted of non-capital murder and rape would be given 'life' sentences, but usually were released after about 15 years, while those train robbers given 30-year sentences would, even with full remission, still serve 20 years.

'Does this mean that stealing banknotes is regarded as being more wicked that murdering someone?' asked the *Daily Mail*. James Cameron, the distinguished commentator then writing for the *Daily Herald*, pointed out that the robbers would have received far lighter sentences for breaking a baby's legs.

The *Daily Telegraph* defended the harsh sentences by suggesting that murderers might be less susceptible to deterrence than thieves. It recalled the trial-judge's remarks that stiff sentences would discourage the whole criminal fraternity from such outrageous crimes.

DOMINANT PERSONALITY

The train robbers, however, were probably the only criminals in Britain even capable of such a crime. To those present at the trial, the personality of Gordon Goody had dominated the trial. Barristers agreed in private that, if war broke out, Goody and his men would win the highest military awards for valour behind enemy lines.

A PLACE IN HISTORY

The Great Train Robbery remains the biggest theft from a train anywhere in the world. It proved to be a crime without rivals. Before and since, the events at Bridego Bridge, big-time criminals tended to concentrate on fixed points, such as banks and safety-deposit centres. Ambushes of moving vehicles had been known, but they were invariably of smaller targets, such as security trucks and postal vans.

Previously, the most celebrated robbery in history was the theft of nearly $2.8 million dollars (less than half the train-robbery haul) from the Brink's Armoured Car Company in Boston, 13 tears before in 1950.

In July 1983, however, property worth an estimated £30 million was stolen from the Knightsbridge Safety Deposit Centre in London (left). In November that year, the London Heathrow airport base of Brinks-Mat was robbed by six masked men who took 6800 gold bars, platinum, diamonds and cheques worth over £26 million. There have been large art, jewel and gold thefts, but these items are not so easy to dispose of as the largely untraceable banknotes packed onto the Mail train that left Glasgow on 7 August 1963.

Edwards and June joined the Reynolds in Mexico City, but the two men had less in common socially than professionally. The Edwards, who had spent their entire lives in Elephant and Castle, London, became desperately homesick and felt out of place on the other side of the Atlantic.

Jimmy White was caught in 1966. A bookmaker's shop reported to police that White was placing bets of £500. White fled south to Littlestone in Kent. Both he and his wife were finding the lives of fugitives almost unendurable. In April 1966, a Dover lifeboat crewman recognised White's photograph in a Sunday newspaper. He was arrested, as much to his relief as anguish. White even showed police £6000 in mail-train banknotes, which they had previously missed when searching his caravan.

At Nottingham Assizes in June 1966, White confessed to robbery and was sentenced to 18 years' imprisonment. In the same month, Bill Boal died of a brain tumour in a prison hospital.

In Mexico, Buster Edwards was close to breaking down under the strain. Finally, he decided that an English prison was preferable to a life abroad. After some delicate negotiating through an intermediary, he surrendered in London in September 1966. In December that year, at Nottingham Assizes, Edwards received the comparatively light sentence of 15 years for robbery, with 12 years for conspiracy, both sentences to run concurrently.

Far Left: The London Evening Standard breaks the news of train robber Wilson's escape from Winson Green Prison, Birmingham, in 1964. Left: Bruce Reynolds after appearing in court, following his re-capture in November 1968.

Even the judge had felt moved to comment on Goody's poise and power of leadership.

With the majority of the gang supposedly safely behind bars, public attention turned to the missing robbers – Reynolds, Edwards and White. British detectives and the Interpol service in Paris, which pools information about known criminals from police forces in different countries, kept their ears to the listening posts, patiently waiting for news of the missing robbers.

DASH FOR FREEDOM

Bruce Reynolds, with his usual ingenuity, fled to France in August 1964. His wife Frances and their son Nick, also travelling under false passports after evading the police pursuit, joined Reynolds in October and the family soon flew to Mexico City. Jimmy White and his wife Sheree moved from hideout to hideout. By the time his former accomplices were being sentenced, White had bought a hill farm in Derbyshire, working alone and, for much of the time, unrecognised.

Buster Edwards, too, was lying low, living as a house-bound recluse in south London. He had plans to meet Reynolds in Mexico but neither he nor his wife could face the upheaval immediately.

In the same month that Reynolds slipped out of Britain, Charlie Wilson made a spectacular escape from Winson Green Prison near Birmingham. A month later, Ronnie Biggs escaped from Wandsworth Prison in London. To the public, Biggs' 30-year sentence placed him in the hierarchy of the train robbers, despite the fact that he had contributed practically nothing to the operation.

Life on the run was not easy for any of the men who eluded capture. Had their accomplices received 15-year sentences, with the prospect of being free men in 10 years or less, Edwards and White would almost certainly have surrendered.

Inside prison, Roy James had shrewdly calculated that, as the years rolled by, the parole laws would become milder and prisoners could be freed before two-thirds of their sentences had passed. This echoed a remark shouted out in court by Rene Wisbey, when her husband was taken down: 'The country won't stand for it.'

But the sheer horror of a 30-year sentence kept Reynolds on the move. He had also succeeded in getting much of his share of the money out of the country.

Right: Claverley Mansions, Littlestone-on-Sea in Kent, where Jimmy White, his wife and baby lived until he was arrested on 21 April 1966.

TO THE LAST MAN

The relentless Det. Chief Supt. Tommy Butler of the Flying Squad had postponed his retirement to pursue the train robbers to the last man. He took their liberty as a personal affront and his patient zeal paid off. Charlie Wilson was tracked down living peacefully and legally with his family in the Canadian town of Rigaud. One morning in January 1968, Wilson answered

a knock at the door to find Butler and 50 members of the Royal Canadian Mounted Police. The jet-setting, confident Reynolds was also trapped by Butler during an incognito visit to a hotel in Torquay in November that year.

'Hello, Bruce, it's been a long time,' Butler remarked. '*C'est la vie*,' was Reynolds' weary reply.

At Aylesbury Assizes, in January 1969, Reynolds admitted to conspiracy and robbery. His counsel could offer little in mitigation except to say that Reynolds had returned

£5500 and felt contrite. It seemed that the train robbers had nothing left to trade with. Reynolds received a 25-year sentence as his wife, Frances, wept openly in court.

Outside the courtroom, a journalist asked Butler if that was the end of the hunt. 'No, got to catch Biggs first,' he replied.

Biggs was soon discovered to be living in Brazil, and was the subject of an abortive attempt to have him extradited in 1974. The Flying Squad had received word that a British journalist was to interview Biggs in Rio de Janeiro. Butler's colleague, Det. Chief Supt. Jack Slipper, was sent to arrest the fugitive train robber. To the lasting anger of the British officers, however, Biggs was released. Under Brazilian law, the fathers of Brazilian children are seldom extradited and Biggs' local girl-friend Raimunda conveniently proved she was pregnant.

PUBLIC ENEMIES

Many of the train robbers inspired an awe among the prison authorities which reflected the general bewilderment in response to their crime. At Durham Prison, soldiers with machine-guns were posted around the fortress-like prison walls while Wisbey and James were held there. Others had to endure long periods as Category-A prisoners, scarcely allowed out of their cells. At first, some were not even allowed to kiss their wives during normal visiting hours.

Outside, however, the world was changing rapidly. The belief that half a lifetime in jail was appropriate punishment for thieves was crumbling. New laws allowed prisoners to be released on probation after serving one third of their sentence, if they earned it by good behaviour.

By the mid-1970s, the men who, over a decade earlier had been effectively put away for the rest of their lives, were quietly released: Cordrey in 1971, Edwards, James, White, Hussey and Goody in 1975. Wisbey and Welch followed in 1976. Wheater, the solicitor, and the two Fields had long since

Above: The London Evening News announces the re-arrest of Bruce Reynolds, in November 1968, after five years on the run.
Below: Ruth Edwards waits for husband Buster, who was imprisoned for 15 years after his surrender in 1968.

INSIDE VIEW
DEATH OF A DRIVER

Jack Mills (above with his wife Florence), the driver who tried to fight off the robbers, died in February 1970, after years of controversy over his reward and injuries. After the attack, he was transferred to mild duties on full pay, but his reward from the Post Office amounted to only £250. Years later, public indignation mounted when Charmian Biggs sold her stor for £30,000. A belated public appeal for Mills raised £34,00 He bought a bungalow in Crewe, Cheshire, his home town, but died soon after of leukemia. A West Cheshire coroner ruled that Mills' injur at Sears Crossing on the nigh of the robbery had not contributed to his death.

Mills was ever afterwards plagued by suggestions that he had exaggerated his injuries an consequent physicaldisabilities when giving evidence at the 1964 trial.

But, by any reckoning, the head wounds he received as a direct result of the assault on h train, were serious injuries.

regained their freedom and anonymity.

Most of the train-robbery money was gone, swallowed up in legal fees or by so-called friends, or paying for families who could not support themselves. Goody was one of the few to leave prison and return to his money, which had been invested for him in property.

LIVING LEGENDS

One by one, the robbers returned to their old haunts in south London, slowly picking up the threads of their family lives and, for some, their business interests. It is certain that, in 1963, they had never suspected that their next 'job' would make history, to be condemned, saluted, discussed and remembered across the world. As individuals, the names of Reynolds, Goody or even the colourful Buster Edwards have never been very famous. Together, however, as the Great Train Robbers, they became a legend larger than life.